THE UNITED STATES
IN THE
MIDDLE EAST

THE UNITED STATES
IN THE
MIDDLE EAST

Interests and Obstacles

Seth P. Tillman

Indiana University Press
Bloomington

094939

Library of Congress Cataloging in Publication Data
Tillman, Seth P.
   The United States in the Middle East: interests and obstacles.

   Includes bibliographical references and index.
   1. Near East—Foreign relations—United States.
   2. United States—Foreign relations—Near East.
   3. Jewish-Arab relations—1949-   I. Title.
DS63.2.U5T54   327.73056   81-47777
ISBN 0-253-36172-9   AACR2
     3 4 5 86 85 84 83

To My Wife, Baldwin,
and to
My Teacher, Ruhl Bartlett

CONTENTS

FOREWORD

IT IS A RARE occurrence that there is published a book as timely and as relevant to current affairs as this volume by Dr. Seth Tillman. Dr. Tillman is a long-time student of Middle Eastern affairs, as an academician and as a senior member of the professional staff of the Senate Committee on Foreign Relations. There are few men in our country as well qualified by training and experience to write about this subject.

In the opening chapter, Dr. Tillman presents a succinct and lucid account of the history of the area from ancient times, giving the reader an accurate perspective for the evaluation of current developments. In subsequent chapters, his analysis of the interests of the American people in the Middle East is thorough and objective. The chapters on Israel, Saudi Arabia, the Palestinians, and the Soviet Union present the reader with a discriminating analysis of the disparities in the cultures of the parties involved, of their political interests, and of their relevance to the restoration of peace in the area.

There is no doubt that the most volatile and dangerous area to the peace of the world today is the Middle East. It is dangerous because of the unceasing violence and terrorism that afflicts the area together with the fact that vast deposits of petroleum, vital to the economic health of the noncommunist world, lie beneath its desert sands. Japan, Western Europe, the United States, among many others, are dependent on the energy from the Gulf States.

Beyond that, such a unique concentration of an essential resource attracts the special interest of the two superpowers who are vigorously competing for power and influence in the world. This competition, focused as it is on the fragile and explosive tinderbox of the Middle East, is the cause of profound apprehension about a major conflict erupting between these superpowers. The possibility of such a major conflict gives particular urgency to the effort to find a comprehensive peace in this area.

The United States, because of its enormous financial and undeviating political support of Israel, is generally regarded abroad as being responsible for Israeli policy and as the only power which has the capacity to influence that policy. Whether or not the U.S. government uses its power to achieve a comprehensive settlement depends on our domestic politics. This elusive but crucial aspect of U.S. policy is not generally understood by the American people.

Dr. Tillman's analysis of what "needs to be done and how to do it" raises the most sensitive, emotional, and controversial issue in the current political scene— and surely one of the most important to the security of the country. If our democratic system functions as it should, his analysis should be the basis for a healthy and useful examination by the Congress, and by the people, of the wisdom of our policy in the Middle East.

J. W. FULBRIGHT

Washington, D.C.

PREFACE AND ACKNOWLEDGEMENTS

THIS BOOK GREW out of my experience as a member of the professional staff of the Senate Foreign Relations Committee and of its Subcommittee on Near Eastern and South Asian Affairs. Between 1970 and 1976 I had the occasion to make a number of extended trips to the Middle East under the auspices of the Foreign Relations Committee and also to put together several series of Committee hearings on American policy in the Middle East. Having previously been a generalist in foreign relations, I found myself increasingly absorbed during the years of my Senate employment in the politics of the Middle East—particularly in the range and interplay of American interests in the region. I traveled to the area again in 1978 and early 1981, on these occasions as a private citizen.

When I left the Foreign Relations Committee in 1977, I undertook at the outset to write an article on American policy in the Middle East. As my research continued and my curiosity remained unsatisfied, it became apparent to me that the subject required fuller treatment than could be provided even by a long article. I thereupon undertook this book.

I have many debts. I am grateful to Ruhl J. Bartlett, my former teacher at the Fletcher School of Law and Diplomacy; to the late Robert B. Stewart, dean-emeritus of the Fletcher School; and to Senator J. William Fulbright for reading the manuscript. I appreciate their thoughtful, if perhaps too generous, comments. I am also grateful to my friends Nathaniel Kern and Malcolm Peck, both Middle East experts, for their critical suggestions on parts of the manuscript, particularly relating to Saudi Arabia. In addition, I am indebted to numerous individuals from both politics and the academy who gave generously of their time and knowledge in interviews conducted in Egypt, Israel, Jordan, Syria, Lebanon, and Saudi Arabia, as well as the United States. For cheerful and highly professional typing and editing I am deeply grateful to Sandra Walker, Joanna Yusko, and Jackie Tillman, all of whom gave generously of their time and talent. I wish also to express my appreciation to the American Enterprise Institute for the fellowship that enabled me to do much of the work on the manuscript. Finally, I thank the staff of Indiana University Press for their highly professional editing, for their encouragement, and for their patience.

SETH TILLMAN

October 1981

[xi]

THE UNITED STATES
IN THE
MIDDLE EAST

CHAPTER ONE

The Long Road
to Camp David

WHEN PRESIDENT ANWAR SADAT of Egypt went to Jerusalem in November 1977 to breach the "psychological barrier," Jews and Arabs were galvanized for the moment into an awareness, hitherto suppressed, of each other's humanity. He had come, Sadat said, to "get rid of the psychological barrier, which in my idea was more than 70 percent of the whole conflict. . . ."[1] Visiting informally with members of the Knesset on the day after his formal speech, President Sadat singled out former Prime Minister Golda Meir, whom he had often referred to as the "old lady." "When you sit here," said Mrs. Meir, "and I look at you and I heard you last night, it's not the same. I believe in your sincere desire for peace."[2]

Mrs. Meir was extolling the advantages of direct contact, after decades of nonrecognition and communication only through intermediaries. Individuals who for years had known each other and speculated on each other's motives and character were suddenly face-to-face, and the effect was galvanic. In the weeks and months that followed, the initial effects of President Sadat's "electric shock" diplomacy wore off, and the old antagonists rediscovered what they had disliked and feared in each other. Communication became more difficult, and the parties found themselves sending messages once again through their momentarily sidetracked American intermediary. Ten months of tortuous, acrimonious diplomacy were required, after President Sadat's trip to Jerusalem, to produce the

Camp David accords of September 1978—and another six months to produce the Egyptian-Israeli peace treaty of March 1979.

FIRST ENCOUNTERS

The significance of President Sadat's visit to Jerusalem was in the act itself, in the attempted breaching of the "psychological barrier." Neither side otherwise departed at that time from long-held positions on territory, the "nature of peace," and the Palestinian problem. Israelis, however, could scarcely believe their ears as President Sadat declared, ". . . we really and truly welcome you to live among us in peace and security." Less audible to his listeners at the time—dismissed perhaps as "bargaining points"—were President Sadat's insistence on complete Israeli withdrawal from the territories occupied in 1967, "including Arab Jerusalem," and on the right of the Palestinian people to self-determination, "including their right to establish their own state."[3] Little attention was paid either, at the time, to President Sadat's warning, before his departure, that "hard and drastic decisions" had to be made.[4] Prime Minister Begin, for his part, extended his blessing to President Sadat and commended his courage in coming to Jerusalem. He expostulated his sense of the meaning of Israel— "this small nation, the remnants of the destruction of the Jewish nation that has returned to our historical homeland. . . ." The Prime Minister spoke of Israel's longing for peace, for normal relations and joint Arab-Israeli economic ventures—to "change this region into a 'Garden of Eden.' " He evoked memories of the ancient Jews—"Here we became a nation. Here we established our kingdoms"—and of their long and bitter exile, in the course of which "we never forgot this land, even for one day. We prayed for her. We longed for her." As always, Begin stressed the Holocaust and the lesson he perceived in it: that only in their own homeland can the Jews be safe from the threat of destruction.[5] Prime Minister Begin had little to say in public during the Sadat visit regarding borders, security guarantees, or the future of the Palestinian people. In an interview he replied "no" when asked if he could foresee an independent Palestinian homeland,[6] but otherwise Begin avoided the divisive, volatile issues.

Events in the weeks that followed showed that the two sides placed quite different meanings on this first encounter between Egyptians and Israelis. Offering no immediate, substantive concessions, the Israelis made it clear that they regarded the visit as a ceremonial curtain raiser, to be followed by protracted, detailed negotiations on the difficult substantive issues. President Sadat, for his part, went home in the belief that, in offering Israel "security and legitimacy," he had given "everything," as he was later to put it,[7] and that Israel could now be expected to respond with comparable magnanimity on matters of territory and Palestinian self-determination. "I feel that the barrier of suspicion, the lack of trust and confidence, has been shattered," Sadat reported to his Parliament on his return to Cairo. As a result, it should now be possible to convene a peace conference and settle matters "within months."[8]

Soaring optimism was not confined to Egyptians and Israelis. On the eve of the next meeting between Prime Minister Begin and President Sadat, held at Ismailia on Christmas Day 1977, the *Washington Post* judged the two leaders to be on a course toward peace "almost irreversibly fixed," with the outlook "genuinely thrilling."[9] The *New Yorker* pictured the world as a "vast stadium, in which the people of the earth are seated as a single audience," looking down on the unfolding drama of peacemaking.[10]

President Sadat and Prime Minister Begin failed at Ismailia to reach agreement on the principles of peace, or even on the language of a joint communiqué. President Sadat called again for a Palestinian state on the West Bank and the Gaza Strip; Prime Minister Begin proposed Palestinian "self-rule" and denounced "the organization called the PLO."[11] The two leaders agreed, however, to set up two negotiating committees, a political committee to meet in Jerusalem and a military committee to sit in Cairo. The atmosphere at Ismailia, according to Ezer Weizman, the Israeli minister of defense, was much different from that in Jerusalem the month before. The welcome accorded the Israelis was "chilly," and in the meetings Begin "engendered boredom" with an exhaustive discourse on details rather than principles, to the visible annoyance of Sadat.[12] Back in Israel Begin reported that the difference of opinion was "fundamental."[13] On December 27, 1977 Begin unveiled his plan of "administrative autonomy" for the Arab population of the West Bank and Gaza. The plan called for an elective administrative council, to sit in Bethlehem, with jurisdiction in fields such as health, housing, education, agriculture, and law enforcement, while "security and public order" would remain under Israeli authority. Israelis would have the right to acquire land and to establish settlements in the West Bank, and Palestinian Arabs who chose to become Israeli citizens would have reciprocal rights in Israel proper. The return of Arab refugees "in reasonable numbers" would be regulated by a joint committee in which Israel would retain the right of veto. Israel, under the Begin plan, stood by "its right and its claim" to sovereignty over the territories but proposed "for the sake of the agreement" to leave the question of sovereignty open. The entire plan would be "subject to review" after five years.[14] In submitting his proposal to the Knesset, Prime Minister Begin stressed the importance of retaining Israeli forces in the West Bank and Gaza. Without them, he feared, the territories would fall under the domination of "the murderers' organization known as the PLO," which he described as "the vilest organization of murderers in history with the exception of the Nazi armed organizations."[15]

To the dismay of American diplomats, among others, Israel and Egypt fell into a fast-mounting war of accusation and recrimination in the first weeks of 1978. The Egyptians continued to insist on "self-determination" for the Palestinian people as well as the dismantling of Israeli settlements in Sinai, while the Israelis insisted on retaining their settlements in the Egyptian Sinai, to be administered by Israel and protected by Israeli forces, and refused to concede more than limited "self-rule" for the Palestinians on the West Bank and in Gaza, under (along with) a continued Israeli military presence. President Carter, on a world trip in early January, made a brief, hastily arranged stop at Aswan in Upper Egypt. Here he attempted to bridge the gap between self-determination and its denial with a formula suggesting that the Palestinians be permitted to "participate in the determination of their own future."[16] The Egyptians, at least tentatively, found this formulation acceptable. Prime Minister Begin, in Jerusalem, reiterated his opposition to the suggestion of self-determination for the Palestinians. "We are not beating around the bush," he said. "To us self-determination means a Palestinian state, and we are not going to agree to any such mortal danger to Israel."[17]

On January 15, 1978 the Egyptian magazine *October* published an interview in which President Sadat gave vent to his own growing frustration and dismay. Noting that Israelis readily described themselves as "stiff necks" and seemed to take pride in it, President Sadat said that "if this is one of their qualities, then I reject it and suggest they look for someone else to tolerate it or to sing its praise." He was aware, he said, that the Jews were "clever tradesmen," but they were mistaken, nonetheless, in believing that they could "take without giving." The Israelis sought "secure borders," Sadat went on, but the concept as they used it was a "myth" because, whatever territory they have held, they have lived nonetheless "in constant fear." Sadat said that he had offered Begin "everything" and "got nothing in return." He had agreed to demilitarized zones, early warning stations, areas of limited arms, freedom of navigation, peaceful coexistence, the opening of borders, and normal relations. But no Israeli—not a single one—might remain on Egyptian territory; on that the president was adamant. He believed that the Israeli leaders had failed to perceive the significance of his initiative. The military and political committees agreed on at Ismailia were supposed to produce a declaration of principles, but, President Sadat concluded, "I declare now that I have no hope whatsoever that this declaration will be issued."[18]

Under these inauspicious auguries Egypt and Israel, with increasing American participation, undertook to frame a broad statement of principles to guide future negotiations. The military committee convened in Cairo, and the political committee gathered in Jerusalem, but the latter meeting was quickly aborted. On arriving in Jerusalem on January 15, the new Egyptian foreign minister, Mohammed Ibrahim Kamel, warned that there could be no peace if Israel continued to occupy Arab lands and to deny the "national rights" of the Palestinians. Highly provoked, Prime Minister Begin cast aside diplomatic niceties at a state dinner on January 17 for the participants in the peace talks. Before an astonished audience, including a delegation of visiting American Congressmen, Begin castigated Kamel—a "young man"—for his arrival statement, rejected the 1967 borders ("the fragile, breakable, aggression-provoking and bloodshed-causing lines") and went on to expostulate the shortcomings of Wilsonian self-determination, notably its "misuse" in the 1930s—an apparent reference to the invocation of that principle by Nazi Germany.[19]

President Sadat responded to the affront to his foreign minister by calling the Egyptian delegation home, rupturing the negotiations. An official statement on January 18 explained that Sadat made this decision "to avoid the talks continuing in a vicious circle or going into side issues. . . ." Reiterating Egypt's insistence on Israeli withdrawal from the territories occupied in 1967 (including East Jerusalem) and on the right of the Palestinian people to self-determination—principles that conform with "justice" and "international law"—the statement affirmed Egypt's view that "it is no longer acceptable that bargaining, outbidding, and wasting time and energy are the ways for achieving them." The statement also said that "in doing what it has done, Egypt may have offered all it can afford."[20]

Israel reacted with astonished anger to the recall of the Egyptian delegation. The Israeli Cabinet, after an emergency meeting, issued a statement asserting that this "extreme" action proved "that the Egyptian government deceived itself that Israel will submit to demands it has never considered feasible." Referring to the Begin autonomy plan of December 27, 1977, the Cabinet statement asserted that "only the Egyptian government in its astonishing rigidity sees in our plan stalling and deceit."[21]

Less than two months after President Sadat's visit to Jerusalem sent hopes for peace soaring on both sides, as well as in the outside world, Israelis and Egyptians had discovered that their initial expectations of each other had been euphoric if not wholly mistaken. The Israelis seem genuinely to have believed that both sides regarded the Sadat visit to Jerusalem as the curtain raiser to an extended process of bargaining in which each party would lay its proposals on the table to be negotiated in detail, bargained over, and in due course compromised. When Sadat called his delegation home from Jerusalem on January 18, 1978, it appeared to the Israelis that the Egyptian President had inexplicably, petulantly given up the game when it had scarcely begun. President Sadat, however, made it clear that he regarded the offer he had made in Jerusalem as definitive—security and acceptance for Israel in exchange for the return of territories and Palestinian rights. He seems to have assumed—or gambled—at the outset that he had found in Menachem Begin a like-minded counterpart, a leader who, like himself, would willingly cast aside the endless haggling over phrases and commas that had characterized previous indirect negotiations and reach a general agreement in principle without delay. When the Israelis showed that they expected to negotiate in detail and, more important, that their conception of a general settlement was markedly different from Sadat's, it appeared to President Sadat that they simply wished to "take without giving," that they had picked up all that he had given them in coming to Jerusalem, put it in their pockets, and then proposed to settle down to the arduous process of getting more.

Euphoric hope thus gave way to disappointment and anger in this first full-scale encounter between Egyptians and Israelis since the founding of the state of Israel. "They are a people who do not desire peace," President Sadat said in his *October* interview of mid-January 1978. "They want war and hatred to continue in order to profit from them. They prefer this situation so as to bargain with it."[22] A few weeks later Israeli Foreign Minister Moshe Dayan, while touring the United States, said of Sadat, "He asks us to do the unthinkable, give back the Golan Heights, the West Bank, Sinai, the settlements, Sharm el-Sheikh. What will happen with our security in the future? Should we really do what would eventually lead to the destruction of Israel? Is it as simple as that?"[23]

Sadat in due course acquiesced in the protracted bargaining process favored by the Israelis, abandoning his initial hopes for a shattering breach of the "psychological barrier" to be followed by an early, general settlement. The acrimony and recriminations that quickly took hold in the aftermath of Sadat's trip to Jerusalem, although reduced in intensity as the two sides came to know each other's ways, recurred throughout the "peace process" leading to the Camp David accords and the Egyptian-Israeli treaty and then continued through the arduous posttreaty negotiations on Palestinian autonomy. Whether a sweeping, dramatic breakthrough (as hoped for by Sadat at the outset) would have drawn the other Arab parties into early participation in the negotiations, acceptance of Israel, and genuine reconciliation, cannot be known. As events unfolded, such expectations were shown to be unrealistic. The psychological barrier had been only partially breached, and although the partial peace of March 1979 would greatly reduce the likelihood of another general Arab-Israeli war, the basic Arab-Israeli conflict—and the core issue of Palestinian nationalism—would remain unresolved and would continue to agitate the politics of the Middle East and the world beyond.

"IN THE BEGINNING . . ."

It is unlikely that there is another region in the world in which the ancient past exerts so vivid an influence on the minds of people now living and so direct a bearing on current events as the Middle East. Both Jews and Arabs have deep historical roots and powerful emotional attachments to the land of Palestine going back to earliest recorded history.[24]

The Jews first came to the area of Palestine under their leader Abraham around 1800 B.C. Later they migrated to Egypt, remaining there for several centuries until Moses led them out into the Sinai, where they wandered for a generation until Joshua led them into the land of Canaan—or Palestine—around 1200 B.C. They were united into a single kingdom by King Saul, whose successor, David, extended the kingdom's boundaries. David's son, King Solomon, built the First Temple in Jerusalem. This united kingdom lasted only about two hundred years and then divided into the kingdoms of Israel and Judah. The Assyrians invaded the northern kingdom of Israel in 721 B.C. and deported much of the population, who then vanished from history as the "Ten Lost Tribes." The southern kingdom of Judah survived until the Babylonians captured Jerusalem in 586 B.C., destroyed King Solomon's Temple, and deported the population. A half century later the Persians, who had conquered Babylonia, allowed Jews to return to Palestine, and a Second Temple was built in the early sixth century B.C. Judah survived first as a Persian province, then, its name hellenized as "Judea," as part of the empire of Alexander and his successors. In 168 B.C. the Maccabees, a prominent Jewish priestly family, led a successful revolt against the ruling Greeks and expanded the power of Judea over the surrounding territories. The

Maccabean kingdom survived less than a century, ending with the Roman conquest around 63 B.C. Major Jewish revolts in A.D. 70 and A.D. 135 were put down by the Romans, who then destroyed Jerusalem and the Second Temple, expelling the Jews from Jerusalem "forever." Thereafter only small numbers of Jews lived in Palestine until the Zionist return in the twentieth century.

Through eighteen centuries of "exile" the dream of "Zion" remained vibrant in Jewish life, culture, and religion. "From my early youth," Menachem Begin wrote in his memoir, "I had been taught by my father . . . that we Jews were to return to Eretz Israel (in English, the "Land of Israel"). Not to 'go' or 'travel' or 'come'—but to *return*. That was the great difference, and it was all-embracing."[25] "Zionism was not born with Theodor Herzl," wrote Arie Lova Eliav, a member of the Knesset and leading critic of Prime Minister Begin's policies, "it was born with the exiles of Babylon. . . . we are the direct descendants of our ancestors born in this land. . . . for a hundred generations we have preserved our uniqueness as a people and our bonds with this land. We have not assimilated, we have not merged, and others have hardly been absorbed among us."[26]

The *idea* of Israel, as it survived through the ages, is expressed in the words of the 137th Psalm:

> By the rivers of Babylon there we sat down; yet we wept when we remembered Zion. How shall we sing the Lord's song in a foreign land? If I forget thee, O Jerusalem, let my right hand forget her cunning; let my tongue cleave to the roof of my mouth, if I remember thee not; if I set not thee Jerusalem above my chiefest joy.

Arabs are hardly less convinced than Jews that they have an ancient historical, even God-given claim to the land of Palestine. A contemporary Arab political leader, in an unsigned paper, purports to show that, even on Biblical grounds, setting aside the question of whether any people can claim title to a land they left almost 2,000 years ago, the Arabs have a better claim to Palestine than do the Jews. According to the Book of Genesis, the Arab writer notes, God promised the "Land of Canaan" to Abraham, who was the ancestor of both Arabs and Jews, and "to his seed." This promise, it is asserted, was first made on the occasion of the circumcision of Abraham's elder son, Ishmael, ancestor of the Arabs, before the birth of the second son, Isaac, the ancestor of the Jews. The writer goes on to question the claim of the Jews to Palestine as their historic "homeland," asserting that even King David's empire at its brief height did not include what is now the heartland of Israel, the coastal plain including Tel Aviv; this territory remained occupied by the Philistines, whose name is the source of the designation "Palestine." Except for a brief period of expansion, the Arab writer asserts, the people of Judea, from whom modern Jews claim descent, occupied only a restricted territory in Palestine; from the time of the expulsion of the Jews, by the Roman Emperor Hadrian in A.D. 135, the land was inhabited by indigenous tribes from whom in large part—so says the contemporary Arab writer—the modern Palestinians descend.

Palestine remained almost uninterruptedly under Roman, and then Byzantine, rule from the first century A.D. until 634, when it was conquered by Arab armies from the Arabian peninsula during the caliphate of Omar, successor to the prophet Muhammad. Palestine thereafter became part of the vast Arab empire conquered by Muhammad's followers. As in the rest of the empire, the inhabitants of Palestine became arabized in culture and language; most of the predominantly Christian population, descendants of the ancient Canaanites, converted to Islam. The Mosque of Omar, also known as the Dome of the Rock, was built in Jerusalem near a spot from which the prophet Muhammad was believed to have ascended to heaven, and Jerusalem became, from the late seventh century, the third most sacred city to Muslims, after Mecca and Medina. The rule of the Arab Empire lasted in Palestine for over four hundred years, until 1071. Palestine thereafter fell under a succession of foreign rulers, including Christian Crusaders in the twelfth and thirteenth centuries. The Ottoman Turks established their rule in 1517, and from then until the end of the First World War in 1918 Palestine remained part of the Ottoman Empire. During all of these periods the population remained predominantly Arab and Muslim, but with a small Jewish minority as well.

ZIONISM AND SELF-DETERMINATION

Dispersed throughout Europe and other parts of the world, the Jews never abandoned their hope of returning to the Promised Land. In prayers and rituals they looked to the coming of the Messiah, who would unite the Jews again in their ancient homeland. In the latter years of the nineteenth century, European Jews, despairing of relief from political persecution and rising anti-Semitism, especially in Russia, undertook to give destiny a helping hand. An Austrian Jew, Theodor Herzl, emerged as the father of modern political Zionism; in response to his efforts the First Zionist Congress met in Basel, Switzerland, in 1897, created the World Zionist Organization, and adopted a resolution calling for a "home in Palestine" for the Jewish people. Various other places, including Kenya in East Africa, were considered as possible Jewish homelands, but primary attention remained focused on Palestine—"the land without a people for the people without a land."[27] Despite all obstacles, Jewish settlements were established in Palestine, and by the time of the outbreak of World War I in 1914 there were over 80,000 Jews in Palestine.

From the outset Zionist leaders sought great power support. From World War I until the end of the British mandate, their efforts were focused on Great Britain, and only to a lesser degree the United States. Decisive influence was brought to bear in Great Britain by Dr. Chaim Weizmann, the Zionist leader and chemist, who provided valuable services during World War I to the British Ministry of Munitions in the organization of chemical works. Weizmann won the support of, among others, the foreign secretary, Arthur Balfour, and the prime minister, David Lloyd George. Balfour, through his contacts with Weizmann, became a sincere advocate of Zionist aspirations; Lloyd George, by his own account, was fearful that Germany's active courting of Zionist sympathy in 1916 and 1917 would attract the support of American Jews to the Central Powers and encourage newly influential Jewish members of the revolutionary Kerensky government in Russia to seek to take Russia out of the war.[28]

On November 8, 1917 Foreign Secretary Balfour issued the declaration that was to be regarded thereafter as the "emancipation proclamation" of modern Zionism. This declaration stated that "his Majesty's Government views with favor the establishment in Palestine of a national home for the Jewish people, and will use their best endeavor to facilitate the achievement of this object, it being clearly understood that nothing shall be done which may prejudice the civil and religious rights of existing non-Jewish communities in Palestine, or the rights and political status enjoyed by Jews in any other country . . . ." Although there was a good deal of sympathy in Great Britain for Zionist aspirations, the Balfour Declaration was, by Lloyd George's account, essentially a war measure, designed to counter the efforts of the Central Powers to attract the support of world Jewry. Further, the British government understood the term "national home" to mean "some form of British, American, or other protectorate. . . . It did not necessarily involve the early establishment of an independent Jewish state. . . ."[29] The Balfour Declaration may also have been motivated, in greater or lesser part, by British imperial interests in securing Palestine as a bulwark for the British position in Egypt and as an overland link to the East.[30]

The United States at this time found itself in an equivocal position: on the one hand sympathetic to Zionist aspirations, on the other hand committed, under President Wilson, to the principle of the self-determination of peoples. Wilson wrote to Rabbi Stephen S. Wise, an American Zionist leader, on August 31, 1918: "I welcome an opportunity to express the satisfaction I have felt in the progress of the Zionist movement in the United States and in the Allied countries since the declaration by Mr. Balfour. . . ."[31] Wilson's peace program, however, was largely rooted in the premise that a lasting peace must be based on the self-determination of established populations. In one of his major statements of war aims, President Wilson had defined self-determination as an "imperative principle of action" and had affirmed as a basic principle that "peoples and provinces are not to be bartered about from sovereignty to sovereignty as if they were mere chattels. . . ."[32] As to Palestine and the other non-Turkish territories under Ottoman rule, Point Twelve of the Fourteen Points called for an "absolutely unmolested opportunity of autonomous development" for the subject nationalities of the Ottoman Empire.[33] Indeed, Prince Faisal, representing the delegation of the Hejaz at the Paris Peace Conference, invoked the principles enunciated by Wilson as the basis of his appeal for the unity and independence of the Arab world.[34] In view of the continuous habitation of Palestine by an Arab population from the seventh to the twentieth century and in view of the fact that Jews made up no more than 10 percent of the country's population at the end of the First World War, Wilson's precepts were not on their face reconcilable with the Zionist program.

Balfour himself, who championed the Zionist cause at the Paris Peace Conference of 1919, noted the ambivalence of American policy. The Allied commitment to the Zionist cause, he maintained, overrode "numerical self-determination," Palestine being a unique area in which the wishes of a *future* community with historical and religious claims must be matched against the wishes of the *existing* community. Balfour told Felix Frankfurter and Justice Brandeis, both Zionist advocates, that he could not understand how President Wilson reconciled his advocacy of Zionism with his commitment to the principle of self-determination.[35] As will be seen in succeeding chapters, the ambivalence—or contradiction—in American policy was to persist through the decades that followed.

No such equivocation was shown in the report of the special American commission headed by H. C. King and Charles R. Crane, which President Wilson dispatched to the Middle East to ascertain the wishes of the nationalities to be liberated from Turkish rule. King and Crane reported to the president from Jerusalem that Muslims and Christians in Palestine were united in the "most hostile attitude" toward continuing Jewish immigration, so much so that the Zionist program could be carried out only by force of arms. The final King-Crane report estimated that nine-tenths of the population of Palestine—virtually the entire non-Jewish population—were "emphatically against the entire Zionist program." The report recommended, accordingly, that only a "greatly reduced Zionist program" of "definitely limited" Jewish immigration be permitted and that the project for making Palestine distinctly a Jewish commonwealth be given up.[36]

The King-Crane report was ignored by the peace makers of 1919, and Palestine came under the British mandate that was to last until Israel's declaration of independence on May 14, 1948. Although the Balfour Declaration was incorporated into the Palestine Mandate agreement between Great Britain and the League of Nations, no provision was made for the establishment of an independent Jewish state and the concept of a Jewish "national home" remained undefined and unclear. Efforts to devise a governmental system in which the two communities would participate failed repeatedly because of Arab objections to the entire mandatory regime; Palestine therefore remained under the direct rule of a British High Commission. During the period of British rule, the Jewish population increased despite limits on immigration, and Palestine became a binational country characterized by mounting national feeling on both sides and steadily rising mutual animosity.

The most inflamed issue during the mandate period was that of Jewish immigration. The Arabs resisted it bitterly, and only small numbers of Jews came to Palestine in the late 1920s. In the thirties, however, the Nazi persecution, rising anti-Semitism in central and eastern Europe, and restrictive immigration policies in the West (including the United States) drove European Jews to flee to Palestine in increasing numbers. Many came illegally, aided by a Zionist underground operating in Europe; by the outbreak of World War II in 1939 there were about 450,000 Jews in Palestine, making up about 30 percent of the population. During the interwar years the Jews also bought up large tracts of land from Arab owners and other sources, assisted by the international Jewish community working through a Jewish National Fund. By contrast with the Palestinian Arabs, the Jews had the advantages of organization, leadership, a high educational level, and the support of Jewish communities all over the world.

Alarmed and frightened by Jewish immigration and land purchases, the

Arabs resorted to repeated, futile violence in the twenties and thirties. Despairing of reconciling the two communities, the British government began in the mid-thirties to consider plans for the partition of Palestine. The Jewish leadership divided over the question of partition, with Dr. Weizmann and David Ben-Gurion leading the group that was willing to accept it as the most practical way of attaining both self-rule and unrestricted Jewish immigration. The Arabs, for their part, objected bitterly to partition and stepped up their violence against the British, who responded by suppressing and disarming the Arab militants and arresting or deporting many of the Arab leaders.

Only in the late thirties, in reaction to German and Italian moves to gain favor with the Arabs, did the British judge it necessary to try to placate the Arabs. Plans for partition were set aside, and, after another futile effort to reconcile Jews and Arabs through a conference held in London in March 1939, the British government issued a white paper extending British rule, limiting the sale of land to Jews, and restricting Jewish immigration to 75,000 over a five-year period, after which further Jewish immigration would be subject to Arab acquiescence. Arab reactions to the new British policy ranged from favorable to skeptical to hostile. The Zionists reacted with shock and outrage to the British white paper, and from that time on Jewish groups resorted increasingly to violence against the mandatory authority. The Jewish Agency, representing world Jewry's interests in Palestine, refused to cooperate with the British authority and stepped up its support of illegal Jewish immigration.

During World War II Palestinian Jews cooperated to the fullest in the fight against Nazi Germany, while also encouraging and assisting illegal immigration. As the dimensions of the Holocaust in Europe became known and as it became clear that the Allies were going to win the war, the Zionists in Palestine resumed their struggle against the British administration. The military arm of the Jewish Agency, the Haganah, stole munitions from British installations; the more militant activist organizations, the Irgun Zvai Leumi (Hebrew for "National Military Organization"), headed by Menachem Begin, and the even more extreme Stern Gang, renewed and increased their attacks against the British. "Two predominating facts determined the condition of the Jewish people at the height of the Second World War," Menachem Begin wrote in his memoir. "Hitler was exterminating millions of Jews in Europe, and—in spite of this—Britain continued to keep the gates of the Jewish 'National Home' tightly shut against the Jews."[37]

During the war years Zionist efforts were also focused, with notable success, on the United States, whose Jewish community now became the world's largest and most influential in the wake of the catastrophe that fell upon the Jews of Europe. American Jews who had shown little interest in Palestine before the war rallied to the cause of a Jewish "national home," and Zionist committees and organizations proliferated in the United States. Spurred by the efforts of these groups, as well as by sympathy for the Jews of Europe, Americans became increasingly sympathetic to the Zionist cause. In 1942 and 1943 over thirty state legislatures adopted pro-Zionist resolutions. In the presidential campaign of 1944 both President Roosevelt and his opponent, Governor Thomas E. Dewey of New York, strongly supported the Zionist program. As World War II ended and the extent of the murder of the Jews of Europe became known, world Jewry, and especially the Jews of the United States, mounted a vigorous and concerted campaign for repudiation of the British white paper of 1939, for unrestricted immigration into Palestine for the surviving Jews of Europe, and for the establishment in Palestine of a Jewish national state.

The Arabs, for their part, also tried to win sympathy by such means as the opening, in 1945, of Arab information offices in London and Washington, but their efforts were of little avail. Viewing the Nazi persecution of the Jews from an Arab perspective, George Antonius, in his classic work first published in 1938, wrote:

> The treatment meted out to Jews in Germany and other European countries is a disgrace to its authors and to modern civilisation; but posterity will not exonerate any country that fails to bear its proper share of the sacrifices needed to alleviate Jewish suffering and distress. To place the brunt of the burden upon Arab Palestine is a miserable evasion of the duty that lies upon the whole of the civilized world. It is also morally outrageous. No code of morals can justify the persecution of one people in an attempt to relieve the persecution of another.

Acknowledging the high hopes invested by a large portion of the Jewish people in the Zionist ideal, Antonius continued:

> it would be an act of further cruelty to the Jews to disappoint those hopes if there existed some way of satisfying them, that did not involve cruelty to another people. But the logic of facts is inexorable. It shows that no room can be made in Palestine for a second nation except by dislodging or exterminating the nation in possession.[38]

Whereas American policy toward the Middle East had been ambivalent at the time of World War I, it was contradictory in World War II. In the election campaign of 1944 President Roosevelt ran upon, and personally endorsed, a Democratic platform provision stating, "We favor the opening of Palestine to unrestricted Jewish immigration and colonizaton, and such a policy is to result in the establishment there of a free and democratic Jewish commonwealth." Roosevelt reiterated the commitment to a "Jewish commonwealth" in Palestine in a message to the Annual Conference of the Zionist Organization of America three weeks before the election, promising that "if re-elected I shall help to bring about its realization." On February 14, 1945, however, President Roosevelt met privately with King Abd al-Aziz of Saudi Arabia aboard the USS *Quincy* on the Great Bitter Lake in the Suez Canal. In a subsequent letter to the king, dated April 5, 1945, Roosevelt recalled that in that meeting, in which the king had expressed strong views on the subject of Zionism, "I assured you that I would take no action . . . which might prove hostile to the Arab people." Since the Arab leaders were committed to the establishment of an independent Arab state in all of Palestine, the president's pledge to King Abd al-Aziz was in clear contradiction to the Democratic platform on which he had recently been reelected. Moreover, on March 16, 1945, President Roosevelt wrote to Rabbi Stephen Wise reiterating his commitment to the Democratic platform. "That position I have not changed," the president wrote.[39]

Between 1945 and 1948 President Truman, after some initial hesitation, brought the United States decisively to the support of the Zionist program. In contravention of State Department advice, Truman wrote to British Prime Minister Clement Attlee on August 31, 1945, urging Britain to allow the immediate immigration of 100,000 Jews into Palestine. Annoyed by this unwelcome advice, the British proposed instead the formation of an Anglo-American Committee of Inquiry to examine the problems of Palestine, including Jewish immigration. Truman agreed, and the committee, made up of six British and six Americans, conducted an investigation both in Palestine and in Jewish refugee camps in Europe over a period of four months. The committee's report, issued on May 1, 1946, expressed concern that most of the Jewish survivors in Europe were still living in miserable conditions on the sites of the former concentration camps and recommended that the British government "authorize immediately" the admission of 100,000 Jews into Palestine. As to the future of Palestine, the committee proposed a United Nations trusteeship to prepare the country for independence as a unified, binational state, "a country in which the legitimate national aspirations of both Jews and Arabs can be reconciled without either side fearing the ascendancy of the other."[40]

The British government rejected the Anglo-American Committee's proposal for large-scale Jewish immigration. To allow such, Foreign Secretary Bevin said, "I would have to put another division of British troops in there, and I am not prepared to do it."[41] The British position had two immediate consequences: the Jewish resistance groups in Palestine stepped up their acts of violence, and President Truman found himself in mounting disfavor with the American Jewish community. Repeated British efforts to reconcile Jews and Arabs failed; violence mounted in the Holy Land; and on October 4, 1946—the day of Yom Kippur, the highest of Jewish holy days, and one month prior to the American congressional election—President Truman called for the establishment of "a viable Jewish state" in Palestine.[42]

Despairing of its own ability either to mediate or impose a solution, Britain, on April 12, 1947, asked the Secretary-General of the United Nations to convene a special session of the General Assembly to recommend a solution to the Palestine problem. On November 29, 1947, by a vote of 33 to 13 (only two more than the minimum for the essential two-thirds majority) the General Assembly adopted its resolution recommending the partition of Palestine into separate Jewish and Arab states, with Jerusalem to be a *corpus separatum* under United Nations administration. Both the United States and the Soviet Union supported the partition resolution, although the United States made only limited efforts to secure its adoption; all Arab members of the United Nations opposed the partition resolution. In the face of bitter Arab opposition, the Palestine Commission set up by the United Nations to implement the partition resolution quickly gave up hope of securing a peaceful transfer of power and, on February 16, 1948, advised the United Nations Security Council that unless adequate military force were placed at its disposal, the commission would be unable to implement partition.[43]

Beset by cold war pressures in Europe and State Department warnings against driving the Arabs into the Soviet camp, the Truman Administration ruled out the commitment of American forces to implement the partition resolution. On March 19, 1948 the United States Ambassador to the United Nations, Warren Austin, called for a special session of the United Nations to reconsider the entire Palestine question. Pending the formation of a permanent regime, the United States now recommended that the Holy Land be placed under a temporary United Nations trusteeship and that efforts to implement partition be suspended since it could not be accomplished by peaceful means. The special session of the General Assembly convened on April 16, 1948, but the United States was unable to win significant support for its trusteeship proposal—and, with violence mounting rapidly in the Holy Land, it became apparent that at least as much force would be required to establish the trusteeship as to implement partition. The trusteeship proposal was soon abandoned.[44]

From the time of the partition, resolution events in Palestine took an increasingly violent and uncontrolled course—at heavy cost to both Jews and Arabs, who reaped a harvest of violence; to the United States, which came to be seen as inconsistent and irresolute in its Middle East policy; and to the United Nations, which was shown to be incapable of carrying out its recommendation. The adoption of the partition resolution on November 29, 1947 set off demonstrations and a general strike by the Palestinian Arabs and scattered fighting between Jews and Arabs in Tel Aviv, Jerusalem, and other cities. Jews and Arabs struggled to take control of the areas being vacated by the British, who had decided to withdraw from Palestine completely by May 15, 1948. Casualties mounted on both sides, while the Haganah converted itself from an underground resistance to a regular Jewish army. In the absence of military force, the Palestine Commission, as noted, was ineffectual. The United Nations General Assembly convened on May 14, 1948 to consider an eleventh-hour mediation proposal offered by the United States, but before the Assembly convened the Jewish Agency had announced the coming into existence, that day, of the new state of Israel.[45]

In the United States, Middle East policy fell increasingly under the pressures of domestic politics. Facing an uphill reelection campaign in 1948, President Truman became increasingly receptive to the importunities of the American Zionists, whose prime objective was prompt American recognition of the Jewish state when it came into existence. Truman's political advisers strongly urged recognition, warning that the Republicans would otherwise exploit the situation to their advantage. Chaim Weizmann wrote to Truman on May 13, 1948, that he "would regard it as especially appropriate that the greatest living democracy should be the first to welcome the newest into the family of nations." At 6:11 P.M. on May 14, 1948—eleven minutes after the expiration of the British mandate and ten minutes after the coming into existence of the state of Israel—the White House announced American de facto recognition of the new state and its provisional government.[46] On that day, too, began the first full-scale Arab-Israeli war.

Little was said of the principle of self-determination in the formation of American policy with respect to Palestine during the period preceding the creation of Israel. Dean Acheson, who was President Truman's Under Secretary of State from 1945 to 1947 and Secretary of State from 1949 until

1953, alluded obliquely to this principle in his memoirs, or at least to its political implications, as a factor in his opposition to the creation of the Jewish state.

> I did not share the President's views on the Palestine solution to the pressing and desperate plight of great numbers of displaced Jews in Eastern Europe. . . . The number that could be absorbed by Arab Palestine without creating a grave political problem would be inadequate, and to transform the country into a Jewish state capable of receiving a million or more immigrants would vastly exacerbate the political problem and imperil not only American but all Western interests in the Near East.[47]

President Truman, for his part, associated the principle of self-determination with the Zionist cause, despite the existence of a sizable Arab majority in Palestine until after the creation of the state of Israel. As he wrote in his memoirs,

> I was fully aware of the Arabs' hostility to Jewish settlement in Palestine, but, like many Americans, I was troubled by the plight of the Jewish people in Europe. The Balfour Declaration, promising the Jews the opportunity to reestablish a homeland in Palestine, had always seemed to me to go hand in hand with the noble policies of Woodrow Wilson, especially the principle of self-determination.[48]

Although he offers no explanation, it is possible that Truman, like Balfour, was thinking of the self-determination of a future community rather than of an existing one. Whatever his precise thinking, and despite the fact that he was by no means unswerving in support of the Zionist program (as evidenced by his temporary abandonment of the United Nations partition plan in March 1948), Truman was celebrated thereafter as a patron father in the founding of Israel. The chief rabbi of Israel visited Truman in the White House in 1949 and is reported to have told the president, "God put you in your mother's womb so you would be the instrument to bring about the rebirth of Israel after two thousand years."[49]

"STRANGERS WITHIN OUR GATES"

On May 15, 1948, the day following the proclamation of the state of Israel, Menachem Begin spoke to the people of the new nation from the hitherto secret radio station of the Irgun Zvai Leumi. He spoke of the "return" of the Jewish people to their homeland, of the "restoration of the whole Land of Israel to its God-convenanted owners. . . ." In impassioned phrases he praised the accomplishment of the Irgun fighters and called for a continuing fight against the partition of the Holy Land: "Our God-given country is a unity. The attempt to dissect it is not only a crime but a blasphemy and an abortion. Whoever does not recognize our natural right to our entire homeland, does not recognize our right to any part of it." Begin called too for justice within the land, and as to the Arabs, he reminded his fellow Jews: " 'Remember ye were strangers in the land of Egypt'—this supreme rule must continually light our way in our relations with the strangers within our gates."[50]

Nurtured by religious and cultural tradition through eighteen centuries of "exile," the dream of the "return" to Zion was transformed in the twentieth century from a spiritual journey to a political movement and then to a militant cause. If the pogroms of nineteenth century Russia were the principal factor in the development of political Zionism, there can be no doubt that its fierce militance was forged in the furnace of the Nazi Holocaust. To the present day the leaders of Israel are members of the generation that was subjected to the genocide, and among a great portion of the Israeli people there still live memories of parents, other relatives, and friends who were consumed in Hitler's furnaces. Official visitors to Israel are all but required to visit the memorial at Yad Vashem, and from this experience the visitor gains not only a vivid picture of the great crime that was committed against the Jewish people but may also gain an insight into the unique psychology of the Israeli people. "In the heart of the Jewish people," writes Arie Eliav, "the terrible aftermath of the Holocaust still remains. Not only corpses were consumed by fire in the ovens and gas chambers, but also a faith in humanity and its values. If this was what people could do to us . . . one can only conclude that man's worst enemy is man, that there is no conscience and no civilization."[51]

Out of this experience, and the inferences drawn from it, came the concept of the "fighting Jew" and a pride in military prowess hardly known in the history of the Jews since the rebellions against Roman rule in the first and second centuries. Menachem Begin wrote,

> Out of blood and fire and tears and ashes, a new specimen of human being was born, a specimen completely unknown to the world for over eighteen hundred years, the "FIGHTING JEW" It is axiomatic that those who fight have to hate. . . . We had to hate first and foremost, the horrifying, age-old, inexcusable utter *defenselessness* of our Jewish people, wandering through millennia, through a cruel world, to the majority of whose inhabitants the defenselessness of the Jews was a standing invitation to massacre them.[52]

Even with allowance made for Begin's penchant for literary hyperbole, it is noteworthy that, writing a few years after the end of the Second World War, he refers to a *"majority"* of the inhabitants of a "cruel world" as having wished to "massacre" the Jews. To Begin the surpassing lesson of the Holocaust is that the world—not just some people at some times, but the *world*—is inveterately hostile to Jews, and only by fighting can Jews hope to survive. "The world does not pity the slaughtered. It only respects those who fight." Rejecting Descarte's proposition—"I think, therefore I am"—Begin proclaims, "We fight, therefore we are!"[53] At the other end of the Israeli political spectrum, Arie Eliav takes note of the national psychology expressed and exemplified by Begin: the lesson of the death camps is "Woe to the weak!"[54]

In this extraordinary frame of mind the Jews of the Diaspora founded their new state and confronted its Arab inhabitants. In their own religious-historical frame of reference they were *returning* to reclaim their own land, and the Arabs, as Begin put it, were "strangers within our gates." To the Arabs, on the other hand, whose continuous habitation over many centuries had caused them to suppose that the land was theirs, the Jews came as intruders—colonialists and invaders. It was they, the Jews, as Anwar Sadat was later to put it, who were the "strangers in a strange land."[55] Having already fought intermittently under the mandate, the two communities had become irreconcilable by the time of the proclamation of Israel. The major Arab states joined the Palestine Arabs in militant rejection of the Jewish state. The resounding "No" of the Arabs, coupled with the slogan of "throwing the Jews into the sea," persuaded the Jews of Palestine, and especially the survivors of the death camps, that they were confronted with the clear and present danger of another holocaust. The "fighting Jew" responded accordingly.

Israeli attitudes toward the Palestinian Arabs reflect ambivalence, guilt, and a strand of moral sensitivity as well as the militancy of the "fighting Jew." On first impression, to an American observer, Israelis may seem unaware of, or indifferent to, the condition of the displaced Palestinians. On a first trip to the Middle East in 1970, I met a group of Israeli students in Tel Aviv soon after having visited Palestinian refugee camps in Lebanon and was struck by the students' apparent lack of interest in the refugees. Efforts to draw them into discussion of the hardships suffered by the Palestinians were unsuccessful; they preferred to discuss the hardships suffered by Jews in the Soviet Union. With some animus I noted in my diary at that time that these Israeli students "seem isolated and preoccupied. . . . Even their humanitarianism seems exclusively Jewish . . . they do not seem to trust anybody." Further examination of Israeli attitudes suggests that many Israelis are neither indifferent to, nor untroubled by, the dilemma that I. F. Stone formulated thusly:

> For me the Arab problem is also the Number One Jewish problem. How we act toward the Arabs will determine what kind of people we become: either oppressors and racists in our turn like those from whom we have suffered, or a nobler race able to transcend the tribal xenophobias that afflict mankind.[56]

Contrasting the mystique of the "fighting Jew" and the "God-convenanted" land there has been a strand in Zionist thinking that has emphasized equality of rights in a binational community. In 1931 David Ben-Gurion asserted that the Arabs' "right to live in Palestine, develop it and win national autonomy is as incontrovertible as is ours to independence. The two can be realized. We must in our work in Palestine respect Arab rights." In a similar vein Chaim Weizmann had told the Fourteenth Zionist Congress in 1925 that "Palestine must be built up without violating the legitimate interests of the Arabs—not a hair of their heads shall be touched. . . ."[57] In theory at least the professed aim of Ben-Gurion in 1931 and Weizmann in 1925 was not wholly dissimilar to Yasser Arafat's "dream" of a "unified and democratic Palestine" including both Arabs and "all Jews now living in Palestine who choose to live with us there in peace and without discrimination."[58]

Whereas Jews have responded to Arabs with attitudes ranging from militancy to dreams of reconciliation, Arabs have responded to Jews with attitudes of fear and awe, with grudging admiration, and with a wracking new awareness of their own inadequacies in a world of modern technology. As felt by Arabs, the Israeli impact is a new variant of the Western impact of the last two centuries—more alarming because, unlike the European colonialists who came only to rule the Arabs, the Jews have come to live among them, to dominate, and, in the case of the Palestinians, to displace them. All that the West conveyed to Arabs in modern times— scorn for their backwardness and poverty, disdain for their mores and culture—as Wilfred Cantwell Smith wrote, came to culminating expression through the impact of Zionism. Having reproached the Arabs for their antiquated ways and having persuaded them of the need to change, to adopt Western ways, the West, in the Arab perception, then betrayed its own converts by supporting the creation of Israel. "The image of the Arab as an uncouth Bedouin," wrote Smith, "unkempt, uncivilized, and essentially unimportant, that was conjured up in order for the West to push aside his claims in favor of the Jews— this was galling."[59]

Successive military defeats at the hands of Israel have humiliated but also galvanized the Arabs, stimulating the desire and determination to emulate Israel—and the West—in education and science and in military and technological prowess. "We are facing a skilled and modern enemy," wrote the Egyptian editor Muhammad Hasanayn Haykal after the military debacle of 1967, "and there is no other solution for the Arab side in the general confrontation but to become likewise skilled and modern." Similarly, a Syrian Arab intellectual, Dr. Salah al-Din al-Munajjid, published a book in late 1967, entitled *The Pillars of the Disaster: A Scientific Inquiry into the Reasons of the Defeat of June 5,* in which extensive note is taken of Israel's superiority in science as against Arab backwardness. The author concludes, "Our age is an age of science. He who masters science is in a position to rule and in a position to impose his will."[60] Defeat aroused among many Arabs the wish to reshape their societies in casts of modernity, with Israel as the exemplar, "primarily in order to be able to defeat Israel," as Raphael Patai wrote, "but also in order to become progressive, to advance themselves, and to occupy a place of honor in the modern world."[61] Thus, in much the same way that the Holocaust gave rise to the "fighting Jew," defeats by Israel—and especially the overwhelming defeat of 1967—instilled in many Arabs an admiration for, and a determination to emulate, the attributes of the enemy.

To a striking degree the October War of 1973 has become a symbol of Arab progress in the effort to catch up with Israel in military and scientific capacity. A war that ended technically in Arab defeat has become instead, because of a creditable performance, a symbol to Arabs of progress and a badge of renewed self-esteem. On a visit to Egypt a few weeks after the October War, I noted that "the failure to break the magic mid-point between defeat and victory seems less important than the precipitous ascent. The dominant permeating mood in Egypt is one of restored pride."[62] An Egyptian Defense Ministry official compared the effect of the October War on Israel with that of the Tet offensive of 1968 on the Americans in Vietnam: in both instances the military winner was the psychological and political loser.[63] Similarly, an Israeli general reckoned the danger to Israel greater in the wake of the October War than before because the Arabs were no long overawed; they had "broken the curtain of fear."[64]

In the wake of the psychological victory of the October War it became possible, as it had not been before, for responsible Arab leaders to contemplate peace with Israel. Having enabled the Arabs to break their own "curtain of fear," President Sadat became free to recognize and publicly assert that, far from being the coldly arrogant empire builders of the common Arab perception, "the Israelis live in constant fear," that fear indeed is their "second skin," and that, "if they are not in constant fear, then they are in constant doubt."[65] These achievements of attitude and insight raised the Arab-Israeli encounter—or at least the Egyptian-Israeli encounter—to a new plateau in the last months of 1977.

From the premandate years (when Chaim Weizmann secured the qualified acquiescence of the Emir Faisal of the Hejaz to an agreement welcoming Jewish immigration to Palestine) to President Sadat's visit to Jerusalem in November 1977, there have been periodic unsuccessful initiatives toward reconciliation of Jews and Arabs in the Holy Land. In late 1949 and 1950 King Abdullah of Jordan conducted negotiations with Israeli representatives, for which he was accused of betraying the Arab cause and was assassinated by a Palestinian refugee in Jerusalem in 1951. In 1970 Nahum Goldmann, president of the World Jewish Congress, was prevented by a suspicious Israeli government from accepting an invitation to hold talks in Cairo with President Nasser. In all instances these initiatives for peace, and the attitudes that gave rise to them, have been overwhelmed by countervailing fears, animosity, and militancy. Not without cause, Jews have perceived Arabs as implacable enemies, and they have responded to Arabs with attitudes composed in varying measure of militancy, fear, contempt, and moral ambivalence. The Arabs, on the other hand, have perceived the Jews as powerful invaders, and they have responded with feelings of hatred, fear, frustration, humiliation, and grudging admiration. To the Jews, the Arabs have seemed aspirant perpetrators of a new holocaust, thwarted only by their own incompetence and by the superior military skills of the "fighting Jew." To the Arabs, the Jews have represented a new European colonialism, more menacing than the old colonialists because they come as settlers, powerful and dynamic, alien and unassimilable, unwelcome strangers within the Arab gates. To the Palestinians who were displaced from their ancestral homes by the establishment of Israel, writes Edward W. Said, a modern Palestinian writer, "it cannot have meant anything by way of sufficient cause that Jews were victims of European anti-Semitism. . . ."[66]

Taken together, these attitudes constituted the "psychological barrier" that President Sadat tried to breach in Jerusalem in November 1977. This obstacle proved more formidable than expected. Like Columbus, who guessed that the earth was round but significantly misgauged its size, Anwar Sadat perceived the existence and significance of the "psychological barrier" but misjudged its dimensions. The insight was important, but so too was the error.

CAMP DAVID AND THE PARTIAL PEACE

Against this background of bitter, historically nourished animosities, Egypt, Israel, and the United States labored to achieve the partial peace of Camp David. Through the early months of 1978 the United States as well as Egypt exchanged recriminations with the seemingly intransigent Begin government, especially over the issue of the continuing emplacement of Jewish settlements on the West Bank, which President Carter denounced as "illegal" and "an obstacle to peace."[67] Confusion and mutual complaint followed over whether or not the United States had endorsed the Begin plan of December 27, 1977 for the West Bank and Gaza. President Carter had in fact praised the plan as a "long step forward" when Begin first announced it,[68] but became increasingly critical as the intensity of Arab opposition became clear, as Israel failed to make further concessions, and as Sadat's peace initiative appeared to be foundering. Through the spring and summer of 1978 Israel held fast to its position despite rising American displeasure and fast-mounting pyrotechnics exchanged between Begin and Sadat. Sadat, for example, called Begin, "the only obstacle to peace,"[69] and Begin retorted that he was only "an obstacle to a Munich-like surrender."[70]

While openly and sometimes severely criticizing Israel, the Carter administration nevertheless took pains to emphasize that it would not use its substantial aid to Israel as a lever to induce concessions. Vice President Mondale, in a visit to Israel in early July 1978, said that there could be no lasting peace without Israeli withdrawal "on all fronts," but also said, emphasizing that he was speaking for the president: "I pledge to you that my country will not fail to provide Israel with crucial military assistance, nor will we use that assistance as a form of pressure."[71] Secretary of State Vance reiterated that pledge in testimony before the Senate Foreign Relations Committee on August 14, producing what one press account described as a "euphoric reaction" on the part of Prime Minister Begin in advance of the summit meeting called by President Carter to meet at Camp David in September.[72] Whether assurances of uninterrupted aid have induced flexibility by bolstering Israel's sense of security or have simply encouraged intransigence has long been debated among American policymakers and Middle East specialists. As will be seen in subsequent chapters, the United States (at least since 1957, when President Eisenhower applied pressure to compel Israeli withdrawal from Sinai after the Suez war of 1956) has adhered, with infrequent exceptions, to the view that Israel would be more forthcoming in an atmosphere of security induced by unstinting American aid and that efforts to induce Israeli concessions should not be carried beyond verbal pressure. There was no known departure from that approach in the meeting at Camp David, although, according to one "inside" but undocumented account, Begin was finally brought to agree to the dismantling of the Israeli settlements in Sinai only under the pressure of Carter's "unstated implication" that future American aid might be jeopardized if Begin, by refusing concessions, caused the conference to collapse.[73] Ezer Weizman seems to substantiate this account to the extent of suggesting that the Israelis at least feared the possible loss of aid if they failed to yield on the Sinai settlements. Weizman says too, but without further specification, that Begin finally yielded on the Sinai settlements under "enormous" and "unprecedented" American pressure.[74]

The Camp David summit was not, as summits traditionally have been, a culmination of successful, painstaking, preparatory diplomacy at a lower level. It was rather a final, desperate throw of the dice by an American administration at the end of its patience and of the resources it was prepared to use. Annoyance with the brawling principals gave way over the summer of 1978 to mounting anxiety as the Saudis informed the United States that they felt President Sadat's peace effort had failed and it was now necessary to reunite the Arabs against Israel.[75] Fearing that the long, arduous American effort to mediate peace in the Middle East was going on the rocks, and that the end of Sadat's peace initiative would not only reunite the Arabs against Israel but would also set in motion a chain of events leading toward another Middle East war, President Carter extended his personal invitation to President Sadat and Prime Minister Begin to meet with him at Camp David on September 5—an invitation that neither, given the source, could refuse.

After thirteen days of polemics, imminent walkouts, and heroic rescue operations by President Carter, the three leaders came out of seclusion and triumphantly presented to the world their two "frameworks" for peace— one outlining a peace treaty between Egypt and Israel, the other a modified version of Begin's autonomy plan of December 27, 1977, defining procedures for the establishment of a "self-governing authority" for the West Bank and Gaza. The framework for the peace treaty called for the phased withdrawal of Israeli forces from all of Sinai over a three-year period and the restoration of the entire territory to Egypt; the establishment of security zones, limitations on national forces, and the stationing of United Nations forces in the evacuated territory; and the establishment, after a peace treaty was signed, of "normal" diplomatic, economic, and cultural relations between Israel and Egypt.[76] The framework for the West Bank and Gaza called for negotiations among Egypt, Israel, Jordan, and "the representatives of Palestinian people" to resolve "the Palestinian problem in all its aspects." For a transition period of five years, an elected "self-governing authority," its powers to be spelled out in negotiations, would replace the Israeli military government; Israeli forces would be reduced and those remaining redeployed in specified security locations. During the period of the transition regime, negotiations would be conducted among the parties to determine the final status of the West Bank and Gaza. Palestinian refugees might be admitted to the territories during the transition period by unanimous agreement of a special committee representing Egypt, Israel, Jordan, and the self-governing authority.[77]

Begin and Sadat each made a fundamental concession to secure the Camp David accords. Begin, with great reluctance, and under heavy pressure, agreed, through an exchange of letters with Presidents Sadat and Carter, to the removal of all Israeli settlements from the Sinai. Sadat in turn agreed to a West Bank–Gaza settlement whose key provisions were left to be determined through future negotiations and that offered no more than the possibility of eventual Palestinian self-determination; he also agreed to the separation of the two agreements, so that progress toward Palestinian self-rule was not to be considered a legal condition for the implementation of the peace treaty, although Sadat would insist that there was a practical political linkage between the two accords. The Carter administration also made a major concession at Camp David, settling for an arrangement that might hold out the promise of a comprehensive agreement but that did not in itself fulfill that objective.

Camp David, in the view expressed soon after by a senior Egyptian diplomat, could have been somewhat better, from the Egyptian and Arab point of view, if Sadat had been less eager and Carter more persevering, but it could not have been *much* better because the result fell, as it had to, within the parameters of what American domestic politics would allow.[78] Sadat's singular achievement, the diplomat added, was that he had freed himself from the Arab mentality of "total right and total wrong." Another Egyptian diplomat, reacting to Arab charges of a "separate peace," recalled that when Egypt was defeated in 1967, the Arab world called it an *Egyptian* defeat, but when Egypt won a partial victory in 1973, the Arab world claimed an *Arab* victory.[79] The American ambassador to

Egypt, Herman Eilts, said shortly after Camp David that President Carter had done "remarkably well" in persuading President Sadat, against the advice of his own delegation, to drop any official linkage between the two Camp David frameworks, but that the Egyptians still wanted "synchronization" in the implementation of the two accords, and that further progress would depend heavily on continued American involvement as a "full partner."[80]

The Camp David agreement thus engendered the prospect of further, profound disagreement. In the view of Ezer Weizman, "Whereas the Egyptians saw the Sinai agreement as the model for similar understandings with Jordan and Syria over the West Bank and the Golan Heights, Begin saw it as the precise opposite. As far as he was concerned, the withdrawal from the Sinai would be the end of the story."[81]

In the weeks following Camp David, euphoria gave way once again to pessimism and recrimination. Disputes arose as to what had been agreed upon: Carter and Sadat left Camp David convinced that Begin had agreed to suspend Jewish settlements in the West Bank and Gaza for the entire five-year transition period; Begin, however, insisted that he had agreed only to a three months' suspension of settlement while Egypt and Israel negotiated their peace treaty, and he adhered to that view despite angry Egyptian and American protests, resuming Israel's settlements policy after a three month hiatus. The PLO, excluded from any role, had been expected to denounce the Camp David accords, and it did; but it had been hoped that Palestinian leaders in the West Bank and Gaza would cooperate under prodding from Saudi Arabia and Jordan. These two moderate Arab nations, however, not only refused to prod the Palestinians but, as will be seen in subsequent chapters, joined more radical Arab states in active opposition to Camp David, while the West Bank–Gaza Palestinians— under threat from, or in shared conviction with, the PLO, or both— firmly refused to play the roles assigned to them or in any way to cooperate under the Camp David "framework." Sadat, who had counted on the United States to persuade at least the Saudis to go along, found himself increasingly isolated and vulnerable to the charge of making a "separate peace"—a charge to which Begin, by word and deed, lent growing credibility, by disavowing any connection between the two Camp David agreements and by reaffirming plans for enlarging Jewish settlements on the West Bank.

Negotiations for the Egyptian-Israeli peace treaty began in Washington on October 12, 1978 and quickly fell into deadlock over the question of "linkage" between the peace treaty and the future of the West Bank and

Gaza. "The link between the two issues is logical, legitimate and consti-tutes a strategic necessity for the sake of overall peace," the official Cairo radio declared on October 20.[82] The negotiations thereafter fell back into the pre–Camp David pattern of accusation, recrimination, and periodic threats of breakdown. The Israeli Cabinet at first rejected but later accepted language in the preamble to the draft treaty loosely suggesting linkage between the peace treaty and the future of the Palestinians, while Egypt demanded a fixed timetable for Palestinian self-rule linked to the implementation of the peace treaty. By mid-November President Carter's patience was sorely tried by the bickering over linkage and other issues, in which he perceived no real importance; compared with the advantages of peace, Carter complained, "little, tiny technicalities, phrases, legalisms have absolutely no historical significance. . . ."[83] A year after Sadat's historic trip to Jerusalem the "peace process" seemed to be foundering and the "psychological barrier" once again seemed impenetrable. The Israeli minister of defense, Ezer Weizmann described the Israeli mood a year after Sadat's visit as a mood of "peace calamity."[84]

On December 10, 1978 Begin and Sadat—the latter by proxy because he did not wish to appear with Begin—accepted the Nobel Peace Prize that they had been jointly awarded, as much, by acknowledgement of the Nobel Committee, to spur them on as to reward them for past efforts. Both recipients used the forum in Oslo to air their still outstanding differences. Sadat, recalling the journey that had started the peace process, said that when he made his "historic trip to Jerusalem," his aim had not been "to strike a deal as some politicians do." His aim had been, and remained, to "leave no avenue unexplored" toward the "cherished goal" of peace, and "to reconcile the sons of Ishmael and the sons of Isaac." He further stated that "any peace not built on justice and on the recognition of the rights of the peoples, would be a structure of sand which would crumble under the first blow."[85] Begin, presenting himself "in humility and with pride as a son to the Jewish people, as one of the generation of the Holocaust and redemption," recalled the murder of the Jews in World War II and the world's failure to come to their rescue, and reiterated the theme spelled out in his memoir, the necessity to fight for human survival, dignity, and freedom. "Only in honoring that command comes the regeneration of the concept of peace," Begin said. "And so reborn Israel always strove for peace, yearned for it, made endless endeavors to achieve it." Begin recalled Sadat's visit to Jerusalem, "the eternal capital of Israel," and the warm reception he received; issued an appeal on behalf of the Soviet Jews, "who are deprived of one of their most basic rights: to go home"; and, in conclusion, said that the award belonged not to him but to his people—"the ancient people and renascent nation that came back in love and devotion to the land of its ancestors after centuries of homelessness and persecution."[86]

The deadlock—and the fireworks—continued into the winter of 1978–1979. Sadat yielded on the timetable for Palestinian self-rule, accepting instead a target date, but Israel would not accept either. Pressed by the unexpectedly strong stand taken by the Arab states, including Jordan and Saudi Arabia, which had met at Baghdad in early November, Sadat too hardened his stand, insisting on some form of linkage between the two Camp David agreements as well as on Egypt's right to meet prior defense commitments to Arab states, As the deadlock deepened, Senator Robert Byrd, the Senate majority leader, suggested that Congress might be reluctant to approve large-scale military and economic assistance to Israel if it refused full autonomy to the Palestinians and persisted in placing new Jewish settlements in the occupied territories. Abba Eban, the former foreign minister under Israel's Labor government, denounced Byrd's threat as "a gross violation of the whole tradition under which our two nations have cooperated in the past."[87] President Carter, his patience wearing thin once again, told a business group on December 13, 1978 that the protracted negotiations since Camp David had been "one of the most frustrating experiences I have ever had in my life."[88] The president's dismay and support at this point of the Egyptian negotiating position provoked bitter complaints from Israel and American Jewish leaders, who charged the president with abandoning his mediating role to become a partisan on Egypt's side.[89] "Coolly, deliberately, he betrayed the Israelis," wrote columnist William Safire.[90] The three-month deadline that the parties, in their Camp David exuberance, had set for themselves for concluding a peace treaty came and passed with the impasse unbroken. The departing Israeli ambassador to the United States said that American statements blaming Israel for the failure to meet the deadline left Israel "bleeding and injured not less than if military or economic aid was being withheld." Former Secretary of State Kissinger, who had issued some rebukes of his own in his time, warned that those coming from the Carter administration could "contribute to breaking the spirit of Israel."[91]

After a three-month suspension of the peace talks in Washington, during which American shuttle diplomacy and other initiatives failed to break the stalemate, formal talks were resumed at Camp David, at the level below heads of government, on February 21, 1979. The peace process was now affected not only by pressures from the Arab world but also by events in Iran, by now caught up in the convulsions of its Islamic revolution. While Israel argued that the Iranian revolution underscored its own importance as a bastion of stability in the Middle East, and also stressed more than ever, with Iranian oil now lost to it, the necessity of access to the oil of the Sinai, Egypt felt more than ever the necessity of escaping the onus, within the Arab and Islamic worlds, of appearing to make a separate peace with Israel. With the loss of what had seemed a bastion of pro-American stability and the threat of turmoil emanating from Iran across the Arab world, the Carter administration felt more urgently than ever the necessity of pinning down at last the maddeningly elusive settlement between Egypt and Israel. Thus, despite the centrifugal forces driving the obstreperous parties even farther apart, President Carter pressed ahead, calling on February 26 for another Camp David summit meeting. President Sadat refused the invitation; the Israeli Cabinet refused to have Prime Minister Begin meet with a lower-ranking Egyptian official but Begin agreed to meet with Carter alone. The latter, seized once again with dismay, told a group of the nation's governors on February 27 that, with agreement so close and the remaining differences "absolutely insignificant," the continuing failure to reach agreement was "almost disgusting."[92]

Prime Minister Begin arrived in Washington on March 1, 1979, announcing immediately on his arrival that the peace talks were in "deep crisis" and that American compromise proposals would turn the peace treaty into a "sham document."[93] In this defiant mood Begin entered talks with President Carter, which quickly broke down as the United States continued to support Egypt's insistence that a target date be set for Palestinian self-rule, that the treaty be designated as not standing alone but as part of a larger process leading to a comprehensive Middle East settlement, and that the treaty be understood as allowing Egypt to come to the aid of any Arab state attacked by Israel. While Carter exhibited mounting frustration, Begin professed to see no need of haste. Conceding that no progress had been made in his talks with the president, Begin, on March 4, counseled a period of "serious reflection." A treaty, he said, would "take some time, since it has been an old conflict."[94]

President Carter was by then in no mood for an extended period of "serious reflection" while his painfully constructed diplomatic edifice crumbled around him. In a last-minute effort to prevent total collapse of negotiations, the president, on March 4, offered new compromise proposals, which Begin referred to his Cabinet in Jerusalem. The Israeli Cabinet approved the new proposals, and on March 5 the White House announced that Carter would fly to Egypt and Israel to try personally to negotiate the final terms of the peace treaty. On the day of the president's departure, March 7, a White House official was quoted as saying that Carter's chance for a second term might well turn on the outcome of his trip: "He has more of his personal prestige wrapped up in this than anything else he has attempted."[95]

The journey was arduous. In Egypt Carter was greeted with a tumultuous reception by the Egyptian public and lingering doubts and counterproposals by Egyptian officials. In Israel Carter encountered strong objections to the latest proposals he brought from Cairo. In both countries the president and his aides held out the prospect of generous new American military and economic aid after a peace treaty was signed. At a state dinner for the president on the evening of March 11, Prime Minister Begin said it was his "duty to say that we have serious problems to solve before we can sign this peace treaty," whereupon, according to a press account, "Mr. Carter's face turned grim and ashen."[96] The president's trials continued on the next day. After addressing an emotional plea for peace to a silent chamber, Carter was obliged to sit stoically through a tempestuous session of the Knesset in which one member denounced the treaty as "a crime against our people," another compared Sadat with Hitler, and others charged the United States with "selling out" Israel.[97] Carter seemed ready on March 12 to abandon his peace mission and go home. The people of Israel and Egypt were ready for peace, he told the Knesset, but the leaders apparently were not.[98]

Once again a miracle at the brink rescued the peace process. A new set of compromise proposals, including provisions for Israeli access to Sinai oil and the timing of an exchange of ambassadors between Israel and Egypt won Begin's approval (subject to the consent of Cabinet and Knesset) on the morning of March 13, altering the mood as the president left Israel from despair to high optimism. "We are happy that we could have helped you to the best of our ability," Begin told Carter in a parting statement.[99] Carter then stopped briefly in Cairo, where Sadat, in an airport meeting, accepted all of the president's new proposals. President Carter flew home in triumph, while Egypt and Israel set their experts to preparing aid requests to be submitted to the United States.

While the Carter administration elatedly prepared for the treaty signing in Washington, indications appeared of the difficulties that lay ahead in the wake of a partial peace. Israel pressed for faster arms deliveries and sophisticated electronic warning equipment against the danger that Syria and Iraq might try to disrupt the Egyptian-Israeli peace treaty. The United

States responded with promises of larger new arms supplies for both Israel and Egypt. The Arab states, moderate as well as radical, condemned the imminent treaty, as did the PLO and Palestinian leaders in the occupied territories. A mission led by the president's national security adviser, Zbigniew Brzezinski, sent to seek support for the treaty, was rebuffed in Saudi Arabia and Jordan. Until the day of the treaty signing, the peace-making parties themselves continued to quibble over technicalities and larger issues, presaging the long, hard struggle to come over Palestinian autonomy in the West Bank and Gaza. Prime Minister Begin opened the debate on the peace treaty in the Knesset on March 20 with defiant assertions, in response to Egyptian claims to the contrary, that Israel would never return to its borders of 1967, never permit Jerusalem to be divided again, and never permit a Palestinian state. "We never agreed to autonomy for the territories," Begin said, "but only for the inhabitants."[100] The Knesset approved the peace treaty overwhelmingly on March 22, but the mood of Israel remained apprehensive. "Zionism has waited sixty years for this great moment," columnist Amos Elon wrote in *Ha'aretz*, Israel's leading daily. "There have been five wars and 12,000 deaths. Now, when the moment has arrived, there is something almost anticlimactic about it; sullen and sour. A gloomy atmosphere."[101] President Sadat too, in the days before the treaty signing, lapsed from his customary public optimism, commenting in anticipation of the hard negotiations ahead on Palestinian self-rule: "Let us sign and start the peace process. I know Begin will be raising hell as he always does but, by God, I shall be raising hell for him also . . . the real peace process starts only after the signing."[102]

The peace treaty was signed at the White House in Washington on March 26, 1979, in an atmosphere more of relief than of elation. Despite six months of negotiation, recrimination, and recurrent threats of total breakdown, the final treaty contained no important departures from the Camp David framework. The preamble vaguely suggested linkage with the broader Arab–Israeli conflict by stating that the treaty was an "impor-tant step" toward comprehensive peace. In its main articles and annexes the treaty provided for an end to the state of war between Israel and Egypt; the phased withdrawal of Israeli forces from the Sinai over a period of three years; the establishment of "normal and friendly relations," includ-ing the right of Israel to buy Egyptian oil upon the completion, in nine months, of an interim withdrawal; the establishment of limited force and United Nations buffer zones in the evacuated territory; and free Israeli passage through the Suez Canal. The stubborn question of Egypt's right to come to the aid of an Arab ally attacked by Israel was dealt with by specifying the precedence of the peace treaty, as Israel wished, while also recognizing the primacy of the United Nations Charter with its provision for collective self-defense.

Accompanying letters among the three heads of government specified that ambassadors would be exchanged a month after the completion of the interim withdrawal, and that negotiations on Palestinian autonomy would begin within a month after the exchange of instruments of ratification of the peace treaty with the goal of completing those negotiations within another year, whereupon the transition period of five years would begin, the self-governing authority would take up its responsibilities, and Israeli military forces would be redeployed into specified security zones.[103] In two accompanying memoranda of agreement, the United States promised Israel its support in the event of violations of the treaty, pledged to be "responsive" to Israel's military and economic needs, and reaffirmed and extended its 1975 commitment to provide Israel with oil should Israel be unable to obtain oil itself.[104]

Throughout the "peace process," culminating in the treaty of March 1979, the United States had consistently and deliberately refrained from bringing to bear the full weight of its political and economic power to achieve a result equitable, by American reckoning, to both parties, and also consistent with the considerable interests of the United States. Under pressure from Egypt it had agreed to be a "full partner" in the peace negotiations, but under greater pressure from Israel it had promised not to try to impose a settlement of its own and never to use its aid as an instrument of pressure. The United States thus remained committed to a role as *mediator* in the Middle East, disavowing the role of *arbiter*. More than any of his predecessors, President Carter had played that mediating role with diligence, energy, unbounded patience, and substantial result. But for an exercise in personal diplomacy on Carter's part unequaled since the time of President Wilson, there would, almost certainly, have been no peace treaty between Israel and Egypt. Whether similar means would suffice to resolve the intractable Palestinian problem and to achieve a comprehensive settlement remained, however, much in doubt in the wake of the Egyptian-Israeli treaty. Whether, should mediation fail, other means might then be resorted to—whether, specifically, the United States might choose to become the *arbiter* of peace in the Middle East—would depend on the answers to fundamental questions of national interest and political feasibility.

One of the striking characteristics of the peace process that led to Camp

David and the treaty signed at Washington in March 1979 was the evidence on many occasions that the United States seemed to want the settlement more than Egypt or Israel did. "Why do we keep a wristwatch about a peace treaty?" Begin had asked when the negotiations seemed about to collapse on March 4, 1979.[105] The peace treaty was finally achieved because President Carter, by going to Egypt and Israel in March 1979, made it clear to the parties that the issue was one of surpassing importance to the United States and that to refuse to settle at that point was to incur the wrath of a thwarted, humiliated leader of the world's most powerful nation. Basic questions of American policy thus remained unanswered in the wake of the partial peace of March 1979: How did the settlement serve American interests as against those of Egypt and Israel? What further American interests remained unrealized or in jeopardy, and what means would be required to secure them?

UNFINISHED BUSINESS

The second stage of the "peace process," aimed at some form of Palestinian self-rule, began in May 1979 with the two sides in basic disagreement. Before the talks began, Begin put forth a new autonomy plan, closely resembling his initial plan of December 1977, limiting Palestinian self-rule to administrative, but not legislative, functions in social and educational affairs, while security and public order would remain under Israeli military control; Israel would control water resources and would also retain the right to acquire land and establish new Jewish settlements in the West Bank and Gaza. "I assure you," an aide to Begin said as the new talks were about to begin, "if anything comes out of the negotiations, it will not be a Palestinian state."[106] Egypt, for its part, spelled out its negotiating position in an official communiqué: "Full Palestinian autonomy in the West Bank and Gaza is the first step toward independence and a transitional stage before the Palestinian people claim their full right to self-determination."[107]

The discussions proceeded intermittently over the next year without significant progress. President Carter tried repeatedly and unsuccessfully to break the impasse over the extent of autonomy to be accorded the Palestinians and made an intensive effort in the spring of 1980 to bring the two sides to at least a semblance of agreement before the May 26 target date for the conclusion of negotiations that the parties had set for themselves. In April 1980 Sadat made his first trip to Washington since the signing of the peace treaty thirteen months before, and Carter took the occasion, in Sadat's presence, to recall that Prime Minister Begin had promised full autonomy for the West Bank and Gaza—"not just autonomy, full autonomy"—and that he had made that promise "many, many times."[108] Begin came to Washington immediately thereafter and pledged a renewed, concerted effort to reach agreement. He offered, however, no concessions on the self-governing authority's powers and the continuing establishment of new Israeli settlements in the occupied territories.[109]

The target date came and went with the impasse unbroken. The Arab world, except for Egypt, remained adamant in its rejection of the Camp David peace process, with neither Jordan nor the West Bank Palestinian leadership showing an inclination to play the roles assigned to them by the Camp David framework. Far indeed from moving closer to the Camp David peace process, King Hussein, who had once been America's closest collaborator in the Arab world, became increasingly alienated from the United States and increasingly aligned with the Arab "rejectionist" group. In the autumn of 1980 King Hussein gave active and open support to Iraq in the war it had initiated against Iran the previous month, pointing out that Iraq was the only country that gave the Arabs "strategic depth" since Egypt had signed its peace treaty with Israel.[110] Syria, which had been moving hesitantly toward closer relations with the United States following the American-mediated disengagement agreement of 1974 under which Israel had yielded territory seized in the 1973 war, signed in October 1980 a twenty-year treaty of friendship with the Soviet Union. The Begin government, meanwhile, continued to emplace new settlements in the West Bank, refused even to consider a Palestinian self-governing authority with legislative and judicial powers, and made little secret of its willingness to allow the autonomy negotiations to go on indefinitely without result. President Carter, distracted by the 1980 election campaign and by the detention of American hostages in Iran, made perfunctory statements of optimism from time to time, but he never again, in his remaining months in office, found it possible to bring decisive influence to bear on the apparently intractable Palestinian issue.

In June 1980 the nine members of the European common market, concerned that the Camp David peace process seemed to be foundering, issued what came to be known as their "Venice Declaration." The Europeans endorsed the principle of Palestinian self-determination, called for the association of the Palestine Liberation Organization with the peace process, and condemned Israel's settlements policy, while also reaffirming their commitment to Israel's right to exist and offering to help guarantee Israel's security.[111] What the Europeans hoped would be taken as a judicious proposal, in fact offended everybody. Israel announced that it "totally rejects" PLO participation in peace negotiations as called for by the

Europeans.[112] The PLO condemned the Europeans for failing to recognize the PLO officially and explicitly endorse a Palestinian state. The American Jewish Congress denounced the Venice Declaration as a "cynical and shameful" expression of "eagerness to appease oil-rich Arabs." President Carter reiterated his administration's stand against dealing with the PLO until it recognized Israel's right to exist.[113] Thus rebuffed, the Europeans retreated, at least temporarily, from the field.

In August 1980 President Sadat suspended the flagging Palestinian autonomy talks after the Israeli Knesset adopted legislation formally annexing East Jerusalem. Despite periodic sputterings the negotiations remained in abeyance thereafter as first the United States and then Israel underwent election campaigns. Apparently convinced that little could be accomplished while Carter remained distracted and while Begin remained in office, Sadat placed his hopes, first, on Carter's reelection, and then on Begin's defeat. Whether a reelected Carter would have taken a stronger stand on the autonomy talks—and what effect that might have had—cannot of course be known. Whether the Israeli Labor party, had it won the election of June 1981, would have been able to achieve a breakthrough on the Palestinian question, is also a matter of speculation. It had not done so during its long tenure in office prior to 1977, and it offered no new proposals in 1981.

The Reagan administration came to office solidly committed to Israel. Asked during the campaign if a Reagan administration would continue to adhere to the Camp David peace process, the Republican candidate replied that he would "continue to support that process as long as Israel sees utility in it." Reagan also gave assurances that he would use "all appropriate instruments," including the American veto in the United Nations Security Council, "to insure that the PLO has no voice or role as a participant in future peace negotiations with Israel." The Republican candidate also promised that a "Reagan Administration will not continue to ship massive quantities of sophisticated armaments to so-called 'moderate' Arab states. . . ."[114]

Once in office the Reagan administration, like its predecessors, found it necessary to moderate its campaign promises. The commitment against arms to "so-called 'moderate' Arab states" was jettisoned altogether with the commitment in 1981, subject to congressional veto, of additional sophisticated aircraft and equipment to Saudi Arabia. The new administration also soon found itself in controversies with the Begin government no less tense and acrimonious than those of the Carter administration.

The principal innovation of the Reagan administration was an initial attempt to subordinate the regional Arab-Israeli issue to its own conception of the larger strategic contest between the Soviet Union and the United States. "We feel it is fundamentally important," Secretary of State Alexander Haig told the House Foreign Affairs Committee on March 18, 1981, "to begin to develop a consensus of strategic concerns throughout the region among Arab and Jew and to be sure that the overriding dangers of Soviet inroads into this area are not overlooked."[115] Within the region the new administration, at its outset, began to look favorably toward what came to be called the Jordanian option, a term that referred to the possible partition of the occupied West Bank between Jordan and Israel as proposed by Israeli Labor governments that had preceded Begin. Preoccupied in any case with its domestic economic program, the Reagan administration seemed inclined in the early months of 1981 to await the Israeli election and the Labor party victory that then seemed probable, and then to proceed with the "Jordanian option" and the development of an anti-Soviet "strategic consensus."

By mid-1981 none of these expectations had been, or seemed likely to be, borne out. The Likud government of Prime Minister Begin was returned to office. King Hussein, as he had done repeatedly in previous years, spurned the "Jordanian option" and reiterated his support of Palestinian self-determination in the West Bank and Gaza. Nor did the "strategic consensus" attract Arab support. When Secretary Haig visited the region in April, officials in both Saudi Arabia and Jordan stressed that, however much they feared and disliked the Soviet Union, they feared and disliked Israel more.[116] It was thus demonstrated to the Reagan administration, early in its term of office, that as long as the Palestinian question remained unfinished business, neither a general settlement, a diversion of attention to global strategic issues, nor even an approximation of regional stability was likely to be achieved.

Events reinforced this demonstration, making it increasingly unfeasible for the Reagan administration to ignore the Middle East while acting on its domestic agenda. A series of crises in the spring and summer of 1981 demonstrated anew that, despite the partial peace of March 1979, the Middle East remained an arena of conflict posing dangers not only within the region but to the outside world as well, including the superpowers.

As on previous occasions, Lebanon was the flashpoint. Racked by civil conflict since 1975, partially occupied by Syrian troops, its government reduced to impotence, its life and society disrupted by the presence of 350,000 Palestinian refugees, and with Palestinian guerrilla forces using its territory as their only available base for raids against Israel, Lebanon had become a microcosm of the larger Middle East conflict. Palestinian attacks across the Israeli border had repeatedly brought on punishing retaliation, including a full-scale invasion in March 1978. Another protracted round of violent conflict began in the spring of 1981, involving Israel, the various Christian militias within Lebanon, the Syrian peacekeeping force present under the auspices of the Arab League, Lebanese Muslim forces, and the Palestinian guerrillas. In late April Israeli planes shot down two Syrian helicopters fighting against Christian Phalangist militia, which had been trying to strengthen their position in the Bakaa valley of east central Lebanon. The Syrians thereupon moved Soviet-supplied SAM–6 surface-to-air missiles into Lebanon, challenging Israel's hitherto unchallenged air supremacy over Lebanon. Israel demanded the missiles' removal, threatening to use its air force to destroy them if they were not removed peacefully.

The United States undertook to mediate the issue; it dispatched to the region a special representative, Philip C. Habib. The Reagan administration, which since coming to office had issued a series of statements accusing the Soviet Union of threatening world peace, now also appealed to the Soviets to counsel restraint to their Syrian ally. Habib, shuttling from capital to capital, managed to bring Saudi Arabia into a mediating role between Syria and the Lebanese factions but otherwise met with little success. With Syria refusing to pull back the missiles, Israel repeatedly threatening to bomb them, and both the United States and the Soviet Union bolstering their naval forces in the eastern Mediterranean, the "Syrian missile crisis" by mid-May appeared, by one account, to have grown into "the most ominous and intractable showdown since the 1967 war."[117]

The issue in Lebanon was at least momentarily eclipsed when Israel, on June 7, 1981, using American-supplied aircraft, bombed and destroyed a nearly completed French-built nuclear reactor outside Baghdad in Iraq. Claiming to have incontrovertible evidence that the purpose of the reactor was to produce atomic bombs and that the target for these bombs would be Israel, Prime Minister Begin passionately defended the Israeli action: "There won't be another Holocaust in history. Never again, never again."[118] World reaction, which was harsh, took note of the fact that Iraq was a signatory to the Nuclear Non-Proliferation Treaty that had come into effect in 1970 and, as such, had accepted international safeguards and inspection of its nuclear facility by the International Atomic Energy Agency. Israel, on the other hand, was not a signatory to the treaty, refused international inspection of its reactor at Dimona in the Negev

Desert, and, by authoritative accounts, possessed either nuclear weapons in being or the capacity to produce them. Former Israeli Foreign Minister and Defense Minister Moshe Dayan said on June 24, 1981 that Israel could manufacture atomic bombs "in a short time." In previous years there had been periodic reports of clandestine acquisition by Israel of quantities of enriched uranium; the American Central Intelligence Agency in 1978 released a memorandum dated September 4, 1974, asserting, "We believe that Israel already has produced nuclear weapons."[119]

Israel thus asserted a national right—for the first time in the nuclear age—to mount a preemptive strike against a potential enemy. And it did so while maintaining an unregulated nuclear capacity of its own. An unnamed Israeli official, recalling the early post–World War II years, when the United States held a nuclear monopoly while the Soviet Union was still developing its capacity, observed that "if Begin had been President of the United States instead of Truman in 1949, there wouldn't be an arms race."[120] Begin himself took note of the significance of the precedent he had set for other countries that might be tempted to strike at enemies that seemed on the verge of acquiring nuclear weapons: "Now every country will decide for itself."[121]

President Reagan reacted cautiously to the Israeli raid. He advised Congress that a "substantial violation" of a 1952 agreement, under which Israel assured the United States that its military equipment would be used only for defensive purposes, "may have occurred," and he ordered a delay in the scheduled shipment of four F–16 aircraft to Israel pending a review of the matter.[122] Although the president was reported personally to have been "shocked" by the Israeli raid, it was quickly made known that the United States would veto a United Nations Security Council resolution imposing sanctions against Israel.[123] In any event, the Security Council, on June 19, 1981, adopted a resolution, previously agreed to by the United States and Iraq, stating that the Council "strongly condemns" the Israeli raid but providing for no sanctions.[124]

The question remained whether Israel had violated its agreement to use American equipment only for defensive purposes. A state department emissary, sent to Jerusalem in July to review that question, was rebuffed by Prime Minister Begin. Although Israel always took American interests into consideration, Begin said, "If anybody should think that one sovereign country should consult another sovereign country about a specific military operation, in order to defend its citizens, that would be absurd."[125] "The larger absurdity," the *Washington Post* commented in an editorial, "is his evident expectation that the United States will load Israel up with the hottest weapons going, at cut rates or for free, and then stand by humming 'Hatikvah' while the Israelis use those weapons as they choose, no matter what the effects on American interests."[126]

Just as the Syrian missile crisis was eclipsed by the Israeli raid on Iraq, the latter crisis was overtaken by a major new outbreak of violence in Lebanon. Begin's Likud coalition had been returned to power in the election of June 30 with a bare plurality of seats in the Knesset and in alliance with several small religious-oriented and politically hard-line factions to make up a bare majority. "There are no Weizmans in our new coalition," a Likud official said, referring to the conciliatory approach of the former defense minister.[127] Disinclined to concessions relating to the occupied territories, the reelected Likud government was also in no mood to endure renewed Palestinian provocations across the Lebanese border.

For a period of two weeks starting on July 10, 1981, Israel, in response to reports of a major Palestinian arms buildup, mounted devastating air attacks on Lebanon. The Palestinian guerrillas responded with sustained rocket attacks on communities in northern Israel. In retaliation for the rocket attacks, in which three Israelis were killed and twenty-five wounded, Israeli warplanes struck at Palestinian neighborhoods in Beirut on July 17, killing an estimated 300 people and wounding another 800. Explaining that the attacks had been aimed at PLO headquarters that had been deliberately placed in civilian neighborhoods to gain immunity from attacks, Prime Minister Begin announced that such quarter would no longer be allowed. "We shall give the enemy no rest," he said, "until we have put an end to his bloody rampage and peace will reign between Israel and Lebanon."[128]

The United States government, dismayed by the escalation of violence, again delayed the shipment to Israel of F–16 aircraft, of which ten were by then scheduled. Asked about the Beirut raid and its probable consequences, President Reagan confined himself to an unexceptionable observation, "I don't think violence is ever helpful to the peace process."[129] The Israelis, for their part, although annoyed by the delay in shipping the aircraft, expressed confidence that they would soon be forthcoming, once the immediate crisis were out of the headlines. A close adviser to Prime Minister Begin expressed understanding of Washington's "embarrassment" and added, "I don't think this is an embargo. It's only a matter of style."[130]

Through the mediation of the American special envoy, Philip C. Habib, and with the quiet assistance of Saudi Arabia, a cease-fire was concluded on July 24 between Israel and the Palestine Liberation Organization. The negotiations were conducted by elaborate indirection since neither Israel nor the United States was prepared to talk directly with the PLO. The Palestinian guerrillas took pride, however, in having withstood the Israeli onslaught, albeit at high cost, and in having shown themselves to be a significant party, recognized or not, to the unresolved Arab-Israeli conflict. Shimon Peres, the leader of Israel's opposition Labor party, commented: "The cease-fire was made with the PLO. There is no point in concealing this. The truth must be spoken even when you're in government."[131]

Relieved by the cease-fire of July 1981, the Reagan administration began to look toward fundamental issues—the continuing anarchy in Lebanon, the interrupted Camp David "peace process," and the seminal issue of unsatisfied and seemingly irrepressible Palestinian nationalism. Like the Carter administration before it, the Reagan administration found itself confronted, sooner than it had hoped and expected, with the excruciating question of whether American interests in the Middle East could be realized by means short of the vigorous application of American power. Skillful diplomacy, good will, and infinite patience had enabled the United States to guide recalcitrant parties down the long road to Camp David. Whether these would suffice to carry the peace process further, to resolve the conflict of nationalisms between rival claimants to the Holy Land, was, as of mid-1981, far from certain.

The assassination of President Sadat on October 6, 1981 added to the uncertainty. Since his great initiative of November 1977, Sadat had grown steadily more isolated from the Arab world. Accused at the outset of "selling out" the Palestinian people for a separate peace, he strove to the full extent of his power and beyond to disprove that fatal accusation by bringing the Palestinian question as close as possible to a settlement based on self-determination. That proved beyond Sadat's resources as he was thwarted by the intransigence and political timidity of the other parties. The Israelis, contrary to what Sadat and Carter had believed was agreed on at Camp David in September 1978, expanded their settlements in the occupied territories, moving toward de facto annexation. The Palestinians, from the outset, refused even to consider the possibility of an evolutionary development of the Camp David "peace process" toward something more to their liking. The United States, holding "ninety-nine percent of the cards," as Sadat frequently said, declined, for domestic political reasons, to play them. It failed not only to restrain Israel's settlements in the West Bank. The United States proved unable as well to move the talks on Palestinian autonomy forward in any significant measure; failed to restrain or significantly reproach Israel when it used American warplanes to attack Baghdad and Beirut, soon releasing the delayed F–16s; and seemed, with the accession of the Reagan administration, to lose interest in the Palestinian question, preferring to focus its efforts on the building of "strategic consensus" against the Soviet Union.

These events posed a heavy burden to President Sadat, who found himself increasingly exposed to foreign and domestic enemies as the putative betrayer of the "Arab nation." Whether a more forthcoming attitude on the part of Israel, a more pragmatic approach on the part of the Palestinians, or a greater measure of political courage on the part of the United States would have saved Sadat from the assassins' bullets cannot of course be known. Whether, too, Sadat's passing marked the end of the Camp David road also could not be known at the time, but that seemed distinctly possible.

CHAPTER TWO

American Interests and the American Political System

As COMMONLY UNDERSTOOD, the term "national interest" connotes a selfish and unprincipled, or at least amoral, approach to the conduct of foreign relations. This term seems to imply concern with a nation's geopolitical and economic advantage without regard for morality, law, or the welfare of others, except insofar as these serve as instruments for the nation's own advantage. In this archetypal usage the idea of "national interest" is exemplified by Lord Palmerston's dictum that England had neither "eternal allies" nor "perpetual enemies" but only interests that are "eternal and perpetual."[1]

At the risk of neologism, a broader conception of "national interest" is employed here. This concept is understood to encompass principled behavior, regard for the law, loyalty to friends and commitments, ethical restraints, and even ethical imperatives—as well as the seeking of geopolitical and economic advantage. Moral principles are embraced within the concept of "national interest" because a civilized society's interests necessarily include certain values and standards of conduct, both in its internal affairs and in its international relations. As used here the term "national interests of the United States" refers to the *security* and *welfare* of the American people in all major aspects—political, military, economic, social, and moral—extending even to matters of sentiment or group affiliation. Because a democratic government exists to serve its people and not the reverse, there would seem no reason why even a strong *preference* of the people, or some part of them, may not constitute a "national interest"—as long as that preference is kept compatible with, and proportionate to, other interests (as long, that is, as the good of the whole is given precedence over the desires of groups within the larger community). In its international context the "national interest" implies primacy but not exclusivity for the security and welfare of the American people. Or, to put it another way, the national interest of the United States *requires* decency in the nation's dealings with others, *allows* generosity so far as the nation can afford it, but *prohibits* the subordination of American requirements to the needs or wishes of others.

A CONCEPTION OF NATIONAL INTEREST

Definitions tend either to beg questions or to raise them. We, as Americans, may satisfy ourselves that the national interest embraces moral as well as political and economic considerations, but we then need to know what our true political and economic interests are and, more difficult still, what our legitimate moral interests are. These categories are largely, but not wholly, subjective. Just as geography can tell Americans something about their security interests and resource studies can tell them a great deal about their foreign economic interests, the nation's history and institutions carry strong implications for the kind of values that represent American interests in the world and also for the kind that do not.

It seems useful, in seeking to identify values in foreign relations, to distinguish between ends and means. Being an agent of its people and not a principle in itself, the government of a democracy, in principle, can have no objectives in foreign policy other than those that, in one way or another, are of service to its own people. A dictatorship may pursue objectives that enhance the nation as a *power*, seeking dominance for its own sake, for the honor and glory of the state, or spreading its ideology out of missionary zeal. These are practices to which, as is well known, democratic states often succumb, but in principle the democratic state, being an agent not a principle, pursues only those objectives in its foreign relations that enhance the nation as a *society*, at home, that is, where its people live. This prototypical democracy will commend its political and social values to others, and within limits encourage their adoption, with a view to developing the most congenial possible international environment. It will establish its military power abroad to the extent, but only to the extent, that doing so is essential to the safety of its own people and those other peoples to whom it is bound by common values or other interests. Such a government may exercise world responsibility by reason of its commitment to the development of an international security community or a world regime of law, but it will not proselytize in pursuance of a mission, divine or secular, nor bring its power to bear merely for the "honor" or "glory" of the state.

The democratic state will not do these things—in *principle*, let it be emphasized again—because there is no point. Being the instrument of its people and not of some god, secular or divine, the democratic state is, in Lockian terms, a compact among its citizens, lacking attributes of divinity or even mystery. It is an arrangement, not a living entity, and arrangements, in logic, are no more capable than inanimate objects of the pursuit of "missions" or of the experience of "glory." In the words of a Senate Foreign Relations Committee report of 1969: "Foreign policy is not an end in itself. We do not have a foreign policy because it is interesting or fun, or because it satisfies some basic human need; we conduct foreign policy for a purpose external to itself, the purpose of securing democratic values in our own country."[2]

In practice democratic statesmen—including, and perhaps especially, American statesmen—readily lapse into the rhetoric of foreign policy as a "mission" and then, at some point, start to believe it. Even Secretary of State Henry Kissinger, whose policies were thought to represent a kind of apotheosis of modern realpolitik, declared in a speech in 1973 that "America [is] not true to itself unless it has a meaning beyond itself"—a "spiritual" meaning, he went on to explain.[3] Events during his tenure would suggest that Dr. Kissinger was not swept away with the rhetoric of foreign policy as a "spiritual" adventure. On other occasions the impulse to uplift, the attribution of mysterious or divine mission to the nation's foreign policy, has had more tangible consequences. With due allowance for the rationalization of other important motives involved, notice may be taken of President McKinley's decision in 1898, on moral grounds, to annex the Philippines to the United States. As he later recounted to a group of visiting clergymen, "I walked the floor of the White House night after night until midnight," and more than once "went down on my knees and prayed Almighty God for light and guidance. . . ." Then one night the word of the Lord came: to give the islands back to Spain would be "cowardly and dishonorable"; to turn them over to France or Germany— "our commercial rivals in the Orient—that would be bad business and discreditable;" leaving them to themselves was out of the question—"they were unfit for self-government;" therefore, McKinley concluded, "there was nothing left for us to do but to take them all, and to educate the

Filipinos, and uplift and civilize and Christianize them, and by God's grace do the very best we could by them, as our fellowmen for whom Christ also died. And then I went to bed, and to sleep, and slept soundly. . . ."[4]

Sometimes as rationalization and sometimes as genuine motive, evangelical moralism has been a recurrent factor in American foreign policy. Its probable high point was the imperialism of 1898, but it has been discerned as an influence on undertakings ranging from the Monroe Doctrine to the Vietnam War. It profoundly influenced the American approach to the Cold War with the Soviet Union in the late 1940s, which might have been conducted and explained in traditional geopolitical terms but instead was pursued as what Senator Arthur Vandenberg described as "the worldwide ideological clash between Eastern communism and Western democracy."[5] It emerged again in the Reagan administration in the form of renewed anti-Sovietism and a declared policy of opposing the terrorism of left-wing but not necessarily of right-wing regimes. As viewed by President Reagan at the outset of his administration, the leaders of the Soviet Union "reserve unto themselves the right to commit any crime; to lie; to cheat" to further their cause.[6] Evangelical moralism was a factor too in the human rights policy of the Carter administration, and it appeared in some of President Carter's pronouncements on the Middle East. Shortly after President Sadat's visit to Jerusalem in November 1977 President Carter expressed optimism that "deep religious conviction" would facilitate agreement between Egypt and Israel. Carter said, "I think the fact that we worship the same God and are bound by basically the same moral principles is a possible source for resolution of differences. I was always convinced that if Sadat and Begin could get together, they would be bound by that common belief."[7]

Common monotheism did not in fact bring Prime Minister Begin and President Sadat closer to agreement, any more than the American program to "educate," "uplift," "civilize," and "Christianize" the Filipinos resulted in the happiness and prosperity of the modern Republic of the Philippines. That would seem to be the central difficulty of religious moralism as a factor in a nation's foreign policy, or in the nation's definition of its national interest: it tends not to bring the desired result. Instances do not readily come to mind of belief in the "same God" helping nations to resolve their differences, or indeed preventing them from fighting. Most of the bloodshed in this century of unprecedented bloodshed has taken place among Christians. The human rights policy of the Carter administration, with its threat of sanctions, unevenly applied, for noncompliance, went beyond the mere commendation of democratic values but nonetheless failed to achieve widespread results and, in the case of the Soviet Union, may have provoked a stiffening of repression. At the conclusion in March 1978 of the Belgrade conference on European security and cooperation, convened to review the Helsinki accords of 1975, the American representative, Arthur J. Goldberg, noted that the conference was the first to put the questions of human rights and fundamental freedoms "prominently and legitimately into the framework of multilateral East-West diplomacy."[8] It must also be noted that after eight months of futile discussion at Belgrade not one of the more than one hundred proposals that were submitted to the conference was approved; no mention was made of human rights in the final report of the conference because the Russians would not permit it; indeed, the only agreements reached at Belgrade were agreements to hold certain other meetings, including another review conference at Madrid in 1980.

The pertinence of these observations to an examination of the national interests of the United States is in their implications for what is and is not feasible as a moral dimension of the national interest. Evangelical moralism in its varied forms, from imperialist uplift to intrusive "human rights" and highly selective "antiterrorist" campaigns, tends to be unrewarding for certain fundamental reasons—of which the most important is its extension into realms in which we are unable or, as we sometimes find at the crucial moment, simply unwilling to apply our national power. Evangelical moralism would also seem to exceed our moral and intellectual resources, involving as it does the attempted extension of Western democratic values to societies in which they may be uncongenial, unfamiliar, or unworkable. A useful distinction may be drawn between *morality* and *moralism*, the one having to do with the nation's own conduct, the other referring to its strictures on the conduct of others. A moral dimension to the national interest, in the present view, is properly confined to those few basic norms of international behavior that seem essential to world peace and that give promise of a measure of justice to national communities in a world of nation states—norms as to which there is at least a semblance of international consensus. Aspiring even to these may be dismissed as utopian; to reach beyond them, into the realm, for example, of personal liberty in powerful, oppressive states, would seem not only futile but, in its raising of hopes not likely to be satisfied, irresponsible as well.

The international norms that may, with some realism, be incorporated into a conception of the national interest are, by and large, codified within the United Nations Charter. Honored, to be sure, more in the breach than otherwise, the basic principles of the charter derive neither from divine revelation nor crusading ideology. These principles are the codified product, rather, of the experience of nations, to some degree with social and individual human needs, but primarily with war and the hope of its prevention. The League of Nations Covenant, predecessor to the United Nations Charter, was, to its principal author, Woodrow Wilson, "a practical document and a humane document," with a "pulse of sympathy in it," a "compulsion of conscience throughout it."[9] Wilsonian rhetoric notwithstanding, the covenant of the league, and the United Nations charter that followed it, were no more than blueprints for a rudimentary international security community. They surely ought not to be regarded as the impractical inventions of dreamers who lacked the patience to work with tried and true systems of international relations. Devised in the wake of the two most terrible bloodlettings in the history of the human race (which traditional balance-of-power politics had failed to prevent) the covenant and the charter represented a halting but necessary start toward a new regime of international relations to be built on the ruins of the old. Modest in relation to the demonstrated needs of nations in a century of unprecedented bloodshed, the standards set forth in the charter have nonetheless exceeded the performance of nations. It is only in this respect that the principles of the United Nations Charter may be regarded as unduly idealistic: barely adequate to the world's needs, they still exceed its grasp. For this reason alone the principles of the charter would seem to represent a maximal standard of morality in our definition of the national interest.

The principles of the charter that as international norms come closest to commanding a consensus among nations are those pertaining to the maintenance and enforcement of international peace. As stated in the preamble to the charter, the world organization was founded, in the first instance, to "save succeeding generations from the scourge of war. . . ." For this purpose certain principles, rules, and procedures were spelled out, including the primary requirements that "all members shall settle their international disputes by peaceful means. . . ,"[10] and that "all members shall refrain in their international relations from the threat or use of force against the territorial integrity or political independence of any state. . . ."[11] The Security Council, subject to its great power veto, is charged with the responsibility to take mandatory as well as hortatory action against any "threat to the peace, breach of the peace or act of aggression," either by economic sanctions or, if necessary, by military action;[12] and the members of the United Nations "agree to accept and carry out the decisions of the Security Council. . . ."[13] The charter also specifies, as basic purposes of the United Nations, the development of "friendly relations among nations based on respect for the principle of equal rights and self-determination of peoples,"[14] and the achievement of international cooperation in the solution of international economic, social, cultural, and humanitarian problems and in promoting and encouraging respect for human rights and fundamental freedoms.[15] The last of these categories of international concern seems to be circumscribed by the prohibition of intervention by the United Nations "in matters which are essentially within the domestic jurisdiction of any state," except for purposes of peace enforcement.[16]

Derived from the experience of nations and representing at least a semblance of consensus among them, these secular principles, rather than others deriving from ideology or religion, qualify as proper and feasible objectives of American foreign policy and, therefore, as factors in the national interest. By contrast with religious and ideological precepts, the principles of peace enforcement contained in the United Nations Charter, although ignored and violated in practice, are not openly challenged as international norms. By contrast with the policy of trying to promote human rights or combatting an uncongenial ideology in unpromising surroundings, implementing the charter does not require for success massive intervention in the internal affairs of other countries; it is not an extremely promising undertaking, but neither is it quixotic in its futility. Finally, for reasons and in ways to be suggested in the pages that follow, there would seem to be a reasonable possibility of applying the principles of the United Nations Charter as bases for a settlement in the Middle East.

The core interest of the United States is its own survival as a free society. The experience of the two world wars showed that this freedom could not be assured in isolation; more recent experience has shown that it could be jeopardized by indiscriminate intervention. Experience has also suggested that something more than military security, political influence, access to resources, and the promotion of American commerce are required for an overall conception of the national interest. There is a moral dimension to the national interest, which places limits on the methods that may be employed for the acquisition of strategic and economic advantage, and which also requires adherence to at least minimal standards of justice and fairness to other nations.

Since World War II the United States has employed, at one time or another, three distinct concepts of national interest: the ideological, as exemplified by the Truman Doctrine, which defined the Cold War as a struggle "between alternate ways of life;"[17] the geopolitical, which treats international relations as a perpetual struggle for power for its own sake, an approach associated with the regime of President Nixon and Dr. Kissinger; and the legal-institutional, an approach derived from the time of President Wilson which holds that power politics has become dangerously obsolete and that the national interest requires the imposition of restraints on national sovereignty through the development of international institutions. As the reader will by now have discerned, the preference—or bias—in these pages is for the last of these conceptions. The shortcomings of the ideological approach are that its reach almost invariably exceeds its grasp and that it is fraught with the risk of conflict. The defects of the geopolitical approach are lack of moral content and a tendency to break down, as in the two world wars of the twentieth century—a tendency that can hardly be contemplated with equanimity in the age of nuclear weapons. In international relations, as within nations, stability requires rules and their enforcement; it requires institutions that may inhibit brilliant statesmen from their works of genius but will also inhibit cruel and incompetent leaders from mischief or destruction. As Henry Kissinger wrote of Prince Bismarck, "In the hands of others lacking his subtle touch, his methods led to the collapse of the nineteenth century state system. The nemesis of power is that, except in the hands of a master, reliance on it is more likely to produce a contest of arms than of self-restraints."[18]

Even if it successfully fostered stability, however, it seems unlikely that a strictly geopolitical concept of the national interest, because of its lack of commitment to values other than stability, would satisfy the American people. As applied to the Middle East, this concept would rule out the creation of a Palestinian state as a prospective element of "instability" in the region. Such a concept would also, strictly applied, rule out permanent American support of Israel: if the United States had neither "eternal allies" nor "perpetual enemies" but only "eternal and perpetual" interests, narrowly defined, Israel might be dropped as a liability to an American strategic "interest" in displacing Soviet influence in the Arab world and as an obstacle to the advancement of American economic interests in the Arab oil-producing countries. It seems clear that the bases of American interest in both Israel and the Palestinians lie elsewhere—in considerations of preference and principle.

UNITED STATES INTERESTS IN THE MIDDLE EAST

The United States has four fundamental interests in the Middle East: reliable access, on reasonable terms, at tolerable prices, to the oil of the

region, especially the Arabian peninsula; the survival and se
state of Israel; the avoidance of confrontation and advancen
eration with the Soviet Union; and the fulfillment, so far a
certain principles, including the peaceful settlement of inte
putes, the inadmissibility of the acquisition of territory by
right of peoples to self-determination. Each one of these i....
alone, gives the United States a vital concern with the future of the Middle
East; taken together, and considering as well the extreme volatility of the
unresolved Arab-Israeli conflict, they make the Middle East the most
important single region in the world from the standpoint of American
interests—and the most dangerous.

The first interest, oil, is also the most tangible and obvious. The United
States, despite successful conservation measures and reduced imports
since the peak year 1977, nevertheless remains heavily dependent on
foreign energy sources, of which the most important by far is Saudi
Arabia, with proven oil reserves at the beginning of 1980 of 166.5 billion
barrels, about 25 percent of the world's total.[19] Although forecasts of
steadily rising import demands made in the late 1970s have been modified
to project no increase, and possible decrease, in demand for oil and
therefore in imports in the 1980s, the projections still indicate no realistic
prospect of independence, for the United States or its allies, from sources
of supply encompassed by the Organization of Petroleum Exporting
Countries (OPEC), of which Saudi Arabia is by far the principal
producer.[20] The Congressional Budget Office has estimated that the loss of
Saudi Arabian oil for one year would reduce the gross national product of
the United States by $272 billion, increase the unemployment rate by two
percent, and radically accelerate inflation, while working far greater havoc
on Europe and Japan.[21] For these reasons the United States, like its allies,
has a vital national interest in the oil-producing countries of the Arab
world—in their prices and levels of production, in security of access, and
in the disposition of their vast oil revenues. It would not seem an exag-
geration to say that there is no country in the world of greater economic,
and therefore strategic, importance to the United States than Saudi
Arabia.

This proposition seems clearly to have been recognized in the Carter
administration's decision, in the spring of 1978, to insist on the sale to
Saudi Arabia of sixty F–15 fighter aircraft—the most advanced American
military plane—and in the Reagan administration's decision in 1981,
notwithstanding contrary campaign promises, to enhance these aircraft
with special equipment and also to provide Saudi Arabia with five sophisticated electronic surveillance planes, known as AWACS (Airborne

Warning and Control System). The intense opposition that these transactions aroused on the part of Israel and Israel's supporters in Congress suggested concern not only with the specific military threat these aircraft might pose for Israel but, perhaps even more, concern that the United States might be moving toward a "special relationship" with Saudi Arabia no less special than the bond with Israel. Prime Minister Begin warned in 1978 that, as a result of the projected sale of F–15s, Saudi Arabia "will be turned automatically into a confrontation state," and that Israel regarded the proposed transaction as "very, very dangerous."[22] Foreign Minister Dayan characterized it as a kind of punishment of Israel by the United States. "If they want to punish us then we must accept this," he said before leaving Israel on a trip to the United States in April 1978, "but America is absolutely wrong and we cannot change our opinion on this."[23] Whatever their potential military importance, the Saudi aircraft sales suggested a new, and to Israel most unwelcome, symmetry in American security policy in the Middle East. For the first time—and in a manner symbolized too, although to a lesser extent, by arms supplied to Egypt—the United States appeared to be recognizing and acting on a strategic interest in the Arab world equal to—perhaps even exceeding—that perceived in Israel, backed, moreover, by vital economic interests. That, perhaps, more than the threat of attacks on Israel from Saudi air bases, was what Prime Minister Begin found "very, very dangerous."

The basis of the American interest in Israel is not, in any case, strategy but affiliation. The strategic service that Israel is said to perform for the United States—acting as a barrier to Soviet penetration of the Middle East—is one that is needed primarily because of the existence of Israel, but for which the Arabs would be much less amenable to Soviet influence. The best defense against the spread of communism in the Middle East, Henry Kissinger told a group of American Jewish leaders in 1975, is to strengthen moderate Arab governments. "The strength of Israel," he said, "is needed for its own survival but not to prevent the spread of communism in the Arab world. So it doesn't necessarily help United States global interests as far as the Middle East is concerned. The survival of Israel has sentimental importance to the United States. . . ."[24] Were the United States primarily concerned with the exclusion of Soviet influence from the Arab world, a powerful case could be made for the abandonment of Israel by the United States. It is true that Israel provides the United States with valuable military information and intelligence, and it is conceivable that under one set of circumstances or another the United States might have need of naval or air bases on Israeli territory. These assets in themselves, however, do not seem sufficient to explain the expenditure by the United States between the founding of Israel and the year 1980 of almost $13 billion in military assistance and over $5.5 billion in economic support, making Israel far the largest recipient of United States foreign aid.[25] Nor indeed would strategic considerations seem to underlie such presidential expressions of the American commitment to Israel as that made by President Carter on May 13, 1977: "We have a special relationship with Israel. It's absolutely crucial that no one in our country or around the world ever doubt that our Number One commitment in the Middle East is to protect the right of Israel to exist, to exist permanently, and to exist in peace. It's a special relationship."[26]

The source of a commitment so expressed must be sought elsewhere, in shared values and sentiment, duty and affiliation. This can be exaggerated to be sure; the sentiments involved can be sentimentalized, as in one writer's assertion that "if America does not ensure the survival of Israel, the American people will endure a despondency of spirit beside which the defeat in Vietnam will appear as one restless night. . . ."[27] The evidence seems clear, nonetheless, that the American commitment to Israel is rooted in strong emotions, Biblical and historical, galvanized by feelings of guilt and obligation arising from the holocaust. However these feelings are characterized, they surely cannot be characterized as normal feelings of attachment comparable, say, to those felt toward Great Britain as the motherland of American constitutional and political values. Americans in general, although critical of specific Israeli policies, and actions, would still seem to recognize the return of the Jewish people to their homeland of almost 2,000 years ago as a "unique and unprecedented act," as Nahum Goldmann, former president of the World Jewish Congress, characterized it—so "unique and unprecedented," indeed, as to warrant the world's acceptance and sympathy even though, as Goldmann wrote, "the Zionist demand for a Jewish state was in full contradiction with all principles of modern history and international law. If this demand were to serve as a precedent, the Indians of North America could claim for themselves the United States, and the descendants of other American natives in Mexico, Peru, and so on. All this gives a singular quality to the Zionist idea and makes it one of the great utopian programs of modern times."[28] One recalls, in this connection, Arthur Balfour's characterization of the Western commitment to Zionism in 1919 as one that overrode "numerical self-determination."[29]

Although it may be questioned whether foreigners have the right to override "numerical self-determination" on the part of an indigenous population, it is incontestable that that is what was done and that the willingness to do so, in a special case, has been integral to the American commitment to Israel. It is also questionable how *deeply* felt the attachment to Israel is on the part of most non-Jewish Americans, although polls leave no doubt that the overwhelming majority of Americans are solidly and consistently committed to the survival of Israel. The core of Israel's constituency in the United States, however, is the American Jewish community with its powerful bonds of loyalty and affection for the Jewish state. Just as the Jewish state of Israel is "unique and unprecedented," so too is the Israeli "lobby" in the United States. This is not a lobby in the conventional sense in which farmers, organized labor, the oil companies, the consumer movement, or the National Rifle Association is a lobby, with commitments to specific economic or social objectives. It is rather a commitment to a people and a cause, a commitment rooted in powerful bonds of kinship, in the memory of a common history and the conviction of a common destiny. The root strength of this most formidable of domestic political lobbies—a fact imperfectly understood by Arabs—lies not in its skill in public relations, access to the media, or ample financing, although all of these are impressive, but in the solid, consistent, and usually unified support of the Jewish communities of the United States. The resources thus made available to the Israel lobby heavily outweigh the lobbying power of Arab Americans or of the Arab governments, even, in the case of some of the latter, with the assets of costly, sophisticated public relations campaigns.

As suggested at the outset of this chapter, there would seem no reason why the strong preference of an American ethnic community should not be accepted as a national interest of the United States—especially when the preference is shared by the majority although with less intensity, and as long as it is harmonized with other national interests. As the government of an ethnically and racially diverse society, the government of the United States is naturally responsive to the wishes of groups within the society, and, because the government is an agent of the people and not a principle in itself, this responsiveness is, within limits, legitimate and desirable. The national interest is *greater* than the sum of group interests within the country, but it is not, and cannot be, something wholly *different* from these. It cannot be antithetical to the strong preferences of large numbers of the nation's citizens. Just as groups and individuals owe their primary loyalty to the community as a whole, the nation in turn owes a loyalty to groups within it.

In its African policy, for example, the United States has a commitment to racial justice not only because it *is* justice, or for geopolitical reasons, but also because the United States is itself a multiracial society. Sympathy and support for racial justice in Africa is in part an expression of loyalty that the United States government owes to its own citizens; conversely, and for the same reason, it would seem inconceivable for the United States to oppose racial equality in southern Africa, even if other, tangible national interests would be served thereby. Similarly, the American commitment to Israel is in part an expression of loyalty on the part of the United States government to its own citizens, and for reasons of the same loyalty it is inconceivable that the United States would "sell out" Israel, even though, from the standpoint of other interests, it might be highly expedient to do so. It is, indeed, a "special relationship."

A "special relationship" is not, however, an exclusive one. In addition to the emotional bond to Israel and the essential economic relationship with the Arab oil-producing countries, the United States has a crucial political association with the Soviet Union in the Middle East. For reasons to be elaborated on in chapter 6, the Soviet Union seems to be a necessary collaborator for the making and maintenance of peace in the Middle East—not only because it carries the formal title of cochairman of the Geneva Peace Conference on the Middle East, as it does, or because it might try to disrupt a settlement in the making of which it had no part, as it might, but also because Soviet cooperation in the making and maintenance of a settlement would help to stabilize the settlement and would advance—or help to revive—Soviet-American détente.

Such cooperation, moreover, seems feasible. On October 1, 1977 the United States and the Soviet Union, in their capacity as cochairmen of the Geneva Peace Conference on the Middle East, issued a joint statement calling for a comprehensive settlement under which Israel would withdraw from occupied Arab lands; the "legitimate rights" of the Palestinian people would be recognized; the state of war between Israel and the Arabs would be terminated and normal relations established; and international guarantees would be given to ensure compliance with the terms of settlement, guarantees in which the United States and the Soviet Union would participate. Vigorous protests were raised, by former President Ford, among others, against "letting the Russians back into the Middle East."[30] Although the Carter administration placed no further emphasis on the joint statement in the months following its issuance, administration officials continued (privately for a time at least) to defend it as an opportunity to draw the Soviet Union into cooperative arrangements for bringing about and upholding a peace settlement on terms favored by the United States.

In the present view such cooperation with the Soviet Union is in the

American national interest for reasons both negative and positive. On the negative side, it would seem desirable to advance arrangements that will reduce the danger of Soviet-American confrontation such as almost occurred during the October War of 1973, when United States nuclear forces around the world were put on standby alert. On the positive side, the prospects of an equitable general settlement would be materially advanced were the Soviet Union to apply its not inconsiderable influence for that purpose on Syria, the Palestine Liberation Organization, and the "rejectionist" Arabs in general. Some degree of cooperation might indeed be indispensable, since the Russians can hardly be expected to acquiesce in a process, or a settlement, from which they have been excluded. Finally, from a global perspective, it is in the national interest of the United States to enlist rather than exclude Soviet collaboration in the maintenance of world order in any and all areas in which that becomes feasible. That is the rationale of détente itself, consistent too with the spirit of the Nixon-Brezhnev joint declaration for the prevention of nuclear war, under the terms of which the two superpowers agreed to "act in such a manner" as to "avoid military confrontations" and to "exclude the outbreak of nuclear war," between themselves and between themselves and others. [31]

The final category of American national interests in the Middle East embraces certain principles (essentially those discussed in the first section of this chapter) to which the United States is committed either by its own tradition, by contract as a signatory to the United Nations Charter, or both.

The provisions of the charter pertaining to peace enforcement and the peaceful settlement of international disputes have been amplified as applied to the Middle East through a series of United Nations resolutions and national policy statements that, taken together, constitute a body of principles to which the United States, at least officially, adheres as guidelines to its own national policy. The most comprehensive of these is Security Council Resolution 242 of November 22, 1967, which, in addition to calling for "withdrawal of Israeli armed forces from territories occupied in the recent conflict," "termination of all claims or states of belligerency," and acknowledgment of the right of "every state in the area" to "live in peace within secure and recognized boundaries," also emphasizes the "inadmissibility of the acquisition of territory by war" and the obligation of states to settle their disputes by peaceful means in compliance with Article 2 of the United Nations Charter. [32]

The official American commitment to these broad principles was reiterated and amplified in a notable speech by Secretary of State William P.

Rogers on December 9, 1969. In a key passage Secretary Rogers said:

> We believe that while recognized political boundaries must be established and
> agreed upon by the parties, any changes in the pre-existing line should not
> reflect the weight of conquest and should be confined to insubstantial altera-
> tions required for mutual security. We do not support expansionism. We
> believe troops must be withdrawn as the resolution provides. We support
> Israel's security and the security of the Arab states as well. We are for a lasting
> peace that requires security for both.[33]

The "Rogers Plan," as it came to be known, was never officially
disavowed by an American president or secretary of state, although
President Nixon admitted later that he personally did not take it
seriously,[34] little was done to implement it, and it came to be regarded
widely as a dead letter. The Rogers Plan stands, however, as a statement of
American principle, consistent with the provisions of Security Council
Resolution 242 and with the letter and spirit of the United Nations
Charter. Nor indeed was the key principle—that nations cannot be permitted to increase their territory by force—new to American foreign
policy in general or as specifically applied to the Middle East. In 1957, in
the wake of the Suez War between Egypt and Israel, President Eisenhower
had insisted successfully that Israel withdraw from the Sinai without
conditions lest a precedent be set for the unchallenged acquisition of
territory by force and the use of conquered territory as an international
bargaining lever. In a national television speech on February 20, 1957,
Eisenhower said:

> If we agree that armed attack can properly achieve the purposes of the
> assailant, then I fear we will have turned back the clock of international order.
> We will, in effect, have countenanced the use of force as a means of settling
> international differences and through this gaining national advantages. I do
> not myself see how this could be reconciled with the Charter of the United
> Nations. The basic pledge of all the members of the United Nations is that
> they will settle their international disputes by peaceful means, and will not use
> force against the territorial integrity of another state. If the United Nations
> once admits that international disputes can be settled by using force, then we
> will have destroyed the very foundation of the Organization, and our best
> hope of establishing a world order. That would be a disaster for us all.[35]

From the perspective of the eighties, Eisenhower's definition of national
interest and principle may be dismissed as quaint and antique idealism.
The United Nations has fallen into disrepute if not total disuse as a
peacekeeping organization, and few if any political leaders still speak of
"establishing a world order." This may show that Americans have grown

more sophisticated in their conception of national interest, or, as suggested in the first section of this chapter, the norms of international behavior codified in the United Nations Charter may still represent a valid component of the American national interest, in which event the prevailing disdain for these principles may be more a manifestation of cynicism than of realism—a sign of Americans strayed from their moorings.

Closely related to peaceful settlement as an accepted postulate of international order, and one as well to which the United States has a longstanding commitment, is the principle of the self-determination of peoples. The origins of this principle, especially in American thinking, are both ethical and pragmatic. As an ethical principle, the premise of self-determination is that it is morally unacceptable for larger or more powerful national groups to impose their rule on smaller or less powerful groups. This proposition underlay the traditional anticolonialism of the United States, and, although it did not deter the United States from acquiring overseas territories, it prevented these acquisitions from achieving legitimacy in American minds and contributed to the early decision of the United States to give up the Philippines, to the concession of juridicial equality to the Latin American states in the inter-American system, and to the application of American pressure against European colonial empires after both world wars. Ethical anticolonialism also underlay both the mandates system of the League of Nations and the trusteeship system of the United Nations, both essentially American contributions, under which, in theory, more advanced nations might be commissioned to exercise jurisdiction over the less advanced only as trustees of the world community, to which they would be accountable, and only for purposes of assisting the less advanced through a transition period leading to independence.

As a modern pragmatic postulate, self-determination grew out of the experience of nineteenth-century Europe and the First World War, from which it had become overwhelmingly evident that unhappy subject nationalities are a chronic source of instability and conflict. It was concluded, accordingly, that the world would be safer and peace more secure if as many people as possible could be permitted to live in political jurisdictions of their choice. For those reasons President Wilson judged the principle of self-determination to be more than a phrase or ideal. "It is," he said, "an imperative principle of action, which statesmen will henceforth ignore at their peril."[36]

As has been seen, the United States has been ambivalent toward the application of self-determination in Palestine. There being no way to reconcile Zionism with the self-determination of an established population, the United States has pursued an inconstant course with respect to the Holy Land. From time to time the United States has acknowledged the principle of self-determination as having at least partial applicability to the Palestinian people, as in the unofficial King-Crane report after World War I, or in Secretary of State Rogers' statement that a "just settlement" of the Palestinian problem "must take into account the desires and aspirations of the refugees,"[37] or in President Carter's statement, early in his term of office, that "there has to be a homeland provided for the Palestinian refugees who have suffered for many, many years."[38] The definitive statement of the Carter administration on self-determination was made by the president at Aswan, Egypt, on January 4, 1978. A codification of American ambivalence, the presidential statement said that a settlement should "enable the Palestinians to participate in the determination of their own future."[39] For the most part, however, since President Wilson's time (when Justice Brandeis joined Arthur Balfour in defining American policy as a commitment to the wishes of a *future* community rather than of an *existing* one),[40] the United States has treated Palestine as a special case because of the standing of the Zionist idea, in Nahum Goldmann's phrase, quoted above, as "one of the great utopian programs of modern times."

As will be seen in chapter 5, the Palestinian Arabs hold a different view, both of their own legitimate rights and of the true nature of the Zionist idea. Dispossessed and dispersed, they perceive Zionism as an imperial rather than a utopian program, and they invoke the principle of self-determination—if no longer to be applied in all of old Palestine, then at least for the West Bank and the Gaza Strip. Puzzled and angered by the repeated rejection on the part of American presidents of an independent Palestinian state, they regard the Aswan formula for *participation* by the Palestinians in the determination of their future as a diplomatic artifice, a denial of the *fact* of self-determination, cloaked, however, in its language. The choice proposed by President Carter, among affiliation with Israel, affiliation with Jordan, or rule by an international authority, was perceived by Palestinians as nothing more than a choice of foreign rulers. "He is trying to form the future of people the way he likes it," Yasser Arafat, chairman of the Palestine Liberation Organization, said on May 1, 1978. "Of course we as Palestinians just simply reject that."[41] Palestinians might have noted too, ruefully, that President Carter put forth his equivocal Aswan formula of January 4, 1978, only one day after joining with Prime Minister Desai of India in issuing a declaration that included a statement of the two leaders' belief "that a cooperative and stable world order depends on the right of each people to determine its own form of government and each nation its own political, social and economic policies."[42] The principle of self-determination was in no way qualified, nor were exceptions indicated in the "Delhi Declaration."

The discrepancy is explained in part by the lack of serious attention normally paid to, or warranted by, the grandiose phrases of joint communiqués issued by touring statesmen. But even more to the point is the unchallengeable fact that Israel is indeed a special case in American foreign policy. The question still unresolved is, how special a case? No serious American observer now contests the permanence of the state of Israel: however great the injustice done the Palestinians by the creation of Israel, it would be no less an injustice to displace the established state of Israel, or to try to replace it with the "democratic secular state" officially advocated by the Palestine Liberation Organization. The real question is no longer self-determination for former Palestine with its former population, but whether the Palestinian Arabs living in the occupied territories and those dispersed in Jordan, Lebanon, and elsewhere will be given the opportunity to decide for themselves—not to *participate* in the decision but to *make* it—whether they will form an independent state in the West Bank and in Gaza, affiliate with Jordan, or enter into some other arrangement. In the present view they are entitled to no less, as partial compensation for their lost homeland, and also for the practical reasons that caused Woodrow Wilson to warn in 1918 that statesmen thereafter would ignore self-determination "at their peril." That same theme—a warning of turmoil generated by irredentism—has been stressed by Palestinian spokesmen. Testifying before the Senate Foreign Relations Committee's Subcommittee on the Near East and South Asia in 1976, Professor Hisham Sharabi of Georgetown University warned that

> politically, unless the Palestinian issue is resolved, there will be no peace or stability in the Middle East because the Palestinians have an awesome political and psychological power in influencing events there. No Arab state, no Arab regime, no Arab leader can be freed from the Palestinian cause until Palestinian rights have been achieved.[43]

Concern for the safety of Israel may justify the imposition of restraints on Palestinian sovereignty over the West Bank and Gaza, but past and present American officials have called for its denial altogether. The Carter administration's proposal for participation by the Palestinians in the determination of their future explicitly ruled out an independent Palestinian state as one of the choices to be offered. In an address to a major Jewish group on November 13, 1977, former Secretary of State Henry Kissinger expressed opposition to an independent Palestinian state on the ground that it would be "an element of instability both for Jordan and for Israel; it will compound the crisis not solve it. . . ."[44] In a similar vein Senator Hubert H. Humphrey, two days before his death on January 13, 1978, wrote a letter to Israeli Prime Minister Begin urging concessions for peace, including "a formula in which we give the Palestinians some time to work out their own difficulties," but also stating that "it is absolutely clear that we will not accept an independent and potentially antagonistic Palestinian state, nor will any of Israel's neighbors. There is an obvious danger in the ultimate political objectives of such an entity."[45]

For reasons to be suggested in chapter 5, it is a good deal less than "absolutely clear" that the United States will not, or cannot, accept an independent Palestinian state, or that such a state is foreordained to be "antagonistic." The Kissinger-Humphrey view of the Palestinian problem is an essentially geopolitical one, rooted in the premise that a people may be denied what otherwise would be recognized as legitimate rights if these are considered to be dangerous or inconvenient to others. As applied to the Palestinian Arabs, the approach is of questionable soundness on geopolitical as well as moral grounds. It is not axiomatic that a Palestinian state, with limited armaments and all but surrounded by a far more powerful Israel, would be dangerous to its neighbors, still less that it would fall quickly under Soviet domination as feared by Israel. Conversely, Palestinian irredentism, bitterness, and frustration are an existing "element of instability," with demonstrated staying power to remain so. Granted that the American interest in Israel is a special one, based on powerful bonds of affiliation, it would not seem so special as to override completely the moral and practical considerations that give the United States a national interest in the self-determination of peoples, including the Palestinian people.

Even before President Sadat's peace initiative and the Camp David agreements brought the issue to a new prominence, the principle of Palestinian self-determination commanded wide support among responsible American observers of the Middle East. This principle was endorsed by a variety of witnesses testifying in 1976 before the Senate Foreign Relations Committee's Subcommittee on the Near East, which held extensive hearings in that year on Middle East peace prospects, and it won unanimous agreement from the signatories, including prominent Zionists, to the "Brookings Report" of 1975, which stated, as to Palestinian self-determination, that "for a peace settlement to be viable, indeed for it even to be negotiated and concluded, this right will have to be recognized in principle and, as a part of the settlement, given satisfaction in practice."[46]

For reasons rooted more in domestic politics than in the complexities of the issues involved, the United States has encountered recurrent difficulties in the effort to shape a Middle East policy rooted solidly in the national interest and also commanding steady public support. Presidents since Harry Truman have found that efforts to develop a policy reconciling all four of the basic United States interests in the Middle East—the security of Israel, access to oil, cooperation with the Soviet Union, and the upholding of certain principles—invariably generate intense domestic controversy. The engine of controversy is the so-called Israel lobby, with its solid and effective support from the Jewish communities of the United States. As a result of the lobby's activities and the high degree of receptiveness to its importunities on the part of Congress, successive presidents have been compelled to make a difficult choice—between adopting policies weighted on the side of Israeli wishes at the expense of other national interests and attempting to frame policies based on the totality of American interests, with resulting controversy and political risk to themselves. The forum for controversy has been the American political system itself, with its separated powers and multiple points of access for those wishing to influence policy, a system uniquely amenable to the airing of public differences, but much less so to their resolution.

THE REDRESS OF GRIEVANCES

Although to some degree contradictory principles, the right of interest groups to lobby and the primacy of the general interest are both invoked under mantles of Constitutional sanctity. Lobbying, as a form of petition, can be traced as far back as Magna Carta in 1215 and, as a right that had been impaired, figured importantly in the events leading to the American Revolution. The belief of the American colonists that their "repeated petitions have been answered only by repeated injury" was one of the grievances listed in the Declaration of Independence, and when the Bill of Rights was added to the Constitution in 1791, the First Amendment specified that "Congress shall make no law . . . abridging the freedom of speech, or of the press; or the right of the people peaceably to assemble, and to petition the Government for a redress of grievances." In the United States this right has seldom been exercised—surely not in recent decades—by the decorous submission to Congress of formal petitions. It is more commonly exercised through the rough-and-tumble of promise and threat, and in recent years through the increasingly sophisticated pressure tactics invented by the public relations industry. In modern America, as one writer on the subject has concluded, "lobbying is indeed that First Amendment right to petition for redress of grievances."[47]

The principle problem arising from lobbying, at least with respect to foreign policy, is not so much corruption as preemption. It is unlikely that the lavishing of favors on legislators, even including the payment of bribes, has an effect on American foreign policy as disruptive as the ability of stronger lobbies to preempt the arena of public discussion and, in so doing, to identify their own special interests with the larger national interest. The problem is not simply one lobby overwhelming another; even if means could be devised to equalize their access or influence, the results would not necessarily be salutary since it is by no means clear that the national interest is nothing more than the sum of all the special and group interests in American society.

The Founding Fathers were not unalert to the dangers of "faction." In *The Federalist* Madison defined a "faction" as "a number of citizens, whether amounting to a majority or minority of the whole, who are united and actuated by some common impulse of passion, or of interest, adverse to the rights of other citizens, or to the permanent and aggregate interests of the community."[48] A faction, so defined, became dangerous, in Madison's judgment, only when it commanded the allegiance of a majority: "If a faction consists of less than a majority, relief is supplied by the republican principle, which enables the majority to defeat its sinister views by regular vote."[49] Madison thought too that the larger the republic, the greater the safeguards would be, because a larger republic would necessarily contain a larger number of "fit characters," each chosen by a larger number of citizens, making it "more difficult for unworthy candidates to practice with success the vicious arts. . . ." The large, varied republic also had the advantage, in Madison's judgment, of encompassing a greater variety of interests, making it "less probable that a majority of the whole will have a common motive to invade the rights of other citizens," or even if they did, that they could then "discover their own strength" and "act in unison with each other."[50]

Madison's analysis might well have proven flawless if his premise had been borne out. But the premise—that only majority factions need be feared—has not been vindicated by experience. Two basic factors, neither of which could readily have been foreseen in the late eighteenth century, have enabled organized minorities in the modern age to exercise a profound, sometimes dominant, influence on public policy. First, the "communications" revolution has allowed minority factions—depending on their resources, skill, and motivation—to use the mass media to influence and sometimes shape public opinion. Subjected to the quasi-scientific techniques of modern advertising and public relations, relatively inattentive, unmotivated majorities have proven often to be easy objects of manipulation not only for sellers of detergents and deodorants but also for marketers for political ideas—all the more when the latter, in Madison's phrase, "are united and actuated by some common impulse of passion. . . ."

The second factor that Madison (writing in the "Age of Reason") failed to anticipate, was the large measure of irrationality that has come to characterize the political process and the behavior of those who run it. Madison counted on representative government to "refine and enlarge the public views, by passing them through the medium of a chosen body of citizens, whose wisdom may best discern the true interest of their country, and whose patriotism and love of justice, will be least likely to sacrifice it to temporary or partial considerations."[51] It is unlikely that even the most insistent contemporary advocate of congressional prerogative would now commend that body as an assemblage distinguished for its collective wisdom, patriotism, and love of justice, much less for a habit of placing the "true interest" of the nation above "temporary or partial considerations." Indeed, in much the same way that the communications revolution has made the American people vulnerable to ideas that often do not represent their best interests, it has also made them susceptible to politicans who cannot always be counted on to serve those interests. Candidates as well as causes are packaged and marketed in contemporary electoral politics, putting a premium on those assets of personality that make a candidate marketable and therefore able to win office, rather than on the assets of character and intellect that enable officeholders to carry out their duties with wisdom and reponsibility. In addition, the breakdown of party organizations, coupled with the proliferation of interest groups, causes candidates to seek their support from these very groups rather than from the "general public." The result is that Congress has become something much closer to a brokerage for the special interests represented by its members than a deliberative body composed, as Madison expected it to be, of representatives "whose enlightened views and virtuous sentiments render them superior to local prejudices, and to schemes of injustice."[52]

At the same time that Congress has become fragmented, it has also become more powerful in relation to the executive in the making of foreign policy. The Vietnam War and the Watergate scandal, which discredited the "imperial presidency," also spawned a reassertion of congressional prerogative that, by the mid-seventies, had extended far beyond the legislative specifications of the War Powers Resolution of 1973 or the Case Act of 1972, which requires the reporting to Congress of executive agreements. Supported by greatly increased staffs, and increasingly uninhibited by considerations of party loyalty, especially on the part of the large Democratic majorities that dominated Congress prior to the election of 1980, senators and congressmen began to carve out subjects of special jurisdiction for themselves, in foreign as well as domestic affairs, usually in areas of special interest to their supporters or prospective supporters. The Carter administration did little to resist these disintegrative tendencies and may have reinforced them, inadvertently, by somewhat ostentatiously divesting itself of the trappings of the "imperial presidency," but even more by President Carter's failure to use his office, with its unique command of the media, to define and articulate a conception of national interest. President Reagan, backed by a Republican-controlled Senate, quickly established executive dominance in matters of the domestic economy but, as of mid-1981, had made no commensurate effort to establish his leadership of foreign policy.

In these surroundings, the new foreign policy lobbies, skilled in the methods of modern "communications" and with plenty of money to make good use of them, have flourished, none more so than the pro-Israel lobby. The operating arms of the Israel lobby include such organizations as the American Israel Public Affairs Committee (AIPAC), which, with an annual budget as of 1978 of $750,000, closely monitors legislation in Congress, provides speeches and other research to receptive members of Congress and then circulates these to the media, and is capable on short notice of generating deluges of letters or telephone calls to members of Congress on issues of concern to Israel. Closely associated with AIPAC is the newsletter, *Near East Report*, which AIPAC distributes to all members of Congress and other influential individuals in and out of government. Other important organizations making up the Israeli lobby are the Conference of Presidents of Major Jewish Organizations, which tends to concentrate its efforts on the White House and the State Department while AIPAC works on Congress; the American Jewish Committee, which, in addition to its political activities, publishes the magazine *Commentary*; the Anti-Defamation League at B'nai B'rith; and not least, the Israeli Embassy itself, whose efficient staff maintain close and continuing ties with members of Congress and their staffs as well as with officials in the executive branch.

A critical role in advancing Israel's interests is played by well-placed congressional aides, coordinating their efforts with such groups as

AIPAC. These individuals, acting on personal conviction, are not "lob-byists" in the conventional sense. "It's long been known that several staff people support Israel," an unidentified aide told a reporter. "But we don't do it for money the way some paid lobbyists do. We do it out of a very, very passionate commitment."[53] Morris J. Amitay, former executive director of AIPAC and previously an aide to Senator Abraham A. Ribicoff of Connecticut, explained the contribution of congressional staff mem-bers when he himself was still a Senate aide: "There are now a lot of guys at the working level up here who happen to be Jewish, who are willing to make a little bit of extra effort and to look at certain issues in terms of their Jewishness, and this is what has made this thing go very effectively in the last couple of years. These are all guys who are in a position to make the decisions in these areas for these senators."[54] Besides relying on their own direct efforts, Amitay explained, pro-Israeli congressional aides call, when necessary, for "outside help," which means the application of direct pressure on legislators from influential Jewish constituents and organizations.[55]

Among the Israel lobby's many victory trophies from the legislative arena, one of the most conspicuous and consequential was the "letter of seventy-six" addressed to President Ford by that number of Senators on May 21, 1975. Following the collapse in March of Secretary of State Kissinger's first round of shuttle diplomacy toward a second Sinai disen-gagement agreement, the angry and frustrated secretary of state announced a "reassessment" of American Middle East policy, during which the Ford administration conspicuously delayed the delivery of certain weapons to Israel and suspended negotiations for pending financial and military aid, including the new F–15 fighter plane. In the course of the policy reassessment, experts from within the government and others called in from outside reached a near consensus in favor of the United States calling for a general Middle East settlement based on Israeli with-drawal to the borders of 1967 (with minor modifications), coupled with strong guarantees of Israel's security. In favoring this approach rather than a renewal of "step-by-step" diplomacy, Kissinger's advisers envisioned a national television appeal by President Ford to the American people spelling out the basic issues of American national interest in the Middle East and, on the basis of these, making the case for Israeli withdrawal in return for guarantees.[56]

Declining to wait becalmed while the "reassessment" progressed to-ward an undesired result, the lobby went into action on Capitol Hill. After three weeks of intensive lobbying and three successive drafts, seventy-six

Senatorial signatures were affixed to the letter to President Ford, dated May 21, 1975. This document affirmed in its key paragraphs that a strong Israel was an essential barrier to Soviet influence in the Middle East and that

> withholding military equipment from Israel would be dangerous, discouraging accommodation by Israel's neighbors and encouraging a resort to force.
>
> Within the next several weeks, the Congress expects to receive your foreign aid requests for fiscal year 1976. We trust that your recommendations will be responsive to Israel's urgent military and economic needs. We urge you to make it clear, as we do, that the United States acting in its own national interests stands firmly with Israel in the search for peace in future negotiations, and that this premise is the basis of the current reassessment of U.S. policy in the Middle East.[57]

The letter bore the signatures not only of enthusiastic supporters of its contents but also of some who had reservations, such as Senator McGovern, who issued a statement saying that "it would be folly for Israel to assume that American support means approval of the existing boundaries in the Middle East,"[58] and at least a few who at first had refused to sign the letter—one of whom, John Culver of Iowa, reportedly told a colleague, "The pressure was just too great. I caved," another of whom, Daniel Inouye of Hawaii, explained, "It's easier to sign one letter than answer five thousand."[59]

The "letter of seventy-six" put an effective end to the Ford-Kissinger "reassessment." Kissinger's advisers agreed that the approach favored in the recent policy review, a presidential outline of a general settlement, had become politically unfeasible.[60] The Ford administration resumed thereupon the step-by-step diplomacy that produced the second Sinai disengagement agreement of September 1975 and, after three more years of arduous diplomatic effort by the Ford and Carter administrations, the Camp David accords of September 1978. Edward Sheehan records that he observed once to a Kissinger aide that Israel's American constituency was the greatest restraint on American policy and that the aide replied: "Of course. And the constraint becomes the determinant."[61]

The "new ethnicity,"[62] which enabled American Jews to greatly expand their political influence in the years after Eisenhower virtually ordered Ben-Gurion to evacuate the Sinai in early 1957, has also affected the political activities of other ethnic groups, including the relatively small community of Arab Americans.[63] Until quite recently Arab Americans, by contrast with Jews, were virtually invisible as a distinct ethnic group in the United States. This was true because of the relatively small numbers of

Arabs who had immigrated to the United States; because most of these were Christian rather than Muslim and therefore unrepresentative of the Arab world as a whole; because Arab Americans tended to become assimilated in the larger society rather more than some other ethnic groups and therefore to lose consciousness of their Arab identity; and perhaps mostly because, in the Eurocentric cultural environment of the United States, the Arabs, prior to their conflicts with Israel and the sudden, critical dependence of the Western world on Arab oil, seemed a people living "outside of history."[64] As a result of these factors, while the Zionist movement gained force and momentum as an influence on American politics from the early years of the twentieth century, there emerged within the American political arena "no fundamental challenge representing Arab interests to the Zionist proposition that the United States support the transformation of Palestine into a Jewish homeland."[65] This fundamental asymmetry of interests within the pluralistic American political system was to have profound consequences for American foreign policy.

Only after the 1967 war did Arab Americans, mirroring the shocked reaction of the Arab world itself, acquire the intensified sense of their own Arab identity to provide the basis for the formation of a coherent "interest group" within the United States. In a manner paralleling the way in which Israeli Zionism gave life to a hitherto latent Palestinian nationalism, American Jewish political activism drove American Arabs to participation in the "new ethnicity." In the cultural and educational sphere an important organizational initiative was taken with the formation in 1967 of the Association of Arab American University Graduates (AAUG). In 1972 a group of businessmen and lawyers of Arab descent formed the National Association of Arab Americans (NAAA) as a political action group designed to counterbalance, so far as possible, the various Jewish organizations actively engaged in efforts to influence foreign policy. At the first annual convention of the NAAA, in Detroit in June 1973, Senator James Abourezk of South Dakota urged the members "to identify with their Arab heritage and to organize as an ethnic group so that they might play an effective role in the political process."[66] The NAAA reached a high point of influence when the Senate Foreign Relations Committee, on May 5, 1978, heard testimony on a proposed package arms sale to Israel, Egypt, and Saudi Arabia from *both* Morris J. Amitay, executive director of the American Israel Public Affairs Committee, and John P. Richardson, director of public affairs for the National Association of Arab Americans.[67] In addition to its direct political activities the NAAA serves as a kind of Arab "antidefamation league," protesting reporting it considers biased, the invidious stereotyping of Arabs, and tasteless cartoons. The NAAA has been reduced in effectiveness, however, by the relative lack of intensity of Arab American political feeling—the lack of that "very, very passionate commitment" of which a Jewish Senate aide spoke—and also by divisions within the Arab American community mirroring divisions within the Arab world itself. "We can't represent Arabs the way the Jewish lobby can represent Israel," a former president of the NAAA, Joseph Baroody, explained in 1978. "The Israeli Government has one policy to state, whereas we couldn't represent 'the Arabs' if we wanted to. They're as different as the Libyans and Saudis are different, or as divided as the Christian and Muslim Lebanese."[68]

In addition to such groups as the National Association of Arab Americans, the Arab lobby consists of other disparate elements. The League of Arab States maintains Arab Information Centers in five American cities. The Arab embassies, numerous and divided in outlook, make limited public relations efforts, but their activities are feeble compared to those of the highly skilled and active staff of the Israeli embassy. Several Arab governments also have contracts with law firms and professional lobbyists to promote their interests in Washington. Undertaking for the first time a public relations campaign for a specific legislative purpose, the government of Saudi Arabia in early 1978 engaged a South Carolina public relations firm to lobby in support of the Carter administration's proposal, ultimately successful, for the sale of sixty F–15 fighter planes to Saudi Arabia.[69] On a much smaller scale are the Middle East Resource Center in Washington and the Palestine Human Rights Campaign, the latter of which works to publicize and seek redress for human rights violations in the occupied territories. Supporters of Israel sometimes cite the major oil companies as participants in the "Arab lobby," but the allegation does not stand up under close scrutiny. Outside the realm of energy costs, uses, and taxation, the oil companies have in fact been chary of taking public positions on Middle East issues, much less of pressing these on Congress.[70]

The Israelis, for their part, having long relied on Congress as the main center of support for their policies, increased that reliance as the post-Watergate executive grew weaker in relation to the legislative branch, and as the Carter administration grew, from the Israel viewpoint, less friendly. Familiar (from long experience) with the Congress and its ways, bolstered by a powerful domestic lobby and by personal sympathizers among the membership and staffs of Congress, Israel has had no need of hired American agents. Israeli officials have extensive personal associations with congressmen and regularly meet with them informally as well as through the more formal meetings that regularly take place between legislators and other foreign representatives. In the case of the Saudi arms sale, for example, Israeli foreign minister Moshe Dayan met on April 27, 1978, with members of the Senate Foreign Relations Committee at the Watergate Hotel, in what James Reston described as "sort of a private rump session of the Senate Foreign Relations Committee,"[71] to express Israel's objections to the linking of prospective aircraft sales to Israel with the proposed sale to Saudi Arabia. Dayan was quoted as saying, "We resent the concept of a package deal. We think the provision of selling arms to Israel should be conducted on its own merits and not within any package."[72]

In the summer of 1979 the resignation of the United States ambassador to the United Nations, Andrew Young, over the issue of an unauthorized meeting with the Palestine Liberation Organization's representative at the United Nations, galvanized black Americans into a new interest and surge of activity in regard to the Middle East conflict. Angered by Israel's role in the events that precipitated Young's resignation, prominent black leaders made trips to the Middle East where they met, among others, PLO chairman Yasser Arafat. These highly publicized journeys, especially that of the Reverend Jesse Jackson, precipitated angry recriminations on the part of Israeli and American Jewish leaders. The trips also precipitated a split among the black American leadership—between the new sympathizers with the Palestinians and traditional supporters of the long-standing black-Jewish alliance in civil rights and other American domestic matters. Following the black leaders' meeting with him in New York on August 20, 1979, the PLO observer at the United Nations, Zehdi Labib Terzi, expressed satisfaction with the public impact of the event within the United States, acquiescing in a friendly diplomat's observation that "if the PLO had budgeted $10 million it wouldn't have brought this amount of publicity."[73] On the same occasion columnist Meg Greenfield, pointing to the disintegration of "any sense of common, shared American policy or interest," wrote of "pluralism gone mad."[74]

In circumstances of intensified lobbying and internal fragmentation, the houses of Congress—and especially the Senate—have largely ceased to be deliberative bodies for the consideration of broad questions of the national interest. They have become instead a kind of brokerage of special interests in which, to be sure, a balance of conflicting factions is preferable to the unchallenged preeminence of a single faction. But even if all interests were equally weighted, as no one would contend they are, the resulting sum of factional ambitions would represent something different from, and less than, the general national interest. In such a political environment, open debate, receptiveness to ideas, tolerance of dissent, and the common commitment to the general good—a "politics of variation"—give way to factional struggle, mutual intolerance, the avoidance of debate so far as possible, and the insistent equation of factional interest with the national welfare—which is to say, to a "politics of preemption."[75] *Pressure* rather than *discussion* becomes the catalyst of decision, and the legislature becomes a battleground of groups, preempting when they can, yielding when they must. Compromises are made, to be sure, but they are concessions to necessity rather than logic, and the individuals who make them are more likely to have been overwhelmed than convinced. Madison's conception of the political process as one in which diverse viewpoints are passed "through the medium of a chosen body of citizens, whose wisdom may best discern the true interest of their country," gives way to the conception of a modern political scientist, Harold D. Lasswell, who defined all politics as a question of "Who gets what, when, and how."[76]

There seems no obvious institutional remedy for the politics of faction. Its causes could be eliminated, as Madison observed, only by destroying liberty (a remedy "worse than the disease") or by contriving, somehow, to invest all citizens with the same opinions, passions, and interests, a patently impracticable undertaking.[77] Recognizing that the causes of factional politics could not be removed, Madison supposed that its effects could nonetheless be controlled through the workings of republican institutions. As has been seen, Madison was unduly optimistic, and the politics of faction—or of "preemption"—seems to dominate in the modern American political system. If there is a remedy, it would seem to lie not in institutional reforms but in the reintroduction of rationality, on which Madison counted heavily, into the American political process. This is essentially a matter of placing in office wiser, more competent leaders—individuals, as Madison defined them, of "enlightened views and virtuous sentiments."

The remedy offered is perhaps a lame one, in the absence of concrete proposals for its realization. It is offered nonetheless as the only apparent redress for a state of affairs in which it has proven increasingly difficult to formulate and carry out foreign policies, especially with respect to the Middle East, rooted solidly in the broader national interest. The American people have from time to time placed in power leaders of vision and integrity, and if a mechanism cannot be suggested to assure such leadership in the future, neither does it follow that it is beyond attainment.

Attainable or not, that is the direction in which remedy must be sought, in leadership of the caliber contemplated by Madison. Practitioners of the "politics of variation" are needed, committed to open debate and the synthesis of ideas, tolerant of dissent, committed to the general good over the advantage of one faction or another, and willing, if need be, to be defeated should that be the price of adherence to the larger national interest.

CHAPTER THREE

Saudi Arabia: The Politics of Oil

In 1940 President Franklin D. Roosevelt scribbled a note on a policy paper that had been handed to him by his adviser, Harry Hopkins: "Arabia is too far afield for us. Can't you get the British to do something?"[1] In that same year the American minister in Cairo was accredited to serve also as the first United States representative in Saudi Arabia, despite a negative recommendation by Secretary of State Cordell Hull based on a report that "the development of American interests does not warrant the establishment of any sort of official representation at Jidda."[2] Only in 1942, ten years after the proclamation of the unified Kingdom of Saudi Arabia, was a resident American chargé d'affaires assigned to the court of King Abd al-Aziz (Ibn Saud).

Prior to the 1930s, American contacts with the Arabian peninsula consisted mainly of the limited and transient activities of traders and missionaries. Oil was discovered in Saudi Arabia in the thirties; in 1933 the first concession agreement between an American oil company and Saudi Arabia was signed, and the company that later was to be known as ARAMCO (the Arabian-American Oil Company) began its explorations in the deserts of eastern Arabia. Commercial production of Arabian oil began in 1938, but large-scale production was begun only after the Second World War. ARAMCO's production rose from something over 50,000 barrels of crude oil a day in 1945 to over half a million a day in 1950, surpassing one million a day in 1958 and two million in 1965.[3] By 1977 Saudi Arabia was producing crude oil at the rate of 9.4 million barrels a day and by 1980, 10.2 million barrels a day.[4] Almost all of this output was accounted for by ARAMCO, which was gradually being brought under complete Saudi ownership, although its top management personnel remained predominantly American.

The year 1970 was a watershed in U.S. relations with Saudi Arabia. In that year U.S. domestic oil production reached a peak of over 11.3 million barrels a day before beginning to drop as oil fields became depleted and overall reserves diminished. Production began to rise again in 1977 with the arrival of oil from the Alaskan North Slope, but, by all projections available, no major, sustained increase of conventional petroleum production could be expected. The Exxon Corporation in late 1980 projected a decline in American domestic crude oil production from just over 10 million barrels a day in 1980 to 7 million barrels a day in 1990, and only a slight increase thereafter. Thus even with decreases in imports and overall demand attributable to price-induced conservation and the expansion of other energy sources, the United States would remain heavily dependent on imported energy.[5] The imports would come primarily from the Middle East, especially from Saudi Arabia with oil reserves representing 25 percent of the world's total. By far the largest single foreign supplier of oil to this country, Saudi Arabia exported an average of 1,254,000 barrels a day to the United States in 1980, down from the peak year 1977, but still exceeding by half the amount purchased by the United States from its second largest foreign supplier, Nigeria, and far exceeding all others.[6] There would seem almost no feasible means of avoiding this dependence on Saudi Arabian and other Arab sources, at least through the decade of the eighties, no matter how successful conservation efforts, no matter what new oil resources are derived from the Alaskan North Slope and domestic offshore discoveries, no matter what programs are undertaken to derive synthetic fuels from coal and shale, or further to develop solar and nuclear energy. The prognosis holds even more for America's allies: whereas the United States imported 37 percent of its oil supply in 1980, Western Europe imported 81 percent of its needs and Japan virtually 100 percent.[7] Saudi Arabia is the largest single producer with the largest reserves of a vital resource that neither the United States nor other countries can do without or adequately replace from other sources or technologies for the foreseeable future: therein lies the importance of Saudi Arabia to the national interest of the United States.

THE "OIL WEAPON"

Unlike guns, which have no other purpose, resources are weapons only if they are used as weapons. The vast resources of oil and "petrodollars" at the disposal of Saudi Arabia and its associates in the Organization of Petroleum Exporting Countries (OPEC) unquestionably represent great *power* in the hands of their possessors. Whether they also represent a threat to the United States and other countries, a weapon aimed against their interests, is a question that increasingly troubled American policy after 1973, when the oil embargo was imposed during the October War. Two basic issues have been involved in the debate as to whether Saudi Arabia was to be cast as an inveterate antagonist to the United States or a reliable friend and collaborator. One issue has to do with Saudi practices regarding the supply and price of oil and the disposition of vast reserves of "petrodollars" acquired since the quadrupling of oil prices in 1973–74 and subsequent increases. The other basic issue is the Arab-Israeli conflict, which precipitated the embargo of 1973 and which has involved Saudi Arabia both as the religious leader of the Arab world and as the chief financial backer of the Arab belligerents. This involvement in turn has aroused suspicion and animosity toward Saudi Arabia among Israel's strong supporters in the United States.

On October 19, 1973, five days before the cease-fire ending the October War, President Nixon asked Congress to provide $2.2 billion in emergency security assistance to replace Israel's losses in the war. On the following day Saudi Arabia, which had not gone beyond cutting production and issuing warnings during the fighting up to that point, announced a total embargo on oil shipments to the United States. On October 21 the smaller Arab states on the Persian Gulf followed suit, making the Arab embargo complete—except for Iraq, which never imposed any embargo, Libya having imposed an embargo on October 19. The embargo was officially lifted on March 18, 1974, but only after it had precipitated profound changes in the world economy and energy situation, and only after it had set the United States on an altered course as mediator between Israel and its Arab enemies.

The U.S. government condemned the embargo, declaring that it would not be coerced into withdrawing its support for Israel. It seems clear, however, that the embargo was the driving force behind Secretary of State Henry Kissinger's urgent "shuttle diplomacy," which brought about, in succession, the cease-fire agreement between Israel and Egypt of November 11, 1973; the resumption of diplomatic relations (which had been broken at the time of the 1967 war) between the United States and Egypt; the convening of peace talks at Geneva in December 1973 and their suspension after only two days; the conclusion of the first Egyptian-Israeli disengagement agreement on January 18, 1974; and the conclusion on May 31, 1974 of a disengagement agreement between Israel and Syria. The political, as distinguished from economic implications of Saudi Arabia's oil power will be examined further in the next section. It may be noted here, however, that although Saudi Arabia participated in a limited way in the brief oil embargo imposed during the 1967 war, the October War of 1973 marked the effective end of the traditional Saudi policy of separating oil from politics. Thereafter the two were to be inextricably bound together, less so, to be sure, than partisans of the Palestinian cause might wish, but nevertheless with profound implications for the Middle East, for the world economy, and for the national interest of the United States.

The embargo, followed by the world oil price revolution, brought the United States to shocked awareness of the "energy crisis." In an address to the nation on November 7, 1973, President Nixon called for a crash program to make the United States independent of foreign energy sources by the end of the decade of the seventies. President Nixon likened "Project Independence," as he called it, to the Manhattan Project of World War II that had developed the atomic bomb and to the Apollo Project that put Americans on the moon in 1969. "Project Independence" had no such dramatic results. Within a short time the stated goal had been modified to "reasonable self-sufficiency," and over the next year or so, as memories of the embargo and gasoline lines faded, it became apparent that total, or even substantial, independence of foreign energy sources was neither financially nor politically feasible. More and more Americans came to doubt the reality of the "energy crisis," regarding it as a political invention. In an interview on July 30, 1977, President Carter said that the public had "not responded well" to pleas for energy conservation, that voluntary compliance was "probably not adequate," and that the public was "not paying attention to the energy crisis." The president expressed fear that a "series of crises" might be required to induce the American people to "quit wasting so much fuel," and he warned that the oil embargo of 1973 and the natural gas shortage of the winter of 1976 might just be "predictions of what is to come."[8] Only after another severe oil shortage, accompanied by new gasoline lines and sharply increased prices, in 1979, did it begin to appear that real conservation efforts were being made in the United States.

In the meantime imports rose steadily, as did prices. In 1973, OPEC quadrupled the price of oil, from a posted price of $2.59 per barrel of Persian Gulf crude oil to $11.65. Further increases brought the price up to nearly $13 a barrel in 1977 and a minimum of $18 a barrel in mid-1979. Some producers were selling at $30 a barrel or more by the end of 1979, the year as it came to be known of the "second oil shock." The effect has been a historic change in world economic relations, such that, in the words of *Congressional Quarterly*'s Middle East survey, "never in modern history had such an abrupt transfer of wealth and power taken place without war and in so short a time."[9] By 1977 the major oil-exporting countries, especially Saudi Arabia, had accumulated some $150 billion in financial reserves and liquid assets, giving them the power, should they choose to use it, to destabilize the currencies or disrupt the economies of many of the major industrial countries. As a result of the oil price revolution, both developed and less developed countries suffered reduced economic growth rates, consequent unemployment, and massive balance-of-payment problems, all of which would have been much worse, for the United States and other industrial countries, but for heavy spending by OPEC countries for arms, industrial equipment, and consumer goods. Saudi Arabia and other oil-exporting countries also invested heavily in U.S. Treasury bills and bonds, commercial bank deposits, corporate bonds, and, in smaller but politically significant amounts, educational institutions in the United States and other industrial countries. The exact amount of Saudi Arabia's foreign assets and their disposition are well guarded secrets, but it has been estimated that the kingdom's total financial reserves in 1980 exceeded $110 billion, of which 75 to 85 percent was held in dollars. About $60 billion of Saudi Arabia's foreign assets were believed in 1980 to be in U.S. government securities and other American banking and financial institutions.[10]

Coming to office in January 1977, the Carter administration judged the energy crisis to be a national emergency and offered a program to deal with it—a program that the president asked the nation to accept as the "moral equivalent of war." The Carter administration's program called for reduced overall energy consumption, significantly reduced imports, the establishment of a Strategic Petroleum Reserve, increased reliance on coal, which the nation possessed in abundance, support for synthetic fuels development, higher gasoline taxes, higher prices on domestically produced oil and natural gas, and various tax credits and incentives to encourage more efficient automobiles, home insulation, the use of solar heating, and other energy-saving measures.[11] Congress, at the request of President Carter, also created a new, cabinet-level Department of Energy in 1977.

Whatever measures might or might not be taken to conserve energy and develop new sources, it was evident by the late seventies that reliable access to foreign energy sources would remain a top priority objective of American foreign policy for years to come. Eventually—perhaps by the end of the century, perhaps sooner—it would be essential to convert to new, exotic fuels on a large scale because the world's fossil fuels, finite and nonrenewable, would be steadily depleted. During that interval, it was equally clear, the United States, as well as most other nations, would remain dependent on foreign suppliers of petroleum and natural gas. Although forecasts no longer (as of the early 1980s) projected increases in the demand for oil of the major industrial countries, the comprehensive projection made by the Exxon Corporation in late 1980 suggested that the demand for oil of the major noncommunist industrial countries would decline only from 40 million barrels a day to 35 million barrels a day by 2000, with American demand declining from 18 to 15 million barrels a day.[12]

Until 1974 more than half the oil imported into the United States had come from what were considered "secure" sources of supply, primarily Canada and Venezuela.[13] Thereafter oil imports from the Western Hemisphere declined sharply, and Canada announced its intention of phasing out all oil imports to the United States by 1983. Authoritative projections thereafter showed no feasible alternative—despite promising discoveries in Mexico—to continuing reliance on Middle Eastern sources.[14]

These data and developments give crucial significance to the question of whether Saudi Arabia can be considered a "safe" source of oil supply. The answer can be sought in an examination of Saudi policies, the interests that underlie these, and the stability of the Saudi system.

Saudi-American relations, the embargo of 1973 notwithstanding, have been built on a longstanding tradition of friendship. Even during the heady days of the boycott, when the Saudis were discovering the enormous political implications of their oil power, Saudi officials stressed their friendship for the United States and the reluctance with which King Faisal had undertaken the boycott. It was imposed, they were at pains to stress, in the final days of the October War only after the Nixon administration undertook to rearm Israel and thus, in the Saudi view, save it from the necessity of a negotiated peace.[15]

The attraction of Saudis to Americans dates from the 1930s, when Americans first came to Saudi Arabia in large numbers to begin developing the kingdom's oil reserves. According to scholars of the period, King Abd al-Aziz found the easy egalitarianism of the Americans congenial to the Bedouin tradition of accessibility by the rulers to their people—a welcome contrast to the pomp and imperial arrogance of the more familiar British in the Middle East.[16] No less important, perhaps, were the technical competence of the American oil companies and the fact that the United States, unlike the European powers, had no history of imperial involvement in the Middle East. Saudi Arabia is the only major member of OPEC whose oil was developed entirely by American companies, and the kingdom's favorable disposition toward the United States has had much to do with its cordial relations with ARAMCO. While Great Britain and Iran fell into a bitter dispute in the early 1950s over nationalization of the Anglo-Iranian Oil Company (ARAMCO), and Saudi Arabia initiated a system of "fifty-fifty" profit sharing; subsequently Saudi Arabia gradually increased its "participation" in ARAMCO, acquiring 25 percent of its producing assets in 1973, 60 percent in 1974, and the remainder in 1980. Even as the Saudis took over the company and brought Saudi personnel into top management jobs, it was understood that ARAMCO, with its still largely American management and technical staff, would continue to operate the vast concession and also conduct explorations for new reserves of petroleum. At the insistence of the Saudi government in the mid-1950s, ARAMCO's corporate headquarters had been moved to Saudi Arabia, facilitating consultation and, it would appear, good relations as well between the Saudi leaders and the company's American management. As of 1981 ARAMCO remained the largest oil producing company in the world; prior to the Saudi takeover, it had been the largest single American investment in any foreign country.[17]

Although the Saudis largely instigated the price revolution of 1973–74, and then, through complex pricing procedures, effectively joined and even led in OPEC price increases throughout 1974 and 1975, from 1976 on Saudi Arabia pursued policies of price restraint within OPEC, while generally maintaining production to meet the needs of the industrial countries. Steadily mounting foreign monetary reserves resulting from oil exports far in excess of imports gave Saudi Arabia a tangible stake in the economic health of the major industrial economies. Accordingly, in their capacity as the effective arbiter of OPEC prices—a role made possible by their large excess capacity—the Saudis, from 1976 on (if not before) resisted pressures for oil price increases in excess of the worldwide rate of inflation, even when other OPEC nations pressed vigorously to raise prices above the rate of inflation. At least until the Iranian revolution reduced Iran from a large and steady supplier to a much reduced and wholly unreliable source of oil, making for a tighter world market, Saudi Arabia had only to increase—or threaten to increase—its own production to thwart what it might judge to be excessive price increases by other members of OPEC. This power was brought to bear decisively in 1976 and 1977 when Saudi Arabia and the United Arab Emirates used the leverage of their spare capacity, greatly in excess of that of other OPEC countries, to compel price restraint. Saudi Arabia's capacity to regulate the world market was reduced by the Iranian revolution, but the Saudis retained much of their power to discourage the other OPEC members from raising prices greatly beyond the level approved by Saudi Arabia without risking serious financial loss.[18]

Except for the period from late 1978 into the first half of 1979—the period between the conclusion of the Camp David accords and the Egyptian-Israeli peace treaty—Saudi Arabia continued to pursue a policy of price restraint within OPEC, adjusting its own production levels to meet the industrial world's requirements and with the objective of bringing market pressures to bear on high-price producers so as to establish unified OPEC prices. The Saudis increased production in the summer of 1979 to alleviate the world oil shortage existing at that time and again in the fall of 1980 to insulate the international petroleum market from the effects of the Iran-Iraq war that had broken out in September. At the OPEC meeting at Geneva in May 1981, a time of oil surplus on the world market, Saudi Arabia, accounting by itself for over 40 percent of OPEC's production, declined to participate in a 10 percent cutback in production; it also held its price at $32 a barrel while other OPEC prices ranged from $36 to $41 a barrel.[19] The Saudis thus adhered firmly to their objective of linking world oil prices, on a continuing basis, to world inflation, economic growth, and currency fluctuations.

Price restraint and high production levels are by no means the totality of American economic interests in Saudi Arabia. Oil being a finite energy source whose depletion is probably no more than a generation away, all possible incentives are required to make the transition from an oil-based economy to an economy based on other sources as smooth and painless as possible. The question must be asked, wrote oil economist Walter Levy in late 1978,

> whether it is really in the interest of the oil-importing countries to put undue emphasis on the availability of ample supplies of oil at low prices, as this would inevitably, within a relatively narrow time span, be followed by shortages of oil with a price explosion. Any freeze of current oil prices, or even more so their reduction, would particularly affect all endeavors to develop non-OPEC-based energy resources, be they oil or non-oil based, as such efforts will be very costly.[20]

Substantial intellectual energies have been expended on the task of discerning Saudi Arabia's "true" motives in pursuing policies so ostensibly favorable to the noncommunist industrial world. Such inquiries lead quickly, inevitably to the discovery that Saudi policies are not rooted in altruism, pure-hearted devotion to the interests of the West, or a predilection for self-sacrifice. It is apparent that in acting to stabilize world oil markets, so far as they can, the Saudis are acting in clear self-interest. In the first instance, underselling other OPEC countries has enabled the Saudis to increase their own share of the world market and therefore their earnings. It also appears to be true that the Saudis wish, by dominating OPEC's price structure, to establish their preeminence in the organization. More important still, with many billions of dollars invested in the Western economies, Saudi Arabia has excellent reason to contribute to the stability of these economies. The Saudi leaders have demonstrated keen awareness of the damage that would be done both to the industrialized countries and the less developed countries by a policy of limiting oil production in order to maximize prices. They are also aware, as some other OPEC producers appear not to be, that radically increased oil prices, by accelerating the pace of conservation and the development of alternative energy sources, would undercut demand, especially in the longer run, for OPEC oil. Finally, the Saudi leaders regard the United States as their necessary protector against radicalism and the possibility of aggression or subversion in the Arabian peninsula. As the *Washington Post* has commented editorially, "The Saudi Government likes the western countries to keep thinking about their interest in its perpetuation in power."[21]

Nation states not being eleemosynary institutions, the fact of Saudi self-interest is itself unremarkable. The fact that the Saudis cooperate with the United States because it is to their advantage suggests in no way that they are unreliable collaborators; on the contrary, it may be argued that in dealings among nations mutuality of interest is not only a more common motive than altruism or compassion but also by far the more reliable. Nor does the presence of self-interest suggest that cooperation will be ephemeral, to be continued or abandoned opportunistically and capriciously. The interests that Saudi Arabia perceives in its collaboration with the West are neither ephemeral nor capricious in the manner, for example, of some of the pretensions of the late shah of Iran. Saudi interests in the West, it would seem, are based on rational calculations of the kingdom's long term political and economic needs.

It would, nevertheless, be a serious misjudgment to conclude, on the ground that "they need us more than we need them," that no special regard need be taken of Saudi Arabia's strong political preferences. The Saudis, as will be seen, care strongly and deeply for the cohesion of the Arab and Islamic worlds in general, and for the national aspirations of the Palestinian people in particular. Cooperation with the West may be regarded as a vital Saudi interest, but it is patently not their only perceived vital interest, and it is far from probable that, if compelled to choose (as they would greatly prefer not to have to do), they would choose their association with the West. Saudi Arabia, as its Oil Minister Sheikh Ahmad Zaki Yamani has shown no reluctance to assert, could reduce oil production substantially and still meet its development needs, while the oil left in the ground would most probably be a better investment than anything that can be done with the money it earns. Yamani has said, "If the Saudis simply cut production to the level needed to meet their own development plans there would be a depression in the United States in which the rate of unemployment would at least double, the price of oil would double again and the inflation rate would rise."[22]

With its mounting monetary reserves—second in the world only to those of West Germany by the end of 1976—Saudi Arabia became in the 1970s a financial "superpower" in world economic relations. Even with a $142 billion five-year plan for internal economic development initiated in 1975, and with large-scale foreign aid programs, mainly in the Arab world, Saudi Arabia's oil income far exceeded its expenditures. Saudi Arabia became a nation beset with what Edward F. Sheehan called "the epidemic of money."[23] This vast surplus wealth has provided highly profitable opportunities for the sale of Western products and technology, but it also poses a long term threat to the industrial countries' interests if, through greed and opportunism, they encourage wasteful, unbalanced, socially disruptive, and politically destabilizing development programs. The Iranian revolution provides a useful and ominous warning in this respect.[24]

As in the extraction and marketing of Saudi oil, the United States plays a central role in Saudi development projects and in the channeling of "petro-dollars" into foreign investments. A Saudi-American Joint Commission on Economic Cooperation, created in 1974, provides assistance to the Saudi government in planning technical projects, and major American corporations, including ARAMCO, help plan and implement projects that in turn lead to large-scale exports of American goods and services to Saudi Arabia. American exports to Saudi Arabia and the channeling of Saudi funds into the United States mounted steadily through the early and middle 1970s. Evidence began to appear in the late seventies, however, of a decline in American business opportunities in Saudi Arabia and other Arab countries. American exports to the kingdom continued to increase in dollar terms but, with adjustments made for inflation, may actually have declined between 1978 and 1979. In addition, between 1975 and 1980 American construction firms lost substantial ground to other foreign competitors in bids for contracts in Saudi Arabia.[25] Whether these losses were the result purely of economic and technical factors, or whether they also resulted from the effects of antiboycott legislation designed to counteract Arab boycotts of Israel, United States tax laws, or political considerations relating to Israel and the Palestinian question, was not clear, but any or all of these factors may have contributed to the American losses.

The "money weapon," like the "oil weapon," could be used to disrupt the economies of Europe, Japan, and the United States. The fact that this extraordinary economic power has not been so used testifies to the strength of the Saudis' conviction that, even in the face of countervailing pressures arising from the Arab world's reaction to the Camp David agreements and the Iranian revolution, Saudi security and development interests still require a close, indeed "special," relationship with the United States. Whether this outlook changes fundamentally in the future is likely to be influenced by political as well as economic factors—by the status of the Arab-Israeli conflict, by security considerations, by trends and pressures within the Islamic world, and by the continuation in power of a Saudi leadership that identifies its interests with the United States, as well as by the pressure of demand upon the supply of oil foreseen for the middle and late 1980s.

Saudi pricing policies and production levels are obviously and importantly, but not exclusively, influenced by the costs of an ambitious domestic development program. Beyond that, the willingness of the Saudis to continue to produce oil in amounts exceeding their own best economic and financial interests (and perhaps those of the industrial countries as well) and also to hold the line against huge price increases as demand, from time to time, presses upon supply, will surely be influenced too by American policy: if the United States sustains an effective energy program, thereby holding down the pressure of demand for petroleum upon supply, if it continues to meet Saudi security needs, and if it helps bring about a general Arab-Israeli settlement, then its influence upon Saudi policy with respect to oil production, prices, and investment will, it seems reasonable to predict, be maximized.

It would seem to follow too that the less successful the United States is in any of these policy categories, the greater will be the need for responsiveness to Saudi interests in the other areas. If, for example, the United States fails to restrain significantly its energy consumption (on a continuing basis), thereby creating greater demand pressure on the supply of OPEC oil, it will be all the more important to advance the Arab-Israeli conflict toward a mutually tolerable solution, or to continue to supply Saudi Arabia with the advanced military equipment it may consider essential to its security. Otherwise the Saudis would have little political incentive—and surely no economic incentive—to maintain a level of oil production that meets the industrial world's immediate needs and also serves to restrain the drastic price increases its OPEC partners may be expected to continue to demand at regular intervals.

That Saudi policy with respect to oil supply and price and the disposition of petrodollars clearly has been, in comparison with other oil producers, favorable to the United States. Questions are raised, nonetheless, as to whether Saudi Arabia is a "safe" source of oil supply, even for the short run—out of fear of another boycott in the event of a fifth Arab-Israeli war, and out of fear that Saudi monarchy may be displaced by a radical coup or insurrection. These apprehensions are not unrelated, since doubts as to the stability of the Saudi monarchy are often expressed by individuals who are also deeply concerned with the security of Israel. Testifying before the Senate Foreign Relations Committee in May 1978 against the sale of F–15 fighter planes to Saudi Arabia, Morris J. Amitay, then executive director of the American-Israel Public Affairs Committee, expressed the view that "Saudi Arabia's narrowly based feudal monarchy is by no means stable, and a change in its orientation could literally occur overnight."[26] The same theme was developed in the hearings at greater length, and with considerable vehemence, by Amos Perlmutter, an Israeli-born professor at the American University in Washington, D.C., who characterized Saudi Arabia as a "politically and militarily weak state" that tries to placate its Arab "secular rivals" with money and arms in a desperate bid for their "legitimization of a medieval patrimonial Saudi dynasty." "Saudi Arabia's most conspicuous fear," in Professor Perlmutter's view, was "not an Israeli attack on its oil wells, but fear of social and political unrest, of Marxists and Soviet-inspired Arab regimes and movements which it bankrolls." The effect of this "rather risky policy," he advised the committee, is that it makes Saudi Arabia "subject to radical and irredentist Arab blackmail," with the likely result that "the Saudis stand to eventually destabilize their own regime."[27]

Some writers present it as axiomatic that, past experience notwithstanding, Saudi Arabia is inherently unstable, or at least unreliable, and therefore an "unsafe" source of oil supply for the United States and other industrial nations. Listing the range of adverse possibilities, Daniel Yergin, a member of the Energy Research Project at the Harvard Business School, wrote in 1978:

> There could be a natural disaster. Or an accident or a terrorist strike in the oil fields or in the narrow straits leading to the Persian Gulf. Or the growth of the Soviet presence in the region, some new twist of the Arab-Israeli conflict, or a struggle for pre-eminence among Saudi Arabia, Iraq and Iran. Or a shift in the outlook of the elite that runs the Saudi kingdom. Or—and this is the very real danger that Western officials prefer to close their eyes to—a coup in Riyadh and the accession to power of a radical like Libya's Colonel Qadafi.

A similar upheaval, Professor Yergin noted briefly, might also occur in Iran.[28]

That all these calamities are *possible* is beyond dispute; the more pertinent question for American policy, however, is whether they are also *probable*, and if so, what can be done about them. On the question of Saudi Arabia's stability, specialists in the region point to the swift, smooth succession to power of King Khalid and Crown Prince Fahd following the assassination of King Faisal on March 25, 1975. Four royal communiqués were issued on the day of the assassination, announcing the event and the identity of the killer—a royal nephew who, it was quickly announced, had acted alone and not as part of a plot—and most importantly, affirming the allegiance of leading members of the royal family to the new king. It is not entirely obvious how the leading figures in the royal family could have ascertained so quickly that the killer had acted alone, but the very fact that they so affirmed gave evidence of the strong and natural impulse of the royal family to hold together in a crisis. The royal family showed its cohesiveness once again in acting carefully but forcefully, and in close consultation with the religious hierarchy, or *ulema*, when the Grand Mosque of Mecca was briefly occupied by rebellious religious extremists in November 1979.

For a time the episode in Mecca cast doubt on the strength and durability of the Saudi system. It took the Saudi security forces two weeks to defeat the rebels, with heavy loss of life on both sides. The episode also seemed more serious because of riots and demonstrations, unconnected but simultaneous, among the Shiite Muslims of the Eastern Province. In fact the difficulty encountered by the Saudi security forces in subduing the Mecca rebels resulted partly from the complex system of underground passages in which the rebels took refuge and partly from the government's reluctance to use heavy fire power inside the most sacred mosque of Islam. Neither during nor after the siege did disturbances occur among the Saudi population suggesting support for the rebels. The Shiite demonstrations were most probably prompted by militancy induced by the revolution in Iran, where Shiite Muslims predominated, but in Saudi Arabia the Shiite community, constituting no more than 10 percent of the population, represented only a very limited revolutionary potential.

The royal family nevertheless took both occurrences extremely seriously and acted decisively. The governor of Mecca, a senior prince, was replaced, as were a number of high-ranking military officers. Sixty-three of those who had attacked the Grand Mosque were beheaded in public places following trial by an Islamic court. Measures were also taken to tighten the application of Islamic law in the kingdom, but at the same time Crown Prince Fahd announced that an appointive consultative assembly would be formed.[29]

A Senate Foreign Relations Committee staff study of 1978 cited several factors that fostered stability in the Saudi system: the tendency of the royal family to unite in time of crisis; the size and relatively high educational level of the royal family, which has relatives in almost every tribe in Saudi Arabia and holds key positions in major ministries, especially those most crucial to the retention and exercise of state power; the maintenance of close ties with the growing technical elite; the involvement of members of the royal family in all military services; the maintenance, in the Bedouin tradition, of close ties with the people; the outflanking of the right by religious traditionalism and of the left by economic development and increasing social services; and the exclusion of foreign nationals from key military and other sensitive positions.[30] Although the royal family number in the thousands, the core of the kingdom's leadership is made up of a number of half brothers of the late King Faisal, all sons of the founder of modern Saudi Arabia, King Abd al-Aziz al-Saud (often referred to as Ibn Saud). Characterized by a high degree of cohesion and mutual loyalty, the principal members of the royal family hold almost all the politically most sensitive ministries of state—the most notable exception being the Ministry of Petroleum and Mineral Resources, headed by Sheikh Ahmad Zaki Yamani.

Another factor making, paradoxically, for relative stability in the Saudi system is the acute sensitivity of the Saudi leaders to their own vulnerability, so much in contrast to the late shah of Iran. Unfailingly deferential to the *ulema*, or Islamic clergy or scholars, the Saudi leaders also adhere to the principle of *shura*, which refers to a practice of informal but effective consultation by the rulers with their subjects. This consultation, different in form and character from Western majoritarian democracy, nonetheless has the effect of keeping the rulers in continual communication with their subjects. It is institutionalized, to a degree, through the *majlis,* the opening of the ruler's doors to the people, who one by one in open session, informally and candidly, state their views or wishes or petition for the redress of their grievances. Through the *majlis*, a system deeply rooted in the Arab past, the rulers allow, indeed must allow, access to themselves by their subjects, and in this way are made accountable for their rule. Nor is the *majlis* necessarily confined to a single center at the royal court. Arab rulers and lesser sheikhs traditionally travel about their domains, from one town or work site to another, carrying the *majlis* to the people.[31]

Based as it is on the cohesion of the royal family, tribal traditions, and strict adherence to orthodox Wahhabi Muslim religious standards, the Saudi system has been called upon to adapt to the social changes induced by oil wealth, rapidly growing urban centers, a developing middle class, and a whole class of royal princes as well as a large number of commoners educated abroad, mainly in the United States. Perhaps the most important force for long term change are the thousands of young Saudis, prospective leaders of the country, who are sent each year, at government expense, to study abroad and who surely come home with new ideas about how the country ought to be run.[32] There would also seem the real possibility that, when the current generation of Saudi leaders are succeeded by a new generation of the royal family, many of whom will have been educated in the West, countervailing pressures from this new generation, the surviving elders and perhaps the military will complicate the system of rule by family consensus. Although social change in Saudi Arabia seems certain, it is far from axiomatic that the change must be wrought by coup or insurrection. These must certainly be accounted as possibilities, but there is reason for a measure of optimism that the *shura-majlis* system will prove to be a serviceable vehicle for radical modernization. Nor is the process of change impervious to the influence of the United States, which has an obvious interest in continued stability, and therefore in the encouragement of evolutionary social change, in the Arabian peninsula. American influence in this direction has long been exerted through the presence in Saudi Arabia of thousands of employees of ARAMCO, working amicably with Saudi leaders and Saudi workers. A most powerful American cultural influence is being brought to bear through cooperation in education; with ever increasing numbers of Saudis coming to the United States to study every year—3,030 in 1975 and 4,590 in 1976—it seems reasonable to anticipate significant American influence on the character and direction of social change in Saudi Arabia.[33] Educational exchange, it must be added, is not inevitably a positive influence from the standpoint of American interests; as the experience of many thousands of Iranian students showed, extended exposure to the American intellectual and political environment can have a radicalizing as well as a liberating effect on students from traditional societies.

The adverse possibilities that are said to make Saudi Arabia an "unsafe" source of petroleum supply for the United States are, by available evidence, no more than possibilities, neither probable nor beyond the range of American influence. Indeed the likelihood of another embargo, or of a coup or insurrection against the Saudi monarchy, probably depends, as much as anything, on the future development of the Arab-Israeli conflict. If there is another war, there will probably be another oil boycott. If there is no war but if the Arab-Israeli—and particularly the Palestinian—issue is allowed to fester inconclusively for years to come, we may then anticipate recurrent terrorism and the radicalization of Arab states that are now moderate. Saudi Arabia would then, to one degree or another, become susceptible to radical pressures and, in any event, partly to fend these pressures off, partly out of genuine indignation, could be counted on to take a less friendly view of American interests, both as to the price of oil and the amount produced. If, on the other hand, a settlement tolerable to both sides is reached, and if, as would almost certainly be the case, the United States played the decisive role in achieving it, virtually all threat of an embargo would disappear; radicalism in the Arab world would be deprived of its major source of fuel, with salutary effects for the Saudi system; and the United States would find its influence enhanced on such crucial matters as the price of oil, the amount produced, and the flow and uses of petrodollars.

The former governor of Texas and secretary of the treasury, John Connally, running for the 1980 Republican presidential nomination, broke new ground for a presidential candidate by spelling out this connection of issues in a speech on October 11, 1979: "We must secure a clear understanding from Saudi Arabia and other moderate oil-producing nations in the region that a just and comprehensive peace settlement means a return to stable oil prices in real terms. The Arabs must, in short, forsake the oil weapon in return for Israel's withdrawal from the occupied territories."[34]

This view of the "oil weapon," and of its connection with the Israeli-Palestinian issue, is hotly contested by some observers, including economists who contend that the issues are separate and distinct. According to this school of thought, the Saudis have acted and will continue to act in accordance with their own economic self-interest, setting prices and levels of production to suit their own economic and security needs, without regard to American interests or Palestinian aspirations to self-determination, even though they pay lip service and protection money to the Palestinian cause. It is argued that even if the United States were to coerce Israel into withdrawing from the occupied territories and allow the Palestinians to form a state in the West Bank and Gaza, the Saudis would continue to collaborate with the OPEC members in regulating prices and production levels according to their own economic self-interest. The major publication of the Israeli lobby, rejecting "the asumption that oil prices and production have something to do with Israel," denounced Connally's proposal as an "invitation to oil blackmail."[35] The *New York Times* condemned both John Connally and Reverend Jesse Jackson, who had made a somewhat similar proposal, for joining to promote "a wicked and dangerous diplomatic bargain."[36]

A more temperate view of the relationship of oil to the Israeli-Palestinian issue would take cognizance of the fact that "economic self-interest" is not a rigid or even very objective category. Diverse economic factors may pull a country in one direction or another and economists often disagree as to what the national self-interest requires. Applying this proposition to Saudi Arabia, it seems reasonable to expect that economic self-interest will indeed govern oil prices and production levels, but that, within the fairly wide parameters of what economic self-interest allows (especially when diverse economic and security pressures pull in different directions) political factors will exert an important and sometimes decisive influence.

It seems hardly contestable that Saudi Arabian economic interests, taken by themselves, would be served best by limiting oil production well below the needs of the industrial countries. Despite foreign expenditures and purchases exceeding what was once thought possible, the kingdom could make do quite well with imports far short of current and prospective earnings; if necessary, costly construction projects already under way could be canceled or postponed without great hardship. It would be, therefore, to the Saudis' strict economic advantage to leave as much oil as possible in the ground—untapped oil being probably the best investment in the world today, far better indeed than the inflated dollars for which the oil is being currently traded. The Saudis also, however, have a strong economic and security interest in the health and stability of the industrial world's economies, especially that of the United States. If they are to be persuaded to give priority to these over the countervailing advantages of oil in the ground, and if, for this purpose, they are to be persuaded to sustain a high level of production, and also to hold the line on prices during the difficult transition period while new sources of energy are being developed to replace the world's diminishing stores of fossil fuels, political incentives could well prove to be decisive—incentives relating to the Arab-Israeli conflict, the status of Jerusalem, and Palestinian self-determination. The linkage suggested by John Connally on October 11, 1979, might thus, in practice, have to be something short of ironclad, more psychological than contractual, having more to do with the basic disposition of Saudi Arabia toward the United States than with clearly spelled-out, binding obligations. For that, however, the connection would be nonetheless real and nonetheless advantageous to American interests.

POLITICAL INCENTIVES

A powerful nation like the United States seeking to influence a militarily insignificant one like Saudi Arabia may choose to apply either positive or negative incentives. It can try to satisfy the smaller nation's political aspirations, if these are judged to be compatible with its own, or it can try to coerce the smaller country into doing its bidding by military force or the threat of it—either on its own or through a surrogate—or by other forms of pressure. The means employed is necessarily a function of the compatibility, or lack of it, between the perceived interests of the great power and the small one. In the case of Saudi Arabia, there has been a basic compatibility of interests with the United States, reinforced by a tradition of friendship going back to the 1930s, on all major regional issues except that of Israel and its place in the Middle East. Theoretically, the oil-exporting nations, with their control of a scarce, vital resource, and with their enormous monetary reserves, could inflict great damage at any time on the economies of the industrial countries or on the world monetary and financial system. In practice it is unlikely—almost, indeed, inconceivable—that Saudi Arabia and the oil-producing emirates of the Arabian peninsula would pose such a threat. It surely would be against their interests to do so. Their extensive financial holdings in Western industrial countries, although potential weapons against these countries, are also hostage to the good health of these countries' economies, and the oil producers must also have a healthy respect for the countermeasures the United States and perhaps other countries could readily take against them. Only in the event of a surpassing crisis in the Arab-Israeli conflict does it seem at all plausible that the oil-producing countries might incur the terrible risk of making maximum use of their oil weapon. It is therefore over this issue, the Arab-Israeli conflict, and the reconcilability of interests with respect to it, that the question of coercion or accommodation arises in Saudi-American relations.

To suppose, as is sometimes suggested, that the Gulf Arabs do not deeply care about the conflict with Israel, and feel no real solidarity with the so-called confrontation states, and especially with the Palestinians, is, by available evidence, a mistaken notion. Asked to appraise the attitude of the Gulf Arabs toward the Arab-Israeli conflict, a former American ambassador to Kuwait and "old Middle East hand," William Stoltzfus, told a subcommittee of the Senate Foreign Relations Committee in 1976 that the Gulf Arabs shared the feelings of all other Arabs, even the sense of humiliation over the lost wars with Israel, even though they had not participated directly in those wars. "Therefore," Ambassador Stoltzfus said, "one can in no way dismiss, and never forget, that as long as the Arab-Israeli question is in the forefront, the Arabs can never forget it. Barely, beneath the surface it exists, and they feel very strongly about it."[37] Another witness, Professor John Duke Anthony of the Center for Middle East Studies of the Johns Hopkins School of Advanced International Studies, spoke of "the widespread sense of moral commitment of the oil states which identify both politically and psychologically with the Arab side of the Arab-Israeli conflict by virture of their membership in the greater Arab community."[38]

The Saudi attitude toward the Palestinians in general, and toward the Palestine Liberation Organization in particular, is ambivalent but by no means unsympathetic. On the one hand, the Saudis fear the revolutionary potential of Palestinian irredentism within the Arab world, especially in such places as neighboring Kuwait with its large Palestinian population, but also in Saudi Arabia itself—where over 100,000 Palestinian workers, although they make up only a fraction of the foreign work force, are nonetheless regarded with apprehension as a potential source of disruption. It is largely because of this fear, there can be little doubt, that the Saudis provide funds for the Palestine Liberation Organization, so as to limit its radical potential and in any case deflect it from themselves. On the other hand, the Saudis feel bound to the Palestinians by a sense of kinship and common cause. The attitude of the Saudis and other Gulf Arabs toward the Palestinians may even compare in certain respects with that of Americans toward Israel. Perceived by their respective mentors as inflexible, obstreperous, exasperating, and sometimes dangerous, the clients nonetheless retain the patrons' solid support, partly for reasons of politics, foreign and domestic, but also—perhaps to a greater extent than either client recognizes—for reasons of genuine sympathy and conviction. Although the patrons may reproach or try to restrain the clients, they will not abandon them. Each patron remains convinced that its client has suffered a historic injustice and that recompense is due, and although the clients fear otherwise, neither is in real danger of being sold out. There are limits on the extent to which the Arabs can be divided against each other, just as there are limits on the extent to which the United States can be separated from Israel. Calculations to the contrary on both sides, however sophisticated, are likely to prove mistaken.

Although, as noted in the previous section, the Saudis have been, on the whole, restrained and responsible in their policies with respect to oil and petrodollars and although they tend to qualify political linkages either in making them or soon after, they have on occasion been forthright in linking oil and petrodollars with Israel and the Palestinian problem. In December 1976, when Saudi Arabia broke temporarily with its OPEC partners in refusing to go along with the full amount of their oil price increase, Saudi oil minister Yamani warned: "Don't be too happy in the West. We expect the West to appreciate what we did, especially the United States."[39] Crown Prince Fahd struck the same theme in May 1977. "We are capable of increasing oil production," he said, ". . . but we have demands in return for that. First and foremost, we want the United States to throw all its weight into the process of reaching a just settlement of the Mideast crisis based on Israeli withdrawal from all Arab territories occupied in the 1967 war, and the return of the Palestinians' rights to their homeland and a state of their own."[40] Although they readily assert the linkage between Israel and oil, the Saudis also stress their readiness to accept the existence of Israel within the borders of 1967. "The Arabs have learned to be moderate, reasonable," King Khalid told Senator Howard Baker of Tennessee in 1975. "Gone are the days of Nasser's period when the Arabs threatened to exterminate the Israelis."[41] In similar vein Crown Prince Fahd told the chairman of the Washington Post Company, Katharine Graham, in an interview in Riyadh in May 1980, that "if Israel would declare its sincere intention of withdrawing from the lands occupied in 1967, Saudi Arabia would do its utmost to bring the Arabs to cooperate and work for a full settlement."[42]

This Saudi position was formalized in an eight-point peace plan offered by Crown Prince Fahd in August 1981. It called for Israeli withdrawal from the territories occupied in 1967, including East Jerusalem; the removal of Israeli settlements from these territories; freedom of worship for all religions in Jerusalem; recognition of the right of Palestinians to return to their former homes; the establishment of a transition regime for the West Bank and Gaza under the United Nations; the establishment of a Palestinian state with East Jerusalem as its capital; the affirmation of "the right of all countries of the region to live in peace"; and a guarantee of the settlement by the United Nations or some of its members. The reference to the right of all countries of the region to "live in peace" was interpreted by the Reagan administration as implying recognition of Israel, but Israel contested that interpretation.

In the Saudi view the cautious linking of oil to American policy on Israel is no more than a matter of giving the United States—and, through the United States, Israel—the incentive to do what each ought to do in any case. The Saudis note in this connection that the United States had not been backward in the use of economic leverage for political purposes in dealings, for example, with Cuba, North Vietnam, and the Soviet Union. To many Americans, on the other hand, references to possible price increases and limits on oil production in connection with American policy toward Israel have the ring of blackmail and extortion, not to be tolerated by a self-respecting nation.

This fundamental difference in perception of the oil weapon was brought forth in an exchange in 1976 before the Senate Foreign Relations Subcommittee on Near Eastern and South Asian Affairs. Dr. Edward N. Luttwak of the Johns Hopkins School of Advanced International Studies judged it "absolutely preposterous to suggest that in the long term the entire energy basis of the Western economy can be predicated upon developing a relationship with Saudi Arabia." This assessment was prompted by the "nature" of Saudi Arabia, its society and politics, and "the fact that it exists in the Middle East." Earlier in his testimony, Dr. Luttwak had urged that "we must acquire the ability to deter an oil embargo by being visibly ready to break it. . . . the Western world cannot do without Arab oil while the United States for its part cannot allow itself to be forced into a position of visible subjection to the will of others."[43] John Duke Anthony, on the other hand, maintained that "most if not all of the difficulties arising out of our dependence on Arab oil and Arab dependence on our technology and expertise are eminently amenable to solution or amelioration . . . through the political process," and further, that "there need not be anything inimical in such a process to Israel's right to, or capacity to maintain, its national survival."[44] Contesting the contention that Saudi warnings about oil in relation to Israel were an intolerable blackmail, Professor Anthony said that what in fact was happening was that "we are being sent warnings, hints. . . . They don't involve demands, but are warnings and hints between people who have a relationship, as close as the United States and the leaders of Saudi Arabia do, which is fully legitimate. . . ."[45]

Depending on which of these perspectives prevails, the United States will choose coercion or the threat of it on the one hand, or accommodation on the other, as the political incentive to encourage continued Saudi responsiveness to the needs of the industrial countries—needs which, as has been shown, cannot be satisfactorily met, at least over a period of a decade or so, from other sources. In the spring of 1978, by approving the sale of F–15 fighter aircraft to Saudi Arabia, the United States Congress, substantively and symbolically, made at least a tentative judgment that accommodation was the appropriate and feasible political incentive for the United States to use in its dealings with Saudi Arabia. As long as the Arab-Israeli conflict remains unresolved, however—perpetuating the possibility of another war or crisis in which the United States would be required to give Israel decisive support—there will remain one of the possible conditions that might provoke another oil embargo, with consequences far more drastic than in 1973. Should that occur, it is by no means likely that the United States could sustain a policy of accommodation toward Saudi Arabia and the other Arab oil producers. In this frame of reference the Arab-Israeli issue remains a vital key to Saudi-American relations; as long as the issue remains unresolved, the decision for accommodation with Saudi Arabia can remain no more than tentative.

Discussion of possible United States military intervention arose even before the embargo of 1973–74. In the spring of 1973, four and one-half months prior to the October War, Senator J. W. Fulbright, chairman of the Senate Foreign Relations Committee, was disturbed by reports of "contingency plans" for American military intervention in the Persian Gulf.[46] He undertook to "smoke out" these reports in a Senate speech on

May 21, 1973. Warning that American policies were provocative to the oil-producing countries and "could well lead to a selective boycott of the United States," Senator Fulbright expressed apprehension that policy makers might "come to the conclusion that military action is required to secure the oil resources of the Middle East," possibly with Iran or Israel acting as surrogate. He urged the oil-producing countries to exercise restraint on price and to give assurances against the danger of boycott. Noting the tendency of certain officials in oil-producing countries to boast of their growing wealth and power, Fulbright suggested that the countries would be well advised to "treat their oil wealth as a kind of global trust, if for no other reason than for their own protection. The meat of the gazelle may be succulent indeed, but the wise gazelle does not boast of it to lions."[47] Senator Henry Jackson of Washington denounced Senator Fulbright's reference to Iran and Israel as possible military surrogates as "most unfortunate" and "utterly irresponsible."[48]

The feasibility, military and political, of armed seizure of Arab oil fields, either by the United States or another foreign power, was a subject of widespread speculation during the embargo of 1973–74. The American ambassador to Saudi Arabia at that time, James E. Akins, a recognized energy expert, warned the United States government urgently and repeatedly that the Arabs could and would inflict heavy damage on their oil facilities before allowing them to be taken over. Noting that an enormous concentration of fire-fighting equipment was required to bring even a single oil fire under control, he urged anyone who might risk the consequences of intervention to consider the effects of a hundred or more oil fires, all burning at once. It might be years, he averred, before they could be put out or would burn out by exhausting the pressure from within the ground, all the while spewing vast amounts of carbon dioxide and other pollutants into the air.[49] A somewhat different view was expressed by an expert on oil production—an American who thought that, at least as of 1973, nationals of the oil-producing countries acting on their own "could demolish facilities but not to the point that they couldn't be restored pretty fast."[50]

The embargo was ended in March 1974 after U.S. Secretary of State Henry Kissinger had embarked on the "shuttle diplomacy" that had brought the first Sinai disengagement agreement between Egypt and Israel in January 1974. A further disengagement agreement between Syria and Israel on the Golan Heights was concluded in May 1974. Thereafter, talk of possible military action against an oil embargo abated but did not end entirely. In January 1975 Secretary Kissinger stated in an interview, "I am not saying that there's no circumstance where we would not use force," but, he also said, ". . . the use of force would be considered only in the gravest emergency." The White House subsequently confirmed that Kissinger's statement "did reflect the President's views."[51] Several months later, in May 1975, Secretary of Defense James R. Schlesinger said that, although another Arab oil embargo was "very improbable," an American military response to it "could be achieved. . . ." Schlesinger declined to specify measures that might be taken, but, he warned, "we might be less tolerant of such an embargo than we have been."[52]

No further veiled warnings of this nature were issued after the Carter administration came to office in January 1977—although Secretary of Defense Harold Brown, in January 1978, was reported to have issued "guidance" documents to the service chiefs advising them to focus their planning for the early 1980s on developing an American military capacity to fight both a full war against Soviet forces in Europe and a possible "half war" in the Persian Gulf. According to a press account of the directive, Brown stated that "events in the Persian Gulf could soften the glue that binds the alliance as surely as could an imbalance of military forces across the inter-German border. But we are as yet unsure of the utility of United States military power in Persian Gulf contingencies. . . ."[53]

With American dependence on the oil of the Arabian peninsula growing and with the Arab-Israeli conflict still unresolved in the late seventies, the possibility of military intervention, in one form or another, directly or through a surrogate, continued to attract consideration both inside and outside of government. A senate study issued in 1977, when the Shah of Iran still seemed solidly in power, suggested the possibility of Iranian military intervention, sponsored by the United States, in the Arabian peninsula should changes of government or policy in the Arab Gulf states jeopardize the oil supplies of the United States and its allies. Arguing (inaccurately, as subsequent events were to show) that a change of government in Iran would be unlikely to affect the flow of oil because of that nation's high revenue needs, the report contended that in Saudi Arabia, by contrast, a change of government, or of the existing government's policies, could result in a drastic reduction in oil supplies and a drastic increase in price—eventualities that became all the more likely as the Arab-Israeli conflict continued unresolved. Indeed, the report suggested, "if the Arab-Israel conflict continues without progress toward some form of settlement, the Saudis will be less able to produce in quantities necessary to satisfy world oil import demand at reasonable prices even if this is their sincerest intent." To deal with this contingency, the authors of the senate report suggested that Iran might be called on to play a "controversial and extremely sensitive" role. And, they continued, "if Iran is called upon to intervene in the internal affairs of any Gulf state, it must be recognized in advance by the United States that this is the role for which Iran is being primed and blame cannot be assigned for Iran's carrying out an implied assignment."[54] The report was sponsored by Senator Henry M. Jackson, chairman of the Committee on Energy and Natural Resources, who, as noted above, in 1973 had criticized Senator Fulbright's reference to the possible use of Iran or Israel as a military surrogate to secure the oil resources of the Middle East as "most unfortunate" and "utterly irresponsible."

No issue, for obvious reasons, has provoked greater strain in Saudi-American relations than the periodic discussion, open or veiled, of possible United States military intervention in the Arab Gulf states. Despite the volatility of the issue, it cannot be dismissed as "unthinkable," if for no other reason than that *no* contingency can be so dismissed by prudent policy planners, whose job it is to consider *all* possibilities, however improbable or distasteful. With interests of such great magnitude at stake for the United States and other industrialized countries, circumstances could indeed arise in which military action in the Arabian peninsula might be necessary—circumstances such as Soviet military intervention or a radical seizure of power in Saudi Arabia or one of the smaller Gulf states. The threat of these occurrences, even under the impact of destabilizing forces set loose on the region by the Iranian revolution, seems small; and it also seems evident that an Arab-Israeli settlement would reduce the likelihood of such a threat even further. Nonetheless, policymakers have the responsibility to plan for all conceivable threats to the national interest. Returning from a trip to the Middle East in February 1979, Secretary of Defense Harold Brown said that the flow of oil was clearly one of the vital national interests of the United States and that "in protection of those vital interests we will take any action that is appropriate, including military force."[55]

On May 15, 1978 the U.S. Senate voted to permit the sale of sixty advanced F–15 fighter aircraft to Saudi Arabia and, by so doing, confirmed the strong inclination of the Carter administration to rely on accommodation rather than the threat of coercion as the basis of United States policy toward Saudi Arabia and, by extension, the smaller oil-producing states of the Arabian peninsula. How this decision was made will be reviewed in the following section. As suggested earlier, however, it would seem premature to regard this decision as definitive as long as the

Arab-Israeli problem remains unresolved. It should, and very probably would, be overturned if another large-scale Arab-Israeli war were accompanied, as it very possibly would be, by another oil embargo. All previous bets would then be off; proposals for armed intervention, directly or by surrogate (toyed with in 1973–74 but later diminished to occasional rumblings), would quickly rise to a crescendo. For the reasons suggested in preceding pages, the oil of the Arabian peninsula has attained the status of "supreme national interest" for the United States as well as for the other industrial nations. The "oil weapon" has become so powerful that it represents at least as great a threat to those who wield it as to those against whom it might be used. The famished lion has never been known to spare an available gazelle.

"SPECIAL RELATIONSHIPS"

On February 14, 1978 the Carter administration announced a "package" arms sale for the Middle East, including: sixty F–15s—the most advanced fighter plane in the United States arsenal—to Saudi Arabia; fifteen F–15s to Israel, which already had twenty-five, along with seventy-five somewhat less "sophisticated" F–16 fighter-bombers; and fifty much less sophisticated F–5Es to Egypt (to be paid for by Saudi Arabia)—the F–5E being a plane that is not used by the United States Air Force but is widely used by the air forces of "third world" countries. Under the Arms Export Control Act, enacted in 1976, Congress has the authority to veto within thirty days of its being formally notified any significant proposed arms sale to a foreign country. The proposed sales were submitted to Congress as a package on April 28, 1978, with a warning by President Carter that "if Congress should accept a portion and reject another, then my intent is to withdraw the sales proposal altogether."[56]

Even before the formal announcement of February 14, opposition to the proposed sale to Saudi Arabia had arisen in Congress and elsewhere. In a letter to Secretary of State Vance dated January 24, 1978, seven members of the Senate Foreign Relations Committee expressed "grave reservations" about the proposed sale to Saudi Arabia, on the ground, among others, that "sixty F–15s would destabilize the Arab-Israeli balance of power" and "seriously enlarge the threat of an aerial strike against Israeli military and civilian targets."[57] Three additional members of the Foreign Relations Committee, without spelling out reasons, also wrote to the president on January 24, urging a delay in the president's "letter of offer" of the F–15s to Saudi Arabia.[58] Columnist James Reston commented that, although there was something to be said on both sides of the emerging F–15 issue, "right now it only doubles trouble."[59] Rowland Evans and Robert Novak perceived the "spectacle of the United States superpower once again squirming in public over an arms sale in the Middle East clearly tailored to its own interests."[60]

Despite mounting pressure from lobbying groups sympathetic to Israel and entreaties from members of Congress, the Carter administration, under countervailing pressure from Saudi Arabia, proceeded with its plans for the "package" arms sale. As the debate mounted, it became increasingly evident that the issue transcended the technicalities of the military balance; it had come to encompass the political and psychological aspects of the "special relationships" between Israel and the United States and between Saudi Arabia and the United States. In the past the exclusivity of Israel's hold on that unique status had been unchallenged and seemingly unchallengeable. "Our Number One commitment in the Middle East is to protect the right of Israel to exist, to exist permanently, and to exist in peace," President Carter had said early in his term. "It's a special relationship."[61] However, as it became evident in the years following the October War and embargo that the United States as well as other industrial nations would remain heavily dependent on Saudi Arabia for oil for years or decades to come, the idea increasingly took hold that another "special relationship" was in the making—a relationship rooted in tangible need and mutual advantage, a relationship that, although not likely to supplant the bond with Israel, seemed likely to achieve parity with it, imputing symmetry to American commitments in the Middle East where previously there had been virtual exclusivity.

On the eve of the Senate vote on the sale of the F–15s, Hyman Bookbinder, Washington representative of the American Jewish Committee, which had lobbied vigorously against the sale, commented, "There is a psychological meaning to this package that goes beyond the military. This suggests to people that the United States has made a decisive turn against its special relationship with Israel." Making the same point more obliquely, Senator Javits of New York said, "The President's new concept of conditioning supplies of advanced military equipment to Israel with the supply of comparable weapons to Arab states casts an ominous shadow over the future of Israel's security lifeline."[62] Two and one-half years earlier, speaking to the same theme from a different perspective, former Senator Fulbright had expressed doubt that the suspicion directed toward Saudi Arabia that was mounting even then was "rooted in genuine fear that a close association with Saudi Arabia and the other Arab oil-

producing countries will be bad for the United States. It is rather rooted
. . . in a deep-seated, perhaps not even wholly conscious fear that the
association will be good for the United States—so very good indeed as to
erode or undercut our all-out, emotional commitment to Israel."[63]

Both Israel and Saudi Arabia mounted major efforts to influence Congress's decision on the F–15s. Each regarded the issue as crucial, not only
for its military implications but for its symbolism for "special relationships" with the United States. Israeli spokesmen invoked the Sinai
accords of 1975, which contained several promises of continuing American responsiveness to Israel's military needs, including the statement that
"the United States is resolved to continue to maintain Israel's defensive
strength through the supply of advanced types of equipment. . . ."[64] Prime
Minister Begin not only denounced the prospective sale of the F–15s to
Saudi Arabia as "very, very dangerous" from a military standpoint,[65] but,
after it had been agreed to by the Senate, protested the "package" as a
violation of the Sinai accords on the ground that "the commitment given
to Israel in September 1975 was an absolute one and unconditional," and
further that "there was no justification whatsoever to connect it with any
supply to countries which are in a state of war with Israel."[66]

The Saudis, for their part, while disavowing "oil blackmail," made it
clear that they regarded the F–15 sale as the definitive test of American
friendship. They also indicated that, if the American deal fell through,
they were ready and willing to purchase another advanced aircraft, the
Mirage F–1, from France, an available and presumably eager supplier
despite the unlikelihood of the F–1 being available until well into the
1980s. Sheikh Ahmad Zaki Yamani, the Saudi minister of petroleum, was
reported to have asserted on May 1, 1978 that although Saudi oil production and petrodollar policies were based on economic considerations,
refusal by the United States to sell the F–15s would undercut "enthusiasm
to help the West and cooperate with the United States." "We place great
importance and significance on this transaction," Yamani said. "If we
don't get it, then we will have a feeling you are not concerned with our
security and you don't appreciate our friendship." Invoking Saudi Arabia's claim to a "special relationship" with the United States, Yamani
warned that, although Saudi Arabia preferred to continue supporting the
dollar, "this doesn't mean we are not going to change our position."
Yamani also reminded the United States that Saudi Arabia could easily
finance its development program with a much reduced level of oil production and further gain by keeping oil in the ground where it would appreciate in value much faster than any possible dollar investments. Calling as

well for increased American efforts to "bring peace to this area," Yamani expressed doubt that the United States attached as great a value as did Saudi Arabia to the unique association between the two countries. "From our side," he said, "it is developing without any restrictions and at a very great speed. I don't think it is developing in the same manner and speed from your side."[67]

In further statements two days later, both the minister of petroleum and the minister of information backed away from these implied threats, as the cautious Saudi leaders tend to do whenever one of their number seems to have ventured too far in political audacity, emphasizing now that Saudi oil production and dollar policies were based solely on economic foundations and would be maintained or altered only on the basis of economic considerations. The minister of information also asserted that Saudi Arabia was not an aggressive state, that it worked constantly for peace, and that the opposition of Israel and its supporters to the sale of American warplanes to Saudi Arabia was not based on genuine fear of a Saudi threat to Israel but rather on fear that approval of the aircraft sale would lead to a strengthening of the bonds of friendship between the Kingdom of Saudi Arabia and the United States.[68] On May 13, two days before the senate vote on the F–15s, King Khalid addressed a letter to President Carter appealing for the aircraft on an urgent basis because of "recently stepped up Communist expansion in the area." The king also said, without elaboration, that Saudi Arabia's "long and increasingly close relationship with the United States is, even with all of its proven mutual benefits, still at only an early stage of reciprocal worth."[69]

In the public debate in the United States, fear on the part of supporters of Israel that the Saudis might use the F–15s against Israel tended to outweigh consideration of the full range of Saudi security concerns. Saudi leaders stressed their concern with possible threats to their kingdom from the Persian Gulf area and the Horn of Africa as well as from Israel. Both Iraq and Iran, at that time, outweighed Saudi Arabia as military powers to their north and east, and the Saudis are chronically nervous about the activities of the Soviet-supported Marxist regime in South Yemen. They are hardly less fearful of the Marxist regime in Ethiopia, which with Soviet and Cuban support successfully expelled Somali invaders from Ethiopian territory in the spring of 1978. Underlying and permeating Saudi security concerns is the profound conservatism of the Saudi system and leadership, as a result of which the Saudis strongly oppose all forms of extremism and disruption in the Middle East.

Should another general Arab-Israeli war take place, it seems likely that

Saudi Arabia would feel compelled to impose a new oil boycott against any country supporting Israel. There was little reason to believe, however, in 1978 or after, that American-supplied F–15s would be used against Israel by Saudi Arabia if for no other reason than the extreme vulnerability of Saudi Arabia to Israeli retaliation. Both Israel and its supporters in the United States warned, however, that possession of the F–15s would convert Saudi Arabia into a "confrontation" state, exposing it to possible preemptive attack by Israel.[70] With this possibility taken into account, the wisdom of the Saudis in seeking the F–15s might well be questioned. What seemed beyond question, however, was that another Arab-Israeli war would be neither initiated nor provoked by Saudi Arabia. The basic security interest of the conservative Saudi kingdom is the peace and stability of the Middle East, central to which, as Saudi leaders have often emphasized, is the settlement of the Arab-Israeli conflict.[71]

In hearings before the Senate Foreign Relations Committee on the package arms sale to Israel, Egypt, and Saudi Arabia, much of the testimony focused on the Saudi challenge to Israel's "special relationship" with the United States. Morris J. Amitay of the American-Israel Public Affairs Committee contended that the linkage of arms sales to Israel and the two Arab states "calls into question the value of America's original commitment to Israel" under the Sinai accords of 1975, because "this commitment was unrelated to any other United States arms sale." "The linkage," said Amitay, "could only create consternation" in Israel, because if the Israelis felt that, "as a requirement for them to receive arms for their defense from the United States there must be balancing transactions made to its Arab neighbors, who have not yet signed peace agreements with her, this will have a chilling effect on Israel's calculations as to whether they should give up buffer areas, and whether they should trade territory for assurances."[72] Amitay also warned against the sale of the F–15s as a "reward" for Saudi moderation with respect to oil prices and the Arab-Israeli conflict: "A cycle of blackmail could be established as the United States attempts to keep Saudi Arabia moderate."[73]

John P. Richardson, director of public affairs of the National Association of Arab Americans, commended the linking of arms sales to Israel and to Arab states on grounds of the national interest of the United States. Richardson contended that the real threat to Israel and its supporters represented by the F–15s was not a military threat but rather "the development of a special relationship between the United States and one or more Arab countries based on mutual economic and political interests." "Such a relationship," said Richardson, "would differ from the strong but basically sentimental relationship between Israel and the United States. . . ."[74] Senator Case of New Jersey expressed his belief that, if Saudi Arabia understood its own interest, it would recognize that it was "utterly dependent upon the combination of Israel's strength and United States support for Israel, because this regime in Saudi Arabia would be wiped out in a minute in intra-Arab fratricidal strife if Israel and American intervention in that area were removed." Accordingly, the Senator found the contention that the need for Saudi oil compelled the United States to comply with Saudi wishes "intolerable" and "utterly false" in its conception of the national interest of the United States. Richardson, in reply, observed that the United States was a highly developed industrial economy, that the "development of our industrialized economy is not the result of a moral judgment," but that, having come to those circumstances, "and without putting any moral component to it, I think we would all agree that this industrialized economy basically runs on one commodity, and that is oil." Therefore, while disavowing submission to blackmail by any party, Arab or Israeli, Richardson urged Americans to "face up to the fact that interests include continuing access to the one commodity that makes this whole thing go."[75]

Both the Carter administration, for fear of the possible policy consequences, and Congress, for fear of the possible political consequences, tried to avoid a congressional debate on the Saudi arms sale. The Senate Foreign Relations Committee, however, having divided evenly by a vote of eight to eight (on May 11, 1978) chose to send the issue to the Senate floor without recommendation, although the tie vote in effect upheld the administration because a majority vote was required to disapprove the arms package. As a result, on May 15, 1978 a reluctant Senate conducted an all but unprecedented debate on the national interests of the United States in the Middle East.

Early in the debate Senator Case, then in his twenty-fourth year in the Senate, said that he considered the issue "perhaps the most important" of his Senate career. He said that he thought it involved, "in a very direct way, the whole matter of the strength of the West in its confrontation with the Soviet Union." Case said that he detected an erosion of the American commitment to Israel and a tendency to "equate our relationship with Israel with our relationship with all other countries in that area"—a tendency that his "conscience" and "judgment" told him was "the worst possible error we can slip into." Israel, the Senator contended, was much more than an object of sentimental interest to the United States. "I suggest it is time," he went on, "that we recognized again and kept bright and shining in our eyes this truth: The existence of Israel, its strength to defend itself, is essential to the preservation of the West, to the preservation of NATO, and inevitably, in the end, to the preservation of the United States. More than that, it is essential to the preservation of the moderate Arab regimes."[76]

Other opponents of the Saudi arms sale also stressed the importance of Israel to the United States, although stopping short of asserting Israel's essentiality to the preservation of the United States. Senator Moynihan of New York said the proposal to sell F–15s to Saudi Arabia made the security of Israel an "item of barter in United States-Arab relations" and further, signified not a true measure of support for Saudi Arabia but rather "another disguised American retreat of a kind that is taking place around the world."[77] Senator Weiker of Connecticut said that the Arab nations were united only by hatred of Israel and that "if we permit the Saudi Government to guide our hand in drawing the mark of shame upon this body, all the bloodshed it will risk and all the tears we may shed over its almost inevitable consequences will not serve to wash that mark away."[78] Senator Metzenbaum of Ohio asserted that the proposed sale "says to the Israelis that they can no longer rely on the one great nation which has stood side by side with them for thirty years," and "says to the Arabs that we are so hopelessly addicted to overconsumption of oil that they can hold our foreign policy hostage almost at will if only they will promise that the oil will continue to flow."[79] Senator Packwood of Oregon denounced the State Department, contending that it had opposed the creation of Israel, had been hostile to it ever since, and now "somehow hornswoggled this president into swallowing their line." Packwood also equated the sale of F–15s to Saudi Arabia with the surrender of the Czech Sudetenland to Nazi Germany at Munich in 1938.[80]

Senator Riegle of Michigan expressed the view that "much of the rush to embrace Saudi Arabia is by people who have dollar signs in their eyes." Although much emphasis was placed on the fear of an oil cutoff, Riegle thought the real concern was "just as much about fear of a cutoff of Arab oil dollars flowing into the income statements of many of the private interests in the United States."[81] Senator Jackson of Washington thought the sale of F–15s to Saudi Arabia would "have a profound and destabiliz-ing effect on the delicate military balance between Israel and her neigh-bors" without meeting the real security threat to Saudi Arabia, which, in Jackson's judgment, was not external but the internal danger of a coup.[82] Senator Javits of New York said it was a "very spurious argument" to contend that the F–15s were essential to the defense of Saudi Arabia. The sale indeed would accomplish "nothing except to scare the living daylights out of Israel," and by so doing make Prime Minister Begin even less flexible as to peace terms.[83]

A tone of reluctance and distress permeated the speeches of Senators supporting the Saudi arms sale. Senator McGovern of South Dakota said that he was joining the debate "reluctantly," and not because he saw clear merit on one side of the issue or the other but "because I have come to the conclusion that, difficult and hazardous as it may be to approve these sales, the consequences of disapproval represent even greater difficulties and hazards." The "key factor," McGovern said, was to reassure moderate Arab leaders of American confidence in them. "I plead with my Israeli friends," said McGovern, "not to press the American public and the United States Congress too one-sidedly. Do not ask us to spurn Egypt and Saudi Arabia to demonstrate that we treasure our important relationship with the people and government of Israel."[84] Senator Mathias of Maryland expressed "outrage" that "the foreign policy of the United States has been allowed to drift so aimlessly that the Senate is presented with an issue guaranteed to embarrass our national interests." With emotion Mathias rejected contentions that the sale of warplanes to Saudi Arabia and Egypt would alter the American commitment to Israel, a commitment that he regarded as "unique and unalterable. . . . forged in the fierce crucible of the Holocaust. . . . the lodestar of our Middle East policy. . . . our only 'special relationship' in the Middle East." Nevertheless, because of the variety of American interests in the Middle East, including the need of oil, Mathias said, he supported the administration's package.[85]

Senator Gravel of Alaska declared that he would support the arms sales, "with some ease with respect to the logic of the issue," but with pain as to its "personal aspects," "as much personal pain as I have ever suffered in my tenure in the Senate." The reason for his discomfort, Gravel explained, was that, despite his hitherto "100 percent voting record for Israel," his vote against Israeli preferences on this issue, "if it is not done properly, kisses away in the future all kinds of financial support," but even more painful still, would cost the Senator "some very important personal friendships." "These are Jewish friends of mine whom I have held dear all my life," Gravel continued, "some of the closest friends I have on this earth, who are lost to me today because of this decision I make in conscience."[86]

Several other proponents of the arms sale placed less emphasis on Israel and more on the positive aspects of Saudi-American relations. Senator Ribicoff of Connecticut, whose influence on the outcome probably exceeded that of any other single Senator, elaborated in his address on the American and Western need of Saudi oil, on the responsiveness to Western needs shown by the Saudis in their oil production policies, and on the responsibility and restraint of their financial policies. Ribicoff emphasized that Saudi Arabia has "emerged as a significant world power," whose leaders sought "help, friendship, and ties with the United States." "This is a new relationship and skepticism is understandable," Ribicoff continued, but "we must remind ourselves that we are here to serve our national interest. Our Middle East policy has remained virtually unchanged for thirty years, while the region itself has changed dramatically. . . . Ecopolitics has a place side by side with geopolitics in the affairs of nations. And petropolitics has a particularly decisive role."[87] Similar themes were struck by Senator Stennis of Mississippi,[88] Senator Bentsen of Texas,[89] and Senator Bellmon of Oklahoma.[90]

The approval by the Senate of the arms package by a vote of 54 to 44 represented a watershed in the Middle East policy of the United States, an acknowledgment by a reluctant Senate, in the face of powerful countervailing political pressures, that the region had indeed changed dramatically and so too had the interests of the United States. The decision signified the acceptance of Saudi Arabia into a special, although not necessarily preeminent, relationship with the United States. It was undoubtedly facilitated at the time by the success of President Sadat of Egypt in gaining new favor for the Arab cause through the peace move initiated with his trip to Jerusalem in November 1977 as well as by the adverse reaction of the American public and Congress to certain of the policies of Prime Minister Menachem Begin of Israel. The major factor, beyond question, however, was oil and the recognition by responsible public officials that a vital national interest was at stake. It had carried Saudi Arabia from the position "far afield" that it occupied in Franklin Roosevelt's time to the center stage of American national interest.

CAMP DAVID AND IRAN

As events subsequent to the Camp David agreements were to demonstrate, there was considerable misunderstanding between Saudi leaders and United States Senators as to the exact nature of the bargain symbolically struck with the Senate vote of May 15, 1978. Both agreed, to be sure, that "moderation" was to be practiced by each party in matters affecting the other's interests, but disagreement soon arose as to exactly what "moderation" required. Many Senators seemed to have assumed that the

F–15s had purchased a Saudi commitment to support of the American-sponsored "peace process" as between Egypt and Israel, and when this turned out not to be the case, some Senators, including a few who had voted for the F–15 sale, charged betrayal.[91] The Saudis, on the other hand, evidently felt that they had committed themselves to something considerably less precise, in the nature of a generally sympathetic attitude toward the industrial world's energy needs, but surely not to anything approaching a contractual promise to support the Carter-Begin-Sadat "peace process." From the Saudi standpoint, the bargain implicit in the F–15 sale seems to have been one of American support for Saudi security needs in return for Saudi responsiveness to American energy requirements, with the Arab-Israel issue not directly involved—although, as events progressed the Saudis, no less than the Americans, found it difficult to keep the issues wholly apart. The misunderstanding about who had promised what to whom probably reflected basic cultural differences as to how promises are made and what exactly a contract or promise implies. This cultural disconsonance might well have remained latent but for two events that put the issue quickly to the test: the conclusion of the Camp David accords in September 1978 and the Iranian revolution climaxed by the fall of the shah in January 1979.

Whether the Saudis under any circumstances would have supported, or even acquiesced in, the Camp David accords is at best doubtful. Whatever chance, if any, there ever was of a favorable Saudi response to Camp David was dispelled, however, by the crumbling of the shah's regime in Iran. The ambivalent attitude of the Saudis toward the Palestinians will be further explored in chapter 5;[92] it may be noted here, however, that whatever their feelings of wariness and even fear of Palestinians and the PLO, the Saudis, with their deeply ingrained sense of themselves as the custodians of Arabism and Islam, have always retained a sense of kinship with and obligation toward their Palestinian "brothers" and coreligionists. That sense of kinship is rooted in the Arabic conception of the *umma*, referring to the Arabs as a single nation or people in the spiritual and cultural sense. Whatever the reservations and anxieties of various Arab regimes toward the displaced and often troublesome Palestinians, loyalty to the Palestinian cause has become, over the years of the Palestinian diaspora, the test and symbol of loyalty to Arabism itself, the modern expression of fealty to the *umma*. When President Anwar Sadat of Egypt divided the Arab world by signing the Camp David agreements, the natural Saudi impulse was to reaffirm solidarity with the "Arab cause," which, practically and symbolically, had come to mean the Palestinian cause. When the Iranian regime of the shah crumbled and then collapsed under the assault of a movement based on resurgent Islamic fundamentalism, the impulse to stand by their Palestinian brothers was elevated for the Saudis to a necessity.

The Iranian revolution, instead of causing the Saudis to feel a greater dependence on the United States as some American officeholders more or less plausibly suggested it should, in fact had the opposite effect. It impelled the Saudis strongly, as Professor Bayly Winder has put it, toward "things that are Arab and things that are Muslim," despite their "natural tilt" toward the United States.[93] Instead of suggesting to the Saudi leaders that they must more than ever rely on the United States to escape a similar fate, the fall of the shah showed the inability or, as the Saudis suspected, the unwillingness of the United States to rescue even an ally in which it had made an enormous investment. The lesson of Iran to Saudi Arabia was that safety lay not in reliance on the United States, whose vast military support had failed to save the shah, but in Arab unity and Islamic orthodoxy. For this as well as other reasons (to be discussed in chapter six) the Saudis rejected American offers in the early months of 1979 to bring significant new military power to the Arabian peninsula.[94] They were later, in 1981, to show equal reluctance, despite their fear of the Soviet Union, to join in the Reagan Administration's proposed "strategic consensus," with the implication of *de facto* alliance with Israel.[95] Iran thus strongly reinforced for the Saudis the shock of the Camp David accords, which postponed to an uncertain future both Palestinian self-determination and an arrangement for Jerusalem that would restore Muslim sovereignty over the Muslim holy places. Under these conditions the "natural tilt" toward the United States was heavily outweighed by the even more natural, and now countervailing, tilt toward Arab and Islamic solidarity.

It was in these circumstances that Saudi Arabia, to the shocked disappointment of American officials, adhered to the tough sanctions against Egypt proposed by the Arab "rejectionists" at the Baghdad meetings of November 1978 and March 1979. At the first Baghdad meeting, following Camp David but preceding the Egyptian-Israeli peace treaty, the parties, including Saudi Arabia, agreed that when the peace treaty was signed Egypt would be automatically expelled from the Arab League and that the League's headquarters would be transferred from Cairo. The oil-producing states also agreed to provide substantial new annual subsidies to the remaining "confrontation" states, Jordan and Syria, and to the PLO.[96] Although Saudi Arabia did not at that time indicate that it would cut off aid to Egypt, President Sadat reacted with bitter astonishment at the Saudis lining up with the hard-line Arab states, and also with dismay at the manifest failure of the United States to have persuaded Saudi Arabia to go along with the Camp David accords. "Today, Sadat is realizing that the Americans don't hold 99 percent of the cards," an Egyptian official commented.[97]

The second Baghdad meeting, in late March 1979 following the signing of the Egyptian-Israeli peace treaty, went considerably further, calling for the severance by all the participants of diplomatic relations with Egypt and the imposition of a total economic embargo, including now the cutting off of economic aid. The only important exception to the financial boycott was that no action was taken to end remittances to Egypt by Egyptians working in other Arab countries, a major source of Egypt's foreign earnings. As agreed at the first Baghdad meeting, Egypt was now expelled from the Arab League and its headquarters were transferred to Tunis. Once again, as in the previous November, Saudi Arabia, after some hesitation, acquiesced in the program of the Arab "hard-liners," including Iraq, Syria and the PLO. The Saudi decision to join in the total embargo of Egypt was made, according to reports, on the personal intervention of King Khalid himself. Again President Sadat and the United States government were taken aback by the harshness of the sanctions adopted at Baghdad and by Saudi Arabia's acquiescence in them.[98] Crown Prince Fahd explained the Saudi attitude in an interview in Riyadh in June 1979 with *New York Times* columnist Anthony Lewis. President Sadat, he said, had misled the Saudis all along:

> Five days before his trip to Jerusalem, Sadat was here. We spoke with him, and he never mentioned anything about his projected trip. . . . Even after Camp David we were hoping that the United States Government would push in the direction of getting Israel to withdraw to its 1967 boundaries and recognize the legitimate rights of the Palestinian people. But the signing of the Egyptian-Israeli treaty shattered all hopes.[99]

In the months following the Egyptian-Israeli peace treaty, Saudi Arabia took further measures against the apostate Egypt. In May 1979 the Saudi Defense Minister, Prince Sultan, announced that the Arab Organization for Industrialization—a consortium formed to develop an Arab arms industry based in Egypt, which by then was providing some 15,000 jobs for Egyptian workers—would be shut down, because "the signing by Egypt of the peace treaty contradicted the reason and purpose for which the organization was established." President Sadat also predicted at this time, bitterly and accurately as events would show, that the Saudis would withdraw their promise to pay for the fifty F–5E fighter planes that Egypt was to receive under the arms sale package that accorded the F–15s to Saudi Arabia.[100] Even before the scuttling of the Arab arms consortium, Secretary of State Vance had acknowledged a deterioration in Saudi-American relations because of "clear and sharp differences" over the Egyptian-Israeli peace treaty.[101] Columnist James Reston at this time referred to the "vicious" Saudi reaction to Egypt;[102] the *Washington Post* commented that "without burning their bridges to Washington, the Saudis have made camp on the other side," and further, that "what once promised to be a formidable conservative grouping of Israel, Egypt, Iran, Saudi Arabia and the Persian Gulf states with the United States is now down to the Camp David Three."[103] In an interview published in the Paris newspaper *Le Monde* on May 15, 1979, Saudi Crown Prince Fahd observed that it was "unpleasant" to have to act against Egypt but there were "political problems that cannot be ignored."[104]

The United States and Egypt were repeatedly shocked and dismayed by Saudi actions in the wake of the Camp David accords. Counting heavily on the "special relationship," American officials had expected to be able to win, if not active support, then at least passive Saudi acquiescence in the Camp David "peace process," and President Sadat had shared their confidence. That the United States and Egypt were mistaken in their expectations was beyond dispute; whether they could and should have foreseen the harsh Saudi stand against Egypt and the second-stage negotiations for Palestinian autonomy is less certain. Secretary of State Vance told the House Foreign Affairs Committee on May 8, 1979 that "since the Baghdad conference, the position, the declared position of the Saudis has changed. It's a fact, and nobody can or should gloss over it."[105]

By available evidence Saudi attitudes had indeed changed under the impact of the Iranian revolution and pressures for Arab solidarity, but *not in all respects*, and the changes that occurred were not reversals of previously held viewpoints but unexpected intensifications of these viewpoints. As will be seen in chapter 5[106] the Saudis made their dislike of the Camp David accords unmistakably clear from the time the accords were signed, specifying their objections to the absence of provisions for Israeli withdrawal from the occupied territories other than Sinai, for Palestinian self-determination, and for the restoration of Arab sovereignty in East Jerusalem. It seems not unlikely that, in their style, the Saudis spoke more cryptically to American officials and diplomats in private, but no evidence has been brought forth to suggest that the Saudi leaders at any time, before or after Camp David, had indicated approval of the *kind* of agreement that emerged. If American officials were astonished by the fact, as distinguished from the intensity, of Saudi opposition to the Camp David accords and the Egyptian-Israeli peace treaty, it was largely because of wishful thinking, because of reluctance on the American side to believe that the Saudis actually meant what they said.

In the more specific matter of sanctions against Egypt, the Saudis, it appears, actually did change their minds, acquiescing at the two Baghdad meetings in measures they had previously led the United States and Egypt to believe they would not accept. By at least one press account, a representative of President Sadat, former Speaker of the People's Assembly Sayed Marei, was invited to Saudi Arabia in October 1978, prior to the first Baghdad meeting, and assured by Prince Fahd that the Saudis would defend Egyptian interest and continue their financial aid to Egypt.[107] As explained by a Saudi foreign ministry official in an interview on October 25, 1978, one week prior to the first Baghdad meeting, the official Saudi policy at that time was close to what President Sadat understood it to be. The official said that, although Saudi Arabia could not accept Camp David as a "final settlement," it was not Saudi practice to interfere in other countries' affairs; if Egypt wished to proceed, that was its own business, and no move had been made to cut off Saudi aid or military support for Egypt.[108] The same point was made even more forcefully, on the same day, by Prince Turki al-Faisal, the director general of intelligence, who said that Saudi Arabia most assuredly would oppose sanctions against Egypt or any move to expel Egypt from the Arab League at the forthcoming Baghdad summit meeting.[109] The Saudis thus, it would appear, misled Egypt and the United States as to their intentions toward Egypt in the wake of the Camp David accords. They do not appear to have done so deliberately, however; rather, under the pressure of the other principal participants at Baghdad (including King Hussein of Jordan) and against the background of mounting turmoil in Iran, the Saudis changed their minds about how Egypt should be treated and went along with the Arab consensus.

If the Carter administration was in any way deceived by Saudi Arabia as to its attitude toward Egypt, it was self-deceived as to the Saudi attitude toward the Palestinians, the West Bank and Gaza, and Jerusalem. Repeated Saudi statements on the need of a settlement based on Israeli withdrawal, Palestinian self-determination, and Arab sovereignty over East Jerusalem tended to be dismissed or downgraded in importance by American officials, who chose, quite possibly with encouragement from President Sadat, to believe that the Saudis did not really mean what they were saying. A full year after Camp David, President Carter clung to the view that, although Arab leaders publicly espoused an independent Palestinian state, "I have never met an Arab leader that in private professed the desire for an independent Palestinian state."[110] The president's statement elicited a reply from Saudi Foreign Minister Prince Saud al-Faisal: "Any interpretation of our position that says that we do not support a Palestinian state is erroneous. I cannot speak for other Arab leaders, but the Saudi position is clear. It is based on the right of the Palestinians themselves to determine whether they want an independent state, or an entity with links to another country, or another solution."[111] If it is once accepted that the Saudis actually meant what they were saying about the Palestinians and Jerusalem, it can then be seen as entirely plausible that a lack of confidence in the will or ability of the United States to carry through the Camp David process to anything meaningful beyond the Egyptian-Israeli settlement was a primary factor in its own right in the tough Saudi stand against Egypt at the two Baghdad meetings—all the more for the fact that the Palestinian autonomy negotiations were scheduled to run well into the American election campaign of 1980. This factor, coupled with the radical change in the Middle East scene wrought in the months between Camp David and the Egyptian-Israeli treaty by the Iranian revolution, would seem to explain amply the direction and changes in Saudi policy during that period. In February 1979 the Saudis, with some embarrassment but without hesitation, turned aside American proposals for a much expanded security arrangement between the two countries.[112] Intensive American efforts in the early spring to win Saudi acquiescence for the Egyptian-Israeli peace treaty, including a trip to Saudi Arabia by National Security Adviser Brzezinski, were also firmly rebuffed. Pulled in opposite directions by American and pan-Arab pressures—by the desire for American security backing and the need for Arab and Islamic solidarity—the Saudis, forced to choose, made their choice for the latter.[113]

They would very much have preferred not to choose. From the standpoint of American national interest there would have seemed much to be gained by releasing the Saudis from an unwanted role (one that in any case they most probably would never accept) in the Camp David peace process, and adhering to the more realistic *quid pro quo* implicit in and symbolized by the sale of the F–15s in 1978: American support for Saudi security in return for a favorable disposition toward the industrial world's energy needs. To press the Saudis in other areas, especially in the most sensitive area of the Camp David political process, was to jeopardize the fundamental bargain on energy and also, in effect, to urge the Saudis to expose themselves to the same destabilizing forces that destroyed the imperial regime in Iran. To the extent that the United States has an interest in the stability of Saudi Arabia—and this interest in the present view is a vital one—American no less than Saudi interests are served by the prudent Saudi policy, however inconvenient it may be to the United States in the short run, of close and continuing adherence to "things that are Arab and things that are Muslim."

In the wake of the Camp David agreements, the Iranian upheaval, the Egyptian-Israeli peace treaty, and steady American pressures to secure Saudi adherence to it, Saudi Arabia also began to show diminished responsiveness in 1979 to American wishes in the energy field. As events progressed, neither side, despite the bargain implicit in the F–15 sale, found itself able or willing to completely separate economic and security issues from the Palestinian question. The Saudis acquiesced, with publicly stated reluctance, in large OPEC price increases in December 1978 and again, in the immediate aftermath of the Egyptian-Israeli treaty, in March 1979, while strongly urging conservation and reduced consumption on the United States and other industrial countries. While declining itself to impose surcharges authorized for individual countries at the March OPEC meeting, Saudi Arabia also agreed at that time to reduce its own production when Iranian production increased, thus insuring—if they followed through—that the world market would remain tight and their own price moderation would be largely negated. In characteristically disguised fashion the Saudis thus, it would seem, expressed displeasure with American energy policies and American political policies. An Algerian delegate to the OPEC meeting of March 1979 commented, "The Begin-Sadat treaty is like a ghost hovering over this meeting. You can't see it clearly, but everyone knows it's there, and they are frightened."[114]

In the spring and early summer of 1979 a sudden, severe oil shortage threw millions of Americans into long gasoline lines and their leaders into political crisis. The apparent and probable cause was the substantial loss of Iranian production, although suspicion ran high that the oil companies were deliberately holding back supplies in order to force up prices. Meanwhile Saudi Arabia, which had been producing 9.5 million barrels of oil a day earlier in the year, held its production to about 8.5 million barrels a day. The Saudis themselves disavowed political motives while rebuffing repeated requests from the Carter administration for increased production, but oil industry officials took to describing the Saudi posture as "the price of peace."[115] Beset by energy pressures and unexpectedly strong and persistent Saudi opposition to the Egyptian-Israeli treaty and the Camp David proposals for the Palestinians, the Carter administration began to try to repair the damage that Camp David and Iran had inflicted on the Saudi-American "special relationship" by abandoning further efforts to draw the Saudis into some form of acceptance of the Egyptian-Israeli treaty and also by dropping further appeals to the Saudis to pay for Egypt's F–5E fighter planes, as they had agreed to do under the 1978 package arms-sale agreement. During this period of strained Saudi-American relations, cooperation nevertheless continued in military and security arrangements between the two countries. Differences over Camp David, Prince Fahd said in June 1979, "should not affect relations between the two governments."[116]

OPEC again raised the price of oil sharply on June 28, 1979, with the Saudis once again opting for the lower end of the new range of increased prices. Once again the OPEC conferees, and especially the Saudi oil minister Sheikh Ahmad Zaki Yamani, warned the industrial countries that it was up to them, by curbing consumption, to restrain further price increases.[117] On the same day (June 28) that OPEC announced its big new price increase, President Carter's chief domestic policy adviser, Stuart Eizenstat, gave the president a confidential memorandum pointing out that growing gasoline lines and fast rising energy costs were taking a heavy political toll on the administration—nothing else had "added so much water to our ship." With Carter low in the polls and the Congress "beyond anyone's control," Eizenstat wrote, "this would appear to be the worst of times." Nevertheless, the president's adviser perceived an opportunity "to assert leadership over an apparently unsolvable problem, to shift the cause for inflation and energy problems to OPEC, to gain credibility with the American people, to offer hope of an eventual solution, to regain our political losses." Eizenstat went on to suggest a number of measures to alleviate the energy problem and concluded that "with strong steps we can mobilize the nation around a real crisis and with a clear enemy—OPEC."[118]

President Carter repudiated the Eizenstat memorandum when it became public and on July 15 and 16, after protracted deliberations at Camp David, offered a new energy program in terms that carefully avoided castigation or provocation of the OPEC countries. The significance of the Eizenstat memorandum lay not in its policy consequences—it apparently had none—but in its delineation of the tempting possibilities for alleviating domestic political pressures by attacking OPEC and, with OPEC, Saudi Arabia as its principal member. Thus, in much the same way that Camp David and Iran put severe strains on the "special relationship" from the Saudi side, gasoline shortages and high energy prices, along with charges of oil blackmail on behalf of the Palestinian cause, stirred congressional and public sentiment against OPEC. This organization, despite its sizable non-Arab membership, was associated in the public mind with the "Arabs," who in turn were scarcely distinguished from each other. As the quintessential "Arabs" and the leading OPEC producer, Saudi Arabia stood squarely in the line of this waxing and waning, potentially explosive, political fire.

In July 1979 Saudi Arabia, in response to President Carter's pleas, increased its oil production from approximately 8.5 million to 9.5 million barrels a day for a projected period of three to six months. The Saudi leaders, according to State Department officials, regarded the increase in production as an act of friendship for the United States, reflecting uneasiness over recent strains in relations and signaling a desire to prevent disagreements over the Egyptian-Israeli peace treaty from interfering with economic and military cooperation between Saudi Arabia and the United States.[119] Carter welcomed the increase in Saudi production as a "positive decision,"[120] and the State Department promptly gave approval to a sizable new sale of arms for the Saudi national guard.[121] Private commentators were skeptical and even scathing in assessing Saudi motives in increasing oil production, citing with disapproval Prince Fahd's reported note to President Carter, "This is your gift on Independence Day."[122] The *New York Times,* suspecting a deal on the Palestinian question, had "a premonition of catastrophe;"[123] columnist Jack Anderson fulminated against the "royal gouging" of the American people by "a few avaricious Arabs;"[124] the cartoonist Herblock pictured the United States as a quivering addict gratefully accepting an oil "fix" from a venal Saudi "pusher," preparing to apply an additional fix labeled "Saudi Middle East policy."[125]

The Saudis thus found themselves in the position of being condemned, more or less equally, for either *limiting* or *increasing* oil production. Limiting production provoked charges of forcing up prices by limiting supply and of political blackmail; increasing production called forth charges of encouraging the United States in a dangerous dependence and thus also of political blackmail. In addition the Saudis found themselves rebuked for acquiescing in repeated OPEC price increases, when they expected to be thanked for their restraint compared to other OPEC countries. Their explanations for the rising price of oil, although often patronizing in tone, were drawn, after all, from the American college classrooms where so many Saudi officials had first become familiar with the inexorable workings of the law of supply and demand. Invitations and accusations notwithstanding, President Carter offered what would appear to be an accurate summation of Saudi motives in a meeting with Florida newspaper editors on August 30, 1979: "They would rather keep the oil in the ground. They are producing the extra oil in effect as a favor to the rest of the world, to provide world stability, which helps them."[126]

Disclaimers on both sides notwithstanding, Saudi-American relations in the energy field continued in 1979 to be inextricably linked with the Israeli-Palestinian issue. In the summer of 1979 the United States made a brief, cautious, ultimately unsuccessful effort to draw the PLO into the "peace process" through a new United Nations resolution, supplementing Security Council Resolution 242 of November 1967, under which Palestinian "rights" would be recognized while the PLO in turn would accept Israel's right to exist and live in security. American officials disavowed any connection between overtures to the PLO, pressures applied to Israel to make concessions on Palestinian autonomy, and the July increase in Saudi oil production. But American policy makers noted too, according to one press account, "that the Saudis operate according to the Bedouin code that a favor by one party begets a return favor."[127] The Israelis, for their part, had no doubt about the existence of a linkage between this and other American efforts to draw Palestinian Arabs into the Camp David autonomy talks and American energy concerns. Foreign Minister Moshe Dayan, on August 7, denounced American moves toward the Palestinians as "not just an erosion, but a shift in U.S. policy toward Israel, to Israel's detriment." He added: "It is a result of American concern about economic and energy problems, concern about quantities of oil and their prices."[128] Despite strong State Department denials of any such connection, Dayan's accusation was echoed among supporters of Israel in the United States. Senator Moynihan of New York, addressing a Jewish group, declared, "American foreign policy is not for sale. . . . We are not going to let this Administration buy oil at the expense of the freedom of Israel."[129]

The evidence of events supports Dayan and Moynihan in their allegations of linkage between oil needs and American policy toward the Palestinians and the PLO. The more pertinent question, it would seem, was not the fact of linkage but its justification. With several important national interests at issue—access to oil, Israel's security, and implementation of the principle of self-determination—the United States could hardly have consigned each interest to a separate, airtight compartment, each to be pursued in artificial disregard of the existence of the others. When a diversity of interests are involved in the same set of circumstances, the task of statesmanship is to devise a policy that, so far as possible, reconciles interests with each other. Oil has been a central factor in the Arab-Israeli conflict since the 1973 oil embargo, which was triggered by the October War, and which compelled the United States to move from a position of almost all-out supporter of Israel to that of mediator between the conflicting parties. The United States did not invent the connection between oil, Israeli security, and Palestinian rights; the three are closely interlocked because the local parties have interlocked them and can be neither persuaded nor forced to separate them. The United Staes must deal with them, perforce, as problems inextricably linked. It can separate them in its policy only insofar as it is prepared to sacrifice one national interest to another. It can revert to a policy of uncritical support of Israel and be compelled, as a result, to rely principally on force to insure access to Arab oil, while also abandoning its own historic commitment to the principle of self-determination of peoples; or the United States, theoretically, could abandon Israel to whatever fate might await it in order to cultivate the good will and develop the closest possible ties with the Arab oil-producing countries. In practice the United States has not, and almost surely never will, pursue either of these courses. It will continue, almost certainly, to practice the linkage that its interests require but that, for political reasons, it feels compelled to deny.

Just as the United States found it necessary to try to balance diverse interests, the Saudis, in the wake of Camp David and Iran, felt compelled to try to maintain an equilibrium between their economic, technological, and security ties to the United States on the one side and their political, cultural, and religious ties to the Arab and Islamic world on the other. In September 1979 the Saudis indicated that they would maintain their high level of oil production and at the same time placed renewed emphasis, unofficially but unmistakably, on their expectation that the United States would press for resolutions of the Palestinian problem and the status of Jerusalem. The Saudi dilemma became intensified as the Camp David peace process failed to advance and the Ayatollah Khomeini's Islamic revolution in Iran sent new shock waves of Islamic xenophobia through the Arab and Muslim worlds. The seizure of the Grand Mosque of Mecca by religious extremists in November 1979, as noted, heightened the ever acute sensitivities of the House of Saud to its own vulnerability. Whatever else these events signified, they made it clear that, from the Saudi standpoint, the relationship with the United States, although "special" and highly valued, also exposed the kingdom to certain perils and therefore was not and could not be exclusive.

From the American standpoint the task of diplomacy was to spare the Saudis, so far as possible, the excruciating choice between their American and Arab and Islamic connections, while at the same time protecting

America's other interests in the Middle East. The task was made more formidable by the apparent breakdown of the second phase of the Camp David peace process relating to Palestinian autonomy and by the Iranian revolution, which had not only placed in jeopardy a principal source of oil and thus increased the industrial world's dependence on Saudi Arabia and other producers, but had also shattered the strategic theory of Israel and Iran as the twin bastions of stability and order in the Middle East. The United States therefore found itself, to its discomfiture, in a condition of increased dependence on Saudi Arabia at a time when the Saudis found themselves pulled in an opposite direction.

AWACS: TESTING THE "SPECIAL RELATIONSHIP"

The outbreak of war between Iraq and Iran in September 1980 once again brought home to both Saudi Arabia and the United States the degree, notwithstanding other strains, of their interdependence. The Carter administration, in response to a Saudi request, promptly dispatched four radar surveillance planes (called AWACS for "airborne warning and control system") to bolster the Saudi air defense system. In January of 1980 President Carter, in response to Soviet military intervention in Afghanistan, had declared, in what came to be known as the Carter Doctrine, the readiness of the United States to use force, if necessary, to repel "an attempt by an outside force to gain control of the Persian Gulf region."[130] In acting to help protect Saudi Arabia against possible Iranian air attacks in retaliation for Saudi support of Iraq, and in offering as well to extend the protection to other Arab Gulf states, the United States, in effect, extended the Carter Doctrine to assist the states of the Arabian peninsula against threats arising from within their region as well as from any "outside force."

The Saudis, for their part, thus moved closer to direct military collaboration with the United States but still, because of Camp David and the unresolved Palestinian question, held back from full-scale strategic cooperation, most particularly in their rejection of possible American bases on their territory. In their sometimes indirect and euphemistic manner the Saudis let it be known to both the Carter and Reagan administrations that they accepted and perhaps welcomed the "Rapid Deployment Force" initiated by President Carter for possible emergency action in the Persian Gulf. They also made it clear that they wanted no foreign bases on their territory or in their immediate vicinity. They preferred American sea power and the Rapid Deployment Force to be available but "over the horizon."[131]

The early hopes of the Reagan administration that Middle East regional issues could be subordinated to a "strategic consensus" against the Soviet Union were quickly dispelled. Secretary of State Haig, in a visit to several Middle East countries in April 1981, was pointedly reminded of standing Arab objections to the Camp David agreements. Seeing Haig off at Riyadh Airport on April 8, Saudi Foreign Minister Prince Saud al-Faisal said that the United States and Saudi Arabia shared the same "overall direction and perception" on a number of issues, but he added that the Saudis believed "the main cause of instability" in the Middle East to be Israel and not, as Secretary Haig had been contending, the Soviet Union.[132]

The Reagan administration also had to deal, early in its tenure, with renewed requests for military aircraft and equipment from Saudi Arabia. Despite assurances given to Congress in 1978 by the Carter administration that no additional equipment would be sought for F–15 fighter planes committed at that time, the Saudis in early 1980 requested additional fuel tanks, bomb racks, air-to-air missiles, and aerial refueling tankers for the aircraft so as to extend their range and attack capacity. Contending that the fall of the shah of Iran and the Soviet invasion of Afghanistan had created new threats in the Persian Gulf, the Carter administration responded sympathetically but delayed a decision on the politically sensitive issue until after the 1980 election. After the election, according to "former high officials in a position to know," the outgoing administration made quiet overtures to the Reagan transition team to join in approving the sale of at least some of the additional equipment.[133]

The Reagan administration announced on March 6, 1981, that, to meet a "growing threat" from the Soviet Union in the Middle East and Persian Gulf, it was prepared to sell the requested additional equipment, except for bomb racks, to Saudi Arabia.[134] The administration then went even further and agreed in April 1981 to sell Saudi Arabia, in addition to the F–15s, five AWACS of their own; pending their delivery, scheduled for 1985, the four American-manned AWACS sent by the Carter administration in the autumn of 1980 would remain in Saudi Arabia.[135] Having made this public commitment, the administration then delayed giving the required formal notification of the sales to Congress lest the Israelis, then involved in an election campaign, and their strong supporters in Congress engage the administration in a bruising, and quite possibly losing, battle over the new Saudi arms sales.

The F–15 equipment and the AWACS now became a "package," and, more than that, in Saudi eyes, a symbol once again of American friendship and support. Refusing to break up the package or, at first, even to postpone the issue, Saudi officials told a delegation of visiting American senators that if the United States could not deliver on the sale, the larger American security commitment would be questioned, and that if the AWACS were cut out, "we will forget the F–15 altogether."[136]

The issue of competing "special relationships" was thus joined once again. The Israelis, who in early 1981 had restrained their eager congressional supporters from launching in all-out campaign against the F–15 equipment lest a premature challenge alienate the new Reagan administration,[137] in April announced "unreserved opposition" to the AWACS sale, contending that this highly sophisticated intelligence equipment, in Saudi hands, would create a "grave danger" for Israel. Israeli foreign ministry officials said that "friends in the United States" would be expected to take into account Israel's strong objections; Israel's deputy defense minister, Mordechai Zippori, said on April 22 that Israel would "try to reason" with the United States but, failing that, would apply "as much pressure as possible," because, he added, "for us, it is a question of existence."[138]

Congressional opposition mounted steadily thereafter. Major newspapers carried an almost full-page advertisement sponsored by the Anti-Defamation League of B'nai B'rith urging opposition to the sale of AWACS to "an oil arrogant, oil greedy nation" that opposed the Camp David accords and financed "PLO terrorism."[139] The Saudis activated the services of American public relations and law firms that had supported their initial bid for F–15s in 1978. Both sides, responding to the Reagan administration's by now well-known predilection, emphasized what they regarded as their own unique strategic value to the United States. In June majorities in both the Senate and House of Representatives recorded their opposition to the sale of AWACS to Saudi Arabia.[140]

By the time the $8.5 billion arms sale package was formally conveyed to Congress, the opposition had grown to formidable dimensions. Under the law the sale would go through unless both houses disapproved it by October 31, 1981. Striking the by now familiar theme of the Reagan administration, Secretary of State Haig, in testimony before the Senate Foreign Relations Committee on September 17, made reference as follows to Israel's opposition to the proposed sale: "We must not let our friends' worries about one another diminish our commitment to their security or hinder our plans to extend strategic cooperation with them."[141]

In the heated debate that followed, opponents of the sale stressed the possible threat to Israel and the instability, as they perceived it, of Saudi Arabia, while proponents argued that the choice to be made was between "Reagan and Begin." The latter theme was echoed in President Reagan's statement, in a news conference on October 1, 1981, that "it is not the business of other nations to make American foreign policy." The president also took the occasion to say that the United States would not permit Saudi Arabia "to be an Iran." Asked to elaborate, Reagan referred to the Western world's dependence on Saudi oil and added, "There's no way that we could stand by and see that taken over by anyone that would shut off that oil."[142]

The two Middle East antagonists, in the meantime, found themselves torn between strong feelings regarding the proposed arms sale and the advisability, dictated by prudence, of abstention from the internal American debate. The Saudi minister of commerce, writing in the *Washington Post*, complained that "we cannot fail to see the contrast between the way the United States treats Israel and the way we are treated."[143] The Israeli foreign minister, Yitzhak Shamir, speaking in New York on October 5, bitterly challenged contentions of Saudi moderation, asserting that the Saudis in truth were extremists motivated by a "fanatic hatred of Jews and Israel."[144]

The House of Representatives disapproved the arms sale on October 14 by the resounding majority of 301 to 111. The Reagan administration, however, had not expected to prevail in the House and concentrated its lobbying efforts on the Republican-controlled Senate. Largely on the strength of arguments that failure to support the AWACS sale would cripple the president's authority to conduct foreign policy, the Senate, after first seeming inclined to reject the sale, finally approved it on October 28, 1981, by a vote of 52 to 48. The president, in a letter to the Senate majority leader, promised that the transfer of the aircraft would take place only after the United States was assured that American technology would be secured; that information gained by the AWACS would be shared with the United States but denied to other parties; that the planes would be flown only within the boundaries of Saudi Arabia; and that the sale would contribute, "with the substantial assistance of Saudi Arabia," to progress toward peace in the Middle East.[145]

As in the debate of May 15, 1978, on the sale of F–15 aircraft to Saudi Arabia, the Senate debate of October 28, 1981 reflected apprehension, reluctance, and intense concern for Israel, even on the part of supporters of the transaction. Senator William S. Cohen of Maine, for example, who changed his vote from opposition to support of the sale, expressed doubt that Saudi Arabia would contribute to stability or moderation in the region. "They are in my judgment as moderate as Yasser Arafat," he said. Cohen explained that he would nevertheless support the sale because its defeat would make Israel a "scapegoat" and because President Reagan had given assurances that he would not permit Israel's military superiority to be eroded.[146] Israel's ambassador to the United States, Ephraim Evron, observed, following the Senate's decision, that Israel would now expect increased military assistance from the United States.[147]

The Reagan administration, like its predecessor, labored in vain to escape the dilemma of competing "special relationships." Neither Israel nor Saudi Arabia, however, could be convinced of the advantages—at least on terms remotely acceptable to the other—of joining together, with the United States, in a "strategic consensus" against the Soviet Union. To Prime Minister Begin the Saudi monarch remained a "reactionary, medieval regime," bent on *jihad*, or holy war, against Israel, and "not capable of playing any useful role whatsoever."[148] The Saudis, for their part, continued to base their relations with the United States on the hope that American leaders could in due course be convinced of the primacy of the Palestinian problem, of the necessity of resolving it *before* there could be full-scale and reliable Saudi-American cooperation in other areas, and of the preeminent responsibility of the United States for bringing about that resolution.

Were the United States able and willing to take decisive steps toward a Palestinian solution based on self-determination, a different policy on arms sales might well prove feasible. Moving to satisfy Palestinian aspirations—as well as Islamic religious concerns for the status of East Jerusalem—would go far to respond to Saudi desires; would also, for reasons previously suggested, serve the national interest of the United States; and would also, in the present view, represent the course of justice in the Middle East. It is in the absence of such action on the part of the United States that arms sales have acquired their status as the measure of Saudi-American friendship, as the decisive test of a "special relationship."

The United States and Saudi Arabia thus confronted each other with profound dilemmas. Each recognized a vital interest in the other; neither, however, for compelling albeit quite different reasons, felt able to take the steps required by the other to secure these mutual interests. The relationship therefore remained troubled, ambivalent, and insecure. Saudi Arabia had indeed come to the center stage of American national interest, although there could be little doubt that, despite the energy crisis, and Israeli fears notwithstanding, the Saudis would not occupy that stage alone. They would be obliged, to their own discomfiture, to share it indefinitely and uneasily with the formidable, dynamic, anxiety-ridden Jewish state whose creation and rapid growth has so radically altered the life and politics of the Middle East.

CHAPTER FOUR

Israel: The Politics of Fear

UNTIL PRESIDENT SADAT acknowledged that "the Jews have been living in fear for thousands of years," and that the Israelis saw themselves as "surrounded by millions of hostile Arabs,"[1] Israel's often-stated security concerns were dismissed by almost all Arabs as a shallow pretext for expansionist ambitions. Only gradually, belatedly, and incompletely have Arabs begun to recognize that their formidable antagonist, his victories notwithstanding, lives in the shadow of an historical legacy of persecution, pogrom, and holocaust.

The phenomenon that is all but incredible to Arabs is an axiom of daily life to Israelis. Their picture of themselves in the modern world, wrote the Israeli writer Amos Elon, is one of "utter loneliness," of a people surrounded by implacable enemies, in constant military conflict, and without membership in any formal military, political, or economic alliance. Over thirty years of independence under conditions of constant threat and tension have reinforced the conviction, engendered by the Holocaust, of a world coldly indifferent to the tribulations of the Jewish people. Elon quotes the poet Nathan Altermann:

> When our children under the gallows wept,
> The world its silence kept. . . .[2]

THE "CONTINUAL TRAUMA"

Israelis make no secret of the fear that permeates their national life and of the profound influence that it exerts on their attitudes and policies. Military defeats may be costly to the Arabs politically, economically, and in loss of lives, wrote Yigal Allon, Israel's minister of foreign affairs from 1974 to 1977, but they pose no threat to their national existence. For Israel, by contrast, a military defeat "would mean the physical extinction of a large part of its population and the political elimination of the Jewish state. . . . To lose a single war is to lose everything. . . ."[3] Arie Lova Eliav, a former member of the Knesset and outspoken critic of the policies of a succession of Israeli governments, wrote of the "continual trauma" wrought by the perceived Arab desire to end Israel's existence. Only one who grasps the fact of this trauma and the pent-up mental and spiritual energy of a two thousand years' history that finally brought about the creation of the Israeli state, Eliav wrote, "can comprehend the constant fear and misgivings that gnaw at our hearts and sometimes craze us. . . . This fear, under whose shadow we live, governs what we do and refrain from doing in this country; it dictates our psychological reactions, which appear so incomprehensible and sometimes irrational to our enemies and friends."[4] The same theme was emphasized by Nahum Goldmann, former president of the World Jewish Congress, who wrote that two thousand years of persecution of the Jews, climaxed by the Nazi holocaust, had "necessarily created in the Jewish psyche a persecution mania and, coupled with it, a deep distrust of non-Jewish peoples, particularly Christians."[5]

The terrorism practiced by the Palestine Liberation Organization has perpetuated the trauma. An Israeli psychiatrist, Dr. Moshe Isac, who has treated victims of terrorist attacks, was quoted as observing that "the worst cases are often the old victims of the Nazis," who begin to dwell again on "all the things they buried when they remade their lives." The effect, however, is not the effect apparently sought by the Palestine Liberation Organization. The victims, according to Dr. Isac, do not become discouraged and consider leaving Israel; instead, "the urge to stay and fight becomes greater."[6]

The deep-seated fear that conditions Israeli behavior has evoked both sympathy and exasperation from American officials. In a report to the Senate following a trip to the Middle East in 1975, Senator McGovern noted that the memory of genocide was "branded upon the Israeli mind, as it would be on the minds of any people who suffered the worst crime in human history" and that this memory, coupled with military self-confidence and courage, made the Israelis "largely immune from the incentives and threats of pressure diplomacy." Nevertheless, McGovern warned, "any American who would encourage an unyielding position by Israel . . . would be doing a good friend a bad deed."[7] Secretary of State Henry Kissinger, on the occasion of the failure, in March 1975, of his first effort to secure a second Sinai disengagement agreement between Israel and Egypt, had an agitated and emotional exchange with Israel's top leaders, in the course of which he was reported to have said: "I'm not angry at you, and I'm not asking you to change your position. It's tragic to see people dooming themselves to a course of unbelievable peril." Prime Minister Rabin retorted with a reference to the mountain fortress where a thousand Jewish patriots of the first century, besieged by Roman soldiers, had killed themselves rather than surrender. "This is the day you visited Masada," Rabin reportedly said.[8] Later, the secretary of state was reported to have commented: "Israel has no foreign policy, only domestic politics. . . . It is the recalcitrance, the excessive caution, the lack of vision, that have caused the Israelis to refuse this agreement. . . . They're so legalistic, so Talmudic."[9]

In a visit to Israel in 1975, I noted the frequency with which Israeli officials and intellectuals seemed to equate the refusal of Arabs to speak directly to them with a determination to destroy the Israeli state. "We are treated by the Arabs as lepers, as people who have no right to exist," a professor of political science declared. If the Arabs would state forthrightly and explicitly that Israel had the right to a permanent, secure, recognized national existence, the dean of the Tel Aviv University Law School, Professor Ammon Rubinstein, said at that time, Israeli opinion on the terms of peace "would change overnight."[10]

So accustomed had Israelis become to their isolation in the Middle East environment, so much in keeping was it with the pariah status that history had taught them to expect, that, when President Sadat in November 1977 undertook to break down the psychological barrier, the Israelis reacted with ambivalence—first with gratitude, then, increasingly, with suspicion and disbelief. An Israeli public opinion poll taken soon after President Sadat's visit showed that for the first time since the war of 1967 a majority of Israelis believed that Egypt really wished to make peace with Israel.[11] As it became apparent in the weeks following President Sadat's visit to Jerusalem that Sadat's offer of security, legitimacy, and recognition of Israel, as then stated, was conditional upon withdrawal from the territories occupied in 1967 and some approximation of Palestinian self-determination, doubt, and disillusion quickly reasserted themselves. A poll taken in January 1978 showed that 72 percent of Israelis opposed the return of Israeli settlements in the Sinai to Egyptian sovereignty and that 71 percent opposed a return to the borders of 1967 "even in exchange for peace treaties with the Arab states."[12] After President Sadat called home the Egyptian delegation from Jerusalem in January 1978, aborting negotiations that had not yet gotten underway, Prime Minister Begin angrily challenged the proposition that Israel ought to make concessions in return for recognition. "We never asked your President or your government or any other president or general to recognize our right to exist," Begin said.[13] By the time the peace treaty was signed in March 1979 after protracted controversy, little was left of the optimism and good will that had been let loose by Sadat's initiative, and the spirit of reconciliation was further drained by the long deadlock over Palestinian autonomy that followed. Defense Minister Ezer Weizman, who more than any other Israeli official had established a personal bond with President Sadat, resigned his post in May 1980 and subsequently wrote: "For thirty years, we lived in a beleaguered society, growing accustomed to dwelling in the shadow of the wall of hostility enclosing us. Unfortunately, when the wall was torn down, the light was too bright for some eyes."[14]

There is a strain of defiant independence in the Israeli national character. It is the result in part of the Israelis' success in building and defending their nation, but also the result of the Jewish experience of centuries past, which has made it an article of faith among Israelis that they can rely only on themselves, and to a lesser but crucial degree on the Jews of the Diaspora. "The world its silence kept," while Jews were persecuted and slaughtered through the ages, and the lesson drawn from that experience is that only those who can take care of themselves will find safety in a cruel and pitiless world. "The world does not pity the slaughtered," in the words of Menachem Begin quoted in chapter 1, "it only respects those who fight."[15] Abba Eban, the former Foreign Minister, made the same point, more cryptically, in his assertion that "a nation must be capable of tenacious solitude."[16]

The feeling of isolation runs deep in Jewish history, and it has been reinforced by the considerable success of the Arabs in winning away from Israel former friends and supporters in Europe, notably France, and even more in the "third world." In the United Nations, Israel has been treated, along with such countries as South Africa and Chile, as a favorite target of condemnation by the third world majority. What little faith Israel might have retained in the capacity for fairness of the United Nations was probably shattered with the adoption by the 30th General Assembly in November 1975 (by a vote of 72 to 35, with 32 abstentions) of Resolution 3379, which declared Zionism to be "a form of racism and racial discrimination." Such experiences, and the attitudes they engender, would seem to account, as will be seen later in this chapter, for the deep suspicion with which Israelis view international guarantees, including a possible guarantee by the United States.

Living alone means living dangerously. Through their two thousand years in dispersion, wrote Nahum Goldmann, the Jews lived from hand to mouth, in constant fear of persecution, expulsion, or worse. Jewish "policy" consisted only of "the desperate attempt to survive, to maintain their identity, not to allow themselves to be exterminated, waiting for the Messiah who would come and solve all their problems."[17] With the founding of Israel and the coming to the fore of what Menachem Begin called the "fighting Jew,"[18] the passivity of waiting for the Messiah gave way to an energetic activism, but the need to live dangerously and by improvisation was, if anything, reinforced. War and the threat of it, and the awful sense that a single defeat will bring annihilation, have become familiar features of life to Israelis; anxiety rises and falls but never disappears; living on the edge is the normal way of life and the fear of sudden violence is ever-present. The native-born Israeli, regardless of age, has known war and terrorism since birth, and anyone born before independence in 1948 has also experienced the civil strife between Jews and Arabs and between Jews and the British under the mandate. The immigrant from Europe in the wake of World War II has known even more of death and destruction, and is haunted for life by the memory of the Holocaust. Amos Elon quotes from the personal story of a native-born Israeli writer, Moshe Shamir, who wrote in 1968 a passage that may be taken as representative of the Jewish experience:

> My son is named after my brother who fell in the War of Independence. This was exactly twenty years ago, when the almonds of 1948 were in full bloom. I am named after my father's brother, who fell in the ranks of the Red Army at the gates of Warsaw. This happened in 1920. My father was named after the brother of his father who was murdered in the Ukraine during a pogrom by rampaging peasants. This was in 1891. . . . Are we now still at the beginning of the road? At the middle? At the end? I only know this: in this half-century in which I live and breathe, fear of death has never left our house. . . .[19]

Against this background it has been all but impossible for Israelis to view the Palestinian question on its discrete merits, apart from largely unrelated historical memories. The Palestinian writer Edward Said writes: "For Zionism, the Palestinians have now become the equivalent of a past experience reincarnated in the form of a present threat. The result is that the Palestinians' future as a people is mortgaged to that fear, which is a disaster for them and for Jews."[20]

From the time of President Sadat's trip to Jerusalem in November 1977 the Israelis were confronted with a dilemma that goes to the heart of the Jewish experience. On the one hand, they could continue their course of "tenacious solitude," retaining the territories conquered in 1967, building Jewish settlements on them, and relying on these expansive borders for a measure of security. It was a dangerous course, to be sure, guaranteeing the continued enmity of the Arab world, requiring Israel to remain in a state of constant readiness for war, but with the reassuring attribute that, except for the need of arms and money from the United States, it would enable Israelis to rely on themselves. On the other hand, this people, for whom acts of faith in the past had led to disaster and death, could risk another act of faith, trading territories for guarantees and for the promise of peace. It would mean, in some degree, entrusting their fate to the good will of others, for a future filled with the promise of long-sought ease and tranquillity, but also filled with terrors for the children of pogrom and holocaust.

THE "FIRST JEWISH LEADER"

More than any previous leader of Israel, Prime Minister Menachem Begin exemplified the Jewish experience. Born in August 1913 in Brest-Litovsk, Begin grew up in the semifascist, anti-Semitic environment of Poland during the interwar years—"a country," as Begin described it, "with millions of poverty-stricken Jews, persecuted, dreaming of Zion."[21] At the age of thirteen he became a member of a Zionist youth group and at sixteen joined the Zionist youth movement *Betar*, then gaining adherents among the Jews of Poland. He became a devoted intellectual and ideological disciple of the founder of *Betar*, Vladimir Ze'ev Jabotinsky, who advocated an aggressive Zionist policy and stressed the importance of military training. To Begin, Jabotinsky was "the greatest Jewish personality of our era after Herzl. . . .[22] Begin became one of the leaders of *Betar* and then in 1938, its head, in which capacities, as he put it, "my friends and I labored to educate a generation which should be prepared not only to toil for the rebuilding of a Jewish State, but also to fight for it, suffer for it and, if needs be, die for it."[23]

In 1939 Poland was overrun and partitioned by Nazi Germany and the Soviet Union. Having escaped the Nazis, Begin was arrested by the

Russians and sent to an Arctic work camp. He was released along with other Polish citizens when the Germans invaded the Soviet Union in 1941. When the Nazis occupied Brest-Litovsk, Begin's birthplace, the local Jews were marched to the river, shot, and their bodies dumped in the river. His father and brother were among the victims, and his mother, then in a hospital, was murdered there. Begin learned later that his father, whom he revered, led the march, singing the prayer heralding death and the Zionist anthem *Hatikva*.[24]

Upon his release by the Russians, Begin joined the Polish army and was sent to Palestine, arriving there in May 1942. He was discharged from the Polish army in late 1943 and immediately became commander of the *Irgun Zvai Leumi*, the militant Jewish underground that had been founded by the revered Jabotinsky and that waged guerrilla warfare against British rule under the Palestine mandate. "Here began the first counter-attacks against those who sought our destruction," Begin wrote, "and, for that purpose, the production of the first Jewish arms." Breaking with the policy of "self-restraint" practiced by the established Jewish leadership in Palestine, Begin and his associates in the *Irgun* conducted their "Hebrew revolt" from 1944 until the Jews of Palestine won their independence in 1948. "To me and to many thousands of young people," Begin wrote, "all this was a work of sublime justice."[25]

Begin and the *Irgun* bitterly opposed the United Nations partition resolution of November 29, 1947. The *Irgun* warned that partition would lead to war and asserted the credo of the underground fighters: "The partition of the Homeland is illegal. It will never be recognized. . . . It will not bind the Jewish people. Jerusalem was and will for ever be our capital. Eretz Israel will be restored to the people of Israel. All of it. And for ever."[26] In an "Order of the Day" following the partition plan, the leaders of the *Irgun* called on their soldiers to tell the rejoicing populace: "We who have offered our lives for the day of redemption are not rejoicing. For the Homeland has not been liberated but mutilated."[27]

The *Irgun* disbanded when the state of Israel came into existence in 1948, but Begin continued to pursue its basic objectives of a strong "Eretz Israel" in all of old Palestine. Begin led his Herut party in eight national elections, failing in all of them to win national power. In all the years of opposition—and three years as a minister in a national unity government after the 1967 war—Begin adhered consistently and tenaciously to his basic themes: the restoration of the "whole Land of Israel" to the Jewish people as its "God-covenanted owners" and the necessity of arms and militancy—by the "fighting Jew"—to achieve this objective and protect the state.[28] Begin's ninth election campaign ended in victory for his Likud coalition on May 17, 1977, and Menachem Begin became prime minister of Israel.

Begin's policies in office remained consistent with the themes of three decades in opposition and of the underground struggle of the *Irgun* before that. The occupied West Bank and Gaza Strip, populated by Arabs and the only possible territory for one form or another of Palestinian homeland, remained, in Begin's view, part of the patrimony of Eretz Israel. His predecessors had emphasized Israel's security interest in the territories occupied in 1967 but had also indicated willingness to restore to Arab sovereignty at least some parts of the West Bank, as well as the Sinai and part of the Golan Heights. To Begin the West Bank—to which he referred by its Biblical designation as "Judea" and "Samaria"—had profound religious as well as security significance. To part with these provinces might even be seen as a violation of God's covenant. In a statement apparently made in jest but also suggestive of his basic outlook on the other Biblical lands, Begin said of Mount Sinai (where the Bible says Moses received the Ten Commandments) "Moses can be angry with us if we give it away. . . ."[29] "In a very real sense," the Israeli-born professor Amos Perlmutter wrote three months after Begin became prime minister, "Begin is the first Jewish leader of Israel. He is the first one to believe—in the traditional sense—in the God of Israel."[30]

With his background and belief, Menachem Begin would have seemed incapable of "striking a deal," no matter how advantageous politically, if it involved the violation of his principles and convictions. These may be summed up as a deep religious nationalism, a belief in the continuing validity of God's promise to the Children of Israel: "And I will make of thee a great nation, and I will bless thee, and make thy name great. . . ."[31] A nation called into existence by the Creator could hardly be expected to yield its claim to the Promised Land on the basis of temporal claims by others, even claims based on centuries-long habitation. To reclaim the land for the Children of Israel, in Menachem Begin's perspective, would seem not just a right but a religious duty. More than that, the Jewish homeland had been earned through millennia of tribulation. Of the founding of Israel in 1948 Begin wrote:

> A nation had been driven out of its country after the loss of its liberty and the utter failure of its uprisings. It had wandered about the face of the earth for nearly two thousand years. Its wanderings had been drenched in blood. And now, in the seventy-first generation of its exile this wandering people had returned to its Homeland. The secular tour was ended. The circle of wanderings was closed and the nation had returned to the Motherland that bore it.[32]

All this in Begin's view—the wanderings, the killings, the persecutions, the banishments, and the torture—had been "necessary," the price extracted by God, it would seem, for the right to live in the Promised Land.[33]

Purchased with blood and sacrifice, the Motherland, Begin never doubted, would also have to be defended with blood and sacrifice. "It is Hebrew arms which decide the boundaries of the Hebrew State," Begin declared in his radio address to the new nation on May 15, 1948. "So it is now in this battle; so it will be in the future. . . . There is only one kind of peace that can be bought—the peace of the graveyard, the peace of Treblinka."[34] Elsewhere in his memoir Begin wrote of

> the paradox in the life of every man who fights in a just cause: He puts on a heavy, sometimes too heavy, yoke, in order to throw off a yoke. He makes war so that there should be peace. He punishes himself so that there should be no suffering. He employs physical force and believes in moral force. He sheds blood so that there should be no more bloodshed. . . . That is the way of the world. A very tragic way beset with terrors. There is no other.[35]

More than any other leader of the young Israeli nation, Menachem Begin was a product of the long, tragic history of the Jewish people. His speeches were filled with references to the Jewish past and with the inferences he drew from it. These inferences, which formed the bases of Begin's policies as prime minister, may be summarized as follows: The land of Israel belongs, by the gift of God, to the Jewish people, and no mortal force, no alien occupancy, however prolonged, can sever the mystic bond. For two thousand years the Jewish people wandered the earth, in forced exile, but never for a moment did they cease to dream of Zion. And in that dream, and the promise of return, they found their solace and strength. The hardships and persecutions of the Diaspora were "necessary," a kind of test through which the Jewish people were required to earn their right to the Promised Land. The persecutions, the pogroms, and above all the Holocaust proved that there could be no safe quarter for the Jewish people except in their own homeland.

"With your own eyes you saw what has happened to our nation when this, its homeland, had been taken from it," Begin told Sadat before the Knesset in Jerusalem after Sadat had visited the memorial to the victims of the Holocaust at Yad Vashem. And while those six million were being destroyed—this theme recurs in Begin's statements—"no one came to their saving—not from the East and not from the West."[36] Now the two thousand years' journey was at an end and the Jewish people were restored to their homeland, but no more than in the Diaspora could the Jewish nation be at ease: it must continue, for as long as its enemies persisted, to fight for the survival of the state—"We Fight, Therefore We Are," is the title of a chapter in Begin's memoir.[37] The basis of the continuing struggle was not political in the ordinary sense but nothing less than a covenant of the generations, between those who survived and those who perished. "We have sworn an eternal vow," Begin told Sadat, "this entire generation, the generation of destruction and rebirths: We shall never again place our nation in such a danger."[38]

RIVAL CLAIMANTS

Whatever else might divide people in Israel's vigorous and contentious politics, few Israelis question that the greatest danger by far to Israel's survival is the possible creation of an independent Palestinian state. Prior to the coming to office of the Carter administration in January 1977, the diplomacy of the Arab-Israeli conflict was focused on less central issues— on the effort to draw Arabs and Israelis from limited agreements on the Sinai and the Golan Heights "step-by-step" toward the more difficult questions relating to the West Bank, the Gaza Strip, and East Jerusalem. When the Carter administration undertook to mediate a general settlement, and even more when President Sadat initiated in November 1977 his bid for peace based on security guarantees for Israel in return for Israeli withdrawal from the occupied territories, the West Bank and Gaza came perforce to center stage, and Israelis were confronted with their most feared specter, the prospect of a radical, irredentist, Soviet-dominated Palestinian state.

The Israeli fear of Palestinian nationalism is different in character from the Israeli fear of Arabs in general or of Egypt and Syria as "confrontation" states. The latter threatened Israel with what they might *do*, militarily or otherwise; the Palestinians threaten Israel with what they *are*, rival claimants to the same land. To whatever extent the Palestinian Arabs are acknowledged to have national *rights* in the territory of old Palestine, Israeli rights are called into question. The very term "rights," as applied to the Palestinians, has alarming connotations to Israelis, who took it as an ominous sign when the Carter administration began to use that term in lieu of the previously favored term "interests" in reference to Palestinian aspirations. After the Camp David agreements were signed, Begin assured the Israeli people that the phrase, "legitimate rights of the Palestinian people," as contained in the Framework for Peace, "has no meaning." He had accepted it, he said, to please Presidents Sadat and Carter, "and because it does not change reality."[39] While sensibilities about the legitimacy of Palestinian claims cause Israelis acute anxiety, draconian threats, the

Palestinian Covenant calling for the displacement of Israel, and acts of terrorism—all to be discussed further in chapter 5—strike at the very heart of historic Jewish fears. They raise the specter of pogrom and holocaust.

Israeli fears being what they are, and Menachem Begin's background being what it was, there could be no doubt that the offer of administrative autonomy for the Palestinian Arabs contained in Begin's proposal of December 27, 1977—and still more the "self-governing authority" proposed for the West Bank and Gaza under the Camp David agreement of September 17, 1978—represented to Prime Minister Begin and his followers of the Herut party significant, even audacious concessions for peace. "Never before," Begin said in defense of his intial home rule plan when it came under attack, "have the residents of these areas been given such freedom to run their own lives."[40]

The territory in question, the West Bank and the Gaza Strip, representing 23 percent of the territory of old Palestine, was occupied by Israel in the 1967 war. Except for about 22,000 Jews living in 120 settlements as of 1981, the population of the West Bank and Gaza consists of about 1.3 million Palestinians. Another half million or more Palestinian Arabs live within the 1967 borders of Israel, and at least 2 million more are dispersed among the Arab states, in what the Palestinians have come to call their "diaspora," adapting the term used by the Jews to refer to their own dispersal outside of the Holy Land.

The Begin plan of December 27, 1977 and the Camp David proposal for a self-governing authority for the West Bank and Gaza were described in the first chapter. The plans differed in that the latter was to be implemented on the basis of an international contract, binding on Israel as well as on all other parties, rather than on the basis of a unilateral, and therefore presumably revocable, grant on the part of Israel. In other important respects, however, the two proposals as interpreted by Israel, amplified by subsequent Israeli statements and proposals, had certain common features that were indicative of the basic position of the Likud government with respect to the Palestinians. The essentials of the Israeli position may be summarized as follows: there could be no separate Palestinian state, whether or not the Palestinian people desired it; for an interim period of five years the Palestinians resident in the West Bank and Gaza might be permitted self-government with respect to certain local and domestic matters, but security would remain under Israeli control, with Israeli forces reduced and confined but not wholly withdrawn; Jewish settlements would continue to be emplaced in the West Bank and Gaza; Israel might permit but would retain the right to veto the return of any

Palestinian refugees to the territories; a permanent regime to follow the transition period might be formed through negotiations among Israel, Jordan, Egypt, and Palestinian representatives, but no commitment regarding the nature of that regime would be made by Israel in advance, and the Palestine Liberation Organization, as such, might not be a participant in the negotiations. As will be seen in the next section, the Labor party opposition tended to differ from the Begin government as to the kind of regime that should be emplaced in the West Bank and Gaza but concurred in ruling out a separate Palestinian state, in the necessity for retaining Israeli forces in the West Bank, and in the exclusion of the Palestine Liberation Organization from negotiations.

Almost immediately after the conclusion of the Camp David accords in September 1978 the Framework for Peace began to come unstuck over the questions of Jewish settlements, the retention of Israeli forces, and Israeli claims to sovereignty over the West Bank and Gaza. In the days following the Camp David meeting, Prime Minister Begin contested President Carter's understanding that a five-year moratorium on new settlements had been agreed upon, insisting that he had agreed to a moratorium only for the three months, within which Israel and Egypt had pledged to try to conclude a peace treaty. Furthermore, Begin interpreted the Framework, which authorized "all necessary security measures . . . during the transitional period and beyond,"[41] as thereby sanctioning the retention of Israeli troops in the West Bank beyond the five-year interim period. Speaking to members of Congress on September 19, two days after the signing of the Camp David accords, Begin said, "I believe with all my heart that the Jewish people have a right to sovereignty over Judea and Samaria." The source of that right, he said, were the "books of the Bible."[42] On the following day Begin spoke to Jewish leaders in New York: "I hereby declare the Israeli defense forces will stay in Judea, Samaria and the Gaza Strip to defend our people and make sure Jewish blood is not shed again. I hereby declare they will stay beyond five years."[43]

These statements, and others that followed, caused acute distress to American officials and dissipated much of the euphoria to which the Camp David agreements had given rise. The statements were, in fact, consistent with views that had been expressed by Israeli officials repeatedly and insistently since the Begin government had come to office in May 1977. In an introductory address to his staff on June 22, 1977, the new minister of foreign affairs, Moshe Dayan, said that the new government would seek a solution for the West Bank "not by dividing it into two parts, one of which would belong to Israel and the other to an Arab state, but by finding a way to coexist there, without annexing any part to Jordan, without handing over any part of the West Bank or of the Gaza Strip to the rule of another government."⁴⁴ Again, on August 10, 1977, on the eve of talks between Foreign Minister Dayan and U. S. Secretary of State Cyrus Vance, the Israeli embassy in Washington issued a "precis" of Israel's positions, which stated among other things that "Israel will not return to the previous boundaries nor agree to the creation of a Palestinian state in any form," that "Israel is unwilling to countenance in any form the participation of the Palestine Liberation Organization in the Geneva Conference," and further, that "Israel is not ready to accept any foreign government on the West Bank and in the Gaza."⁴⁵ Dayan reiterated the tough Israeli position on the Palestine Liberation Organization on September 25 and again on September 30, 1977, stating that Israel would not negotiate with the Palestine Liberation Organization even if the United States did, or even if it amended the Palestinian Charter, accepted Security Council Resolution 242, and recognized the existence of Israel.⁴⁶

Prime Minister Begin was, if anything, even more forthright than his foreign minister in rejecting the idea of a Palestinian state, and in refusing any dealings with the Palestine Liberation Organization, both before and after President Sadat's visit to Jerusalem in November 1977. At a dinner in Jerusalem for Secretary of State Vance on August 9, 1977, Begin startled his guests with an emotional denunciation of the Palestine Liberation Organization, provoked apparently by the tentative, ultimately fruitless, initiative the United States government was then engaged in toward drawing the Palestine Liberation Organization into peace discussions if it would accept Israel. "That organization," declared Begin, "the philosophy of which is based on an Arabic *Mein Kampf,* is no partner whatsoever, and never will be for us to hold any talks. . . ."⁴⁷

President Sadat, following his visit to Jerusalem, issued an invitation to all parties to the Middle East conflict to attend a preliminary peace conference in Cairo. Lest anyone suppose, in the wake of the Sadat visit, that the Prime Minister had softened on the Palestine Liberation Organization, which he termed a "Nazi Organization," Begin told reporters on November 27, 1977 that "no Israeli delegation will negotiate in any way at any place with the so-called Palestine Liberation Organization, whether it is Geneva or Cairo or the moon."⁴⁸ Then, in a statement reminiscent of former Prime Minister Golda Meir's famous assertion that "there was no such thing as Palestinians,"⁴⁹ Prime Minister Begin told the American columnist Joseph Kraft in late 1977 that the word "Palestine" did not exist in the Hebrew language; the term, he said, was "jargon."⁵⁰

Recurrent conflicts between the Carter administration and the Begin government of Israel reflected the underlying, long-standing conflict of interests between the two countries over the principle of self-determination. The United States, as suggested in chapter 2, has a historic commitment to this principle, a commitment that, in the present view, qualifies as a national interest. Zionism, by contrast, based as it is on the religious and historical claims of the Jewish people to a land long inhabited by others, necessarily depends on the denial of self-determination to the rival claimants. To accord even the slightest degree of legitimacy to Palestinian national aspirations is, in the Israeli perspective, to call into question their own legitimacy as a nation-state. The difference between Israel and the United States in this respect is not, therefore, one of mere misunderstanding, or of the lack of a diplomatic formula sufficiently ingenious to bridge the gap. It is, rather, a fundamental difference of outlook over an international norm, and from the Israeli standpoint an issue filled with implications for Israel's own right to exist.

Virtually alone among the statesmen and politicians who have attempted to devise an Israeli-American understanding on this seminal issue of the Arab-Israeli conflict, Menachem Begin understood that the gap was unbridgeable, that two irreconcilable principles were at stake, and that if agreement was to be reached, it would not be the result of an authentic compromise but rather the result of one party or the other, Israel or the United States, yielding its own principle and acquiescing in that of the other. The denial of self-determination to the Palestinians became, under Menachem Begin, the explicitly stated policy of the government of Israel. "We are not beating around the bush," Begin was quoted in chapter 1. "To us self-determination means a Palestinian state, and we are not going to agree to any such mortal danger to Israel."[51] This basic proposition, variously phrased, became official Israeli doctrine under Begin, turning up repeatedly in official statements and documents. A "Policy Background" paper issued by the Israeli embassy in Washington on April 6, 1978 stated that:

> an independent Palestinian state . . . would quickly fall under the sway of Palestine Liberation Organization terrorists. It would be a powerful focus for Palestine irredentism, a center of anarchy open to Soviet penetration and a threat not only to Israel, but to the entire area. *Israel and the United States fully agree* that there can be no room for such a state and that the *Palestine Liberation Organization cannot be a party to any negotiations for the establishment of peace.*[52]

When Prime Minister Begin and his principal associates quickly reverted to these themes in the wake of the Camp David accords, American officials, although dismayed, took hope in the hypothesis that Begin was protecting his flanks against domestic criticism. Supporters of the Camp David agreement in Israel as well as in the United States commended this thesis, asserting that Begin was fighting a rearguard action against an inevitable Arab "destiny" for the West Bank, which he, or more probably some successor, would ultimately be compelled to accept. So argued, for example, former Foreign Minister Abba Eban, who, with other leading figures in the Labor party, advocated partition of the occupied territories, and believed that the Camp David autonomy plan could serve as a "natural bridge" to such a solution.[53] Professor Shlomo Avineri, a director general of the ministry of foreign affairs under the Labor government, expressed the opinion after Camp David that Begin's Cabinet understood that they were giving up the West Bank as an integral part of Israel, although its final status would remain uncertain for the five-year transition period called for in the Camp David agreement. Avineri speculated that Begin himself probably expected no more than "some residual Israeli presence" after the five-year transition period.[54] To this school of thought the equivocation of the Camp David agreement as to the final status of the West Bank and Gaza was a political necessity, if not an asset, enabling history to move in its necessary direction without requiring recognition of that direction by those to whom it was politically and otherwise distasteful. Begin, wrote Abba Eban, "is too precise and intelligent a man for us to believe that he does not comprehend how short a step separates this kind of 'self-government' from some form of eventual Arab sovereignty."[55]

If indeed Begin was fighting a "rearguard action" after Camp David, as Avineri suggested,[56] it was nonetheless vigorously prosecuted. There "will be no plebiscite" in the West Bank and Gaza, Begin declared in debate in the Knesset on September 25, 1978, "and there is and will not be under any conditions or in any circumstances a Palestinian state." Furthermore, declared the Prime Minister, "The murderers' organization known as the PLO is not and will not be a factor in the negotiations. . . ." Begin also reiterated that, contrary to President Carter's understanding, he had promised to suspend the emplacement of new Jewish settlements on the West Bank only for the projected three months' negotiating period with Egypt, and that even during this period Israel would reserve the right to expand existing Jewish settlements.[57] A month later, following the visit to the West Bank of Assistant Secretary of State Harold Saunders, in which the American official suggested to Palestinians that the status of the Israeli settlements after the five-year transition period would be subject to negotiation, Israeli offiicials emphatically reaffirmed their intention to retain Jewish settlements.

Prime Minister Begin announced on October 25 that Israel intended to enlarge its West Bank settlements as soon as possible.[58] Foreign Minister Dayan made the same point even more emphatically the next day: "This is our policy, whether other people like it or not."[59] Dayan also said the same day, "We don't dream about removing or dismantling one single Israeli settlement."[60] At a political rally in Tel Aviv on the evening of October 26, Begin reaffirmed "the inalienable and full right of the Jewish people to settle any part of the land of Israel—including Judea, Samaria and Gaza."[61]

There seems no doubt that the emphatic reaffirmation after Camp David of Israeli claims to the West Bank and Gaza were provoked by countervailing American and domestic Israeli pressures. With reference to the announcement on October 25 that existing settlements would be expanded, an aide to Prime Minister Begin commented, "If Saunders hadn't come here, there wouldn't be any announcement. It's like physics—for every action there is a reaction."[62] In the period following the Camp David agreements, as the negotiations with Egypt bogged down over the issue of "linkage" with the West Bank and Gaza, the Begin government found itself caught between the need to protect its domestic base through assurances that Israel would not give up the West Bank and Gaza and the need to keep the "peace process" going by allowing the Egyptians and Americans to hope that Israel might eventually do exactly that. Taking note of these political factors, experienced observers in both Israel and the United States continued to insist that the evasions and ambiguities of the Camp David accords were salutary and that, as long as the United States did not force Israel into specifying prematurely what might lie at the end of the process, the self-rule plan could be expected to evolve toward some form or other of "Arab destiny" for the West Bank and Gaza. A member of Begin's Likud coalition, Zalman Shoval of the La'am party, observed in early November 1978, when the Egyptian-Israeli treaty negotiations were going badly, that the worst mistake the United States had made was pressing Israel to say what might be expected after the five-year transition period for the West Bank and Gaza. It was, he said, "politically and psychologically wrong," and had caused the Israeli government to give "all kinds of evasive answers." Shoval himself envisioned, at the end of five years, either the partition of the West Bank or some form of "functional" compromise between Israel and a Palestinian-Jordanian state.[63]

For precisely the reason that most Israelis found the Camp David plan for the West Bank and Gaza tolerable—its lack of clarity as to the long term future—the rival claimants to that territory, the Palestinians, rejected the plan from the outset as a scheme not for self-government but for the perpetuation of Israeli domination, as a West Bank academic put it, by "using the natives" to help run the occupation.[64] Rejecting the argument that the post–Camp David statements of Begin and Dayan were a "rear-guard action" not to be taken as definitive, Palestinians took these statements very seriously indeed, as literal and accurate proclamations of Israeli intent. Suspicious and fearful from the outset because of the failure of the Camp David agreement to specify or even imply ultimate self-determination, Palestinian opinion leaders in the West Bank and outside became hardened in their suspicion and dismay as Israeli leaders, for whatever reason, reiterated their unalterable opposition to a future Palestinian state.

Self-determination remained the central issue after Camp David, as it had been before. If the United States would give public assurance of ultimate Israeli withdrawal from the occupied territories, said Khalid Fahoum, chairman of the Palestine Central Council (in October 1978 in the presence of PLO Chairman Yasser Arafat) then "everything could be discussed."[65] A leadership delegation from the National Association of Arab Americans reported in late 1978, after a tour of eight Arab countries, that a "consensus" had taken form within the Arab world for a settlement based on Arab acceptance of Israel in return for Israeli withdrawal from the occupied territories and Palestinian self-determination.[66] The Israelis, on the other hand, although divided between proposals for "functional" and "territorial" compromise for the West Bank and Gaza, remained— except for a small group of "doves"—solidly united in their own national consensus, that a separate Palestinian state would pose a mortal threat to Israel—a threat consisting not only in what such a state might do but in the very fact of its existence. As Prime Minister Begin expressed it in October 1978,

> A state has a parliament, a government, an army, diplomatic relations with other states, other symbols of statehood. The inhabitants of Judea, Samaria and Gaza cannot have these things, because, if they had them, they would determine not only their own fate, but also ours—a fate of killing, murder and war. We will never agree to that. Never.[67]

THE NATIONAL CONSENSUS

Born of the Nazi Holocaust and the solidarity generated by the "state of permanent siege," Amos Elon wrote, "there is among Israelis today an elemental, almost tribal sense of sticking together which sometimes confounds outsiders from the fragmented societies of the West."[68] Although often masked by partisanship and vigorous debate, this deeply rooted solidarity forms the basis of the Israeli national consensus regarding the survival of the Israeli state and the mortal threat, as it is perceived, of a Palestinian state.

At times, during the arduous, discouraging efforts for peace that followed President Sadat's visit to Jerusalem in November 1977, American as well as Arab leaders betrayed a longing for what had come to seem the "good old days" of the Labor governments that had preceded the rule of Menachem Begin. President Sadat flirted openly and without profit in the period before Camp David with the leader of the Labor party opposition, Shimon Peres. In fact, on the basis of their recorded and public pronouncements, the principal figures of preceding Israeli governments held positions on the occupied territories hardly more acceptable to the major Arab leaders, including President Sadat, than those of Begin and his Likud colleagues. Before Sadat's trip to Jerusalem and prior to the accession of the Carter administration, when the United States was seeking peace in the Middle East "step-by-step," the diplomacy of the Arab-Israeli problem had been focused on what Sadat was later to call the "side issues" of the Egyptian Sinai and the Syrian Golan Heights,[69] and Israeli governments were under little pressure to spell out their proposals for a permanent regime for the West Bank and Gaza. Except for a few dissenters, however, the major figures in Israeli politics under the Labor governments were virtually unanimous in their insistence that withdrawal could be only partial, that Israel must retain military installations in the West Bank, and that there could be no independent Palestinian state. The premise of their policy was that Israel must have "defensible borders," and although Israeli officials were disinclined to specify where these borders might be drawn before Presidents Carter and Sadat brought the question to the fore, it was evident that, to Begin's predecessors as to Begin himself, these meant something quite different from the "insubstantial alterations" of the borders of 1967 once recommended by the United States.[70]

Although no official plan for the West Bank was put forth by an Israeli government prior to the Begin plan of December 27, 1977, the so-called "Allon Plan" suggested by Yigal Allon, Israel's minister of foreign affairs from 1974 to 1977, spelled out in considerable detail the Labor government's conception of "defensible borders." The plan called for an Israeli strategic frontier along the Jordan River, with Israel to retain, or annex, a strip of territory of varying width along the Jordan River, stretching back to the hills of Samaria and Judea. In those territories Israel would develop—was indeed developing before the Labor party was voted out of office in May 1977—extensive rural and urban settlements as well as permanent military installations. Between the territories retained along the Jordan River, however, and Israel proper to the west, the heartland of the West Bank where the Arab population was concentrated would be left to what Allon called an "Arab solution," demilitarized under a form of Arab sovereignty with a corridor to Jordan across the Allenby Bridge. Israel, under the Allon Plan, would retain "greater Jerusalem" including the new Jewish residential areas established around its periphery after the 1967 war, but the religious rights of all faiths would be guaranteed. In addition, Israel would retain much or most of the Syrian Golan Heights. The Sinai peninsula would be demilitarized under joint Israeli-Egyptian policing, but Israel would retain actual control of eastern Sinai from Sharm el-Sheikh at the mouth of the Gulf of Aqaba in the south to the Mediterranean coast in the north.[71]

The Allon Plan was somewhat imprecise about the Gaza Strip, specifying, however, that under no circumstances would it be restored to Egypt.[72] In one description, ultimate Israeli annexation was called for, with only the Arab population who lived there before 1948 to be permitted to remain and the unabsorbed refugees to be resettled either in the West Bank or in Sinai.[73] Elsewhere Allon suggested that the city of Gaza and its environs "could comprise part of the Jordanian-Palestinian unit that would arise to the east of Israel" and would be linked to it by a traffic route across Israel. Israel, however, would control the desert area from the southern part of the Gaza Strip to the dunes east of the Sinai town of El Arish, which itself would be returned to Egypt.[74]

Two major premises underlay the policy of "defensible borders." One was that the Arabs would not, under foreseeable circumstances, reconcile themselves with the permanence of Israel. "Whereas the Arab states seek to isolate, strangle and erase Israel from the world's map," Yigal Allon wrote in 1976, "Israel's aim is simply to live in peace and good relations with all its neighbors."[75] The other premise was that Israel could safely rely only on her *own* military power, a conviction which has deep roots in Israeli minds, and which, as will be seen, has much to do with the Israelis' disdain of international, or even American, guarantees. "We want the kind of boundaries we can defend and defend by ourselves," Prime Minister Rabin told Senator McGovern in 1975, because, as he explained, anything else would "change the very nature of Israel. . . ."[76] "We must be capable of defending ourselves, of ourselves, by ourselves. . . ." Allon emphasized.[77]

Building on these two premises, the Israelis made their case for borders that would allow of strategic depth. The Allon Plan was designed to meet this requirement and also to satisfy Palestinian aspirations by "territorial compromise." From the standpoint of pure strategy, Allon pointed out, it would have served Israel better simply to move the borders eastward from the vulnerable borders of 1967. That, however, would have placed a large Arab population within the boundaries of Israel, a prospect hardly less distasteful to Israelis than to the Palestinian Arabs themselves. Allon therefore came up with his proposal for Israeli deployment along the Jordan River, to the east of a surrounded, disarmed Palestinian Arab political unit, which would be linked to Jordan by a narrow corridor through the Israeli-held territory along the Jordan River.[78]

Closely examined, the Allon Plan seems not so radically dissimilar from the Begin plan of "administrative autonomy" of December 27, 1977, or from the Camp David self-rule plan, as many acrimonious debates in the Knesset between Begin and his opposition seemed to suggest. None of these proposals would permit a separate Palestinian state; all would require the demilitarization of the area—Allon specified that "apart from civilian police to guarantee internal order, these areas would have to be devoid of offensive forces and heavy arms."[79] Allon would have Israeli forces withdrawn from the Palestinian unit but stationed around it on territory detached from it; under the Begin plan of December 1977 "security and public order" would remain "the responsibility of the Israeli authorities;" and under the Camp David plan, Israeli forces would be partially withdrawn and otherwise regrouped, pending the creation of a permanent regime for the West Bank and Gaza. Under all three plans the Palestinian Arab unit would itself be defenseless, restricted in its authority over its own population and territory, denied the right to form a political unit separate from either Israel or Jordan, and completely at the mercy of Israeli military power. The principal difference was that the Allon Plan would permit—whereas the Begin Plan and the Camp David Plan, as interpreted by the Begin government, would deny—Arab "sovereignty" over the West Bank unit.

In opposition after May 1977 and even after the Sadat visit to Jerusalem in November 1977, the Israeli Labor party continued to adhere to the policy of "defensible borders." On the eve of the Camp David summit meeting in September 1978 former Prime Minister Rabin wrote that Egyptian demands for total Israeli withdrawal from the West Bank and Gaza Strip and the creation of a Palestinian entity whose future would be decided "solely by Arabs" was "totally unacceptable to Israel."[80] Writing in August 1978, the leader of the opposition, Shimon Peres, noted that on certain basic issues there was "something like a national consensus." Both coalitions, Peres wrote, his own and Begin's, rejected the creation of a separate Palestinian state, which both felt certain would be militant, dangerous, and subject to Soviet influence. Both coalitions also required that Jerusalem remain united under Israeli sovereignty, because, Peres wrote, in words that Begin might have used, "Jerusalem is not only the heart of Israel; it is also the soul of the Jewish people." Israelis are united too, said Peres, in their insistence on "secure boundaries." These most assuredly could not be the borders of 1967, described by Peres as "inherently indefensible," nor could the changes be limited to "minor rectifications." These, said Peres in his article, were the main elements of Israel's national consensus.

Turning then to the differences between his own Labor party and Begin's Herut party, Peres cited as the principal difference Labor's willingness to accept—by contrast with Herut's intense opposition to—the partition of Palestine, or, more exactly, the partition of the occupied West Bank between Jews and Arabs. Peres did not dispute Begin's rationale for retaining the West Bank. "There is no argument in Israel about our historic rights in the land of Israel," Peres wrote. "The past is immutable and the Bible is the decisive document in determining the fate of our land." Labor would accept partition of the West Bank, nevertheless, historically just claims notwithstanding, for the sake of peace. The partition plan envisioned by Peres was essentially—or exactly—the Allon Plan, requiring Israeli defense positions along the Jordan River, and Israeli installations at other strategic points as well. The remainder of the West Bank and Gaza, disarmed and militarily surrounded by Israel, in compulsory union with Jordan, would be permitted to live "under an Arab flag," freeing the Palestinians of an unwanted Israeli rule and freeing the Israelis of an unwanted Arab population who, with their high birth rate, "would eventually endanger the Jewish character of Israel. . . ."[81]

An almost identical outline of a peace settlement had been put forth early in 1978 by the former Labor minister of foreign affairs, usually regarded as a "dove" in Israeli politics. Abba Eban, like Peres, ruled out a separate Palestinian state, favored the restoration of "substantial areas" west of the Jordan River to Jordan "after territorial changes essential for Israel's security were made," and rejected out of hand a return to the borders of 1967, which, as Eban put it, "none of us would accept." Eban, like Peres, pointed to the principle of *partition* as the essential issue between the Begin government and its opposition. "For over four decades there has been only one essential debate in Zionist and Israeli diplomacy," Eban wrote in March 1978. "It is the debate between the partition logic and its opponents."[82]

So intense and agitated was the debate in Israel over the "partition logic" that at least two pertinent considerations were obscured, to Americans no less than Israelis. First, the issue of partition, which until 1967 had to do with the disposition of Palestine as a whole, was redefined after 1967 to apply only to the 23 percent of the territory of old Palestine that remained outside of the control of Israel after the 1948 war and that was occupied by Israel in 1967. Second, whereas previously the discussion of partition applied to hypothetically equal parties, it came perforce after 1967 to apply to the relationship between a militarily dominant Israel and a projected Palestinian enclave with severe restrictions on its sovereignty, surrounded and disarmed, permitted to live "under an Arab flag" but otherwise denied the right of self-determination.

Another basic element in the Labor-Likud consensus has been the palpable desire for a separate peace with Egypt. Even before President Sadat's visit to Jerusalem, leading Israelis and supporters of Israel in the United States had pointed to the tractability of the territorial issue of Egyptian Sinai compared to the more difficult questions of the West Bank and the Golan Heights. Throughout the protracted negotiations preceding and following the Camp David meeting, it was widely assumed—by many Arabs as well as by Israelis—that Egypt's economic difficulties, along with the desire to recover Egyptian national territory, had motivated Sadat to seek what would amount to a separate peace, provided some diplomatic facade, or vaguely worded statement of principles, could be devised to give the appearance of Egyptian loyalty to its Arab brothers.[83] In advance of the Camp David summit in September 1978 Prime Minister Begin spoke favorably of the possibility of a "permanent partial peace" between Israel and Egypt.[84] In a presummit article in the *Jerusalem Post*, former Foreign Minister Eban urged the summit participants to "climb down from the slogan of 'a comprehensive overall settlement,' " because "the only realistic aim at this stage is an Egyptian-Israeli accord accompanied by a statement of principles on the Palestine question that would enable Anwar Sadat to avoid implications of a 'separate peace.' "[85] Realistic or not, the possibility of a separate peace with Egypt was attractive to Israelis of otherwise diverse persuasion for exactly the reason that it was greatly feared by Egypt's Arab brothers: it would detach from the Arab coalition its most significant military force, allowing Israel greatly increased latitude in its subsequent dealings with Syria, the

Palestine Liberation Organization, and the restive Palestinians living in the West Bank and the Gaza Strip.

A final tenet of the Israeli national consensus often called up to explain and justify the Israelis' rejection of any dealings with the Palestine Liberation Organization was that Jordan would ultimately provide fulfillment for Palestinian national aspirations. Noting that Palestinians made up a majority of east bank Jordan's population and, except for the army, most of its governing elite, Israelis of both the Likud coalition and the Labor party opposition have tended to see Jordan as the future "Palestinian state," although views vary as to whether the prospective Jordanian-Palestinian state would remain under the Hashemite monarchy or take some other form. General Ariel Sharon, minister of agriculture in the first Begin government and a strong proponent of Israeli settlements in the occupied territories, made the point more bluntly than others when still in opposition in 1975, asserting that he would annex the West Bank to Israel and turn Jordan over to the Palestinians. "Hussein," said Sharon, "is not a partner in this thing."[86]

The foregoing is not intended to suggest that there were no important differences between Begin and his predecessors in their respective approaches to peace but only that these differences were less significant than the vigorous debates that characterize Israeli politics made them appear. More important still, neither Begin nor his opposition offered a program for a *general* settlement with any real prospect of acceptance by any of the Arab parties except Egypt. In the view of Arie Lova Eliav, the prominent dissenter and member of the Knesset until 1979, a Labor government would have been hardly more responsive than Begin's to the initial Sadat peace initiative: "They would still be sitting in their councils and fighting. Peres would fight Rabin, Rabin would fight Peres. And I don't think they would give Sadat any answer of any kind. . . ."[87] Asked in August 1978 if he thought that an Israeli Labor government would have acted like Begin's government, the Palestinian-born president of the National Association of Arab Americans replied: "Yes, I do, except probably with more cleverness, with greater ability to mystify the issue than Begin who is a sincere, outspoken person for which, as a Palestinian, I'm most grateful."[88]

At the heart of the Israeli national consensus, as noted in the previous section, second only to the shared sense of Israel's destiny and mission, is the fear of Palestinian nationalism. Lacking a territorial base or conventional armed forces of their own, the Palestinians threaten Israel's existence only in the long run—by challenging the Jewish state's legitimacy.

Drawing on their own experience, the Israelis appreciate well the potential power of an exiled people with a shared sense of historic injustice and a tenacious yearning for a lost homeland. Whatever their differences as to the best means of suppressing or deflecting it, Begin and his opposition, with minor exceptions, were united in their view of Palestinian nationalism as a mortal threat to Israel.

In earlier times it had been plausible to deny the fact of Palestinian nationhood. Before the coming of the Jews the Arabs of Palestine did not have a strong sense of themselves as a separate and distinct nationality. The early Zionists, bemused by their own missionary zeal, permitted themselves to believe, as David Ben-Gurion put it in 1917, that in the "historical and moral sense" Palestine was a country "without inhabitants."[89] After Theodor Herzl, the founder of modern Zionism, visited Palestine in 1898, according to the modern Israeli writer, Amos Elon, his report contained no reference to the Arab population, although they probably numbered over half a million at the time; nor did Herzl take notice of the Arabs in his extensive private diary.[90] An entry made in Herzl's diary in 1895, however, reveals that the Zionist leader was not wholly unaware of the existence of a native population and of the problems it might cause:

> We shall have to spirit the penniless population across the border by procuring employment for it in the transit countries, while denying it any employment in our own country. . . . Both the process of expropriation and the removal of the poor must be carried out discreetly and circumspectly.[91]

Golda Meir's assertion in 1969 that "there was no such thing as Palestinians," was referred to in the previous section above. In the same interview Meir expanded on the basic proposition: "When was there an independent Palestinian people with a Palestinian state? It was either southern Syria before the First World War, and then it was a Palestine including Jordan. It was not as though there was a Palestinian people in Palestine considering itself as a Palestinian people and we came and threw them out and took their country away from them. They did not exist."[92]

The contemporary Palestinian writer Edward W. Said comments on this tenet of Zionist thought: ". . . in order to mitigate the presence of large numbers of natives on a desired land, the Zionists convinced themselves that these natives did not exist, then made it possible for them to exist only in the most rarefied forms."[93]

As will be seen in chapter 5, the perspective of the old-time Zionists was not wholly without basis in reality. Palestinian self-awareness was spawned and nourished by Zionism itself, by the incursion of an alien population and by the bitter experience of expulsion and exile. The apparent callousness of the assumption that Palestine was a land "without inhabitants" should not obscure the fact that Palestinian self-awareness is of recent vintage, a by-product, by and large, of Zionism itself. It is not wholly surprising, therefore, that the sudden appearance of Palestinian nationalism and the militancy of its expression through the Palestine Liberation Organization caused old-time Zionists to feel not only perplexed but, in a sense, betrayed. As Amos Elon wrote,

> They did not imagine that the Arabs who had been living there for centuries could possibly object to becoming a minority—a fully respected minority that would live in more comfort and wealth under the most liberal of regimes—through the advent of massive Jewish immigration from abroad. . . . There are few things as egocentric as a revivalist movement. For decades the Zionist leaders moved in a strange twilight zone, seeing the Arabs and at the same time not seeing them. Their attitude was a combination of blind spots and naivete, of wishful thinking, paternalistic benevolence, and that ignorance which is often a factor in international events, and sometimes their cause.[94]

Since the establishment of Israel and the expulsion of a large part of the Palestinian population, Israeli leaders—Begin's predecessors no less than Begin himself—have sought to deny the legitimacy of Palestinian nationalism and at the same time to absolve themselves from responsibility for the Palestinian refugees. They have done so by pointing out that there are twenty-one Arab states covering a vast territory and only one small Jewish state and arguing, accordingly, that it was the responsibility of the Arab states to take care of "their own." Asked in November 1977 whether Israel might ever accept a Palestinian homeland as called for by President Carter, former Prime Minister Meir commented, "I think not. It is not necessary for the Palestinians. It's dangerous for Israel. It is a threat to Israel's existence and of no necessity for Palestinian refugees."[95] "We rejoice," said Prime Minister Begin in early 1978, in the expression by the "great Arab people" of their right of self-determination in "twenty-one sovereign Arab states. . . ."[96] But as for Palestine, Begin contended on more than one occasion, the Jews were no less "Palestinian" than the Arabs of old Palestine. "Everyone should say Palestinian Arabs and Palestinian Jews."[97]

While mainstream Israelis, with a few exceptions,[98] adhered to their view of Palestinian nationalism as essentially bogus, as a thin disguise for the destruction of Israel, a few Israelis, outspoken but outside of the national consensus, argued not only for the authenticity of Palestinian nationalism but for the necessity of Israel—for the sake of its own long term security—coming to terms with it. "Even if in some miraculous way a temporary or permanent settlement is reached with the Arab states that are south, north, and east of us," wrote Arie Lova Eliav, "the problem of the Palestinian Arabs will still not be solved. We will not achieve true peace, and the Jewish-Arab conflict will not come to an end, until a solution is found to this problem."[99] The problem, in Eliav's perspective, was moral as well as practical: "We struggled for the right of self-determination of Jews, and succeeded. How can we deny this right to others then, to people who wish to see themselves as a nation?"[100] Nahum Goldmann, who would allow the Palestinians to decide freely between confederation with Jordan and a separate West Bank state,[101] rejected the claim that Palestinian nationalism was illegitimate or bogus because it was of recent vintage: "The Israeli and Zionist leaders refuted this claim when they raised their demand for the Jewish state without being able to show that a Jewish state and people had existed during the last two thousand years. In recent years dozens of states have been established that did not exist before, so what is this claim which says that no Palestinian state or entity can be established in the future because it did not exist in the past?"[102] What was really meant by the contention that "there are no Palestinians," wrote Meir Merhav, a senior correspondent of the *Jerusalem Post*, in 1977, was that "those who call themselves Palestinians *have no right to be*," because the label was false, masking their true, hostile purpose. The rejection on this basis of Palestinian self-determination, Merhav commented, was "partly the result of a false perception of reality, partly the outcome of faulty logic and partly the product of an irrational mixture of mystical beliefs, aggressive romanticism and traumatic fears, which cannot be upheld in today's world."[103]

When peace with Egypt became a palpable prospect in the wake of the Camp David accords, the Israeli doves turned their thoughts to the new possibilities, and new pitfalls, the accords opened up for a Palestinian settlement. Simha Flapan, editor of the journal *New Outlook*, warned that a separate peace would "not survive the tensions" of an unresolved Palestinian problem because Egypt could not, even if it wished, separate itself from the Arab world. He feared too that the vague provisions of the self-rule plan gave the Palestinians insufficient incentive to cooperate. Uri Avnery, a former member of the Knesset—who was to become a member again in 1979 as part of the minuscule, dissident Sheli party—observed that if the Palestine Liberation Organization and West Bank leaders had a

Zionist psychology of pragmatic incrementalism, they would take the opportunity offered by Camp David, inadequate though it was from their standpoint, and build on it just as the Zionists had built on their once modest opportunities, year by year and step by step, until at last they had their state. "But they cannot; it is not their way."[104] Arie Lova Eliav made the same point: the great Zionist leaders, he said, especially David Ben-Gurion, had known the art of the possible and prospered by taking opportunities as they arose, whereas the Palestine Liberation Organization, by contrast, would not take small openings. It was their way, rather, said Eliav, to demand all or nothing—and get nothing. If, he observed, the autonomy plan were left to the Begin government and the PLO they would collaborate to reduce the plan to a "shambles."[105]

Taking into account the prospect, as it seemed to them, of both Palestinian intransigence and resistance by the Begin government to a prompt, liberal implementation of the autonomy plan, the Israeli dissenters saw merit in the opening of dialogue between the United States and the Palestine Liberation Organization as a means of breaking the prospective impasse. Israel cannot be expected to move, said Flapan, "unless there is a thaw in U.S.–Palestinian relations."[106] Eliav urged that the United States pursue a two-part policy of bringing forth moderates within the Palestine Liberation Organization and applying pressure to the Begin government. Conceding that such an approach would draw the American administration into deep controversy, domestic as well as international, Eliav conceded, "It's a quagmire but not Vietnam."[107] The generally held view of the Israeli dissidents—a view that, as will be seen in chapter 5, was also strongly put forth by the West Bank Palestinian mayors—was that only the Palestine Liberation Organization could bring the West Bank leaders to participate in the Camp David autonomy plan, and that the only prospect of gaining the Palestine Liberation Organization's acquiescence was through some form of dialogue between the PLO and the United States. Eliav stressed the importance of seeking a simple, forthright, unqualified statement by the PLO: "We will recognize Israel if Israel will recognize us." If they did this, Eliav said, Begin's government would be "cornered," because the only good argument mainstream Israeli politicians had against dealing with the PLO was its refusal to disavow unequivocally the intention of annihilating Israel. This simple option, which the PLO thus far had declined to exercise, remained, in Eliav's view, the best hope for realizing Palestinian aspirations—"a million times better than terror."[108]

Unlike the vast majority of their countrymen, the Israeli dissenters accepted with equanimity the prospect of a Palestinian state. They did so in the belief that Palestinian nationalism was authentic, legitimate, and, in an age of national liberation movements, irrepressible; it posed, therefore, a far greater threat to Israel's security if forcibly suppressed than if allowed fulfillment within the territorial confines of the West Bank and Gaza. The dissenters had little doubt—in 1978—that the Camp David autonomy plan, after much conflict and commotion, would nonetheless evolve toward Palestinian self-determination. They expected this to occur because world opinion would support Palestinian aspirations; because the United States, in keeping with its own tradition, would be drawn toward a solution based on self-determination; and because Israel itself could be expected to become less fearful of Palestinian nationalism—and more responsive to its own democratic impulses—in the wake of peace with Egypt.

Whatever prospects the dissenters' views had for gaining wide acceptance through the evolution of events following the conclusion of Egyptian-Israeli peace, the "doves" remained, at the time of the signing of the peace, an isolated minority. Notwithstanding the extraordinary events culminating in the treaty-signing at Washington on March 26, 1979, the national consensus seemed solid: that Israel must have "defensible borders," extending well beyond those of 1967, and that, except insofar as Jordan might be defined as "Palestinian," there could be no separate Palestinian state. Perhaps even more important as a factor shaping their national policy, the Israeli people adhered still to the ancient Jewish conviction that they were a people alone in the world and that the only difference of attitude toward them among the nations of the world was between those who actively sought Israel's destruction and those who would be indifferent to it. All the assurances and exertions on their behalf from President Truman's time to President Carter's notwithstanding, Israelis continued to find reasons to doubt the loyalty and steadfastness of the United States. They could rely, they felt sure, only on themselves and on the Jews of the "Diaspora," welcoming help where they could find it but trusting no one.

"Begin, Begin, King of Israel"

Lost to view in the polemics and fireworks generated by the Israeli election campaign of 1981 was the survival, virtually unimpaired, of the Labor-Likud national consensus against Palestinian self-determination and Israeli withdrawal from the occupied territories. The Camp David autonomy talks had been suspended since August 1980, having gotten

virtually nowhere in the preceding fifteen months. The Begin government, far from moving closer to the Egyptian position, had, if anything,
added to its stringent conditions for Palestinian autonomy. The Labor
Alignment, under the leadership of Shimon Peres, reiterated its proposal
for "territorial compromise," that is, for partition of the West Bank along
the lines of the Allon Plan. Rejecting a Palestinian state and negotiations
with the PLO, Shimon Peres reiterated Labor's willingness to relinquish
parts of a demilitarized West Bank to Jordan—"itself already in reality a
Palestinian state because a majority of its citizens are Palestinians." This
plan came to be known as the "Jordanian option."[109]

At the outset of the campaign a sizable Labor victory seemed all but
certain. The nation was beset with economic and social ills, including an
annual inflation rate exceeding 130 percent in 1980, government spending
exceeding the gross national product, declining immigration, and a high
rate of emigration. The Begin government had come to seem incompetent
in the management of domestic affairs and its original Cabinet had largely
disintegrated. Begin, however, managed, as the campaign progressed, to
draw public attention away from domestic economic issues to the emotionally charged issue of national security, with its connotations of national survival. Peres could not compete. He chastised Begin, with little effect,
for relinquishing all of Sinai to Egypt and stressed the essentiality of
"defensible borders" on the Golan Heights and at the Jordan River.[110]
Begin, for his part, cited the peace treaty with Egypt and challenged
Peres's claim that he could successfully negotiate a "Jordanian solution."
On June 4, 1980, Begin had announced that a series of leaders of previous
Labor governments had met secretly at various times with King Hussein,
had offered "territorial compromise," and had been rebuffed. Begin said
his own foreign minister, Moshe Dayan, had also held unsuccessful, secret
negotiations with King Hussein on the future of the West Bank.[111] Raising
the ultimate bugbear of Israeli politics, Begin had even suggested, in
August 1980, that "the election of the alignment would lead to an
Arafatian state in Judea and Samaria."[112]

Whatever advantage Labor might have derived from the "Jordanian
option" was negated by King Hussein's outspoken rejection of it. Increasingly alienated from the United States since the Camp David agreements, King Hussein had actively supported Iraq in its war against Iran,
stating that an Iraqi victory would be the beginning of "victory here in
Palestine."[113] In January 1981 the king told a group of visiting Americans
that, from the Jordanian perspective, the essentials of peace included Israeli
withdrawal from all territory occupied in 1967 including Arab Jerusalem,

and Palestinian self-determination including the right to form a Palestinian state. The "Palestinians alone" had the right to determine their future, the king said; to that there was no alternative for Jordan, and "no substitute" for the PLO as representative of the Palestinian people. In an apparent allusion to the traditional American commitment to the principle of self-determination, and to the exception made in the case of the Palestinian people, King Hussein added: "We resent the treatment of our just cause by a different yardstick from that applied to other just causes in the world."[114] The king reiterated his unequivocal position at the Islamic summit meeting in Taif, Saudi Arabia, on January 29: "There is no Jordanian option. There are no options. There is a reality—Palestine and the Palestinians."[115]

Unable to make a persuasive case for its Jordanian option, the Israeli Labor party was reduced to complaining more of Begin's foreign policy methods than of his policies. The raid on Iraq's nuclear reactor on June 7, coming in the wake of Begin's tough stand against the Syrian missiles in Lebanon, galvanized Israeli patriotic feeling and further strengthened the Likud's electoral prospects. Peres was at pains to insist that he approved the raid but accused Begin of timing it for electoral purposes and criticized Begin for failing to explore diplomatic alternatives.[116]

Begin, for his part, assailed the opposition for questioning the Iraqi raid, claimed credit for expanding Israeli settlement in the occupied territory, and ridiculed the Jordanian option. He told a rally that his government had developed 55 new settlements: "You should see Judea and Samaria now: this empty country that even the British said you couldn't build on. . . ." And as for the Jordanian option: "Abba Eban would give 70 percent of Judea and Samaria to King Hussein. And he says he would turn it over to Arafat." On occasion after occasion excited crowds, taking up the Biblical cry from the time of King David, chanted, "Begin, Begin, King of Israel."[117]

With strong support from Israel's Sephardic Jews—those with origins in Arab countries—Begin's Likud won a narrow victory, with 48 seats in the Knesset to Labor's 47 seats. To gain a bare majority of 61 Begin formed a coalition with three small religious parties, which extracted major concessions on religious and educational matters as the price of their support. Begin retained as foreign minister Yitzhak Shamir, a strong supporter of Jewish settlements on the West Bank who had opposed the peace treaty with Egypt. The post of defense minister went to Ariel Sharon, the former general and minister of agriculture in the first Begin government, in which capacity he had conducted an aggressive settlements policy on the West Bank. Sharon in the past had advocated the displacement of King Hussein so that Jordan could become a Palestinian state. The new Begin government was thus more staunchly committed than before the election to the expansion of Jewish settlements in the West Bank and to constricted conditions of Palestinian autonomy.

Nor was the reelected Begin in a mood to endure pressures and reproaches from the United States. American criticisms of the Israeli air attack on Beirut on July 17, 1981, in which 300 civilians were killed, prompted Begin to retort, "I don't want to hear anything from the Americans about hitting civilian targets. I know exactly what Americans did in Vietnam."[118]

"Tenacious Solitude"

Pride in self-reliance, the direct outgrowth of the Jewish sense of aloneness in a hostile world, coexists in Israeli minds with the incongruous but incontestable fact of Israel's dependence on the United States. The beneficiary of by far the largest American foreign aid program in the world,[119] Israel recognizes that neither its chronically strained and inflation-ridden economy nor its military superiority over its Arab neighbors could be sustained without approximately $1 billion a year in American military assistance—half of it grants and about $800 million a year in economic aid—to say nothing of periodic supplementary assistance, such as that provided to compensate Israel for its Sinai bases in the wake of the peace treaty with Egypt, and sizable annual contributions from private individuals and organizations in the United States.[120] The conviction of self-reliance in Israeli minds cannot, therefore, represent a literal belief in Israel's ability to make its own way in the world unassisted. It appears rather to be a kind of inspirational national myth, the practical consequence of which is to induce an extreme resistance to actual or perceived pressure from abroad and to foster the conviction that, even if Israel cannot survive on its own economic resources, it can and must rely on its own human resources, military and other. Something of this order apparently was what was meant by Abba Eban's assertion that "a nation must be capable of tenacious solitude."[121]

One major manifestation of this attitude has been an extreme mistrust of international, including American, guarantees as the basis of peace in the Middle East. "History has taught them to place no faith in third-party assurances that they will be safe," wrote I. L. Kenen, former executive director of the American-Israeli Public Affairs Committee.[122] This refrain is echoed across the Israeli political spectrum. "We have never asked for guarantees," Prime Minister Begin said on December 13, 1977. "When the test comes, guarantees do not stand the test. . . . Guarantees do not give you any security whatsoever. We are experienced people. We have survived. . . . We can sustain ourselves. We don't believe in guarantees."[123] On March 23, 1978 Begin said: "We don't want even one American soldier to fight our battles. . . . We can sustain our independence. From time to time we need some tools. . . ."[124] The same theme was emphasized by Begin's predecessors. "There are no international guarantees," Prime Minister Rabin said in 1975. "A bilateral American guarantee would be equally meaningless—wrong from the very beginning." On the same occasion Foreign Minister Yigal Allon commented that, beyond seeking assurances of a steady supply of modern arms, Israel would not wish to be a "burden" to the United States; nor indeed would Israel dare to rely upon the United States in any other way, Allon said, because "the mood is changing; isolationism is growing; people can change their minds."[125] Arie Lova Eliav, at the other end of the spectrum, wrote, "The Americans will help us fight, but they will not fight for us. They will not shed their blood for our existence."[126] The instance most frequently cited by Israelis in support of their contention that even an American guarantee is not to be trusted is the failure of the Johnson administration to have challenged President Nasser's reimposition in May 1967 of the Egyptian blockade of the Gulf of Aqaba—despite Secretary of State John Foster Dulles's *aide-mémoire* of February 11, 1957, issued prior to Israel's final withdrawal from Sinai in the wake of the 1956 Suez War, stating that the United States recognized the Gulf of Aqaba as an international waterway and that the United States "is prepared to exercise the right of free and innocent passage and to join with others to secure general recognition of this right."[127]

In the years following the October War of 1973, in which Israel was caught by surprise and required a massive resupply program from the United States to turn the tide, Israel built up its stockpiles to a level that it was hoped would enable the Jewish state to win a new war without need of additional American supplies. Such a force level, combined with plans for a quick, decisive victory, would also free Israel from foreign intervention, such as that mounted by the Nixon administration in 1973, to compel a cease-fire before a clear victory could be won. In an analysis by a Defense Department official published in the *Armed Forces Journal International* in 1977, it was stated that the Israeli buildup and requests for American assistance into the mid-1980s were of a magnitude that would give Israel the capability to launch lightning offensives against all of its Arab neighbors before the great powers could intervene or before an oil boycott could have effect. The number of medium tanks, for example, requested for the decade from 1976 to 1986 would approach the number to be deployed by the United States within the North Atlantic Treaty Organization. Israel would thus gain virtual immunity from the kind of pressure applied by Secretary of State Henry Kissinger to gain the cease-fire in the October 1973 War.[128] The article was denounced by the Anti-Defamation League of B'nai B'rith as "anti-Israeli and anti-Jewish."[129] In addition to its power in conventional weapons, Israel has been assumed by the Central Intelligence Agency, at least since the mid-1970s, to possess an indeterminate number of usable nuclear weapons.[130]

Israel's doubts about American reliability, and the concomitant concern for self-reliance, were intensified in 1978–79 by the termination of the American treaty commitment to Taiwan, and even more by events connected with the Iranian revolution. Having itself recognized the People's Republic of China in January 1950—one of the first noncommunist states to do so—Israel made no official comment on President Carter's announcement of December 15, 1978, that the United States would sever formal relations and terminate its security treaty with Taiwan. There was, however, unofficial commentary. An assistant to Prime Minister Begin was quoted as saying: "So now we know how the United States honors its treaty commitments, if Vietnam weren't proof enough." The Hebrew newspaper *Ha'aretz* cited Carter's action as "proof of the inconsistency of the Americans, and of a cynicism which does not shrink from betraying an ally."[131]

Far more drastic in its impact on Israel was the Iranian revolution. The cutoff of what had been Israel's principal source of oil, the expulsion of the Israelis from their mission in Teheran, and the warm embrace of the Palestine Liberation Organization by the revolutionary regime shocked Israelis and intensified their sense of isolation in a sea of now not only Arab but Islamic hostility. The downfall of the shah wrenched from Israel its one friend in the region, and the prompt recognition by the United States of the new government reinforced Israel's doubts about America's will and ability to protect its friends. "As Iran has shown," an unnamed Israeli official was quoted as commenting, "the U.S. is no longer in a position to say to anybody, 'Trust us. We will stand behind you.'"[132]

Even before his triumphant return from exile, the Ayatollah Khomeini had declared his movement's rejection of Israel and refusal of oil sales and other dealings with Israel as long as it was at war with Arab states.[133] When the revolutionary Islamic government took power in February 1979, the Palestine Liberation Organization, which said it had trained Iranian revolutionaries with its own units, hailed the victory of the Ayatollah's forces as a triumph of Muslim people over "repression, imperialism, Zionism and colonialism."[134] Oil sales to Israel were terminated as promised, and in mid-February 1979 Chairman Yasser Arafat of the Palestine Liberation Organization was received as an honored guest in Teheran, where he formally opened PLO offices in the building that had previously housed the Israeli mission. "In the name of the Palestinian fighters," Arafat proclaimed on that occasion, "I undertake to free the land of Palestine with you under the leadership of Imam Khomeini."[135]

In the winter of 1979 the Iranian revolution drove Israel in two, somewhat conflicting directions with respect to the still uncompleted peace treaty with Egypt. On the one hand, it intensified Israel's dependence on the Sinai and Gulf of Suez oil fields, which were to be given up under the projected treaty. On February 3, 1979 the Israeli Minister of Justice, Shmuel Tamir, declared that "with the new developments in Iran, people all over the world will agree with us that unless our permanent supply of oil is assured there is no point for Israel to quit Sinai."[136] On the other hand, the increased isolation of Israel and uncertain prospects arising from what appeared to be a spreading Islamic revival, made peace with Egypt more attractive and may have provided incentive to conclude the treaty before the Camp David framework fell apart. Already fearful of the military possibilities of the recently formed alliance of Iraq and Syria—which was to prove short-lived—Israelis began to fear that Iran might join with Iraq, Syria, and Jordan as an active military partner against Israel. How and in what ways these two factors—oil and the fear of a hostile Iran—interacted to help produce the Egyptian-Israeli peace treaty remains a matter of speculation. It seems probable, however, that the prospect of deepening solitude, combined with the specter of a formidable military coalition on its eastern front, gave significant added incentive for the prompt conclusion of peace with Egypt.

Throughout the protracted, tortured "peace process" that culminated in the Egyptian-Israeli peace treaty of March 1979, the Israeli negotiators, in further evidence of their penchant for "tenacious solitude," responded with resentment and defiance whenever they perceived themselves to be under pressure from the United States. In the final, climactic stage of negotiations in March 1979, after President Carter addressed the Knesset in Jerusalem, Prime Minister Begin commented pointedly in his reply: "No, it is not true that you came to bring pressure on us. I may add that if pressure had been exerted on us, we would have rejected it."[137] The statement was similar to many that had been made over the years, representing a deep-seated sensitivity to foreign pressure, which, even in its milder forms, was perceived as an intolerable incursion on Israel's sovereign independence. Having survived at the sufferance of others through the centuries of the Diaspora, the Jews, gathered at last in their own homeland, took it as cardinal to their statehood that they would neither be dictated to by others nor allow their survival to depend on the good will—or guarantees—of others. Recognizing this acute sensitivity, American leaders made it a practice to assure Israel on all possible occasions that continued American support, including military and economic assistance, would never be used as a lever on Israeli policy. "With or without a peace treaty," President Carter told the Knesset on March 12, 1979, "the U.S. will always be at Israel's side."[138]

Israelis have exhibited a kind of ambivalence toward their dependence on the United States and the power that the United States could, if it chose, exert on them. On the one hand, they have been acutely, painfully aware of their vulnerability to American pressure; on the other hand, they have shown confidence in their ability to defy pressure, and that confidence, with few exceptions, has proven justified. On the one hand, as indicated above, they have expressed a lack of confidence in the will and ability of the United States to honor its commitments; on the other hand, they have appeared to have little doubt that American military and economic support would continue to be forthcoming, while also attaching great importance to assurances of continuing American support. The desire for assurances was in evidence in the Israeli attitude toward the "Memorandum of Agreement" with the United States relating to security that accompanied the Israeli-Egyptian peace treaty. The agreement, containing qualified assurances of American support for Israel in the event of Egypt's violation of the treaty, was, according to the State Department, eagerly solicited by Israel,[139] and, despite its highly qualified provisions, welcomed by Prime Minister Begin as a "beautiful document . . . well written, and what it contains is very important."[140]

The complex and less than wholly consistent attitude of Israelis toward American guarantees would seem to be explained by the following three factors, in ascending order of importance: first, official American assurances that aid would not be used as an instrument of pressure; second, the historical familiarity of the Jews with having to take risks and live dangerously; and third, the reliance of Israel on the Jewish community of the United States. Implicit—and sometimes explicit—in the strong Israeli preference for self-reliance has been the belief that Jews could ultimately only rely on Jews. "The lack of confidence in guarantees," Nahum

Goldmann wrote in 1975, ". . . is the result of distrust of non-Jewish promises. . . ."[141] Or, in the more pungent phrase attributed to David Ben-Gurion, "It is not important what the *Goyim* are saying but what Jews are doing."[142] The application of these attitudes to Israel's relations with the United States goes far to explain the paradox of deep mistrust combined with high confidence. As Arie Lova Eliav put it: "In one sense we relate to a superpower having vested interests of its own in the region, and in another sense we are dealing with a state where six million Jews, constituting about one-half of the Jewish Diaspora, now live."[143]

Whatever doubts Israelis of otherwise diverse persuasion have harbored as to the reliability of the United States in its superpower capacity, they have had few apparent doubts as to the commitment of American Jewry to Israel or as to the influence that American Jews could bring to bear upon the policy of the United States. Israeli officials had become familiar visitors to the halls of Congress and the American political hustings long before the accession of the Begin government in 1977. At that time it was thought possible that a rift would open between the American Jewish leadership and the Likud government, but this fear proved short-lived. Even before Begin made his own first visit to the United States as prime minister, his personal representative, Samuel Katz, told American Jews, "We are confident that the Jewish community in America will stand out courageously and challenge its government if it becomes necessary."[144] On September 30, 1977, in advance of a tour of American Jewish communities, Foreign Minister Dayan identified American-Jewish opinion leaders as Israel's "key and lever" in winning American public support for the Begin government's policies. "They should go and explain to the Senate, the Congress, the press, the communities, on television and to their gentile friends."[145] In the first week of March 1979, when peace with Egypt still seemed uncertain, Prime Minister Begin, after talks with President Carter in Washington, addressed a conference of Jewish leaders in New York. Observing that the American Jewish community wielded great influence, Begin added, "When the time comes, don't hesitate to use that influence."[146]

Because of the influence of American Jews, Israelis have felt confident of their own influence on the American political process. Support for Israel has been a political imperative for every American administration, Eliav wrote in the early seventies, and "the most active and influential factor in this commitment is the tremendous identification of American Jewry with Israel."[147] When President Carter flew to Cairo and Jerusalem in March 1979 in a last, desperate, and finally successful bid to secure the Egyptian-

Israeli treaty, his personal position was one of extreme vulnerability but also of a peculiar kind of strength—the kind accruing to a politician with nothing left to lose if his gamble failed. The Israeli leaders, and President Sadat no doubt as well, could not have been unaware of the president's low standing in the polls at home and his uncertain prospects for a reelection campaign in 1980. Politically if not substantively the president appeared to need the treaty more than Begin and Sadat did, and this gave the two Middle Eastern leaders significant bargaining power. Asked if Israel might send the president back to Washington without an agreement, an Israeli official described as being close to Begin commented, "There's been some discussion about whether to send him back to Washington or back to Atlanta."[148] This power over the American president was in fact too great to be safely used: if he were sent home empty-handed, he might have nothing to lose by resorting to a policy—hitherto disavowed by his administration—of political and economic sanctions against the recalcitrant parties. Under these circumstances making peace may have seemed the more prudent course of action.

Occupation and Colonization

The focus of American policy shifted after the Egyptian-Israeli peace treaty—to the unresolved Palestinian question—but the underlying dilemma of American policy did not. If anything, it intensified because, as attention now shifted to the intractable, core issue of the Arab-Israeli conflict, the United States, more than ever, was forced to confront the question of the adequacy of its policy to its interests. The issue was the ability of the United States, as a "full partner" to the peace process, to translate the second Camp David framework, calling for a resolution of the "Palestinian problem in all its aspects," into the reality of full autonomy if not ultimately self-determination for the Palestinian people in the West Bank and Gaza.

Time worked against the Camp David peace process and against the American objective. The target date for agreement on Palestinian autonomy, May 1980, passed with neither agreement nor prospect of it, and all the while Israel continued to expand its settlements and consolidate its control of the occupied territories. The settlements became a key symbol of, and principal obstacle to, the ability of the American government to deliver on its promise.

Even the most humane of military occupations creates intolerable strains between the occupier and the subject population, especially if the occupation is of long duration. The Israeli occupation of the Arab-populated West Bank and Gaza Strip has been one of the less onerous of modern times, but the benefits accruing to both sides from the comparative mildness of the occupation were largely dissipated as it extended into the second decade beyond the 1967 war during which the territories were seized. When an occupation is described as *comparatively* mild, the emphasis, in any event, should fall on the word "comparatively." By definition an occupation regime is based on foreign force rather than indigenous consent; the subject population has only those rights that are accorded to it by the occupier, which is to say it has no *rights* at all in the sense of legal entitlement, but only certain privileges that may be withdrawn for punitive purposes or simply at the caprice of the occupier. In such circumstances a relationship of good will, or mutual trust and respect, must be judged impossible, even if, as in the case of the Israeli-occupied territories, the subject population has enjoyed a measure of economic prosperity. In the absence of trust and good will the police power becomes paramount, and the occupier, whether or not he wishes it, is compelled to employ, in one degree or another, police state methods, including arbitrary arrest, detention without trial, and collective punishment.

The single most agitated issue involving the occupied territories, however, because of its implications for a permanent Israeli presence, has been the continuing emplacement there of Jewish settlements. The legal status of the settlements depends on the meaning and applicability to them of the fourth Geneva Convention of 1949, which relates to the protection of civilians in time of war. Article 49 of that convention (to which Israel, the United States, and the principal Arab countries are all signatories) states that "individual or mass forcible transfers, as well as deportations of protected persons from occupied territory to the territory of the Occupying Power or to that of any other country, occupied or not, are prohibited, regardless of their motive." The only exception allowed is evacuation for reasons of "the security of the population" or for "imperative military reasons." In its other most pertinent clause, Article 49 states that "the Occupying Power shall not deport or transfer parts of its own civilian population into the territory it occupies."[149]

The official Israeli position has been that the fourth Geneva Convention did not prohibit its settlements and, in any event, was not binding on Israel as to the West Bank. An "overall" reading of Article 49, it was contended in an official Israeli statement of 1977, made it evident that the purpose of the article was to protect local populations from displacement and that the transfer of parts of the occupying power's own civilian populations into the territory occupied was prohibited only if it involved the displacement of the local populations. "Since no Arab inhabitants have been displaced by Jewish settlements," the document concluded, "it is clear that the situation envisaged in Article 49 of the Geneva Convention does not apply to the Jewish settlements in question." The document also made a moral case for the Jewish settlements: that peace and prosperity were advanced by Jews and Arabs living together, and further, that "the notion that Judea-Samaria should be the one place in the world today where Jews would be barred from living is reminiscent of the racist 'Judenrein' notion developed forty years ago by the Nazis."[150]

The other Israeli legal argument for the settlements has been that Israel could not properly be regarded as an "occupying power" on which the Geneva Convention was binding because the party that was driven out in 1967, Jordan, was not itself the "legitimate sovereign." So contended Yehuda Avi Blum, Professor of International Law at Hebrew University in Jerusalem, and subsequently chief Israeli representative to the United Nations, in testimony in October 1977 before a subcommittee of the United States Senate Committee on the Judiciary under the chairmanship of Senator James Abourezk of South Dakota. Blum, who appeared before the subcommittee on the recommendation of the Israeli Embassy in Washington, said that Jordan had itself acquired the West Bank in the 1948 war by using force in violation of the United Nations Charter in the wake of Arab rejection of the United Nations partition plan of 1947, and that this "could not give rise to any valid legal title." Since it was not a legitimate, internationally recognized "sovereign" that was expelled from the West Bank in 1967, it followed, in Professor Blum's analysis, that Israel was not bound by the obligations of an occupying power as spelled out in the fourth Geneva Convention. Israel, Blum argued, had a better "relative" title to the West Bank, as part of the old Palestine mandate, than anybody else, and he concluded, "The moment Israel wishes to extend its law and jurisdiction and administration to Judea and Samaria, it is entitled to do so. . . ."[151]

No other state or party, including the United States, has accepted the Israeli claim to the legality of its settlements in the occupied territories. On October 28, 1977, the United Nations General Assembly adopted a resolution declaring that the settlements "have no legal validity and constitute a serious obstruction" to Middle East peace efforts. The vote was 131 to 1, with only Israel opposed.[152] In the debate preceding the vote, Israel's ambassador to the United Nations said that the intent of the resolution was to exclude Jews from the occupied territories simply because they were Jews, indicating a "vicious, anti-Semitic, Nazi philosophy behind this resolution."[153] The United States and six other countries abstained.

The legal basis for the worldwide consensus against the legality of the

Jewish settlements was spelled out before Senator Abourezk's subcommittee by W. T. Mallison, Professor of Law at George Washington University. Asserting that the Geneva Conventions of 1949 were indeed applicable to the territories occupied by Israel, Professor Mallison noted that the common Article 2 of all four conventions stated that they "shall apply to all cases of declared war or of any other armed conflict which may arise . . . even if the state of war is not recognized" and further, that they applied to "all" situations of partial or total occupation of territory. Emphasizing that the conventions, under their own explicit terms, applied to the *facts* of an international conflict and not to its *merits* as interpreted by one of the belligerents, Mallison went on to observe that "the negotiating history makes it clear, since the application of the conventions is mandatory, that questions as to *de jure* titles to territory are not involved and that the convention must be applied in occupied territory whatever the claims concerning the *de jure* status of that territory." As to Blum's claim that Israel was not bound by the fourth Geneva Convention because it did not regard Jordan as having been the legitimate sovereign before 1967, Mallison commented that "the idea that, in order to apply the law of belligerent occupation, it is necessary for the belligerent to recognize the displaced government's title to the territory, finds no support in either the text of the convention or its negotiating history. In addition, it is contrary to the well-established customary law based upon state practice." Even during the American Civil War, Professor Mallison recalled, the United States treated the Confederacy as being subject to the international law of belligerent occupation. Referring again to the Israeli claim that Jordan lacked title to the West Bank because it had acquired that territory, in Israel's view, by aggression, he commented that "if the humanitarian law were to be changed so that its application was made contingent upon recognition by the belligerent occupant of the justness of the war aims of its opponent, it is perfectly clear that the humanitarian law would be rarely, if ever, applied." The illegality of the Israeli settlements was established, Mallison concluded, by the clear and explicit prohibition of the sixth clause of Article 49 of the fourth Geneva Convention, that "the Occupying Power shall not deport or transfer parts of its own civilian population into the territory it occupies." There were, he noted, "no qualifications or exceptions to this provision."[154]

Subscribing to the international consensus, the United States government, prior to the accession of the Reagan administration, took the official position that the Israeli settlements were illegal and an obstacle to peace, but also made clear that the United States would take no action to enforce that view. President Carter said on July 28, 1977: "This matter of settlements in the occupied territories has always been characterized by our Government, by me and my predecessors as an illegal action."[155] Carter reiterated this stand in a news conference a month later: the settlements, he said, were in violation of the Geneva Convention, therefore illegal, and an "unnecessary obstacle to peace," but he also disavowed the use of American leverage, such as Israel's reliance on American military assistance, to bring about Israeli compliance. "Obviously," he said, "we could exert pressure on Israel in other ways, but I have no intention to do so."[156]

Over the next year, culminating in the Camp David meeting of September 1978, Carter raised the issue of the settlements with Israeli officials on several occasions, but each such exchange was followed by disagreement as to what, if anything, had been agreed. When Prime Minister Begin visited the United States in July 1977, and again when Foreign Minister Dayan came in September 1977, the president was left with the understanding, as he later expressed it, that no new settlements would be authorized although existing settlements might be expanded under the aegis of the military.[157] A new settlement was established at Shiloh on the West Bank in January 1978, ostensibly as an archaeological exploration project. Carter sent a personal message to Begin expressing his "regret" at the emplacement of "another illegal settlement," and he added: "However, I am confident that Prime Minister Begin will honor the commitment personally made to me, and thus will not permit this settlement to go forward."[158] Members of the Gush Emunim, or "Faith Bloc," an organization committed to Israel's Biblical claim to the West Bank (which they refer to by the Biblical designation of "Judea and Samaria") told reporters at their settlement site at Shiloh that the archaeological explanation was a "cover" and that they planned to establish a permanent community. In addition to the settlement at Shiloh, three new emplacements, described as previously planned military outposts, were established in January 1978.[159] Unnamed American "officials" told reporters on January 30, 1978, that Foreign Minister Dayan had assured President Carter the previous September that no new civilian settlements would be established in the occupied territories for a year, but that Israeli officials had subsequently redefined Dayan's commitment as applying only to the remainder of the year 1977.[160] Dayan himself denied that he had pledged an end to new settlements. He told the Knesset on February 1, 1978, that he had in fact told Carter the previous September that future governments of Israel, like all past governments, would continue to establish Jewish settlements in Judea and Samaria, and that all he had promised the president was that, "taking into consideration the special situation of intensive peace negotiations with the Arabs, land settlement in the next few months will be in the framework of military camps."[161]

So confused was the situation in mid-winter 1978 as to what Israel had or had not promised with respect to the settlements, that the *New York Times*, although frequently sympathetic to Israeli policy, commented that the effect of Israel's various explanations of its settlements policy was "to portray Israel's leaders as tricksters determined to drive huge tractors through the loopholes of solemn policy declarations."[162] The *Washington Post* found Begin's policy "provocative and devious," and commented, "A policy of sneaking new settlements in between the lines of assurance to the United States is offensive to the United States, and to Jimmy Carter personally."[163]

Confusion as to what had or had not been promised to the United States continued, but there seemed little basis for doubt that the Begin government was committed to a policy of continuing Jewish settlements and land acquisitions on the occupied West Bank. Controversies arose between West Bank Palestinians and the occupation authorities with respect to land titles and acquisitions, and in some instances seizures of land were restrained by court orders and in others the Israeli government backed down.[164] In May 1978 Defense Minister Weizman acknowledged that the "archaeological dig" at Shiloh was not that, but, as the Gush Emunim readily acknowledged, a settlement.[165] On August 13, 1978, the Israeli government acknowledged, in the wake of news leaks, that the Cabinet's security committee on June 28 had secretly approved five new settlements for the Jordan River Valley.[166] The next day, in the wake of foreign and domestic criticism, the Cabinet shelved plans for the five settlements until after the forthcoming summit meeting at Camp David.[167] Anfractuous tactics notwithstanding, the Begin government made no secret of its basic commitment. "Jews in the land of Israel have a right to settle there," the prime minister had said in February 1978.[168] A spokesman for Gush Emunim summed up the settlements policy candidly in a news conference in June 1978: "There has never been settlement in Israel without confiscation of land."[169]

The Camp David summit meeting of September 1978 was followed immediately by another rancorous American-Israeli disagreement as to what in fact had been agreed with respect to settlements. In his triumphant address to a joint meeting of Congress on September 18, President Carter announced that "Israel has agreed that the legitimate rights of the Palestinian people will be recognized. After the signing of this framework and during the negotiations concerning Palestinian self-government, no new Israeli settlements will be established in this area. The issue of future settlements will be decided among the negotiating parties."[170] Differing sharply with the president, Prime Minister Begin, as has been noted,[171] insisted in the days after Camp David that he had not agreed to a suspension of Israeli settlements for the projected five-year negotiating period on Palestinian rights, but only to a moratorium for the three months within which Egypt and Israel were to try to conclude a treaty.[172] As a result of this disagreement a planned exchange of letters among the three Camp David parties regarding the suspension of new settlements never took place. While Begin, back in Israel after the Camp David meeting, reiterated his firm stand on the settlements,[173] President Carter insisted, on September 27, 1978, that he had "a very clear understanding" with Begin that there would be no new settlements during the five-year period of negotiations on the permanent status of the West Bank and Gaza, and the president warned that "a very serious problem" would arise if Begin persisted in his contention that he had agreed only, in effect, to a three-month moratorium.[174] Testifying before a House subcommittee the next day, Assistant Secretary of State Saunders said, "The understanding we have is that as long as serious negotiations are going on there would be no new settlements."[175] President Carter, however, appeared on September 28 to view the matter less seriously than he had the day before, saying at his news conference that his disagreement with Begin—with whom he had spoken on the telephone since the previous day about what had been agreed regarding the settlements—was "an honest difference of opinion" that "would certainly be no obstacle to the progress toward peace." Disavowing any charge of bad faith on Begin's part, the president stressed, no fewer than three times, that the disagreement was "an honest difference of opinion."[176]

The United States thereafter reverted to its traditional policy of verbal disapproval of the settlements while Israel, apparently convinced that the United States would not or could not back its protests with either action or sanctions, adhered to its policy of expanding the settlements and ignoring protests. "Settlements," Begin declared in the Knesset on March 20, 1979, "are part of the security setup of the state of Israel," and "the security of Israel is the center of our lives."[177] On March 22, 1979, the United Nations Security Council voted to establish a three-member panel to "examine the situation relating to settlements in the occupied Arab territories." The United States abstained on the vote, and Israel made it known that the panel would not be admitted to the occupied territories.[178] The Israeli

Cabinet on April 22 approved the creation of two new settlements, one of which, Shiloh, was actually over a year old but was now, in effect, legitimized. The State Department revealed the next day that Ambassador Samuel Lewis had urged the Israelis not to proceed with the two settlements, and the State Department spokesman also recalled that Israel and the United States "had different interpretations of the agreement reached at Camp David" regarding the settlements, adding that "We are continuing to have discussions with Israel on that issue."[179] Secretary of State Vance, in testimony before a Senate subcommittee on April 26, observed that Israel was no longer abiding by a freeze on new settlements, that this represented a "serious, difficult problem," and that the United States still adhered to its belief that the settlements were "contrary to law and an obstacle to peace."[180]

The Israeli position with respect to these protests may be summed up in a statement that columnist Joseph Kraft reported was made to him by Foreign Minister Dayan: "I know you Americans think you're going to force us out of the West Bank. But we're here and you're in Washington. What will you do if we maintain settlements? Squawk? What will you do if we keep the army there? Send troops?"[181] President Carter, in effect, concurred with Dayan's assessment of the American role. Asked at a news conference about the two new settlements authorized by the Israeli Cabinet in April 1979, and whether, in view of the costs to be incurred by the United States to implement the Egyptian-Israeli peace treaty, it would not be reasonable to expect Israel to desist from a settlements policy that violated international law, the president reiterated his position that the settlements were indeed illegal and an obstacle to peace, and he added, "But there's a limit to what we can do to impose our will on a sovereign nation."[182]

Apart from their purported defensive value, the expanding West Bank settlements have served to create new facts, which many Israelis hope will be unalterable. Established communities, with extensive housing and public services and a settled population, may reduce the prospect of a negotiated Israeli withdrawal from the West Bank to a practical impossibility. As time passes and the settlements grow and consolidate, it becomes steadily more difficult—and even comes to seem unreasonable—for the United States to press for withdrawal. In due course the cause of Palestinian self-determination may thus be reduced to ceremonial litany, comparable, say, to the annual rhetorical pieties in which American congressmen engage on behalf of the "captive nations" of Eastern Europe. To whatever degree the West Bank settlements represented a defense system or the carrying out of a Biblical mandate, they also represented—

and that perhaps most of all—a political strategy, outside of the peace process and all other avenues of diplomacy, to determine, finally, the outcome of the struggle for Palestine.

While the settlements grew larger and more numerous, American policy grew more ineffectual. On March 1, 1980, the United States joined in voting for a unanimously adopted United Nations Security Council resolution condemning the settlements as illegal and calling on Israel to cease building new settlements and to dismantle the existing ones. The United States ambassador to the United Nations, Donald F. McHenry, said after casting his vote: "We regard settlements in the occupied territories as illegal under international law, and we consider them to be an obstacle to the successful outcome to the current negotiations, which are aimed at a comprehensive, just and lasting peace in the Middle East."[183]

The American vote provoked angry protests from Israel and its American supporters. On March 3 President Carter announced that the American vote had been a mistake, the result of an error in the transmission of his instructions to Ambassador McHenry, and that the United States should have abstained. Secretary of State Vance accepted responsibility for the "failure of communications," but the outcry was not stilled. Prominent senators challenged the credibility of the administration's explanation; the Israeli Cabinet, unassuaged by Carter's disavowal, expressed "deep resentment" of the American vote for the "repugnant resolution;" White House political advisers expressed fears for the loss of Jewish votes in upcoming Democratic primaries in Illinois and New York; and American Jewish leaders were only partially mollified by the president's disavowal of the vote. While the American reversal failed to mollify Israel and its American supporters, it elicited expressions of scorn and dismay on the part of European as well as Arab countries. Ambassador McHenry judged that the United States had gained "the worst of all possible worlds."[184]

Whatever its other effects, the Security Council resolution of March 1, 1980, had no effect on Israel's settlements policy. Having previously confined the Jewish settlements to sparsely populated locations, Israel in early 1980 authorized Jewish civilians to settle in the occupied Palestinian city of Hebron. In March additional Arab-owned lands were expropriated in East Jerusalem for a Jewish housing project. The United States deplored the action, which it feared might disrupt or prejudge the outcome of the "delicate negotiations" then still in progress on Palestinian autonomy.[185] The American protest, following the Security Council vote of March 1 and its retraction, was, like many preceding protests, ignored.

American policy toward the Israeli settlements was debated in the

Senate on June 17, 1980. On that occasion Senator Adlai E. Stevenson of Illinois offered an amendment to the foreign aid bill purporting to withhold $150 million from the almost $2.2 billion earmarked for Israel for fiscal year 1981, an amount representing 43 percent of all foreign aid, until the president determined that Israel had ceased the expansion of its settlements and also ceased planning new settlements in the occupied territories. Reminding his colleagues that the official American position was that the settlements were in violation of international law and an impediment to the peace process, Stevenson said that the $150 million he proposed to withhold represented an estimate of what Israel was spending annually on the West Bank settlements. To allow this sum to go forward, Stevenson said, was to subsidize the Begin government in its "defiance of our policy and our interests." It would be wiser, the Senator argued, to reward accommodation instead of intransigence. As matters stood, "aid, always more aid, is proposed as if to signify that the way to our purse is through resistance to our policies." He offered his amendment, therefore, as an opportunity for the Senate to signal its intent "to represent U.S. interests and to implement U.S. policy in the Middle East."[186]

No other Senator spoke in support of the Stevenson amendment. In opposition, Senator Javits of New York argued that the amendment amounted to coercion of the Israelis—"hitting their jugular"—and would therefore drive them "into a corner" and make them even more stubborn.[187] Senator Percy of Illinois said that, although he opposed Israel's settlement policy, he thought the timing wrong and that the amendment would disrupt the Camp David peace process. He feared too that "the action might be looked upon as coercion, might get people's backs up, might imply that a policy has a price tag on it."[188] Senator Packwood of Oregon took the view that Israelis "have as much right to settle in the West Bank as does anyone else. . . ."[189] Senator Mathias of Maryland opposed "the approach of taking punitive action against a friend."[190] Senator Dole of Kansas contended that, in fact, no U.S. funds were used by Israel to establish settlements, that the amendment was therefore unnecessary, and further, would be "most detrimental" to peace negotiations.[191] Senator Church of Idaho, chairman of the Senate Foreign Relations Committee, warned against coercion—"do not put a gun to the head of the Israeli government"—lest Israel lose its trust in the United States.[192]

Senator Stevenson, in rebuttal, argued that he was not suggesting coercion or punishment. "I am suggesting that we make it very clear that we in the United States will no longer let ourselves be coerced."[193] The Stevenson amendment was defeated by a vote of 85 to 7.[194]

Israel, since annexing the Arab sector of Jerusalem after the 1967 war, had steadfastly maintained that East Jerusalem was therefore to be distinguished from the occupied West Bank. On July 30, 1980 the Israeli Knesset enacted a law declaring united Jerusalem to be the permanent capital of Israel. It was this action, as noted in chapter 1, that provoked President Sadat to suspend the deadlocked Palestinian autonomy negotiations. Prime Minister Begin responded to Sadat's decision, conveyed in a stern letter, with a defiant letter of his own affirming that "Jerusalem is and will be one, under Israel's sovereignty, its indivisible captial," and also affirming the legality and legitimacy of Israel's settlements. "None of them will ever be removed," Begin added.[195]

The United States, in the wake of these events, continued to act with less than full consistency with its own official position. That position, with respect to Jerusalem, had been spelled out in a statement before the United Nations Security Council by U.S. Representative Charles W. Yost on July 1, 1969:

> The United States considers that the part of Jerusalem that came under the control of Israel in the June 1967 war, like other areas occupied by Israel, is occupied territory and hence subject to the provisions of international law governing the rights and obligations of an occupying power. Among the provisions of international law which bind Israel, as they would bind any occupier, are the provisions that the occupier has no right to make changes in laws or in administration other than those which are temporarily necessitated by his security interests, and that an occupier may not confiscate or destroy private property. . . . [Under international law] the occupier must maintain the occupied area as intact and unaltered as possible, without interfering with the customary life of the area, and any changes must be necessitated by the immediate needs of the occupation.[196]

The Carter administration neither repudiated nor reaffirmed this position in the summer of 1980. The United States abstained when the Security Council on August 20, by a vote of 14 to 0, censured Israel for its formal annexation of East Jerusalem and called on those countries maintaining embassies in Jerusalem to remove them to another place. The resolution would not in any case affect the United States, which maintained its embassy in Tel Aviv. Nevertheless, Secretary of State Muskie, addressing the Security Council, denounced the call for removing the embassies from Jerusalem. "It is without force," he said, "and we reject it as a disruptive attempt to dictate to other nations."[197] In the following weeks the Netherlands and several Latin American countries transferred their embassies to Tel Aviv.

While the United States, under the Carter administration, maintained its position against the Israeli settlements, Israel continued to alter the landscape of the occupied West Bank. The architect of Israel's settlements policy, Minister of Agriculture Ariel Sharon (who was to become defense minister in August 1981) explained in 1980 the strategy of the settlements:

> You just can't do anything about it any more. That is why it is impossible any more to talk about the Jordanian option or territorial compromise. We are going to leave an entirely different map of the country that it will be impossible to ignore. I don't see any way any government will be able to dismantle the settlements of Judea and Samaria.[198]

It fell to the Reagan administration to bring the declared policy of the United States into an approximation of consistency with actual practice. In a press interview on February 2, 1981, President Reagan said of the settlements: "I disagreed when the previous Administration referred to them as illegal, they're not illegal." He added, however, that, under existing circumstances, rushing the settlements, might be "ill-advised" and "unnecessarily provocative," detrimental to the spirit of Camp David.[199]

Should policy on all sides fail to resolve the future of the West Bank, as seems possible, the issue may in due course be resolved by demography. Should Israel annex or otherwise maintain control of the West Bank and Gaza Strip, the Palestinian Arabs, with birth rates substantially higher than those of the Israeli Jews, would eventually become a majority, turning Israel into a binational state. Such a result would represent a fundamental negation of Zionist ideology, which lays down as basic criteria for the salvation of world Jewry the creation of a Jewish state—one, that is, in which Jews constitute an overwhelming majority—and the governing of the state according to democratic principles. Israel thus faces a profound dilemma: the acquisition of a large new Arab population with full political rights would compromise Israel's character as a Jewish state; the denial of such rights would compromise its character as a democracy.[200]

Israel thus confronts a moral dilemma, as to its own character and also as to the future of a large and growing subject Arab population. Even before the occupation and colonization of the West Bank, Israelis had been increasingly and uncomfortably aware of the parallel between their own tragic experience and that of the Palestinians—a parallel that the Palestinians themselves played on by appropriating the term "disapora," hitherto commonly associated with the eighteen centuries' dispersal of the Jews, and even by calling themselves the "new Jews." Amos Elon described a series of interviews conducted by young kibbutzniks after the Six Days War of 1967 with Israeli soldiers who had fought in the war. One soldier recalled witnessing the flight of Arab refugees and associating the scene with the Jewish Holocaust, and another admitted that when he entered a refugee camp to put down a disorder he felt "like a Gestapo man."[201] Mainstream and official Israelis were more disposed to disavow moral responsibility for the Palestinians. A foreign ministry official said in an interview that it was hypocritical to expect Israel to live up to an exalted moral standard, that others did not do so, that Israel indeed was in the "ivy league" when it came to morality.[202] A former high official under Labor governments commented simply that Israel's moral claim to the West Bank was as good as that of the Palestinians: "We think it's our land; they think it's theirs."[203]

CHAPTER FIVE

The Palestinians:
Nation in Diaspora

METAPHORICALLY, IF NOT FACTUALLY, Golda Meir was by no means wholly inaccurate in her assertion that, as a national unit, separate and self-aware, the Palestinian people "did not exist."[1] Prior to 1948, and perhaps for some years after that, the Palestinian Arabs, however strongly they may have felt it, asserted no strong sense of national identity distinct from that of all other Arabs. The Israeli Jews could not have failed to be fully aware that the Palestinians were being uprooted from their *homes* in 1948 and again in 1967; it was much less clear that they were being expelled from their *country*.

Nationalism, in its essence, is a state of mind, the shared belief of a sizable number of individuals that they form, or ought to form, a separate national community. There are no formal requirements, no criteria of eligibility, no objective factors essential for the formation of a nationality, although most nationalities in fact possess certain distinguishing attributes such as a common history, religion, language, culture, or descent. None of these, however, is essential. What is essential, is the "living and active corporate will" to form a nation, regardless of when and how that will came into being.[2] By this definition the Palestinian people have become, since 1948, a nation—a nation born of war and expulsion, occupation and exile, its nationalism fueled by memories of lost homes, the abiding conviction of having been wronged, and a militant ideology of "armed struggle." As defined by a refugee in one of the camps, the source of Palestinian nationalism is easily explained: "A foreigner came and took our land, took our farms and our homes, and kicked us out."[3]

THE CRUCIBLE OF "ARMED CONFLICT"

The war that followed the creation of the state of Israel in 1948 resulted in the displacement of more than 700,000 Palestinian Arabs. Whether they fled of their own accord in response to the urging of Arab leaders, or were forcibly driven from their homes by Israeli force and terror, is hotly disputed by the parties but otherwise of little consequence. Whichever was the case, it is clear that the Palestinian exodus was not an uncoerced migration of people seeking new homes in a new land in the way of the successive immigrant groups that came to the United States in the nineteenth and early twentieth centuries. For whatever specific causes, the Arab refugees fled in fear, and the Israelis, wishing to create a Jewish state, barred their return. On December 11, 1948 the United Nations General Assembly adopted Resolution 194 creating a Conciliation Commission for Palestine and resolving, among other provisions, "that the refugees wishing to return to their homes and live at peace with their neighbors should be permitted to do so at the earliest practicable date, and that compensation should be paid for the property of those choosing not to return. . . ."[4] Efforts by the Conciliation Commission to achieve a settlement on this basis were thwarted by Israel's refusal to accept more than a limited number of refugees and the refusal of the Arab states to accept a refugee settlement that recognized the Jewish state.

Unwelcome as well in the surrounding Arab states, the homeless Palestinians settled into stark refugee camps in Jordan, Syria, and Lebanon. Some were made refugees again when they fled the West Bank in the 1967 war. As of 1980 there were approximately 4 million Palestinians in the world, almost half of whom were still registered as refugees with the United Nations Relief and Works Agency (UNRWA), with some 688,000—one-third of the total refugee population—still living in over sixty refugee camps.[5] In 1950 the Israeli Knesset enacted a "Law of Return," which provided that every Jew had the right to immigrate to and become a citizen of Israel.[6] In the years following, the questions of return and compensation for the Palestinian refugees remained unresolved while Israelis expropriated Palestinian homes, farms, and businesses. Palestinians and their sympathizers sometimes invoked Article 13 of the Universal

Declaration of Human Rights, which states that "everyone has the right to leave any country, including his own, and to return to his country."[7] Such appeals were ineffective, although Article 13, as invoked in the United States Congress on behalf of Soviet Jews, was apparently persuasive in helping to secure the enactment in 1974 of the Jackson-Vanik Amendment making equal trade treatment for the Soviet Union contingent on the dropping of emigration controls. Senator Fulbright, the chairman of the Senate Foreign Relations Committee, asked at that time, "Is the right of Palestinians to return to homes from which they were expelled any less fundamental than the right of Soviet Jews to make new homes in a new land?"[8]

In exile the Palestinians nurtured and cherished memories of their former homes. Israeli soldiers interviewed after the 1967 war recorded their astonishment, on entering refugee camps, at encountering a kind of "Arab Zionism," with the inmates, in some instances, organized within a camp according to the towns, villages, or even streets in which they had lived until 1948.[9] Yasser Arafat, in an interview published on January 7, 1975, asked rhetorically: "Do I have to force myself to forget the house where I was born in Jerusalem a few yards from the Wailing Wall, a house whose destruction Mrs. Golda Meir ordered under the occupation regime? Do I have less right to be there than this Russian lady, naturalized American, who has come to install herself in my ancestral land?"[10]

Palestinian nationalism took root and flourished in the refugee camps. The camp Palestinians came increasingly over the years to perceive themselves as Palestinians, not, in the view of one sociological study, as an alternative to their Arab identity, but rather as a "more intensive, more exemplary form" of Arabism. The study suggested certain outstanding features of the Palestinian identity as it took form in the camps: far from forgetting the events that had made them refugees, the camp Palestinians retained a keen awareness and bitter resentment of their expulsion from Palestine and of their statelessness and subordinate status in the countries that gave them refuge. Further, the land of Palestine, once taken for granted, or indeed hardly considered as a distinct national unit, became a powerful symbol of national identity, comparable, it would seem, to the symbolism of "Eretz Israel" in the minds of the Jews. Hardship, exile, and oppression, far from breaking the spirit of the Palestinians, generated self-confidence and solidarity, giving force and militancy to the emerging concept of a "Palestinian people." As militancy grew, the camp Palestinians came to despise and then reject the conception of themselves as "refugees," replacing this with a new identity as freedom fighters and revolutionaries. There took hold an ideology of armed struggle, and a responsiveness to leaders who disdained coming to terms with an adverse reality and called instead for sustained struggle for recovery of the lost homeland.[11] The prevailing spirit was summed up in one of Yasser Arafat's favorite phrases: "We are tigers"—because, as he explained, "we have nothing to lose."[12]

In a first visit to a Palestinian refugee camp—outside Beirut on November 14, 1970—I recorded my impressions of both the physical conditions and prevailing spirit of the camp:

> It was physically as hateful and ugly, squalid and degraded a place as the worst "favelas" in Brazil or even the slums of Calcutta. The houses were wretched shacks, the stores makeshift huts, the streets—if they can be called that— filthy alleyways lined with open sewers. The population is dense, especially with ragged children. One sees how the 750,000 refugees of 1948 have become 1,400,000. There are differences, though, from the shanty towns of Lima in Peru and Recife in Brazil. First of all there is law and order, enforced by the indigenous soldiery which calls itself the "Armed Struggle Command." Second, there is a semblance of social cohesion: we visited a school within the camp and the children seemed well-tended and were neatly uniformed, although the schoolhouse was makeshift. There also appears to be no hunger—at least not starvation—thanks in part to the pittance—about ten cents per person a day—provided by UNRWA, which also runs the schools and hires and pays the teachers. The most important difference between the refugee camp and the slums I have seen in Asia and Latin America is that these people are not submissive, hollow-eyed, subrevolutionaries. They are political and angry and sometimes violent: they are refugees and their anger and hatred flourish in the fetid soil of the camp. It is not judged wise for visitors—American visitors at any rate—to enter the camp unescorted by the armed guard. They accompanied us everywhere— they were friendly enough themselves—and I would not have wanted them to leave us. As we left the refugee camp, a Palestinian employee of UNRWA called me aside. "Tell the people in Washington," he said, "that we are disappointed with the United States."

Disappointment ripened into anger—"fury," Arafat says[13]—as it became increasingly clear over the years that neither the ministrations of UNRWA, the accumulating archives of United Nations resolutions, the cultivation of the great powers, nor appeals to the conscience of the world would bring redress for the injustices suffered by the Palestinians. "Through bitter lessons," Professor Hisham Sharabi wrote in 1973, "they have found that neither the laws of nations nor the acts and resolutions of international bodies can bring about the conditions of right and justice. The justice which the world will recognize is that which the oppressed can by their struggle and sacrifice bring about. . . ."[14] The proposition is the same as Menachem Begin's, quoted in chapter 1: "The world does not pity the slaughtered. It only respects those who fight."[15]

With support from various Arab governments, Palestinian guerrilla operations on a small scale began in the early 1950s. Egypt trained and equipped Palestinian *fedayeen*—the word translates as "those who sacrifice themselves"—who mounted raids into Israel from the Gaza Strip, raids that were increased in scale after the Israelis began mounting large-scale retaliatory attacks into Gaza in early 1955. In the mid-fifties there came into being the first autonomous Palestinian resistance group, called "al-Fatah," the word meaning "victory" or "conquest." The group was founded principally by Yasser Arafat, who had fled Jerusalem with his family in 1948 and subsequently resided as a refugee in the Gaza Strip, as an engineering student in Cairo, then as an engineer in Kuwait, where he founded his own firm in 1955. During this period Arafat worked among Palestinian students in Cairo, Baghdad, and Stuttgart, West Germany, gathering funds and recruits for al-Fatah. In Kuwait Arafat built a solid financial base for al-Fatah by enlisting the support of well-paid Palestinians employed there in the oil industry. New support, including training facilities, came from Algeria after it gained independence in 1962, and then from Syria with the coming to power in that country in 1963 of the Baath (Arab Rebirth) party, whose ideology of Arab socialism also included a commitment to the liberation of Palestine.[16]

Under the sponsorship of the Arab League, the Palestine Liberation Organization was established by the first Palestine National Congress meeting in Arab Jerusalem in May 1964. The PLO committed itself to armed stuggle but did not become a major militant force until after the 1967 war in which Israel occupied the West Bank and the Gaza Strip. Arafat himself credited Israel's early occupation practices, such as the blowing up of houses of suspected fedayeen and the confiscation of property, with greatly strengthening the resistance movement. "Thank God for Dayan," he was quoted as saying. "He provides the daily proof of the expansionist nature of Zionism."[17] The period following the 1967 war, in which the Arab armies were shattered and Arab morale momentarily broken, became, in Professor Sharabi's description, "the heroic period of Palestinian resistance." The fedayeen mounted daring raids across the Jordan River, helping to revive the spirits of the defeated and demoralized Arabs. "Never before in their history," wrote Sharabi, "had the Palestinians felt so strongly bound together."[18] The prestige and morale of the PLO soared after a small band of fedayeen inflicted sizable losses on a large

Israeli armored force that attacked the al-Fatah camp in the Jordanian village of Karameh on March 21, 1968. Young Palestinians flocked to al-Fatah recruiting stations, and even King Hussein, whose army was later to crush the fedayeen in Jordan in the "Black September" of 1970, said in a news conference on March 23, 1968, "The time may come . . . when we will all be fedayeen."[19]

Meeting in Cairo in July 1968, the Palestine National Congress adopted the "Palestinian National Covenant," which became the PLO's charter and which called for the dissolution of the state of Israel. The covenant stated that "Palestine with its boundaries that existed at the time of the British Mandate is an integral regional unit" (Article 2), to which the Palestinian people held "legal right" (Article 3), but "Jews who were living permanently in Palestine until the beginning of the Zionist invasion will be considered Palestinians" (Article 6). The covenant also stated that "armed struggle is the only way to liberate Palestine and is therefore a strategy and not tactics" (Article 9), and that "fedayeen action forms the nucleus of the popular Palestinian war of liberation" (Article 10). Purporting to "purge the Zionist presence from Palestine" (Article 15), the covenant declared the partition of Palestine in 1948 and the establishment of Israel to be "fundamentally null and void" (Article 19). Another provision, which reciprocates (although it preceded) Golda Meir's celebrated assertion that as a people the Palestinians "did not exist,"[20] defined Judaism as a religion not a nationality, and went on to state that "the Jews are not one people with an independent personality. They are rather citizens of the states to which they belong" (Article 20).

In the years following the adoption of the convenant, various modifications were introduced in the form of public statements by PLO leaders and resolutions adopted by the Palestine National Congress, although the covenant itself was not formally amended. Most of these changes, as will be seen later in this chapter ("Arafat and the PLO"), were in the direction of grudging, hesitant, often euphemistic, but increasingly explicit acceptance of a two-state solution for Palestine, with Israel acknowledged as a sovereign state within its boundaries of 1967. At the same time the PLO leadership, especially Yasser Arafat, who became chairman in 1969, spoke of a unified "democratic, secular" state of Palestine in which Jews, Muslims, and Christians would live as equals.[21] No longer purporting to limit the Jewish population to those "living permanently in Palestine until the beginning of the Zionist invasion," as specified in the charter, Arafat, in his United Nations speech of November 13, 1974, included within his conception of the "Palestine of tomorrow" "*all Jews* now living in Palestine who choose to live with us in peace and without discrimination."[22] Increasingly, too, PLO leaders began to disavow "armed struggle" as the essential means of achieving a "unified and democratic Palestine." Arafat himself began to reconcile the ultimate goal of a unified Palestine with the practical necessity of a two-state solution by referring to the former as a long-term goal to be sought by peaceful means. "Is it a crime to dream?" Arafat asked in an interview in early 1975.[23] In a conversation with Senator McGovern a few months later, Arafat stressed that the "democratic, secular" state was a "vision of the future," to be realized through a process of "intellectual transformation" and "political persuasion," not by "force or terror."[24]

Anathema though it is to most Israelis, Arafat's vision of a "democratic, secular" state, as was suggested in chapter 1,[25] is not wholly dissimilar from the idea of a binational state that formed a significant strand of classical Zionist thought. Starting with the awareness that Palestine was not indeed an empty land, this school of Zionist thinking looked to the creation of a single state containing two nations, Jewish and Arab, with two official languages, Hebrew and Arabic, and with full political rights and cultural autonomy for both national groups. One of the foremost proponents of this "Other Zionism," as I.F. Stone has called it, was the German-Jewish philosopher, later to become an Israeli, Martin Buber, who espoused a "Hebrew humanism" and called on the Zionist Congress of 1921 to proclaim "its desire to live in peace and brotherhood with the Arab people and to develop the common homeland into a republic in which both peoples will have the possibility of free development."[26]

The binational movement among Zionists expired with the establishment of Israel in 1948, and since that time the prospect of a unified state composed of coequal Arab and Jewish communities has become steadily more remote. Arafat's "vision" seems highly unlikely to become anything but that in the current era, as the PLO has recognized through its grudging acceptance of the idea of a two-state solution for Palestine. So, too, with little tangible prospect for achieving even the lesser goal of a West Bank-Gaza state, the PLO has remained committed to the theory and practice of "armed struggle."

The "heroic period" of the Palestinian resistance ended with the "Black September" of 1970, when King Hussein, weary of the punishing Israel countermeasures provoked by the fedayeen and by the fedayeen's virtual takeover of his kingdom, turned his Bedouin soldiers against them and, over a period of months, broke the fedayeen's power and expelled them from Jordan. Thereafter the Palestinian guerrillas used Lebanon as their principal base of operations. Their presence became a major factor in the outbreak of the Lebanese civil war in 1975, and their actions against Israel provoked recurrent violent Israeli countermeasures including the large-scale invasion of Lebanon of March 1978 and the heavy bombing of July 1981.

During this period, despite continual, intermittent acts of terrorism, the thinking of the Palestinian leadership evolved haltingly in the direction of negotiation, compromise, and reliance on diplomacy. The PLO pursued, in effect, a dual strategy of peaceful settlement and armed struggle, neither of which brought lasting, tangible rewards. The Palestine Liberation Organization was recognized by twenty Arab heads of state, meeting in Rabat, Morocco, in October 1974, as the "sole legitimate representative of the Palestinian people on any liberated Palestinian territory." On October 14, 1974 the United Nations General Assembly voted to recognize the PLO as "the representative of the Palestinian people;" the vote was 105 to 4—Israel, the United States, the Dominican Republic, and Bolivia—with 20 abstentions. On November 13, 1974 Yasser Arafat became the first head of a nongovernmental organization to participate in the General Assembly. These diplomatic successes brought the PLO to a high point of international standing, but, with Israel and the United States adamant in their refusal to deal with the PLO, diplomacy had brought the Palestinian people no closer to recovery of their lost homeland or any part of it. The PLO leadership remained ambivalent as between peaceful settlement and armed struggle. In his address to the United Nations General Assembly, Arafat said: "I have come bearing an olive branch and a freedom fighter's gun. Do not let the olive branch fall from my hand."[27]

THE THEORY AND PRACTICE OF TERROR

On March 11, 1978 a band of Palestinian raiders came ashore on the coast of Israel south of Haifa, seized a bus filled with Israeli passengers, and raced south to the outskirts of Tel Aviv, firing from the windows at motorists and throwing hand grenades. The bus was finally halted at a roadblock outside of Tel Aviv, where an exchange of gunfire with police ensued until the vehicle exploded in flames. A Palestinian military spokesman in Beirut announced that the attack, in which 37 Israelis and nine fedayeen were killed, had been carried out by al-Fatah.[28] Commenting on the raid, one of the most costly in Israeli lives since the founding of the Jewish state in 1948, an unnamed "source" close to PLO Chairman Arafat said: "This is a liberation movement; we can't just sit around and do nothing."[29]

Prime Minister Begin, who was to have left on March 12 for the United

States, postponed his trip and summoned Defense Minister Ezer Weizman, who was in the United States, to return immediately. The prime minister held a press conference on March 12 at which, according to reports, his voice trembled and faltered, his eyes were rimmed red, and his manner was that of a mourner. "What I can say," he said, "is that those who killed Jews in our times cannot enjoy impunity." Begin expressed condolences to the bereaved families: "May God console them in their grief," he said in what was described as a frail voice. He compared the PLO once again to the German Nazis and said that al-Fatah, as a political organization, was "one of the meanest and basest in the annals of mankind. This brutal enemy wants to break our spirit," Begin said. "But he will not succeed. We shall overcome."[30]

Three days later, on March 15, 1978, an Israeli force estimated at the time at 20,000 soldiers struck across the Lebanese border, attacking on land and from the sea and air, bombing and strafing Palestinian camps and enclaves as far north as Beirut, and seizing what Israeli officials called a "security belt" up to six miles deep along the entire 63-mile border. Minister of Defense Ezer Weizman said that the operation was not for reprisal in the usual sense, but "to destroy and uproot, as far as possible, terrorist concentrations in southern Lebanon." A statement issued by the Army Chief of Staff's office said that since the October War of 1973 there had been 1,548 attacks across the Lebanese border, costing 108 Israeli lives.[31] Prime Minister Begin announced that Israeli forces would remain in southern Lebanon until some kind of agreement was reached to insure that the area could never again be used for attacks on Israel. "We want an arrangement," he said, "in which all those places from which the murderers were ejected shall not return there."[32]

Israeli forces remained in Lebanon until June 1978, having advanced beyond the original six-mile strip to occupy all of southern Lebanon up to the Litani River. When they finally withdrew in June, they turned only a portion of the territory they had occupied over to the United Nations peacekeeping force that had been assigned to Lebanon by the Security Council in late March. Along the six-mile wide "security belt" adjacent to their border, and in defiance of the United Nations, the departing Israelis installed Lebanese Christian militia, with whom Israel had long been allied, and who operated in defiance of the Lebanese government in Beirut. A United Nations official estimated that even before the Israelis had completed their withdrawal, some 250 Palestinian guerrillas had infiltrated back into the border area.[33]

The PLO, for its part, was not unduly dismayed by the invasion and its aftermath. Its main forces, to be sure, had been driven north of the Litani River and were compelled to remain there by the United Nations force, but PLO leaders expressed satisfaction that their irregular forces had stood and fought and conducted an orderly retreat in the face of an enemy with overwhelming firepower. "The fight in the south was a chance—the first chance of its kind—where the Palestinian fighters had a direct confrontation with the Israelis," said Shafik al-Hout, head of the PLO office in Beirut. "They fought and they resisted beautifully. No panic, no running away."[34]

The strategy employed in "Operation Litani," as it was called in Israel, proved costly to the civilian population of southern Lebanon. The Israelis themselves lost nineteen men in combat and another twelve in accidents; the Palestinian fedayeen lost between 250 and 300. Lebanese and Red Cross estimates placed the number of Lebanese and Palestinian civilian dead at close to 1,000; other estimates ran higher, but the exact number remained unknown. Approximately 200,000 Lebanese and 65,000 Palestinians were made refugees, driven from their homes to temporary refuge in and around Beirut. In order to minimize their own casualties, the invading Israelis mounted heavy artillery and air attacks ahead of their advancing forces and made no effort to put blocking forces behind the fedayeen; the main PLO forces were therefore allowed to withdraw intact while the Israelis pounded undefended villages with artillery and air strikes. American-supplied F–15s—the most advanced American warplane—were used for the first time in combat, as were a variety of other weapons, including lethal, American-supplied "cluster bombs." "The damage to Lebanese villages," the *New York Times* commented, "will do much to erase the horror felt universally over the terrorist raid near Tel Aviv."[35]

A preliminary summary of the Litani campaign made public by the Israel Defense Force stated that

> every move and advance by our forces was preceded by an artillery softening up, bombing from the air and shelling from the sea. It was clear that these bombings and shellings would cause suffering to the civilian population in southern Lebanon and would give the terrorists time to get out. . . . We took into consideration the suffering of our own residents, the destruction and damage to our settlements in the north in the course of recent years—the direct result of the collaboration, even if under compulsion, of the residents of southern Lebanon with the terrorists. We also took into consideration the large number of deaths in the terrorist raid on the coastal road. . . . We decided to carry out the operation with an advance softening up all along the front in order to reduce our losses to a minimum.[36]

The United States protested, and Israel apologized for its use of American-supplied "cluster bombs" in southern Lebanon. Developed for use in Vietnam, the cluster bomb is an antipersonnel weapon consisting of a canister filled with separate little bombs that are scattered over an area, exploding separately and spreading shrapnel. In a letter to the Speaker of the House of Representatives dated April 5, 1978, Secretary of State Vance recalled that under a 1952 agreement certain weapons were to be provided to Israel only on condition they were used for self-defense, and the secretary went on to say that "a violation of the 1952 agreement may have occurred by reason of the Israeli operations in Lebanon," but because Israel had agreed to United Nations Security Council Resolution 425 calling for Israel's withdrawal from Lebanon, he contemplated no further action.[37] The secretary also commented, on April 6, that although he had no doubt Israel considered itself to have been acting in self-defense in south Lebanon, there was a question of "proportionality."[38]

Chairman Arafat of the PLO took a stronger view of the matter. At a press conference on July 30, 1978 in Havana, where he was attending the eleventh World Festival of Youth and Students, Arafat said that Israel had killed 1,180 civilians in its invasion of Lebanon, and he accused President Carter of having ignored this "massive liquidation" of civilians. "Why doesn't Carter remember it as a violation of human rights?" Arafat asked—and then answered, "Carter thinks our blood is cheap because we belong to the Third World." Arafat also took the occasion to reject the word "terror" as applied to the actions of the PLO, which, he said, were more to be compared with the anti-Nazi resistance movements of World War II.[39]

The Fatah raid of March 1978 and subsequent Israeli invasion of Lebanon were on a larger scale but otherwise of a similar pattern with previous instances of terrorist attack followed by swift, severe retaliation. Among the major occurrences were the following: On April 11, 1974 Palestinian gunmen killed Israeli civilians in a raid on the village of Kiryat Shemona; Israel retaliated with attacks on six villages in southern Lebanon and General Dayan, then minister of defense, warned that if Palestinian guerrilla attacks did not cease, "the Lebanese villagers will have to abandon their homes and flee. . . . All of southern Lebanon will not be able to exist." On May 15, 1974 Palestinian fedayeen massacred twenty-two Israeli teenagers in a school in the northern Israeli town of Maalot. A grieving Prime Minister Golda Meir said the next day, "One doesn't conduct wars on the backs of children," and on that same day, Israeli planes bombed and strafed several Lebanese towns and Palestinian refugee camps, killing some fifty civilians and wounding 200 others.[40] Israeli planes bombed Palestinian refugee camps several additional times in May and June 1974, using American-supplied Phantom jets and Skyhawks and American-supplied phosphorous and antipersonnel bombs. The Associated Press reported from a refugee camp after the June raid: "Weeping children watched as parents dug frantically in the debris for bodies and bits of furniture." The article also gave the account of one of the raids by a blacksmith who took refuge with some of his children in a trench and then summoned two other sons: "I shouted for them to join us. But they were blasted to pieces before my eyes."[41] There were further occurrences in 1975. In March, Palestinian guerrillas, landing from the sea, took over a Tel Aviv hotel and killed eleven persons. On July 7, three days after the explosion of a bomb hidden in a refrigerator killed fourteen persons in Jerusalem, Israel launched land, sea, and air attacks against suspected guerrilla bases, killing, according to Lebanese officials, seventy-three persons and wounding another 159. On November 9, 1977, in reprisal for rocket attacks that killed three Israelis, Israeli warplanes assaulted Palestinian guerrilla strongholds in southern Lebanon, killing eighty-seven persons and wounding 105, according to Palestinian and Lebanese officials.[42] In almost all of these occurrences the same pattern obtained: a surprise Palestinian terrorist attack against Israeli civilians followed by massive retaliation resulting in the killing of many more people, civilian as well as fedayeen, on the other side.

"Operation Litani" resulted in the forced withdrawal of the main Palestinian guerrilla forces beyond the Litani River, but it failed to break the cycle of terrorist attacks and retaliation. On August 3, 1978 a bomb went off in a crowded market in Tel Aviv, killing one Israeli and injuring fifty, and five hours later Israeli jets struck at a Palestinian training base south of Beirut. An Israeli Cabinet statement said, "The murderous organizations will be hit wherever they may be"; the PLO said the base had been deserted for a year.[43] On August 19, 1978 terrorists attacked an Israeli El Al Airline crew in London, killing a stewardess, whereupon Israeli planes strafed a Palestinian refugee camp and village in Lebanon.[44]

In the autumn of 1978 Syrian peacekeeping forces, which had entered Lebanon under the auspices of the Arab League in the wake of the Lebanese civil war, undertook to subdue the Christian militias in the area of Beirut. Israel thereupon mounted several limited military operations in support of its Christian clients, with whom Israel had formed a de facto alliance against the PLO. On October 5, in the wake of intensified fighting between Syrian troops and Christian militias, Israeli gunboats shelled a

Syrian-controlled section of western Beirut, apparently to apply pressure on the Syrians to relent in their attack on the Christian militias.[45] The Israeli government officially denied this intention, claiming to have been attacking a PLO naval base. "We had information that they were about to have an attack against Israel," Foreign Minister Dayan said in an interview.[46] In fact, Israeli officials had frequently expressed concern for the fate of the Lebanese Christians; Dayan himself was reported to have told his staff on August 31 that the United States would be urged to consider the "humanitarian" aspects of the Lebanese situation, notably the threat of a mass slaughter of Christians, the prospect of which, Dayan reportedly said, "brings up to the memory of the Jewish people a very dark era of Jewish history."[47]

The conflict between Israel and the PLO thus became inextricably linked with the tangled internal conflicts of war-wracked Lebanon. Whether Israeli intervention was motivated in significant measure by humanitarian concern for the Lebanese Christians—more exactly, those, by no means all, within the Lebanese Christian community who sought and welcomed Israeli support—or solely by the desire to strike at and weaken the PLO in every possible way, was a question of academic interest, because both objectives were advanced by Israeli support of the Christian militias, which had fought against the Palestinians as well as Lebanese Muslims in the civil war and whose animosity toward the Palestinians was hardly less than that of the Israelis themselves. Israel therefore continued to provide arms and money to the Christian militia forces in their six-mile-deep "security belt" along the length of the Israeli-Lebanese border. These irregular forces, under their leader Major Saad Haddad, engaged in periodic duels with the Palestinians, barred the Lebanese government from reasserting its authority in the border region, repeatedly attacked United Nations peacekeeping installations and personnel, and prevented the United Nations force from carrying out its mandate under Security Council Resolution 425 of March 19, 1978. This resolution, sponsored by the United States, called on Israel to withdraw its forces "from all Lebanese territory" and established the United Nations Interim Force in Lebanon (UNIFIL) for the purpose of "confirming the withdrawal of Israeli forces, restoring international peace and security and assisting the government of Lebanon in ensuring the return of its effective authority in the area. . . ."[48]

As the recurrent conflict within Lebanon abated once again in late 1978, the pattern of Palestinian provocation and Israeli reprisal resumed, with periodic terrorist raids followed by Israeli air or ground attacks on Palestinian concentrations within Lebanon. On January 18 and 19, 1979, after a bomb explosion injured twenty-one Israelis in an outdoor market in Jerusalem, an Israeli force of several hundred soldiers moved under an artillery barrage into Lebanon, advancing for the first time north of the Litani River and killing, according to reports, forty Palestinians and Lebanese. Palestinian guerrillas retaliated with rocket fire against two northern Israeli towns.[49] Israeli Defense Minister Ezer Weizman said at a news conference on January 19, "We have to continue to hit them in Lebanon as long as the Lebanese government, even by default, allows them the use of its territory."[50] Another exchange took place on January 23. On the same day, Defense Minister Weizman threatened retaliation against civilian targets in Lebanon if Palestinian attacks on Israeli civilians continued, and Foreign Minister Dayan, reacting to expressions of sympathy for the Palestine Liberation Organization by Israeli Arabs, threatened Israeli Arabs and those in the occupied territories with expulsion. Reminding them of "what happened with the Arab people" in the 1948 war, Dayan said that they had become refugees because they were unwilling to live in peace with the Israeli Jews, "and that should serve as a lesson."[51]

Dayan's and Weizman's warnings went unheeded. Following the signing of the Israeli-Egyptian peace treaty in March 1979, the PLO and other groups stepped up terrorist attacks. One group, calling itself "Black March" in honor of the peace treaty, attempted unsuccessfully on April 16 to attack an Israeli airliner in Brussels. In the wake of a terrorist attack in the Israeli town of Nahariya on April 22 (in which four persons including two small children were slain), Prime Minister Begin declared to an assemblage of mourners, "The blood of him who raises his hand against a child of Israel in the land of Israel should be spilled."[52] And so it was, as well as the blood of many others who had no part in the killings at Nahariya. A four-day retaliatory campaign of heavy bombardment in south Lebanon by Israel and its ally, the Christian militia, resulted in about sixty dead—half Lebanese and half Palestinian—about 100 wounded, and heavy property damage, while 45,000 to 50,000 people were forced by the bombardment to flee their homes.[53]

As time passed, Israel adopted a policy of preemptive strikes against Palestinian concentrations in southern Lebanon, rather than waiting for terrorist attacks and then retaliating. In August 1979 the United States delegate to the United Nations, Andrew Young, appealed forcefully for an end to preemptive strikes and to the "deadlock of terror and counter-terror." Prime Minister Begin replied that the Israeli policy was "the most legitimate national self-defense ever seen on earth," and that anyone who said there was symmetry in the actions of the two sides "performs an act of revolting injustice."[54]

The recurrence of terror, counterterror and preemptive attack continued thereafter, with the United States expressing repeated but unavailing disapproval. In 1980 there were major terrorist occurrences in the increasingly restive occupied West Bank. On May 2 Palestinian terrorists, using hand grenades and automatic rifles, attacked a group of Jewish settlers walking from prayers at the Tomb of the Patriarchs, where Abraham is thought to be buried—in the Arab city of Hebron—killing six and wounding sixteen.[55] Within hours of the ambush Israeli troops seized the mayor of Hebron, Fahd Qawasmeh, the mayor of nearby Halhoul, Mohammed Milhem, and a Muslim religious leader from Hebron, flew them by helicopter to the northern border, and expelled them into Lebanon. The Israeli military government explained that, although there was no evidence of direct involvement in the Hebron attack on the part of the three leaders, they had previously made inflammatory statements that constituted incitement.[56] On June 2 Jewish terrorists planted bombs in or near the cars of three other West Bank leaders. Mayor Bassam Shaka' of Nablus lost both legs above the knees; Mayor Karim Khalaf of Ramallah had his left foot blown off; Mayor Ibrahim Tawil of Bireh escaped, but an Israeli explosives expert, who had come to give warning, was blinded when the bomb meant for the mayor exploded in his face.[57] Mayor Shaka', after receiving medical treatment in Jordan, returned in July to a triumphal welcome in his town of Nablus. He addressed the rejoicing townspeople: "They wanted to kill me but I lived even though they didn't want me to live. I live in the name of God and in the name of Palestine."[58]

Sporadic fighting continued in Lebanon throughout 1980 and early 1981 as Israel attempted to keep the Palestinian guerrilla forces off balance. A major new outbreak of violence, as noted in chapter 1, occurred in July 1981, climaxed by Palestinian rocket attacks on communities in northern Israel and the Israeli bombing of Beirut on July 17. Three Israelis were killed and twenty-five were wounded in the rocket attack on the Israeli town of Nahariya, although casualties would have been higher if many civilians had not evacuated the town. At least 300 were killed and 800 wounded in the bombing of the densely populated Palestinian neighborhood in Beirut. The brunt of the July violence of 1981 fell on neither Israelis nor Palestinian guerrillas but on Lebanese and Palestinian civilians. Almost all of those killed in Beirut were civilians, although the attack was meant to strike at PLO headquarters. Witnesses to Israeli air attacks on roads and bridges in southern Lebanon in July 1981 said most of the casualties appeared to be civilians trapped in clogged traffic and burned alive in their cars.[59]

The foregoing is by no means a definitive catalogue of the terror and counterterror practiced by Palestinians and Israelis on each other. Israelis would not fail to recall the terrorist attack on Israel's Lydda airport in May 1972, in which twenty-six persons were killed and about eighty wounded, or the atrocity committed at the Munich Olympic Games in September 1972, when terrorists of the Black September group murdered eleven Israeli athletes—two in an initial melee, the rest after many hours of intrigue and fruitless bargaining for their lives while they were held hostage.[60] Palestinians, for their part, emphasize the heavy Israeli reprisals that have followed every incident, including the Munich massacre. A representative expression of their embittered, ironic view of the "cycle of violence" was offered by a professor of philosophy at Bir Zeit University on the West Bank in 1978:

> In the last five years, Palestinian guerrillas have killed about 140 Israelis, but the Israelis have killed more than 2,000 Palestinians. As head of the Irgun in the 1940's, Begin organized bombings and attacks that killed hundreds, mostly innocent people, and now he is Prime Minister of a Jewish state. How can Palestinians look down on violence when we have such a shining example of what it can accomplish in Mr. Begin?[61]

Unwelcome though they are to most Israelis, comparisons between the practices of the PLO and of the preindependence Israeli resistance forces, especially Begin's Irgun Zvai Leumi, suggest certain parallels. One such is the disclaimer of "terror" as the proper characterization of each group's activities—on the ground that the nature of the act must be distinguished from its *intent*, and it is the latter which is determining. "The difference between the revolutionary and the terrorist," Arafat said at the United Nations in 1974, "lies in the reason for which each fights. For whoever stands by a just cause and fights for the freedom and liberation of his land from the invaders, the settlers and the colonialists cannot possibly be called terrorist."[62] Similarly, Begin wrote in his memoir of the Irgun's fight against the British: "The historical and linguistic origins of the political term 'terror' prove that it cannot be applied to a revolutionary war of liberation. . . . what has a struggle for the dignity of man, against oppression and subjugation, to do with 'terrorism'? . . . historically we were not 'terrorists.' We were strictly speaking anti-terrorists."[63] A few Israelis—only a few—have accepted the comparison. Commenting on his own unsuccessful effort to bring Israeli and PLO moderates together, Arie

Lova Eliav, who had participated himself in the struggle against the British, commented in 1978: "Begin said, 'How can you shake hands with a man whose hands are dripping blood? These people are killers.' Well, Begin was a killer. I was a killer. And besides, here are some killers who are ready to talk sense."[64]

Whatever it is called—"terror" or something else—both sides have resorted to it when it has seemed necessary for their purposes. Terror, in general, is the political instrument of movements that lack other means—such as the armed forces or political and economic leverage of states—to advance their objectives, and that also possess little or no confidence in the likelihood of their goals being realized through appeal to international law, international organizations, or the "conscience of mankind." For such movements, terror, which strikes at only a few but frightens almost everybody, is an efficient and economical means of making their grievances known to the world, and it is also usually perceived as the *only* available alternative to abandoning their goals. "For seventeen years," Arafat told Senator Baker in 1975, "we sat in our camps and did not shoot one bullet against anyone." During that period, he noted, the Palestine issue was even removed from the United Nations agenda. "We gained more misery and remained in our camps."[65]

In an interview in Beirut in December 1973, Chairman Arafat's second-in-command, Salah Khalaf (usually known as "Abu Iyad"), who was reputed to be the executive head of Black September, volunteered his views on "what is called terrorism." Terrorist actions, he said, were not carried out for the sake of their immediate results and certainly not for the purpose of terror in itself or personal revenge. Their purpose was broadly political—to draw the attention of the world, and especially that of the United States, to the Palestinian movement and its purposes. He wondered, he said, why the American government and people, instead of simply condemning terrorist acts, were not seeking out the underlying reasons for them. Abu Iyad acknowledged that fedayeen activities could not be expected to bring early, substantive results; their intention was to keep the struggle going, to keep the Israelis engaged.[66]

Palestinians have accused the United States of applying a double standard to the violence practiced by the PLO and that practiced by Israel. Americans, they have said, react with vocal horror at Palestinian attacks on Israelis, but take little apparent notice of Israel's "state terrorism," of the bombing of refugee camps in which women and children are killed just as they are killed by fedayeen—except in greater numbers. Would the United States, a PLO member asked rhetorically, approve if the Palestinians had tanks and planes with which to "carry out terrorism in a civilized fashion?"[67] Arafat too has stressed the double standard, and he compares the PLO's struggle with that of other revolutionary movements. "George Washington himself," he said to Senator Baker, "was a terrorist in the view of the British. So, too, was de Gaulle to the Germans." So indeed were the Israelis, he added, half of whose leadership at the time he spoke, Arafat said, had once been under sentence from the British imperial government for terrorist activities. "Terrorist," said Arafat, was a title accorded to "people engaged in this kind of struggle."[68] Israelis do not deny that their retaliatory forays often take more civilian lives than the raids that provoked them; but they say that a distinction must be recognized between provocation and response, between those who initiate terror and those who retaliate against it. Palestinians, for their part, urge a different distinction—between, as one PLO member put it to Senator Baker, "the terrorism of the oppressor and the terrorism of the oppressed."[69]

Menachem Begin, in his memoir, denied that the most commonly cited instances of Israeli "terrorism" during the struggle for independence—the blowing up of the King David Hotel, the hanging of British soldiers, and the killing of Arab civilians in the village of Deir Yassin during the 1948 war—were in fact bona fide acts of terror. More than two hundred persons, by Begin's own account, many civilians as well as British officers, were killed or injured in the Irgun's destruction of the King David Hotel in July 1946 with bombs smuggled into the basement in milk cans, but Begin denied culpability on the ground that ample warning to evacuate had been given but was ignored.[70] The hanging of two captured British sergeants in July 1947, in retaliation for the hanging of three Irgun commandos by the British, was explained by Begin as a justified reprisal ("We repaid our enemy in kind") but also as a useful act of policy. Begin quotes with satisfaction the statement of a British official, "The hanging of the two British sergeants did more than anything to get us out."[71]

The killing of approximately 250 people by the Irgun in the Arab village of Deir Yassin in April 1948 has been described as a deliberate massacre designed to spread panic and provoke flight on the part of the Arab populations.[72] Begin in his memoir vehemently contested the generally accepted view of the events at Deir Yassin, contending that the attackers sacrificed the element of surprise in order to give the civilian population warning of the attack and that its characterization as a massacre was "enemy propaganda." Begin did not contest, however, the *usefulness* of the panic and terror associated with Deir Yassin. In a footnote to the revised edition of *The Revolt*, published in 1977, the year he became Prime Minister of Israel, Begin comments: "Out of evil, however, good came. This Arab propaganda spread a legend of terror amongst Arabs and Arab troops, who were seized with panic at the mention of Irgun soldiers. The legend was worth half a dozen battalions to the forces of Israel."[73] In the original American edition of *The Revolt* (published in 1951), as quoted by I. F. Stone, Begin amplified his comment to note that, in the wake of Deir Yassin, Arabs throughout Palestine "were seized with limitless panic and started to flee for their lives. This mass flight soon turned into a mad, uncontrollable stampede. Of the about 800,000 Arabs who lived on the present territory of the state of Israel, only some 165,000 are still living there. The political and economic significance of this development can hardly be overestimated."[74] Begin thus claimed, in effect, that the terror associated with Deir Yassin precipitated events that enabled the new state of Israel to rid itself of the bulk of its Arab population and thus to acquire its demographic character as a Jewish state.

A review of the terrorist practices of both Arabs and Jews suggests two conclusions: first, both parties have found terror at various times to be an acceptable and useful instrument of policy, appropriate for use by people who have no other means at their disposal; neither party, in practice, has subscribed to the view of terrorism as simply a manifestation of insane and mindless murderousness. Second, both Palestinians and Israelis have seemed convinced that terrorism was to be defined not by the act, but by its motive; and since each party has also been convinced that its own motives were honorable and the other's venal, each has avowed, with apparent sincerity, its own innocence of terrorism and the other's culpability. The phenomenon would seem a manifestation of what Hans Kohn called the moral " 'double-bookkeeping' which is so widely accepted in modern nationalism everywhere—a twofold scale of moral judgment, defining the same action as right for oneself but wrong in the neighbor."[75]

THE "JEWS OF THE JEWS"

Few things have puzzled and dispirited Palestinians more than their failure to elicit popular or official sympathy in the United States. Palestinians in the West Bank and elsewhere believe that they are judged invidiously by a double standard—that their grievances, circumstances, and aspirations have been distorted and misrepresented in the United States, in result of which a basic issue of human rights has been portrayed instead as a problem essentially of terrorism, and a people who were forcibly dispossessed from their homeland have been perceived instead as aggressors against those who expelled them. Palestinians attribute their unfavorable image in the United States to the power and machinations of the "Zionist lobby," but they appear, nonetheless, to be mystified as to how the lobby works and as to the nature and sources of its influence. They are no less mystified, and frustrated, by their own impotence, by their apparent inability to appeal to American idealism and to bring Americans to look beyond terrorism to the tragedy of the Palestinian people, the legitimacy of their grievances, and the justice of their aspirations. Despite many disappointments they have continued to look to the United States, not only because of its power, but also because of their perception of the United States as a nation that, in the definition of a West Bank intellectual, pursues its interests like other nations, but "with a touch of idealism."[76]

Puzzlement and frustration are heightened by the similarity Palestinians have perceived between their own misfortunes and the past misfortunes of the Jewish people. Condemned as the Jews once were to diaspora and second-class citizenship, to discrimination and the loss of rights, the Palestinians became, in the phrase of the poet Rashid Hussein, the "Jews of the Jews." There, however, the comparison ended; the third world might perceive the Palestinians as fellow victims of imperialism, but in the eyes of the mighty—especially the United States, whose power was decisive in the Israeli-Palestinian conflict—the Palestinians were less even than an object of pity. Professor Sharabi wrote:

> 1967 made us see ourselves and our situation in a new light. . . . The Jews were in their homeland, a stirring spectacle in the eyes of the world, while our loss of homeland was of little moment. We suddenly saw ourselves for what we were in the eyes of the 'civilized' world: another species of Third World sub-humanity, existing outside history—the new Red Indians, the Blacks of Israel.[77]

The theme of dehumanization recurs in the writings of Palestinians. Edward Said perceives in the West—and especially the United States—an entrenched cultural attitude toward Palestinians deriving from traditional prejudices about Arabs and Islam. In the West, Said writes, "the Arabs and Islam *represent* viciousness, venality, degenerate vice, lechery and stupidity in popular and scholarly discourse." Arabs indeed, writes Said, are virtually the only ethnic group about whom racial slurs are still tolerated and even encouraged. At the same time Zionism has become identified with liberalism in the West, and as a result liberals, who would otherwise be expected to sympathize with victims of oppression, have shown indifference if not outright hostility to the Palestinian cause. Said writes: "In

Zionism the liberal West saw the triumph of reason and idealism . . . in liberalism Zionism saw itself as it wanted to be. In both cases the Arab was eliminated. . . ."[78]

Haunted by memories of persecution and the Holocaust, Israelis are deeply disconcerted by comparisons of their own experience with that of the Palestinians, especially in the area of human rights. As the occupation extended through two decades and beyond, however, instances of harsh treatment, arbitrary punishment, and even torture accumulated, as inevitably they would under an alien military regime ruling over a sullen, hostile, subject population. The *London Times* conducted an investigation in 1977 of instances of torture in the occupied territories and reported its conclusion that "torture of Arab prisoners is so widespead and systematic that it cannot be dismissed as 'rogue cops' exceeding orders."[79] The *Times* report was condemned in Israel and ignored in the United States, but in due course other reports of abuses accumulated, ultimately receiving cautious official acknowledgment in the United States. The State Department, in its 1978 annual report on human rights around the world, noted that Israel was a democracy whose standards of justice "within Israel" were comparable to those of the United States, but that under the military regime of the occupied territories certain normal human rights guarantees were "superseded on security grounds." Disclaiming knowledge of any evidence of the consistent practice of torture, the report added: "However, there are documented reports of the use of extreme physical and psychological pressures during interrogation, and instances of brutality by individual interrogators cannot be ruled out."[80]

The State Department went further in its report on human rights in 1979. Commenting at length on Israel's democratic credentials and high standards of justice and human rights internally, the report noted that these did not always apply, for security reasons, to the occupied territory. The "complex human rights situation" in the occupied territory, the report noted unexceptionably, was "largely the result of the tension between the occupying authorities and the indigenous population, mostly Palestinian Arabs." "Torture," the report said, "is prohibited by law in Israel, and is virtually unheard of." In the occupied territories, however, the report pointed out, reports of torture and brutality in the interrogation of suspects were both numerous and widely publicized, and there were allegations that mistreatment of detainees was a systematic practice. The State Department cautiously concluded that "the accumulation of reports, some from credible sources, makes it appear that instances of mistreatment had occurred."[81] Alluding perhaps to the domestic political implications rather than the circumspect phrasing of this statement, a State Department official characterized it as "dynamite."[82]

Other reports were less circumspect. The official State Department reports on human rights in both 1978 and 1979 stopped short of charging Israel with the consistent or systematic practice of torture, but two classified cables dispatched through the United States Consulate General in Jerusalem, respectively in May and November 1978, went considerably further, and undoubtedly contributed to the somewhat stronger language in the State Department's 1979 report than in its 1978 report. These cables, as obtained and released by the *Washington Post* in February 1979, suggested, in one instance, that the torture of Arab prisoners in the occupied territories "may be a widespread and even common practice," and in another instance, that "physical mistreatment is systematically used on many Arab security suspects interrogated in the West Bank." These reports, based on interviews with, and examination of court records pertaining to, Palestinian applicants for American visas who had previously been arrested by the Israeli authorities for "security offenses," were drafted by a Foreign Service Officer, Alexandra U. Johnson, who became engaged for a brief period to one of the Palestinians she interviewed and who was subsequently dismissed from the Foreign Service. Johnson's superiors in the Consulate General made it clear, however, that her dismissal was not for reasons of her reporting on human rights violations. Her superiors endorsed these reports as objective and transmitted them to the State Department, with a message of transmittal (in the case of the second of her two major reports), stating that "the weight of the evidence points to the validity of her general conclusion that physical mistreatment is systematically used," and that it seemed clear, on the basis of Johnson's research, that "Israeli practices on the West Bank go beyond acceptable civilian norms."[83]

The Israeli government vehemently denied the allegations contained in the Jerusalem cables and castigated the *Washington Post* for publishing them. In an official statement the government said that the reports of torture and mistreatment were "baseless, and have been refuted over and over again." Suspects were treated with due process of law, the statement said, and it went on to point out that Israel permitted access to prisoners within fourteen days of their arrest, without witnesses, by representatives of the International Committee of the Red Cross, including physicians who were permitted to examine the prisoners.[84] Israeli Minister of Justice Shmuel Tamir, on February 8, 1979, denounced allegations of brutality in the interrogation of Arab prisoners as "utterly false, baseless, and libelous," and as an intentional attempt "to smear our country and way of life" on behalf of "murderers."[85] Prime Minister Begin said on February 11 that the report in the *Washington Post* was "dishonest, libelous and utterly false." "The *Washington Post*," said Begin, "was invited to visit any jail and interview anybody it wanted but the paper chose instead to peddle sensationalism."[86]

The criticism of Israel's human rights standards also elicited a sharp reaction in the United States, shifting the focus of discussion from the accuracy of the charges against Israel to the propriety of their being raised. The chairman of the Conference of Presidents of Major Jewish Organizations, Theodore R. Mann, charged the *Washington Post* with joining "left-wing and extremist groups in the United States in a sensationalist and irresponsible attack" on Israel. The Jewish Community Council of Greater Washington referred to the statements of Palestinian detainees quoted in the Jerusalem cables as "self-serving statements of convicted terrorists dedicated to the destruction of the state of Israel. . . ."[87] The *New York Times*, ordinarily enthusiastic about human rights inquiries, judged the matter to be one of "clumsy public relations" on the part of the State Department, whose annual human rights report "managed to attract unfair attention to some alleged lapses." With prospects looking favorable for the then still uncompleted Egyptian-Israeli peace treaty, the *Times* asked, "Why rile the Israelis again and for policies that have been generally exemplary?"[88]

In the absence of first-hand observation by objective parties, it cannot be stated definitively that Israel has employed torture as a systematic practice. The State Department, however, would seem not to have exceeded the evidence at its disposal in its restrained observation that "instances of mistreatment" appeared to have occurred. Israel's principal basis for defense of its record, the access to detainees granted to the International Committee of the Red Cross, would seem in itself inconclusive, because the Red Cross saw only a fraction of Arab prisoners, and access was granted only within (which is to say at the end of) fourteen days, prior to which the prisoners customarily were held incommunicado. Palestinian detainees who have been released have said that mistreatment usually occurs within the first two or three days after arrest.[89] So numerous and vivid, moreover, were the accounts of mistreatment supplied by former Palestinian prisoners, so persuasive too were some of these accounts—not only to the interviewing officer, Ms. Johnson, whose credentials were questioned, but as well to her superiors in an institution justly famed for caution if not timidity in politically controversial matters—that it seems reasonable to suspect, as did the *Washington Post*, that "there is some fire behind this smoke."[90]

Torture is the extreme abuse of a regime of force, but a people under foreign occupation inevitably are subjected to many hardships and injustices short of the most extreme, ranging from personal indignities to collective punishment through the application of arbitrary security measures. The very fact that the occupation of Arab lands has lasted so long and prospects for its termination remain so uncertain, has intensified the anger and frustration of young Palestinians, while instilling hopelessness in many older people, who have come to doubt that either they or their children will ever live as a free people in their own homeland. In most of the major wars of the modern era, from the Napoleonic wars of the early nineteenth century to the two world wars of the twentieth century, foreign military occupations were relatively brief; and although some, notably the German occupation of Europe in World War II, were exceedingly cruel, few if any compared with the Israeli occupation of the Palestinian West Bank and Gaza in their connotations of permanence, of apparent institutionalization. This factor, perhaps more than any other, has caused the Palestinians to perceive themselves as the "Jews of the Jews."

In these conditions even comparative economic prosperity has earned the occupier neither affection nor gratitude. A research team from Bar-Ilan University in Israel completed in 1977 a five-year study of the attitudes of Palestinian Arabs working in Israel, questioning about 1,000 of the 50,000 who were then commuting from the West Bank and Gaza to work in construction, agriculture, industry, and services in Israel proper. The individuals questioned had worked with Israelis for at least a year, and they registered no significant decrease in hostility. The director of the study, Professor Yehuda Arim, said that the study directly challenged Israeli hopes for harmonious coexistence with the Arab population. "The study," he said, "shows no support for the naive assumption that time will take its course and that if only the Israelis and Arabs will live together, the Arabs after a time will come to accept the situation and change their attitude in a positive direction." Professor Arim offered the summary observation, "If someone hates your guts, living with him will make it worse."[91] A Palestinian professor of sociology, Salim Tamari of Bir Zeit University, told Senator Abourezk's Judiciary subcommittee in October 1977 that Arab workers from the occupied territories were used by the

Israelis as "cheap labor," especially in the construction industry. "Our workers," he said, "are constructing houses for Israeli immigrants . . . often in land which has been confiscated from Arab owners."[92]

There are, in addition, the daily, routine indignities undergone by a subject population. The future is uncertain; property is insecure, subject to one form or another of expropriation or encroachment by the occupation authorities—usually at the start for some ostensible military purpose, sometimes later for a new or expanding Jewish settlement. The wife of the principal of a West Bank school spoke in November 1978 of the importance Palestinian parents had come to place on education, on equipping their children to make a living and contribute to their communities wherever they might be or have to go: "What else," she asked, "can we give our children?" The woman's sister, born in Palestine but now an American citizen, described the difficulties of visits to her family in the West Bank—being detained for two hours at the airport, her belongings searched, made to undress, and interrogated about her family and her birthplace.[93] Everyday talk among West Bank people runs to relatives in Israeli jails, being stopped to show one's identity card, restrictions on the movements of suspected individuals, confiscations of property, encroaching Jewish settlements, insults or bullying by Israeli soldiers, the occasional summary expulsion of individuals from the country, the periodic demolition of the houses of suspected terrorists or of their families or others who may have sheltered them. Under British mandate law, still prevailing and regularly employed by the Israelis, individuals may be arrested and held without charges under "administrative detention" for as long as six months. Arrests in the middle of the night and denial of access by the families and lawyers of the unaccused prisoners are familiar occurrences. To be arrested for political reasons is frightening, but for Palestinians under occupation it is no disgrace; for many young people it is a mark of honor.[94]

Aspects of life under the occupation were described by witnesses before Senator Abourezk's Judiciary subcommittee in October 1977. Professor Tamari testified that all aspects of cultural expression, including drama, literary magazines, and the press, were subject to "extreme control" by the occupation authorities. "All references to Palestinian identity, to express a folk culture, are frowned upon," he said. Tamari recalled too the sudden, summary deportation of Dr. Hanna Nasir, president of Bir Zeit University, on the night of November 21, 1974. Student demonstrations in support of the Palestine Liberation Organization were taking place at the time, and although Dr. Nasir was not a participant in the demonstrations, he was arrested in the middle of the night, handcuffed and blind-folded, and driven by jeep to the Lebanese border, where he and several colleagues were thrust across, without escort, through the dangerous border military zone. Dr. Nasir was subsequently charged by the occupation authorities with having incited the students to riot.[95] Nasir subsequently took up residence in Amman, Jordan. Interviewed by the writer on October 31, 1978 regarding the recently concluded Camp David accords, he noted that, under their provisions, Israel would retain a veto over the return to the West Bank of Palestinians from outside—including, presumably, individuals who, like himself, had been summarily expelled. With no answers in the Camp David framework on such matters as Jewish settlements and Palestinians living abroad, to say nothing of ultimate Israeli withdrawal, Nasir thought the reference in the agreement to self-rule "most disgraceful," a euphemism for continued occupation.[96] Israeli military authorities have said that they ended involuntary deportations, which are a violation of the fourth Geneva Convention, in 1976.[97] This statement was made prior to the expulsion of two West Bank mayors and a religious leader in May 1980.

Administration of the occupied territories has involved constant friction, endless irritations, and occasional violence between the Israeli military government and the sullen, hostile population and their leaders. In April 1976 the Israeli authorities permitted local elections, which resulted in the election of strong supporters of the Palestine Liberation Organization as mayors of most of the major towns. These local leaders, who, as will be seen in the following section, were unanimous in their rejection of the Camp David accords, also came into conflict with the military government over the daily life and management of their communities. Permission of the occupation authorities is required for such matters as building a school or a market, letting a construction contract, or entering an arrangement with one of the several foreign private voluntary organizations that contribute to economic development in the West Bank and Gaza. For example, Mayor Mohammed Milhem of Halhoul, a small community between Bethlehem and Hebron, quarreled with the military government over the location of a produce market at a location on the town's main road, to which the occupation authorities objected on the ground that the noise of the market would be distracting to a nearby boys' school. The mayor pointed out that the normal market hours, early morning and evening, were at times when the school was not in session. With exasperation he commented, "It is not their boys who are studying in the school; it is our boys."[98]

The town of Halhoul came into more violent conflict with the occupying power in March 1979 in the aftermath of President Carter's final mission to Jerusalem to secure peace between Israel and Egypt. On March 15 Israeli soldiers and armed civilians from a nearby Jewish settlement opened fire on protesting, rock-throwing Palestinian youths in Halhoul who had trapped them in their cars. Two Palestinian young people were killed. Then, to punish the town for the violence, its 15,000 residents were placed under a twenty-three-hour-a-day curfew that lasted for sixteen days. During that period the townspeople were confined to their homes except for one hour a day to shop for food and other essentials. Israeli security forces patrolled the streets and barred access to the mayor's home. Milhem later commented that the town had been "kept under curfew to give an example to the rest of the people."[99]

A sensitive and critical issue between the West Bank Palestinians and the Israelis is control of water in that semiarid land. Israel after the 1967 war became increasingly dependent on the West Bank for its water supply and by 1979 was drawing a third of its water from the occupied land. As Jewish settlements were established on the West Bank, some of which engaged in intensive farming, the military government laid down strict rules on water use by Arabs, generally prohibiting the sinking of new wells or the enlargement of existing wells. Palestinians in turn, fearing the loss of control of their water resources, resisted where they could the connection of Arab towns and villages to the Israeli national water system. As negotiations for Palestinian autonomy were initiated in the wake of the Egyptian-Israeli peace treaty, Israeli officials, concerned for the water supply of Israel proper as well as its West Bank settlements, made it clear that continued effective control of the West Bank's water was an Israeli requirement. Palestinians, for their part, saw themselves being drawn into ever tighter dependence on Israeli authority. An autonomy plan that denies water rights, said Mayor Fahd Qawasmeh of Hebron, "doesn't even give us minimum autonomy."[100]

More perhaps than the mistreatment of prisoners or other major violations of rights, the restrictions and humiliations of daily life brought the Palestinians, as the long occupation wore on, to the sense of themselves as the "Jews of the Jews." The Palestinian people had been the "total owners of the land of Palestine," recalled Hikmat al-Masri of Nablus, a former head of the Jordanian parliament; but now, he said in November 1978, the Palestinians were reduced, in the antiseptic phrase of the Camp David accord, to the status of "inhabitants" of the West Bank and Gaza, if not indeed of "Eretz Israel."[101] The very term "inhabitants," as used in the

Camp David agreement, quickly took on a malign symbolism to West Bank Palestinians; it became a term of art invented by diplomats to refer to people they had no other name for, defining the Palestinian people, as it seemed, not for what they were, but for what they were *not*—as "tenants" (in the ironic term of Mayor Khalaf of Ramallah),[102] as squatters in what they had thought was their own land, as "the strangers within our gates" Menachem Begin referred to in 1948,[103] as a nondescript category of humanity in diplomatic or juridical terms, as anything but citizens with rights.

The bitter feelings, the sense of loss and wrong, and the nationalism deriving from these have acquired a center of intellectual expression at Bir Zeit University in the West Bank. There Palestinian students and their professors develop ideas and hopes for a future Palestinian state, denounce and sometimes agitate against the occupation, and cultivate and reinforce among each other a sense of Palestinian nationality. To Israelis Bir Zeit represents, in the words of a military spokesman, "a snake pit, college-sized," where extremist activities and plots are hatched, from behind whose campus walls stones and bottles are thrown at Israeli soldiers.[104] To Palestinians Bir Zeit is a center of patriotism and pride, of resistance to the foreigner's rule and hope for the future. The Israelis have periodically cracked down on Bir Zeit, suspending classes or restricting access in the wake of demonstrations, arresting and holding students under administrative detention, or harassing and humiliating them in various ways. Nafez Nazzal, professor of Middle East studies at the University, estimated in mid-1978 that almost all of Bir Zeit's approximately 1,000 students were supporters of the Palestine Liberation Organization and that at least half had been detained at one time or another by the occupation authorities. "To them the PLO is their dignity, their identity, their loyalty," Professor Nazzal said.[105] On May 2, 1979 the Israeli military government closed down Bir Zeit University for an "indefinite period" in the wake of clashes between Israeli Gush Emunim supporters (conducting a procession in the town of Bir Zeit in celebration of Israel's thirty-first anniversary) and protesting Palestinian students. On May 21 an advertisement signed by sixty Israeli professors appeared in the newspaper *Ha'aretz* protesting the closing of Bir Zeit University as an arbitrary act of collective punishment that obscured "the distinction between criminal acts and the free expression of political views. At a time when the government is shaping policy concerning autonomy," the Israeli professors said, "freedom of discussion is more, not less, imperative."[106]

Whatever sentiment may once have existed for the recovery of all

Palestine as called for in the Palestinian National Covenant of 1968, nationalist aspirations in the West Bank were focused in the late seventies on the achievement of a separate Palestinian state in the West Bank and Gaza. The intellectuals of Bir Zeit rejected the Camp David framework of September 1978, but they also made clear their readiness, if they had a state of their own, to recognize and live in peace with Israel.[107] The only thing that was not negotiable, said the dean of arts, Mohammed Hallaj in November 1978, was the right of the Palestinian people to a national existence of their own. That could be attained, Hallaj and his colleagues believed, if the United States were prepared to apply the necessary pressure on Israel to secure a comprehensive settlement including Palestinian independence. But the United States had "sabotaged" that possibility, Dean Hallaj said, by fostering the separate peace between Egypt and Israel, which left Israel with less incentive than ever to accept Palestinian self-determination. Discouraging though the situation was in the wake of Camp David, Hallaj felt confident, nevertheless, that Israel could not hold the West Bank indefinitely—because the long occupation was a "historical aberration," and because someday the Arabs could be expected to mobilize their real power, human and material, which neither the United States nor the rest of the world could ignore, which indeed could alter the balance of power so as to "make the world treat us differently."[108]

Similar views have been expressed by the exiled West Bank mayors, Mohammed Milhem of Halhoul and Fahd Qawasmeh of Hebron. In May 1981, for example, the two exiled officials reiterated their readiness to live in peace in a Palestinian state confined to the West Bank and Gaza. "We should add," they wrote, "that we also vigorously espouse peace and security for all nations in the area, including Israel." They also reiterated willingness to have the Israeli military withdrawal deferred for five years. This, Milhem had said to an Israeli audience in March 1980 (two months before his expulsion), "is enough time to put the minds of the Israelis at rest and to test the good will of the Palestinians."[109]

Although clear in their aspirations, Palestinian leaders and intellectuals are ambivalent and uncertain in their expectations. They express confidence in ultimate self-determination, which they consider historically inevitable, but they despair of its early attainment, and they fear that Israeli encroachments may drive them from their own land before history can work its will. As to the United States, they see American history, principles, and interests working in their favor, but they also see American policy, for reasons they can scarcely fathom, working against them. In their minds they accept the permanence of Israel and are willing to live in peace with it, but in their hearts they still share the perception expressed by Professor Sharabi in 1973 that Israel's happiness is made of Palestinian tears, that the Israelis have a country because the Palestinians are without one, that Israel's strength is the Palestinians' weakness, its pride their humiliation, that "Israel's being is the Palestinians' non-being."[110]

CAMP DAVID, THE ARABS AND THE PALESTINIANS

At the time of the Camp David agreements, in September 1978, President Carter was apparently convinced that the Palestinians of the West Bank and Gaza would readily accept, if not warmly welcome, the autonomy plan for the West Bank and Gaza. Calling for a transitional "self-governing authority," to be followed after five years by an undefined permanent regime whose nature the Palestinians would "participate" in determining, the plan for the West Bank and Gaza, Carter told Congress, "outlines a process of change which is in keeping with Arab hopes, while also respecting Israel's vital security interests." The two agreements signed at Camp David, the president said, "hold out the possibility of resolving issues that history had taught us could not be resolved."[111]

Euphoria was still at a peak in Washington as messages began to arrive indicating that the Camp David plan was not "in keeping with Arab hopes." Chairman Arafat of the Palestine Liberation Organization, to no one's surprise, denounced the accords as a "dirty deal."[112] On the same day, September 19, to the considerable surprise of the Carter administration, Saudi Arabia, and Jordan, declining to wait for Secretary Vance's imminent mission of explanation, also criticized the agreement. The Saudi Cabinet in an official communiqué, said that the Camp David procedure "cannot be regarded as an acceptable final formula for peace," because it did not outline a plan of Israeli withdrawal from all occupied Arab territory including Jerusalem, because it did not stipulate Palestinian self-determination, and because it ignored the role of the Palestine Liberation Organization.[113] The Jordanian government, in a statement approved personally by King Hussein, criticized the plan for a separate peace between Egypt and Israel and disavowed any "legal or moral commitments" to play the role assigned to Jordan by the accord—which Jordan "played no part in discussing, formulating or approving."[114] On September 20, 1978 Mayor Karim Khalaf of Ramallah, the largest of the West Bank towns, who was in Washington at the time, issued a statement denouncing the Camp David summit as "a big disappointment—maybe the disappointment of the century," and the product of the summit as "two documents that have given the Zionists all that they want and deprived the Palestinian people of their basic rights."[115] King Hussein, having received Secretary Vance and heard his appeal for Jordan's support, recalled at a news conference on September 23 that it was an Egyptian-commanded Arab army that had lost the West Bank and Golan Heights in 1967, as well as the Egyptian Sinai. "When I look back," the king said, "I recall hearing from the leaders of Egypt that they were for a comprehensive settlement. I am absolutely shattered."[116] A concise and, as events were to show, prophetic observation on the Camp David agreements was offered by a PLO official in Beirut, who said: "It's true there can be no war without Egypt, but there can be no peace without the PLO."[117]

To the dismay and puzzlement of American policy makers, rejection of the Camp David accords was quick and overwhelming among the Palestinians in the occupied territories. Not only the intellectuals of Bir Zeit, but the elected mayors (most of them PLO supporters) and, by all indications, the population at large, rejected the autonomy proposal for the West Bank and Gaza, perceiving it not as an avenue toward realization of their hopes but as a thin disguise for the perpetuation of the occupation. A visit to the West Bank in October 1978 by Assistant Secretary of State Harold Saunders won no converts for Camp David among the West Bank notables, who did not believe the State Department official's suggestions that the autonomy plan might evolve toward eventual Israeli withdrawal. The Saunders mission succeeded only in infuriating the Israelis, who, unlike the Palestinians, took Saunders at his word and responded by announcing the enlargement of their West Bank settlements.[118] Some of the leading Palestinians refused even to meet Saunders, and others insisted that the contact be kept secret. Hanna Nasir, the exiled president of Bir Zeit University, refused to see Saunders in Amman, commenting later that it had seemed Saunders was coming not to get the facts but to "sell" a product; if he had come before Camp David, it would have been different. He understood well, Nasir added, that, because of the influence of the Jewish lobby, the United States could do little for the Palestinians, and for that reason "they can't expect much of us either."[119]

Without exception the principal West Bank mayors, in the wake of the Camp David agreements, stressed two requirements for their participation in a transitional autonomy plan: the assurance of self-determination at the end of the transition period and the assent, tacit if not explicit, of the PLO. No Palestinian, said Mayor Fahd Qawasmeh of Hebron in early November 1978, would negotiate whether the West Bank was to be Palestinian or Israeli. It should be understood at the outset that the West

Bank was "Palestinian land" and that the transition period would end with Palestinian self-determination; the details of arriving at that goal would then be an appropriate topic of negotiation.[120] Even if a West Bank leader personally perceived in the Camp David procedure a "chance that had to be grasped," Mayor Mohammed Milhem of Halhoul said, that leader would be acting on his own; the people were for self-determination and the PLO. Milhem said he had little doubt that both the people of the West Bank and the PLO would accept a transitional autonomy plan if there were a clear commitment to self-determination at the end of it.[121] The Camp David autonomy plan, said Mayor Karim Khalaf of Ramallah, "will never be accepted by us," to do so would be "to accept the occupation forever." Like Milhem, Khalaf expressed confidence that the PLO would accept an independent state made up of the West Bank and Gaza; any decision taken by the PLO, said Khalaf, would be accepted by the West Bank population.[122] Mayor Bassam Shaka' of Nablus expressed similar views and said that the Palestinians would persevere in the struggle for their national rights. Asked how the struggle might be carried on, Mayor Shaka' said that determining the appropriate means was the prerogative of the PLO not of the mayor of a town under occupation.[123]

Known for his prudence and pragmatism, Mayor Elias Freij of Bethlehem, the only mayor of a major West Bank town who was not elected on a pro-PLO slate in 1976, would have seemed a likely supporter of the Camp David "self-governing authority." Freij's judgment in November 1978 was that the plan would work if the PLO and Jordan approved, if strong local personalities were involved, if East Jerusalem were included, and if the self-governing authority had legislative as well as administrative powers and also control of state lands, thus enabling it to prevent further Jewish settlements. None of this was likely to come about, Freij thought; the Israelis surely would not agree to these terms, their apparent purpose being to divide the Palestinians and convince the United States that real Palestinian autonomy or independence would bring radicalism and Soviet domination.

What then was likely to come of the Camp David plan for the West Bank? "Nothing," said Freij. "There will be stagnation. There will be confusion." Only in the long term, Mayor Freij suggested, as normal relations between Egypt and Israel took form, would change come in the West Bank. When Israelis could go to Alexandria or Aswan, they might also want then to be free to go to Amman and Jerash in Jordan and might begin to place more value on gaining that freedom than on building West Bank settlements. The opening to Egypt might over time, thought Freij, work major psychological changes, helping the Israelis to "get their fingers off the trigger," which in turn might bring the Palestinians to a point at which "the brave slogans you hear now will be substituted by more practical slogans." Change would come about not as the result of agreements but from the "force of events."[124]

Except for Freij—and he only with the utmost circumspection—none of the principal figures on the West Bank could foresee, in the wake of Camp David, any good coming to the Palestinians from peace between Egypt and Israel. Neither the professors of Bir Zeit nor the West Bank mayors were receptive to the advice offered by some of the Israeli "doves"—that they take the administrative autonomy for whatever it might be worth and build on it, step by step, as the Zionists had once done, putting a foot in any door, building on modest opportunities until at last they achieved their goal.[125] The Bir Zeit professors dismissed this approach as unsuitable and unpromising, arguing that the circumstances of the Palestinians in the late seventies were in no way comparable with those of the Jews in the thirties and forties when Zionism—from a Palestinian perspective—rode a favorable historical tide.[126] Whatever attraction, if any, an approach of pragmatic gradualism might have had for the West Bank mayors in the wake of Camp David, was in any case effectively negated by Prime Minister Begin's uncompromising statements on Jewish settlement and against any Palestinian state.[127] Some Palestinian leaders, it seems clear, were also deterred by the fear of putting themselves outside the consensus of their colleagues and exposing themselves to the sometimes lethal vengeance of the PLO. Another inhibiting factor was cultural: pragmatic incrementalism is not the style of Palestinians, whose tendency has been to stand on principle and pride. Further, in the wake of thirty years of defeat, exile, and occupation, the Palestinians have an acute sense of their own weakness: they do not trust themselves in an open-ended political contest with the politically skilled and militarily dominant Israelis because they fear they would lose it. Palestinians would only have an impact when they proved they were a "party to be reckoned with," Mayor Milhem of Halhoul said, and that was not possible in the aftermath of Camp David.[128] Palestinians in the occupied territories make the point too, when pragmatism is urged on them, that they have demonstrated sufficient flexibility in reconciling themselves to the loss of three-fourths of what was once their homeland, and in their readiness to live in peace with Israel in return for being allowed to set up their own state in the remaining one-fourth of Palestine consisting of the West Bank and Gaza.

Although rejection of the Camp David accords by the Palestinians in the occupied territories was a considerable disappointment to the Carter administration, American policy makers had not counted on "winning" the Palestinians by direct persuasions alone. Greater reliance was placed on their being "delivered" by Saudi Arabia and Jordan, who, with Egypt, were the other designated participants in determining the Palestinian future. No effort was to be made, however, to enlist the cooperation of the Palestine Liberation Organization, whose leaders the administration regarded as having "removed themselves" from the peace process.[129] However, as events were to make increasingly clear (both in the immediate aftermath of Camp David in the fall of 1978 and later in the wake of the Egyptian-Israeli peace treaty of March 1979) neither Saudi Arabia nor Jordan were disposed to cooperate with American policy. Declining to try to "deliver" the Palestinians for the Camp David accords, the two Arab countries went on to become active opponents both of the autonomy plan for the West Bank and Gaza and of Egypt's separate peace with Israel. At the Arab meetings in Baghdad in November 1978 and March 1979, both Saudi Arabia and Jordan joined the hardline Arab states and the PLO in imposing severe sanctions against Egypt.

The intensity of Saudi opposition to the Camp David accords took American officials by surprise. The prevailing impression in the State Department and in the American embassy in Jidda in the weeks after Camp David was that, except for their special concern for Jerusalem, the Saudis had no strong objection to the autonomy plan for the West Bank and Gaza and would in any case accept any settlement that was acceptable to the Arab "confrontation" states. Their interest in a Palestinian state was considered to be an aspect of their own national security policy rather than a commitment on principle, based on the expectation that a state of their own would absorb Palestinian energies that might otherwise be applied, in anger and frustration, to the destabilization of the Arab world. It was also assumed by American officials that the Saudis would continue to place high value on the moderation of President Sadat and would therefore continue to bolster him, financially and otherwise, even though they disliked the separate peace with Israel and other aspects of Egyptian policy.[130]

Although Saudi officials were characteristically restrained in expressing to Americans their dismay with American policy, they made no secret of their dislike of the Camp David accords, and they placed considerable emphasis on Saudi Arabia's support of Palestinian aspirations. Prince Turki al-Faisal, the director general of intelligence, said on October 25, 1978 that the Camp David agreements had been presented to Saudi officials as the initiation of a process leading toward self-determination, but "there are no assurances," he added, and he doubted that a free expression of the Palestinian will was possible without some kind of guarantees. Palestinians were like Israelis in that "they don't trust anyone," the Prince said, and for that reason he felt certain that no Palestinians would participate in the Camp David procedure without the approval of the PLO or without guarantees of ultimate Israeli withdrawal from the occupied territories.

Turning to Saudi Arabia's own role in the peace process, Prince Turki said that his country had only indirect interests in the Palestinian problem, that it would acquiesce in anything the confrontation states decided with respect to their lost territories, but that Saudi Arabia could neither speak for the Syrians, Jordanians, and Palestinians nor tell them what to do. Prince Turki specifically and emphatically disavowed the use of Saudi Arabia's financial support of Jordan and the Palestinians as a means of applying political pressure on them: "We have never used this way of getting a direct return," he said. Saudi financial support, said the prince, gave evidence to the Palestinians of Saudi Arabia's sincerity, reliability, and disinterested judgment and thus won the Palestinians' trust. The United States, he said, could give money or withhold it, and also use other means, to influence other countries; but "our strength is fragile," said Turki, money being his country's only means of influence, and because other sources of finance were available to the recipients of Saudi money, "we can only use it by giving, not by threatening to take it away." Further, on the subject of why Saudi Arabia would not urge King Hussein and the Palestinians to play their assigned roles in the Camp David plan, Prince Turki said that it was not within his country's power to convince Palestinians of the good will of an American administration that, even though it had gone further than any of its predecessors in recognizing Palestinian rights, still would not talk to them. "We have experienced the good will of the United States," he said, "but not the Palestinians. There are things that are beyond our means," the Prince said.[131]

If Saudi Arabia misled the United States in any way after the Camp David agreement, it was, as noted in chapter 3, as to their attitude toward Egypt, not as to the Camp David plan for the West Bank and Gaza. Politely but firmly Saudi officials made it clear from the outset that they would do nothing either to encourage or oppose Palestinian participation in the autonomy plan for the West Bank and Gaza. Their position, in essence, was that it was an inadequate proposal that the Palestinians could not be blamed for rejecting, although they themselves, trusting the good intentions of the United States, might have gone along with it.[132] Raymond H. Close—who had served as CIA Chief of Station in Jidda for over six years until February 1977 and then remained in Saudi Arabia as a business consultant, said in Jidda on October 25, 1978 that he was "positive" the Saudis would not actively try to "deliver" the Palestinians for the Camp David autonomy plan no matter how hard the United States pressured them to do so.[133] If American officials allowed themselves to believe otherwise, it may have been because the Saudis did not make their position clear enough at the time, speaking as they tend to in polite euphemisms; more probably it was because the Americans, wedded to the idea that the Saudi concern for Palestinian self-determination was purely expedient and not a commitment of principle, simply did not believe that the Saudis meant what they said.

The mistake of American policy makers who counted on Saudi support for the Camp David agreements was in supposing that something that was *partially* true was in fact the whole truth. It has long been apparent beyond reasonable doubt that the Saudis feared Palestinians and the PLO as agents of radicalism and were prepared to support Palestinian nationalism and make payments to the PLO largely for purposes of self-protection. It also appears to be true—and this is the point American policy makers have sometimes overlooked—that the Saudis, although fearful of Palestinian radicalism, are by no means without genuine sympathy for the Palestinian claim to a state of their own. The basis of this sympathy, as noted in chapter 3, is the *umma*—the religious and cultural conception of the Arabs as forming, despite all political and ideological divisions, a single people or "nation."

No less than Saudi Arabia, the refusal of Jordan to cooperate with the Camp David procedure came as an unpleasant surprise to American policy makers, who were taken aback as well by the bitterness of King Hussein's opposition. Although not a party to the Camp David agreement, Jordan, under its provisions, was to play an important role in negotiating the details of the transitional regime, in determining the final status of the West Bank and Gaza, and in cooperating with Israel to maintain security during the transition. Hussein found all of these roles unattractive; he found the last offensive. Jordan was being asked, he said some months later, to safeguard "the security of the occupying power against the people under occupation."[134] In an interview on CBS Television's "Face the Nation" on October 1, 1978, King Hussein said that his relations with the United States were at a "rather critical juncture," and he read out a list of questions he said he had submitted to the United States including the following: Would the administrative autonomy apply to Arab Jerusalem as part of the West Bank? Who would exercise sovereignty after the transition period? What would the status of Arab Jerusalem be after the transition period? Would Israeli settlements remain during and after the transition? Would the people of the West Bank and Gaza be accorded the right of self-determination? What is envisaged by the United States for the majority of Palestinians living as refugees outside the occupied territories?[135]

To these seminal questions the State Department prepared answers that it was decided to keep secret lest their publication displease the government of Israel. However, according to columnists Rowland Evans and Robert Novak, who had obtained the secret replies to King Hussein, they included the following: whatever number of Jewish settlers might remain after the five-year transition period "would presumably be agreed to in the negotiations concerning the final status of the West Bank and Gaza." And as to Arab Jerusalem, the United States would "support proposals" permitting the Arabs of East Jerusalem to vote and participate in the self-rule plan.[136] The American answers failed to satisfy King Hussein, who aligned himself with the militants at the Baghdad summit conference of Arab leaders in early November 1978, entered a cautious rapprochement with his erstwhile enemies in the PLO, and continued to denounce the Camp David accords with uncharacteristic bluntness. While failing to satisfy King Hussein, the American reply on the Israeli settlements incensed Prime Minister Begin, who, as previously noted, announced on October 25, 1978 that Israel would enlarge its West Bank settlements as soon as possible.[137]

Relations between Jordan and the United States deteriorated steadily after Camp David, and further still after the Egyptian-Israeli peace treaty of March 26, 1979. Six days before the treaty was signed, and two days after President Carter's national security adviser, Zbigniew Brzezinski had come to explain its terms, King Hussein charged the United States with "arm-twisting" in its efforts to win support for the treaty. The Arab people, the king told a group of American reporters, were being asked to "acquiesce or support a totally unacceptable situation," and were threatened, if they did not, with the displeasure of Congress and American public opinion. Rejecting once again the "humiliating" role assigned to Jordan by the Camp David accords, the king said that Israel had achieved a vital objective in detaching Egypt and consolidating its hold on the occupied territories. The United States was in an "almost impossible position," King Hussein said. "A country cannot claim such a special relationship with Israel, giving large amounts of aid and arms, and be able to be a mediator that can claim to be fair and influence events."[138]

To no one's surprise, Syria, the third "confrontation" state on Israel's borders, also rejected the Camp David accords and, to everyone's surprise, formed a rapprochement (which was to prove short-lived) with its hitherto bitter enemy, Iraq. Distracted by its military involvement in Lebanon, and largely ignored by the United States, which had no expectation of Syrian assistance in "delivering" the Palestinians, Syria played only a minor role in the post–Camp David diplomacy. Syrian officials stressed, however, their readiness to make peace with Israel on the basis of United Nations Security Council Resolutions 242 and 338 (the latter reaffirming the former); and, according to the United States Embassy in Damascus, President Assad seemed not to doubt the sincerity of American intentions to implement the provisions of the Camp David agreements regarding the West Bank and Gaza but greatly doubted the ability of the United States to deliver.[139] Syria, in the wake of Camp David, remained committed, however, to a comprehensive settlement, an approach "totally different" from that of the United States, in the description of a Foreign Ministry official, who also said, regarding the Palestinians, that there could be no partial peace or partial sovereignty or partial self-determination. "No Arab will rest," he said, as long as the Palestinians were denied justice.[140]

In the six months between the Camp David agreements of September 1978 and the signing of the Egyptian-Israeli peace treaty in March 1979, it became evident that the Arab world was all but unanimous in its rejection of Egypt's separate peace and that, except for Egypt, none of the designated Arab parties—Jordan, Saudi Arabia, or the Palestinians of the occupied territories— could be brought to participate in the Camp David plan for a "self-governing authority" for the West Bank and Gaza. All three, for various and overlapping reasons, remained unwavering in their insistence on prior assurance of Palestinian self-determination at the end of a designated transition period. All three insisted too that there could be no progress without the participation of the Palestine Liberation Organization, which was excluded by the Camp David accords.

These attitudes remained unchanged, and even hardened, in the wake of the partial peace. Saudi Arabia continued to pursue an oil policy favorable to the United States and to look to the United States for support of its security; but the Saudis remained firm in their rejection of Camp David, offering instead, in the summer of 1981, a peace plan calling for Israeli withdrawal from the territories occupied since 1967 and the establishment of an independent Palestinian state with its capital in Jerusalem. King Hussein, as was noted in chapter 4, repeatedly and forcefully rejected the "Jordanian option" as an alternative to Palestinian self-determination and to the participation of the PLO in making a general settlement. Camp David, the king said in early 1981, was a "dead horse."[141] Syria became steadily more estranged from the United States and on October 8, 1980 signed a twenty-year treaty of friendship with the Soviet Union.

As the Reagan administration moved slowly toward grappling with the issue of Middle East peace, it encountered an Arab world profoundly divided in many respects but, except for Egypt, united in its support of Palestinian self-determination and the right of the PLO to represent the Palestinian people. Nor, despite tentative initiatives in 1981 on the part of the new Israeli defense minister, General Ariel Sharon, did significant new West Bank leaders come forward to cooperate with the occupying authorities or to participate in the Palestinian autonomy talks.

For the Reagan administration, as for the Carter administration, there seemed no feasible alternative, if peace were to be made, to dealing in one form or another with the PLO. "Any leader who ignores the PLO ignores reality," Mayor Freij of Bethlehem commented after the Camp David accords were signed.[142] "If you are serious about peace," Hanna Nasir, the exiled president of Bir Zeit University said in Amman after Camp David, "deal with the PLO. They are the people who represent us."[143] Reviled by Israel and boycotted by the United States, but still, by all indications, commanding the loyalty and support of the Palestinians both within and outside the occupied territories, the PLO remained the absent party to the "process of change" that President Carter had so confidently told Congress, after Camp David, would be "in keeping with Arab hopes. . . ."[144]

ARAFAT AND THE PLO

In the Arab world, by contrast with the United States, to say nothing of Israel, Yasser Arafat and his principal associates are considered moderates, inhibited from a more forthright policy of accommodation by the intransigence of Israel and the unresponsiveness of the United States, on the one side, and by the extremist pressures of rival Palestinian factions on the other.[145] It was well known, Mayor Milhem of Halhoul said in November 1978, that, unlike George Habash, head of the Popular Front for the Liberation of Palestine, Yasser Arafat would settle for a West Bank-Gaza state, but he had little incentive to emphasize that because he knew it was unattainable under existing circumstances. By denying Arafat and his still-dominant associates in the PLO their limited objective, Milhem said, the Camp David procedure would promote "extremism and rejection."[146] This thesis—of Arafat's moderation and the importance of rewarding it—has been commended to the United States many times by its friends in the Arab world, but without result. Crown Prince Fahd of Saudi Arabia told Senator Baker in 1975 that Arafat was the "best" and "most reasonable" person to represent the Palestinians and that if the United States would cultivate him and so strengthen his position, the extremist Palestinian factions would "wither on the vine." Senator Baker asked the Crown Prince if he thought Arafat had the personal capacity to change from a guerrilla leader to a responsible government leader. The transition would be "almost automatic," Prince Fahd replied, and Arafat would then be able to silence the rejectionists "once America offers him the hand."[147] Crown Prince Fahd reiterated that advice in the wake of the Egyptian-Israeli treaty, judging it "incumbent" on the United States to talk to the PLO and offering Saudi good offices to arrange the dialogue.[148]

In a variety of ways, direct and indirect, Arafat from time to time reached out for the American hand, but was unwilling, or politically unable, to meet the conditions that the United States said were essential: explicit acceptance of United Nations Security Council Resolution 242 and acknowledgment of Israel's right to exist. As will be seen, Arafat and his colleagues have come close to saying these things: they have said them by euphemism and they have said them indirectly; they have allowed them to be said explicitly by intermediaries; they themselves have said them explicitly in private and then not always denied the report later. They had always, however, stopped short of the explicit statements demanded by the United States, explaining that recognition of Israel was the last card in their hand—a card they dared not play except in return for Israeli recognition of the right of the Palestinians to a state of their own. To play that crucial card for less—for nothing more than the privilege of *talking* on an official level with the United States—was something they would not and, politically, could not do.

PLO leaders point, nevertheless, to a steady evolution of their attitudes. In the Palestinian view the proposed democratic secular state represented a major innovation, not toward the destruction of Israel but toward the creation of a bicommunal state based on secular human rights.[149] In his address to the United Nations General Assembly on November 13, 1974, Chairman Arafat invited the Jews of Israel to "emerge from their moral isolation" so that Jews and Arabs might "live together in a framework of just peace, in our democratic Palestine."[150] Received in the United States as a strident attack on Israel, the speech was defended by Arafat as an appeal for reconciliation, and he expressed astonishment and indignation that it had been interpreted otherwise. There had been an orchestrated effort by "Zionist leaders" in the United States to portray his United Nations speech as conveying "something that was not in it," he told Senator McGovern in March 1975.[151] Two months later Arafat made the same point to Senate Baker: the speech, he said, had been greatly distorted by the American press, which had chosen to see in it only the intent to destroy Israel, not the "positive steps we have taken." He and his colleagues were the "first leadership" to have taken these positive steps, Arafat told Baker, but Prime Minister Rabin of Israel had responded to the offer contained in the United Nations speech by saying Israel would meet the PLO "only on the battlefield."[152]

In his meeting with Senator McGovern in Beirut on March 28, 1975, Chairman Arafat cited, as evidence of a "bold" and "realistic" evolution, the resolution adopted by the Palestine National Council, the PLO's legislative body, in June 1974 to seek to establish a Palestinian national authority over any part of Palestine that might be liberated from occupation. Asked by Senator McGovern, specifically and repeatedly, whether this meant the acceptance of Israel with its 1967 boundaries, a Palestinian state confined to the West Bank and Gaza, and mutual recognition, Arafat replied each time, "yes." McGovern announced Arafat's stated willingness to settle for a West Bank-Gaza state in a press conference in Jerusalem on April 4, 1975; no denial was subsequently issued by the PLO.[153] Chairman Arafat was less forthcoming in his meeting with Senator Baker on May 22, 1975, reiterating the decision of the Palestine National Council in June 1974 to raise the Palestinian flag over any liberated territory, but also disavowing any intention to seek to destroy Israel by force. His long-term goal remained, he said, the establishment of a democratic state "for my people and the Jewish people," but "this is not the dream for next year."[154]

PLO attitudes evolved further in the year 1977, encouraged, it would seem, by the newly installed Carter administration's call for a comprehensive settlement in the Middle East and by President Carter's endorsement of a "homeland" for the Palestinian people.[155] The Palestine National Council at its meeting in Cairo in March 1977 adopted a resolution calling for the establishment of a Palestinian state in part of the territory of Palestine, accepting the principle of partition without the qualification that had been attached to the resolution of June 1974, which stated that a "permanent and just peace" could only come with self-determination for the Palestinian people "on the whole of the soil of their homeland." In light of the vehement rejection of past proposals for partition, these resolutions, especially the one of 1977, were regarded by the PLO leadership as major departures, amending in effect the Palestinian National Covenant, implying the acceptance of Israel, and—while not abandoning the goal of the democratic, secular state—relegating it to the status of a "dream" for the distant future that need not be an obstacle to more immediate, feasible arrangements. In addition, the Palestine National Council session of March 1977 elected a new PLO Executive Committee excluding representatives of the "rejection front," who refused to consider peaceful coexistence with Israel under any conditions. In an article published in autumn of 1977, the head of the Israel section of the PLO Research Center in Beirut, Sabri Jiryis, wrote that "the fact that the PLO now calls for the establishment of an independent Palestinian state in part of the territory of Palestine and demands participation in efforts to reach a political settlement in the area certainly means that the Palestinians have adopted a new attitude, very different from all the previous attitudes."[156]

Although pragmatic realism has by no means become dominant in Palestinian thinking, or in the policy of the PLO, it is no longer despised as it was from the time the Zionist impact on Palestine first made itself strongly felt in the early years of the twentieth century until the period following the October War of 1973. Modern Palestinian history can be summed up, Sabri Jiryis wrote, as a series of rejections by Palestinians of all proposals for the solution of the Palestinian problem—from the Balfour Declaration of 1917 to the United Nations partition resolution of 1947 and even the Rogers Plan of 1969, the proposal of the American secretary of state calling for Israeli withdrawal to the borders of 1967 with no more than "insubstantial" alterations and for a "just settlement" of the problem of the Palestinians.[157] In the years of their diaspora, however, beginning in 1948, the Palestinian people were transformed from a semitribal, agricultural society to a modern people including intellectuals, educated civil servants, and trained technicians. Among these groups individuals came to prominence who recognized the futility and high cost of the rejectionism of the past. They recognized too that while the old Palestinian leadership had led their people to disaster by relying on rhetoric unsupported by the power to give it effect, the Zionists, through realism about their own strengths and weaknesses and tactical flexibility, had gained vast rewards. To these Palestinians the enemy became, for strategic purposes, the exemplar.[158] The October War of 1973, resulting in partial Arab success and followed by intensified diplomatic efforts to achieve a Middle East settlement, precipitated a sustained reexamination of attitudes and options within the PLO and among Palestinians both in the occupied territories and in the diaspora. The result was the adoption of an attitude described by Sabri Jiryis as one of "tough and cautious moderation" by Palestinians who learned gradually that "realism, pragmatism and moderation are not to be despised as a means of achieving a people's goals."[159]

Another expression of the new Palestinian realism appeared in an article (in the American journal *Foreign Affairs* in July 1978) by Walid Khalidi, professor of political studies at the American University of Beirut. Khalidi, who was born in Jerusalem, has been regarded as one of the intellectual leaders of Palestinian nationalism, and his article could be read, if not as a direct "signal" from the PLO to the United States, then in any event as an accurate expression of the thinking of Yasser Arafat and his principal colleagues. Until recently, Khalidi wrote, Arab perceptions of Zionism and Israel had been set in an unbreakable mold: the United Nations partition resolution of 1947 was perceived as a travesty of self-determination; Western support of Jewish immigration into Palestine had been an "exercise in charity at the expense of others;" and Zionism itself was seen as a latter-day manifestation of Western imperialism, an intolerable anachronism imposed on the Arabs at a time when the decolonization of the third world was almost complete. These perceptions, wrote Khalidi, which had inhibited the Arabs from coming to terms realistically with the Arab-Israeli conflict, began to give way in the seventies to a new, more pragmatic outlook owing to several factors, including the impact of the defeat of 1967, growing awareness of the extent of the American commitment to Israel, parallel awareness of the limits of Soviet support for the Arabs, a new Arab self-confidence generated by oil wealth and the creditable Arab military performance in 1973, and growing awareness on the part of Palestinians of what "armed struggle" could and could not achieve.[160]

The new Arab and Palestinian realism, wrote Khalidi, provided the basis for an "honorable overall settlement" of the Middle East conflict. The cornerstone of the settlement would be a sovereign Palestinian state in the West Bank, including East Jerusalem—the "natural capital of Arab Palestine"—and Gaza. Only such a state, endorsed by the PLO, could win the support of Arab opinion and the majority of Arab states, wrote Khalidi; that could not be accomplished by a "Bantustan" linked to Jordan, still less by an Israeli-dominated sham autonomy. The Palestinians would thus, for the first time, accept the principle of partition, "with all the implications of such acceptance for Israeli-Palestinian and Israeli-Arab reciprocal recognition and coexistence."[161] The government of the Palestinian state, as envisioned by Khalidi, would necessarily involve the PLO; the "centrist" Fatah would form the "backbone" of the Palestinian government—its centrist tendencies reinforced by the Palestinians who lived under the occupation, by the professional Palestinian elite of the diaspora, by economic dependence on the Arab oil producing countries and other foreign sources, and by the need for cooperation with Jordan.[162] As to the security question and Israel's insistence that a Palestinian state would pose a mortal threat to its existence, Khalidi projects a military balance between the two states "crushingly" in favor of Israel, noting too that the Palestinian state would be divided in two parts, both virtually encircled by Israel. Far from being tempted by adventure, any PLO leadership of the new state would be acutely aware of the risks of confrontation with a vastly more powerful Israel. The real security question indeed was: "For how long would the Israeli brigadier generals be able to keep their hands off such a delectable sitting duck?"[163]

Although Chairman Arafat of the PLO had not spelled out the terms of a settlement, or himself gone beyond grudging generalities, and despite a notorious tendency to take positions not easily reconciled with each other according to whom he was addressing, the evidence seemed persuasive by the late seventies that Arafat and al-Fatah were prepared to make peace on the basis of the West Bank-Gaza state and to accept Israel within its approximate borders of 1967. They were not, however, prepared to concede the moral legitimacy of Israel: Zionism could never represent for Palestinian Arabs anything but a political movement that had occupied their country and expelled them from it. Zionism might represent the fulfillment of an historic dream to the persecuted, wandering Jews, but it was not the Palestinian Arabs who had persecuted them or set them to wandering. The Palestinians were not responsible for the ghettos of Europe, for the pogroms of the Russian tsars, or for Hitler's Holocaust. All these were the actions of European or Western countries, and the support some of these countries then gave to Zionist aspirations in Palestine represented to the Arabs not an act of idealism or an expression of conscience but a further manifestation of the Western colonialist mentality, according to which it was legitimate to compensate the Jews for their sufferings in Europe by permitting them to rob a people who had done them no harm of their country and their homes. Sabri Jiryis wrote: "Realism may require recognition of the existence of a Jewish state in Palestine and that this fact be taken into account in seeking a settlement.

But this can never mean approving the expansionist and exclusivist tendencies of Zionism."[164] Arafat then would go on dreaming his "dream" of the unified, secular state in "Palestine's sacred land;"[165] older Palestinians would retain memories of lost homes and fields and vineyards; and young Palestinians would continue to be fired by calls to militancy and by the abiding conviction of injustice. They would not conceive of loving Israel, of Arafat embracing Begin as Sadat had done, or of sympathizing with the Zionist dream whose fulfillment had shattered their lives. They would remain rueful and embittered, but they would settle, on terms they had rejected when they might have had them, terms that they still considered woefully unjust but that they now accepted because they had come, belatedly, to a realistic assessment of their enemy's resources as well as of their own.

These were the themes of an interview with Chairman Arafat and several of his colleagues in Damascus on October 28, 1978. As on other occasions, the top PLO leaders expressed militant nationalism, bitterness toward the United States, appeals to humanity and idealism, and also stressed their own reasonableness and moderation. The Camp David agreement, concluded the previous month, was a "betrayal" of the Palestinian people, Arafat said, perpetrated by President Carter for his own domestic political purposes, while in Rhodesia, by contrast, Carter resisted as inadequate proposed terms for the black majority that went far beyond what the Palestinians asked. The United States gave Begin everything he demanded, Arafat said, and in so doing betrayed not only the Palestinians but America's own interests, which, he stressed, would be no more reliably invested in President Sadat than they were in the then faltering but not yet fallen shah of Iran. Bitter and disappointed though they were, Arafat and his colleagues stressed, the Palestinian people would persevere, because their cause, said Arafat, was the "conscience" not only of the Middle East but of the whole third world, and it moved with the tide of history, which even the United States could not reverse. Whatever short term benefits the United States, or Carter personally, might derive from Camp David, said Khalid Fahoum (chairman of the Palestine National Council and also of the smaller policy making body known as the Palestine Central Council), conditions would surely change, as the great numbers of unorganized Arabs and Muslims became organized, as they were already changing in Iran. "We are not worried for the future," Arafat added in imperfect English.[166]

Interspersed with these protests and affirmations were repeated assertions of the reasonable and moderate aspirations of the Palestinian leadership. Arafat and his lieutenants stressed their willingness to accept the

West Bank–Gaza state, their rejection of communism, and, despite anger and disappointment, their lack of basic animosity toward the United States. "The Arabs are not against you," Arafat said. The present leadership of the PLO had been ready for five years, and remained ready, said Fahoum, to open a dialogue with the United States, and it accepted the West Bank–Gaza state. "I am astonished that you are willing to tie yourselves to what Kissinger signed," said Arafat, referring to the American pledge to Israel in September 1975 that the United States would not recognize or negotiate with the PLO as long as it did not recognize Israel's right to exist and accept Security Council Resolutions 242 and 338. In fact, said Fahoum, the PLO accepted *all* United Nations resolutions pertaining to the Middle East adopted since 1947 and did so "without any reservations." "With open mind," Arafat added. Arafat and his colleagues laid special stress on their acceptance of the Soviet-American statement of October 1, 1977, which called for the "termination of the state of war and establishment of normal peaceful relations" between Israel and her neighbors, for demilitarized zones and international guarantees of borders, as well as for "insuring the legitimate rights of the Palestinian people." The United States had, however, quickly backed away from the joint statement under Israeli protest.[167] Prince Turki al-Faisal had said on October 25, 1978, that by endorsing the Soviet-American statement the PLO had in fact accepted Security Council Resolutions 242 and 338; they had chosen that route because the Soviet Union gave them political and economic support, and to have taken another route, said Turki, would have jeopardized that support.[168]

When the Carter administration came to office in 1977, Fahoum said near the end of the Damascus interview, the Palestinians had taken heart from his references to a Palestinian homeland. Everything had changed, however, with Camp David, which was a "complete sellout" of the Palestinians, and any extremism following was to be understood as a "natural reaction" to what Palestinians heard from Begin and the Israelis and from the politically motivated American administration. If America was to be governed by these political motivations every four years, Fahoum asked, "What can we do? What can we do?"[169]

Arafat spelled out the PLO's willingness to give de facto recognition to Israel and to renounce violence against it even more explicitly in an interview with Congressman Paul Findley of Illinois, the senior Republican on the House Middle East Subcommittee, on November 25, 1978. On this occasion, Arafat asked again for a dialogue between the PLO and the United States. At the end of a four-hour discussion, in the course of which Findley made specific suggestions on a statement to be made by Arafat, the PLO chairman, with assurances that he would stand behind it, Arafat issued the following statement: "The PLO will accept an independent Palestinian state consisting of the West Bank and Gaza, with connecting corridor, and in that circumstance will renounce any and all violent means to enlarge the territory of that state. I would reserve the right, of course, to use nonviolent means, that is to say, diplomatic and democratic means, to bring about the eventual unification of all of Palestine." Arafat promised too, "We will give de facto recognition to the State of Israel," and gave assurance as well that "we would live at peace with all our neighbors." He then volunteered, "But it is we who would need protection, not Israel. Israel has twelve to fifteen atomic bombs. I know." Findley concluded that Arafat's pledges to him met the conditions for American negotiations with the PLO under the commitment made to Israel in September 1975 and that this justified "immediate talks with the PLO."[170]

Neither the statement made to Findley nor the substance of the writer's interview with Arafat and his colleagues on October 28, 1978, which was conveyed in a cable to the State Department from the United States Embassy in Damascus, elicited a response from the Carter administration. The embassy cable included a comment that stated in part: "The PLO evidently wants a dialogue with us and is willing to go part of the way to get one. But it appears that the PLO cannot go far enough to satisfy our minimum requirements." Representative Findley, in a speech on May 5, 1979, urged again that the United States work toward reciprocal recognition by Israel and the PLO without requiring prior, explicit endorsement by the PLO of Security Council Resolution 242; he also said: "Although it seems clear that the next step must be the opening of a U.S.-PLO dialogue, it is not clear that the United States will take this initiative."[171]

Thwarted by the lack of American response to its signals of willingness to compromise and angered by the Camp David agreement and Egypt's separate peace with Israel, the PLO reverted to bluster and threat and stepped up acts of terror in the wake of the Egyptian-Israeli peace treaty, but did not repudiate its offer of dialogue with the United States and of de facto acceptance of Israel. On the day the treaty was signed in Washington, March 26, 1979, Arafat fulminated before a gathering of guerrilla recruits at a camp in Beirut that he would "finish off American interests in the Middle East" and, topping Begin's threat that Arafat would get his fingers burned if he tried to undermine the treaty, countered that he would "chop off" the hands of Begin, Sadat, and Carter.[172] Less colorfully but more realistically, the director of the PLO's office in Beirut, Shafik al-Hout, visiting the United States in April 1979 on a restricted visa that prevented him from making public appearances, reviewed before a private group the series of concessions the PLO had made: It had started with the call for a democratic, secular state—in effect inviting those who had taken the Palestinians' land by force to remain and share it with them. This, however, was dismissed as unrealistic, so the PLO then, said al-Hout, offered to establish Palestinian authority in any territory from which Israel might be induced to withdraw. When this proposal was objected to on the ground that it did not promise peaceful coexistence, the PLO had moved to its present position of accepting the West Bank-Gaza state and de facto recognition of Israel. Although coming to this position had been an agonizing process, involving "days and nights of deliberation, and mutual accusations," this too, al-Hout continued, was deemed insufficient: the United States continued to demand explicit recognition of Israel—"which we will never do except on reciprocal terms." To pay for a dialogue with the United States by legitimizing Israel was to play the PLO's "last card." What, he asked, would they then have to talk about with Israel?[173]

The obvious next step was to offer to recognize Israel on *condition* that Israel simultaneously recognize the PLO and the right of the Palestinian people to self-determination in the West Bank and Gaza. That had been proposed to the PLO by a group of Israeli "doves" at meetings in Europe in 1976, but, as Arie Lova Eliav, who participated, later ruefully observed, "They couldn't deliver."[174] It was proposed to the PLO again in April 1979, as a personal suggestion, by an official of the National Association of Arab Americans, who said the PLO need not fear the loss of its "bargaining card" because "when one states requirements and commitments together, they must go into effect simultaneously or neither is binding."[175] Another suggestion put to the PLO in the wake of the Egyptian-Israeli treaty was that it call a provisional cease-fire on terrorism, in order to demonstrate good will and discipline within its ranks and to help win American support for Palestinian self-determination.[176] The PLO continued to resist both suggestions—the offer of reciprocal recognition and the provisional cease-fire, although it did agree to a cease-fire in Lebanon after the fighting of July 1981. It still bore—in the terms of Arafat's United Nations speech of 1974—"an olive branch and a freedom fighter's gun," the one with fear and hesitation, the other with dubious effect.

THE UNITED STATES AND SELF-DETERMINATION

From its inception in 1977, the Carter administration acted so as first to raise but then, increasingly, disappoint the hopes of the Palestinian people. When President Carter called for a Palestinian "homeland" at Clinton, Massachusetts on March 16, 1977,[177] a wave of excitement and hope spread across the occupied territories.[178] Carter made the point even more emphatically two months later, stating in a press conference on May 12, "I don't think there can be any reasonable hope for a settlement of the Middle East question . . . without a homeland for the Palestinians."[179] Palestinians heard echoes in these statements of Wilsonian self-determination, of that "touch of idealism" that Palestinians, despite many bitter disappointments, still associated with the United States.[180] Less audible to Palestinians at the time was President Carter's immediate qualification of his statement of May 12, 1977: "The exact definition of what that homeland might be, the degree of independence of the Palestinian entity, its relations with Jordan, or perhaps Syria and others, the geographical boundaries of it, all have to be worked out by the parties involved."[181]

As was noted in chapter 2, the United States has a historical commitment to the principle of self-determination but, for reasons of an essentially irreconcilable commitment to Zionism, has been, over the years, ambivalent and inconsistent in its application to Palestine.[182] The Carter administration perpetuated the tradition of ambivalence but, on the whole, opposed Palestinian self-determination, endorsing instead a measure of autonomy for the Palestinians in the West Bank and Gaza under one or another foreign sovereignty. Having spoken of a Palestinian "homeland" in the spring of 1977, President Carter, in subsequent pronouncements, reverted to the more clinical term "entity" in referring to the hypothetical Palestinian political unit; he also made clear that, whatever form the "entity" might take, he preferred it not be an independent state.[183] The president came to accept as axiomatic the Israeli contention that an independent Palestinian state inevitably would be radical. His own "personal opinion," he said on December 28, 1977, was "that permanent peace can best be maintained if there is not a fairly radical, new independent nation in the heart of the Middle Eastern area."[184]

President Carter also seemed to have subscribed, in the course of 1977, to the proposition that the neighbors of the Palestinians, especially Israel, had at least as much right as the Palestinians themselves to participate in deciding what the Palestinian future would be, and that any attempt on his part to deny them that right would represent an unwarranted incursion on their sovereignty. In asserting, on at least two occasions, that his own preference was against an independent Palestinian state, the president hastened to add that he had no inclination to impose that preference but would gladly accept anything that might be agreed among the "parties."[185] Implicit in the emerging presidential attitude was the decision to *deny* self-determination to the Palestinians, since, by definition, *"self-*

determination" means that the party whose future is to be determined, and not others, will make the fundamental decisions about that future. In conceding to Israel—and to some lesser degree Egypt and perhaps Jordan as well—a measure of freedom of choice, or at the very least a veto, over what would be done with the Palestinians, President Carter appeared to hold the view that he was simply respecting the sovereignty of these nations—in much the same way that he would later acquiesce in Israel's settlements policy in the West Bank, even though he deemed the settlements illegal, because, as he put it, "there's a limit to what we can do to impose our will on a sovereign nation."[186] The sovereignty of one nation was thus defined as extending, for reasons of security, beyond its own affairs to encompass the affairs of its neighbor.

Such was the genesis of the equivocal Aswan formula of January 4, 1978. On that day, President Carter, in the presence of President Sadat at Aswan, laid down the formula, which was to be invoked and repeated many times subsequently, that a Middle East settlement must resolve "the Palestinian problem in all its aspects," recognize "the legitimate rights of the Palestinian people," and "enable the Palestinians to participate in the determination of their own future."[187] The Palestinian people were by this means put on notice that although they might "participate" in deciding their own future, Israel and perhaps others would participate as well, guaranteeing that there would be no independent Palestinian state. The Wilsonian postulate was thus amended so as to retain most of its language while being divested of most of its meaning.[188]

Although State Department officials were at pains to explain that the purpose of the artfully constructed Aswan formula was to begin the process of reconciling divergent positions, its effect was to permit different parties to believe different things. President Sadat declared his and Carter's views "identical,"[189] and an Egyptian journalist was quoted as saying of the Aswan formula, "We got the concept of self-determination now, all but the actual term."[190] Prime Minister Begin expressed satisfaction that Carter and Sadat had said nothing at Aswan about a Palestinian state, to which, he also observed, self-determination was tantamount.[191] The Palestinians—who it was hoped would be pleased with the application of the word "determination" to their future, even in the absence of the companion word "self," and also with President Carter's reference to their "legitimate rights"—were not pleased. A PLO spokesman in Beirut suggested that President Carter "tell us where he wants the rights realized—on the moon or on the earth." The president, the PLO official said, "is still vague and appears to be unaware of what he really wants."[192]

Between the Aswan meeting in January and the Camp David agreement of September 17, 1978, it became evident that, whatever was meant by American references to the "legitimate rights" of the Palestinians and whatever President Carter wanted or did not want, he clearly did not want an independent Palestinian state. The president stated unequivocally in his press conference of March 9, 1978, "We do not and never have favored an independent Palestinian nation."[193] He reiterated that position in late April, expressing his "belief" that "a permanent settlement will not include an independent Palestinian nation on the West Bank," or require complete Israeli withdrawal from the occupied territories. The president on that occasion also expressed his belief that a permanent settlement would be based substantially on Prime Minister Begin's "self-rule" plan of December 27, 1977.[194] Carter during this period, however, was showing mounting irritation with Begin's insistence on his plan for the West Bank and Gaza, and the resulting confusion may have obscured the fact that the president was hardly less firm than Begin himself in his rejection of an independent Palestinian state.

Although it was achieved only after an arduous negotiation among Carter, Begin, and Sadat, the Camp David Framework for Peace, with its provisions for a circumscribed Palestinian self-governing authority, re- tention of Israeli forces, an Israeli veto over the return of Palestinian refugees from the 1967 war, and extensive political roles for Israel, Egypt, and Jordan in determining the final status of the occupied territories, was essentially a spelling out in detail of the Aswan formula as defined and interpreted by the Carter administration in the first months of 1978.[195] Although, like the Aswan formula, the Framework for Peace was inter- preted differently by the parties, it could be interpreted as a precursor to self-determination only on the basis of the assumption that its substance would eventually be changed and that Israel would agree to it being changed. As it stood, the agreement represented a somewhat liberalized modification of the Begin plan of December 27, 1977—a result no less consistent with the official, publicly stated position of the Carter adminis- tration than with that of the Begin government. No question of principle divided the two governments: both were against self-determination. The fireworks and recrimination that characterized their relations both before and after Camp David had to do only with the *extent* of Israel's control over the prospective Palestinian "entity" and the *degree* of participation by the Palestinians, lesser or greater, in the determination of their future. Palestinian hopes, which were raised high by the early references of the Carter administration to a Palestinian "homeland" and the "legitimate rights" of the Palestinian people, were struck low once again by the Camp David accords and the Egyptian-Israeli treaty of March 1979. Palestinians by that time would have readily acquiesced in the view, expressed in 1978 by Hyman H. Bookbinder, Washington representative of the American Jewish Committee, that the Carter administration did not really know what it was doing when it applied those volatile code words, "homeland" and "rights," to the Palestinians. "I am convinced," Bookbinder told a journalist, "they did not understand the fears of a threat to Israel that those words conjure up."[196]

Inseparable from the question of self-determination was the American attitude toward the Palestine Liberation Organization, which, as has been seen, commanded the allegiance of Palestinians both within and outside the occupied territories as the symbol and driving force of Palestinian nationalism. The Carter administration, like its predecessors, refused any official contacts with the PLO as long as it refused to accept explicitly Security Council Resolution 242 and to acknowledge Israel's right to exist. The administration, moreover, considered itself legally proscribed from such contacts under the "Memorandum of Agreement" concluded with Israel on September 1, 1975 by Secretary of State Henry Kissinger, under the Ford administration, in connection with the second Sinai disengagement agreement between Egypt and Israel, which stated that "the United States will continue to adhere to its present policy with respect to the Palestine Liberation Organization, whereby it will not recognize or negotiate with the Palestine Liberation Organization so long as the Palestine Liberation Organization does not recognize Israel's right to exist and does not accept Security Council Resolutions 242 and 338."[197]

Whether in fact the agreement of September 1975 was binding on the Carter administration or any succeeding administration may well be questioned. When the package of agreements of which the PLO pledge formed a part was submitted to the Senate Foreign Relations Committee in September 1975, the committee, in its post-Vietnam wariness of foreign commitments, questioned the executive branch closely as to the binding character of the various "memoranda of agreement." The State Department was at first reluctant to define these as binding "executive agreements" and did so only when pressed by members of Congress. In his testimony before the Foreign Relations Committee on October 7, 1975, Secretary of State Kissinger said it was "extremely important" that, in approving the assignment of U.S. technicians to Sinai, Congress "should take care not inadvertently to create commitments that were not intended." The memoranda of agreement, Kissinger said, "are important statements of diplomatic policy and they engage the good faith of the United States so long as the circumstances that gave rise to them continue. But they are not binding commitments of the United States."[198] Subsequently, in authorizing the assignment of American technicians to the Sinai to oversee the disengagement of Egyptian and Israeli forces, Congress specifically dissociated itself from the related memoranda of agreement.

The commitment regarding the PLO was in any case beyond congressional jurisdiction and also one which no president could make binding on a successor because it had to do with the president's exclusive constitutional authority to negotiate with foreign entities. The Supreme Court, in *United States* v. *Curtiss-Wright Corp.* in 1936, ruled that the president alone negotiates: "Into the field of negotiation, the Senate cannot intrude; and Congress itself is powerless to invade it." In its 1978 report on the Panama Canal Treaty, the Senate Foreign Relations Committee stated that a provision in that treaty barring negotiations with third parties for the right to build a new canal unless the United States and Panama first agreed "may not be construed as precluding a future President from exercising his constitutional power to confer with other governments." The committee added: "A President may voluntarily commit himself not to enter into certain negotiations, but he cannot circumscribe the discretion of his successors to do so, just as they may not be limited in so doing by treaty or by law."[199] The Carter administration thus adhered to the agreement barring negotiations with the PLO as a matter of choice and policy rather than of law.

While adhering to the prohibition, the Carter administration in 1977 repeatedly encouraged the PLO to make the essential statements that would permit contacts with the United States and some form of Palestinian participation in peace negotiations, which, at that time (prior to President Sadat's visit to Jerusalem) were expected to be conducted through a Geneva conference of all parties to the Middle East conflict. In a news conference on July 28, 1977 President Carter said he thought the Palestinians "ought to be represented" in Middle East peace negotiations, but would have to acknowledge Israel's permanence before the United States could advocate their participation.[200] Again, on August 8, 1977, the president raised the possibility of discussions with the Palestinians, even on the basis of a qualified acceptance of Security Council Resolution 242. Carter said, "If the Palestinians should say, 'We recognize UN Resolution 242 in its entirety; but we think the Palestinians have additional status other than just refugees,' that would suit us okay."[201] Repeating the offer in almost exactly the same words on September 29, he added that if the PLO did accept Resolution 242 even with the qualification that the Palestinian interest went beyond the Resolution's reference to the "refugee problem," "we would then begin to meet with and to work with the PLO."[202]

The United States and the PLO in fact came close to establishing contact in the summer of 1977. Through Egyptian and Saudi intermediaries agreement was reached—or substantially reached—on PLO acceptance of Security Council Resolution 242 with a reservation affirming Palestinian national rights. An American proposal for entering a dialogue was conveyed to Arafat through Prince Fahd of Saudi Arabia. As a result of misunderstanding the American proposal was at first conveyed as indicating American agreement to Palestinian self-determination, although in fact the United States had agreed only to enter a dialogue. This was then made clear to Arafat. Although it fell far short of what he had first understood it to be, Arafat submitted the proposal to his executive committee, which, under Syrian urging, rejected it by a vote of 8 to 4.[203]

In November 1977 President Sadat made his trip to Jerusalem, effectively eliminating such prospects as may have existed for a Geneva peace conference and opening the way to a separate Egyptian-Israeli peace through bilateral diplomacy. The PLO remained adamant in its opposition to the "peace process" that came into being at Jerusalem, declining— along with Syria, Jordan, and the Soviet Union—to attend a preliminary peace conference in Cairo, to which President Sadat, upon his return from Jerusalem, invited "all parties of the conflict."[204] From that time on President Carter seemed to write the PLO off. "The PLO have been completely negative," Carter said at his news conference on December 15, 1977. Having "completely rejected" Security Council Resolutions 242 and 338, the president said, and having refused to acknowledge publicly Israel's right to exist, "they have themselves removed the PLO from any immediate prospect of participation in a peace discussion."[205] Carter's national security adviser, Zbigniew Brzezinski (in an interview in late December 1977 with the French magazine *Paris Match*) said that the United States had done everything it could to draw the PLO into the peace process, all to no avail, so it was now "bye-bye PLO."[206] Chairman Arafat retorted that when President Carter says "farewell to the PLO, what he really should be saying is farewell to his interests in this area."[207]

Beset by Israel's adamant refusal of any dealings, direct or indirect, with the Palestine Liberation Organization, Carter and Sadat were more probably relieved than disappointed by the PLO's refusal to attend the meeting in Cairo to which Sadat had invited "all parties." In extending the invitation, Sadat did not explicitly mention the PLO (as he had not in his address on November 20, 1977 to the Israeli Knesset), nor did President Carter refer to the Cairo meeting in his castigation of the PLO on December 15, 1977, although he expressed regret on that occasion that the Soviet Union and Syria had declined Sadat's invitation.[208] The PLO, which might have forced the issue of American and Israeli dealings with itself by accepting the invitation to Cairo, chose instead, possibly for reasons of its own divisions, to spare Israel that excruciating dilemma. Asked about this in October 1978, Khalid Fahoum, chairman of the Palestine National Council, replied in Arafat's presence that Sadat's invitation was designed only to split the PLO: "He was not serious."[209]

Embarked on the long road to Camp David and the Egyptian–Israeli treaty, the Carter administration, from the beginning of 1978, showed little or no further interest in establishing contacts with the PLO. Indirect and unofficial reports that such contacts would be essential to the implementation of the Camp David autonomy plan were turned aside. On one occasion, shortly after Camp David, President Carter likened the PLO to Nazis, as Begin had often done, eliciting bitter dismay from Arafat and approbation from Begin, who told the Knesset, "We have heard from the President of the United States the correct comparison."[210] In an interview on January 9, 1979, Ambassador Andrew Young, the United States permanent representative to the United Nations, commented that the PLO representatives at the United Nations were "very skilled politicians and very intelligent, decent human beings"; that it must be recognized realistically that the PLO had "captured the imagination of the Palestinian people" and had wide influence among the Arab states; that American unwillingness to recognize this "doesn't make it any less true"; and that he thought the United States "should have some way of relating to the Palestinian people."[211] Ambassador Young, as on other occasions, seemed to be speaking for himself and not for the Carter administration. On March 23, 1979, three days before the signing of the Egyptian–Israeli peace treaty, President Carter said that the United States had a "problem" about dealing with the Palestine Liberation Organization but would "immediately start working directly with that organization" if it dropped its opposition to Security Council Resolution 242 and accepted Israel's right to exist.[212]

Israel during this period remained firm both as to its own view of the PLO and as to what it considered the proper American view. Arriving in New York before the signing of the treaty with Egypt, Prime Minister Begin reiterated his familiar characterization of the PLO as "the most barbaric organization since the Nazis."[213] During the celebration of Israel's thirty-first anniversary in May 1979, Begin, in addition to vowing that Israel would never give up the West Bank or the Golan Heights, made it known that he had sent a note to Secretary of State Vance protesting the granting of a visa to the director of the PLO office in Beirut, Shafik al-Hout, who had visited the United States the previous April. Alluding apparently to the memorandum of agreement of September 1, 1975, under which the United States had agreed to "consult fully" with Israel on dealings with the PLO, at least in the framework of a Geneva peace conference,[214] Begin said he had demanded prior consultation with Israel before the United States had any dealings with PLO officials. "That is the duty of the United States," Begin declared, and he added, "If one day the Americans open negotiations with that organization of murderers, it will be a black day for free mankind."[215]

As negotiations on the status of the West Bank and Gaza were begun desultorily in the wake of the Egyptian-Israeli peace treaty, the United States found itself constrained by past agreements and policy declarations. On record itself as opposing an independent Palestinian state, the Carter administration had also committed itself to a procedure, under the Camp David agreement, that virtually assured Israel the authority to deny Palestinian self-determination at the end of the projected five-year transition period. In addition, the Carter administration found itself severely restricted or totally prohibited— depending on its reading of the agreement of September 1, 1975 and on its interpretation of various subsequent statements by PLO officials—from communicating officially with the only Palestinian authority with the power, if it chose to wield it, to make the Camp David procedure work. The Carter administration was not responsible for the agreement of September 1, 1975, but at no time, so far as is known, did it seek to extricate itself from the agreement's terms or to interpret those terms in any but the most restrictive sense. The Carter administration was, on the other hand, wholly responsible for the modification amounting to negation of the principle of self-determination embodied in the Aswan formula as spelled out in the Camp David Framework for Peace.

The Reagan administration, in its early months, showed, if anything, even less willingness than its predecessor to favor Palestinian self-determination or to open dialogue with the PLO. Asked in a press interview shortly after taking office whether he had sympathy for the Palestinians or "any moral feeling toward them and their aspirations," President Reagan did not reply directly to the question but instead condemned undesignated statements challenging Israel's right to exist, denounced terrorism, and questioned whether the PLO represented the Palestinian people.[216] Following the cease-fire between Israel and the PLO in Lebanon in July 1981 President Sadat appealed personally to Reagan to "build on this," drop the 1975 prohibition and open a dialogue with the PLO. Reagan rejected this proposal; according to Secretary of State Haig, the President told Sadat that the United States must keep "all its commitments."[217]

In opposing self-determination for the Palestinian people, the Carter and Reagan administrations, without apparently intending to do so, confirmed the long term tendency of the United States, going back to the time of President Wilson, to make an exception of Palestine from the traditional American commitment to the principle of self-determination as an international standard. There had been other such departures in American history, such as the brief period of empire building in the late nineteenth century, which, however, was followed by an extended process of decolonization that gave independence to the Philippines, statehood to Hawaii, and freedom of choice to Puerto Rico. There were also instances of American *acquiescence* in the suppression of self-determination by others, such as the imposition of Soviet domination on eastern Europe after the Second World War. These, however, were not acts of policy formulated and carried out by the United States government, but rather instances of reluctant acquiescence in circumstances in which there seemed no feasible alternative. The Carter administration itself, indeed, applied a rigorous standard of self-determination to the temporary elected biracial government established in Zimbabwe Rhodesia in 1979, refusing, "as a matter of principle," to lift sanctions against that government because of what the president judged to be shortcomings in the electoral procedure that put it in office.[218]

The Carter administration's policy toward the Palestinian people, based on the Aswan formula, represented an attempt to split an unsplittable difference. The principle of self-determination can be applied in different ways and can also be applied with designated restrictions and qualifications—pertaining, for example, to the level of armament of the political unit in question, to the rights of its citizens, or to the treatment of minority groups within its borders. It cannot, however, be applied under rules and conditions that allow the people whose future is to be determined a voice in shaping their destiny that is no more than theoretically equal with the voices of several designated outsiders, all more powerful than they, all with concerns either different from or antithetical to their own. The

Palestinian poet and author, Fawaz Turki, wrote: "A people are free or not free, independent or not independent, they are a determining force in their own destiny or are ruled by the gun. The problem of choice, in the context of Palestinian rights, is inescapable. Palestinians have rights or do not."[219]

As an international norm, the principle of self-determination is largely an American contribution, an application to international relations of the proposition, set forth in the American Declaration of Independence, that governments derive "their just powers from the consent of the governed." Its origins, as suggested in chapter 2, are both ethical and pragmatic, having to do both with the rights of peoples as codified from the experience of nations and with the maintenance of good order in international relations. Elihu Root wrote in 1922:

> The organization of independent nations which has followed the disappearance of the Holy Roman Empire is in the main the outgrowth of that progress in civilization which leads peoples to seek the liberty of local self-government according to their own ideas. Whatever may be the form of local governments there can be no tyranny so galling as the intimate control of the local affairs of life by foreign rulers who are entirely indifferent to the local conceptions of how life ought to be conducted. National independence is an organized defense against that kind of tyranny. Probably the organization of nations is but a stage of development but it is the nearest that mankind has yet come towards securing for itself a reasonable degree of liberty with a reasonable degree of order.[220]

A succinct application of Root's formulation to the Palestinian problem is provided by I. F. Stone: "If the Palestinians are to have self-rule, what gives Carter the right to cast the first ballot?"[221]

CHAPTER SIX

The Soviet Union: Predator or Partner?

SUCH IS THE REPUTATION of the Soviet Union in world affairs that even when it behaves well it is assumed to have done so for venal or ulterior motives. Except for the brief period of World War II, when the making of common cause against Nazi Germany cast the Russians in a heroic image, the American view of Soviet Russia has been consistently unfavorable. Before World War II the Soviet Union was regarded as exactly what its founder, Lenin, had advertised it to be: a zealous and unappeasable agent of world revolution. In the years after World War II learned debates were conducted in government and the academy as to whether Soviet imperialism was a function more of Marxist ideology or of the Russian tsarist legacy. Stalin, the "crafty giant" of Churchill's description, came to represent a new Hitler in American eyes—a role for which, by reason of temperament and despotic conduct, he was by no means wholly unsuited. Dean Acheson (then under secretary of state), soliciting support for the Truman Doctrine in 1947, characterized the Soviet communist threat in the metaphor of a contagious disease. Soviet pressures then being applied on Greece, Turkey, and Iran "might open three continents to Soviet penetration," Acheson said. "Like apples in a barrel infected by one rotten one, the corruption of Greece would infect Iran and all to the east. It would also carry infection to Africa through Asia Minor and Egypt, and to Europe through Italy and France. . . ."[1] With a nation so abnormal and malevolent it was also judged impossible to make reliable agreements. "I

[230]

think it is a mistake to believe that you can, at any time, sit down with the Russians and solve questions," Acheson advised the Senate Foreign Relations Committee on April 1, 1947.[2]

These themes—the relentlessness of Soviet pressure, the insatiability of Soviet ambition, the contagiousness of Marxist ideology, and the unreliability of Soviet agreements—have, with infrequent exceptions, governed American attitudes and policy toward the Soviet role in the Middle East since the late forties. The forging of a fragile détente in direct superpower relations in the sixties and seventies had only slight fallout effect on their dealings in respect to the Middle East. Whether and to what degree the traditional view of Soviet aims in the Middle East has been proven accurate by events will be examined in this chapter. What is incontestable is that for over three decades the superpowers have acted as rivals rather than collaborators in the Middle East, with the result that each has found itself tied to clients whose conduct has often been inimical to its interests, and with the further result that the regional conflict has retained the constant potential of becoming a global conflict.

THE SOVIET-AMERICAN STATEMENT OF OCTOBER 1, 1977

At the initiative of the Soviet Union, whose role as cochairman of the long-delayed Geneva Peace Conference on the Middle East had dwindled to insignificance since the 1973 war, the United States and the Soviet Union, on October 1, 1977, issued a joint statement on the Middle East. The statement, as noted in chapter 2,[3] called for a "comprehensive" settlement of the Arab-Israeli conflict providing for Israeli military withdrawal from territories occupied in the 1967 war; resolution of the Palestinian question including assurance of the "legitimate rights" of the Palestinian people; termination of the state of war and the establishment of "normal peaceful relations" among the parties; measures to assure the security of borders between Israel and its Arab neighbors including the establishment of demilitarized zones and the stationing in them of United Nations troops or observers; and, if desired, international guarantees of the entire settlement in which the United States and the Soviet Union would be "ready to participate."[4] Although the joint statement was suggested by the Soviet Union, the State Department commended its provisions as a compromise, under which the Soviet Union endorsed "normal peaceful relations" between Israel and its Arab neighbors in lieu of the mere termination of belligerency referred to in Security Council Resolution 242 (adopted after the 1967 war) while the United States, for the first time, acknowledged the Palestinians to have "rights" and not merely—in the antiseptic term previously favored—"interests."

The joint statement of October 1, 1977 was consistent with the *official* policy of the United States as represented by American adherence to Security Council Resolution 242, the Rogers Plan of December 9, 1969,[5] and the Soviet-American agreement of 1973 to serve as cochairmen of the Geneva conference. The reference to Palestinian "rights" was an innovation for the United States but by no means inconsistent with Secretary of State Rogers' statement—in which the concept of "rights" was implicit— that "there can be no lasting peace without a just settlement of the problem of those Palestinians whom the wars of 1948 and 1967 have made homeless."[6] Similarly, the reference in the joint statement to Israeli withdrawal from "territories occupied in the 1967 conflict" was a close paraphrase of language contained in Security Council Resolution 242. Nor, since the Soviet Union had been accepted by the United States in 1973 as cochairman of the Geneva conference, did the fact of a *joint* statement by the two countries represent an innovation in *official* American policy.

It represented a considerable departure, however, from the actual operative policy of the United States and, for that reason, provoked controversy and condemnation. In practice the United States had found itself unable, or unwilling, to implement the central concept of the Rogers Plan, which stated, as to Israel's borders, that "any changes in the pre-existing line should not reflect the weight of conquest and should be confined to insubstantial alterations required for mutual security." The Rogers Plan was neither implemented nor repudiated as subsequent administrations adopted the approach of President Nixon, who later wrote: "I knew that the Rogers Plan could never be implemented, but I believed it was important to let the Arab world know that the United States did not automatically dismiss its case regarding the occupied territories. . . ."[7] Henry Kissinger, according to Nixon, objected to the Rogers Plan on grounds that it "encouraged the extremist elements among the Arabs, gratuitously offended the Israelis, and earned the contempt of the Soviets, who saw it as playing naively into their hands."[8] Kissinger, who became secretary of state in September 1973, two weeks before the outbreak of war in the Middle East, pursued a policy—despite the brief Geneva meeting in December—of rigorous exclusion of the Soviet Union from the "step-by-step" diplomacy that resulted in disengagement agreements between Israel and Egypt in 1974 and 1975 and a disengagement agreement between Israel and Syria in 1974. No further effort to achieve

Soviet-American cooperation for a general settlement was made until Secretary of State Vance and Foreign Minister Gromyko issued their joint statement of October 1, 1977. It came, therefore, as a shock, suggesting that the United States might now set out, in collaboration with the Soviet Union, to achieve what it had officially said it wanted to achieve—a peace based on the "inadmissibility of the acquisition of territory by war" as called for by Security Council Resolution 242 and a "just settlement" of the Palestinian problem as called for in the Rogers Plan.

Such fears quickly proved groundless as the Carter administration beat a hasty retreat under a barrage of Israeli and domestic criticism. While Arab governments and the Palestine Liberation Organization welcomed the Soviet-American statement, the Israeli government rejected it, in the words of Finance Minister Simcha Ehrlich, "with both hands," because it seemed a step toward an imposed solution and because it seemed to indicate American willingness to have the PLO participate in a Geneva peace conference. Speaking in the absence of Prime Minister Begin, who was in the hospital, Ehrlich suggested that the Carter administration's action represented an effort to relieve its frustration from policy failures in other areas by forging ahead at all costs to convene a Middle East peace conference. Maintaining a united front with the Likud government, the Labor party opposition joined in denouncing the Soviet-American joint statement. Former Foreign Minister Yigal Allon pronounced it "unnecessary, ill-timed and ill-phrased."[9] While American officials tried to explain that the reference in the joint statement to the "legitimate rights" of the Palestinians was actually a concession extracted from the Russians (who would have preferred the term "legitimate *national* rights"[10]), Israeli officials charged that the document was essentially Soviet in conception and wording, and they identified the phrase "legitimate rights" as code words for their greatest fear, a Palestinian state in the West Bank and Gaza. Israeli officials were especially dismayed at the absence of specific reference in the joint statement to Security Council Resolutions 242 and 338 (the latter reaffirming the former after the 1973 war). "We hang onto those with all our strength," one official explained, "because they say nothing about the Palestinians."[11] Professor Shlomo Avineri, a former director-general of Israel's ministry of foreign affairs, wrote in 1978 that the Soviet-American statement of October 1, 1977 had "made the Israelis lose whatever trust they still had in the sound judgment of the American Administration. . . ."[12]

The fireworks at home were no less fierce, and even more protracted, as members of Congress, American Jewish leaders, and other influential individuals fulminated against "letting the Russians back into the Middle East." Rabbi Alexander M. Schindler, chairman of the Conference of Presidents of Major Jewish Organizations, said that the joint statement, "on its face, represents an abandonment of America's historic commitment to the security and survival of Israel." Senator Henry Jackson, one of Israel's most vigorous supporters in the Senate, and AFL–CIO president George Meany both denounced the Soviet-American statement, the latter warning that any attempts by the Carter administration to undercut Israel would backfire politically on the president.[13] The joint statement, and especially its reference to the "legitimate rights of the Palestinian people," so alarmed wealthy Jewish Democrats in Los Angeles that they refused to buy tickets to a fund-raising dinner the president was to attend on October 22. "I have never seen them as upset by anything as they are now," said Hershey Gold, a Democratic fund-raiser and cochairman of the scheduled dinner.[14] The *New York Times* in an editorial called for further explanation of this "tortured piece of prose,"[15] while its columnist, William Safire, denounced the "infamous" Soviet-American agreement as a "Carter plan to impose a settlement that turns the West Bank into a Soviet staging area" against Israel.[16]

Against this formidable array of detractors the Carter administration was able to attract only a few supporters, including such unwelcome ones as the PLO and the Russians themselves. The PLO welcomed the joint statement immediately upon its issuance, saying that it contained "positive indications toward a just settlement of the Middle East conflict."[17] As noted in chapter 5, the PLO reiterated its acceptance of the Soviet-American statement on subsequent occasions, using this means, Prince Turki al-Faisal of Saudi Arabia said, to communicate indirectly their acceptance of Security Council Resolutions 242 and 338.[18] Asked in May 1978 whether Israel and a Palestinian state could live under a joint Soviet-American guarantee, Yasser Arafat replied, "I think this is the only possible solution. And this is why I said that the Soviet-American declaration could be considered a fundamental basis for a realistic settlement in the Middle East."[19] A Soviet view of the furor aroused by the joint statement is provided by Sergei M. Rogov of the Soviet Institute of U.S. and Canadian Studies: "The remarks made against the White House by Zionist circles became quite fierce when the joint Soviet-American statement on the Middle East of 1 October 1977 was issued. This campaign was directly ordered by Israeli Foreign Minister M. Dayan, who was then in the United States. . . ."[20]

The controversy began to abate after President Carter addressed the

United Nations General Assembly on October 4. The president called again for recognition of the "legitimate rights" of the Palestinian people, but he allayed Israeli anxieties by adding that how the rights of peoples in the area were defined and implemented was a matter for negotiations, by reaffirming Security Council Resolutions 242 and 338 as the basis for peace, by disavowing any intention of imposing a settlement from outside, and by referring to the Soviet-American statement as a procedural initiative.[21] Israel's ambassador to the United Nations, Chaim Herzog, while still objecting to the Soviet role in peace negotiations, expressed satisfaction at the president's reference to Security Council Resolutions 242 and 338, and Rabbi Schindler, who had feared the "abandonment" of Israel when the Soviet-American statement was announced, called the president's speech "superb."[22]

In a further effort to alleviate the uproar over the Soviet-American statement, President Carter, Foreign Minister Dayan, and their respective advisers met on the night of October 4–5, 1977 in the United Nations Plaza Hotel in New York. After a six-hour negotiating marathon, Dayan told reporters at 2:15 A.M. that agreement had been reached on a "working paper" spelling out procedures for the Geneva Peace Conference that was then, prior to Sadat's trip to Jerusalem, still expected to take place. Israel and the United States also agreed that night on a joint statement of their own. Issued on October 5, the statement reaffirmed Security Council Resolutions 242 and 338 (which were not mentioned in the Soviet-American statement) as the "agreed basis" for resumption of the Geneva Peace Conference, and also said, that "acceptance of the Joint United States-U.S.S.R. Statement of October 1, 1977, by the parties is not a prerequisite for the reconvening and conduct of the Geneva Conference."[23]

It is not definitively known what transpired in the long meeting at the United Nations Plaza Hotel. According to an undocumented "inside" account by two journalists, one an American, the other Israeli, President Carter on that night of October 4 delivered a "virtual ultimatum" to Dayan. Carter threatened to address himself to the American Jewish community and, in effect, to review aspects of American aid—"our promises to you are not in the box," he is quoted as saying—if Israel did not go along with some form of Palestinian representation at a Geneva conference and also accept the eventual establishment of a Palestinian "entity" or "homeland" in the West Bank and Gaza. According to this account (as well as others), Dayan replied that Israel would never accept a Palestinian state under any name, nor would it negotiate with the PLO; he

also rejected the Soviet-American statement as "totally unacceptable."
Then, according to the account, Dayan provided a review of American
pledges repudiated or unkept since the time of President Roosevelt, in
consequence of which Israel counted only on itself to save the Jewish
people from another holocaust. At the end of the meeting, the account
says, Carter acquiesced in the agreement that was subsequently
announced, asked Dayan where he would be going from New York, and,
on learning that he would be speaking to Jewish leaders in Chicago, said
with a smile, "Do me a favor. Don't attack me."[24]

Whatever precisely transpired at the United Nations Plaza Hotel, the
result was an Israeli-American agreement that effectively nullified the
Soviet-American initiative of October 1, 1977. Grateful for a reprieve
from the political fireworks elicited by the joint statement, the Carter
administration showed no visible distress at having abandoned its venture
in superpower collaboration only four days after initiating it. Quite the
contrary: according to the *New York Times'* account of the events of
October 5, the smoothing over of Israeli-American discord was, to President Carter's political aides, "even more important than the substantive
accord. The aides were deeply concerned over the extremely bitter reaction that the Soviet-American document had aroused in the Jewish community, many of whose prominent members are also leading contributors
and supporters of the Democratic Party." Although the administration
continued to insist that Israel and the American Jewish community had
overreacted to the Soviet-American statement, the *Times* article said,
"Mr. Carter and his aides did not seem to mind giving the appearance of
'capitulation' in return for an end to the political warfare."[25]

A month and a half later President Sadat made his trip to Jerusalem,
effectively ending whatever prospects then existed for a Geneva peace
conference of all parties to the Middle East conflict. Sadat's initiative also
derailed whatever slight prospects still existed for superpower collaboration toward a general settlement. Thereafter events were shaped by Egypt
and Israel, each for its own reasons bitterly hostile to the Soviet Union,
with the United States cast in the role of a mediator with uncertain
leverage on both sides. Because history does not reveal its alternatives, it is
impossible to judge whether the Soviet-American initiative of October
1977 would have drawn the Soviet Union into a constructive role in
Middle East peacemaking if it had been carried out with energy and in
good faith. It seems probable, as was pointed out at the time, that the
initiative of October 1 might have been better received had the concerned
parties, foreign and domestic, been forewarned and reassured of the

superpowers' intentions. This was not done partly because State Department officials and others involved did not regard the joint statement as a major innovation but rather as a gesture toward the Russians that, even if it had been adhered to, would have brought about no major changes in the American approach to peace in the Middle East.[26] It also seems highly probable that, even with the most skillful handling, the joint action of the two great powers would have generated alarm and controversy. All that can be said with certainty is that, whatever chances, greater or lesser, had previously existed for drawing the Soviet Union into a constructive joint effort to resolve the central, intractable Palestinian problem, there was no longer any such likelihood as Israel and Egypt moved toward a separate peace. The Soviets, on the contrary, were cast in alliance with the PLO and the Arab rejectionist states as opponents and obstructors of the Begin-Sadat "peace process." President Carter made passing mention of the joint statement in a press conference on December 15, 1977, saying that he had been "well pleased" with it.[27] The reference, however, was valedictory, and the administration thereafter had little more to say about a Soviet role as the active parties proceeded on their tortuous course toward Camp David.

The aborted Soviet–American initiative was not forgotten, living on, after a fashion, in the annals of political infamy. In a speech before the World Jewish Congress on November 1, 1977, Senator Howard Baker, then minority leader of the Senate, expressed strong objection to "the dramatic and sudden reintroduction of the Soviet Union into the negotiating process."[28] The Soviet–American joint statement, Senator Javits said on May 15, 1978, "was a very great mistake; we took in a partner we did not need and who is bound to compromise us, because it is to their interest to keep the Middle East in panic and disorder. . . ."[29] Senator Moynihan on the same day expressed gratitude to President Sadat and Prime Minister Begin for scuttling the Soviet–American initiative and apprehension lest their possible failure be followed by a revival of "the Washington, Moscow, Damascus, PLO policy of October 1. . . ."[30]

Following President Sadat's trip to Jerusalem in November 1977 the view gained wide currency that Sadat had been propelled to launch his peace initiative in part because of fear that the United States might permit the Soviet Union to acquire once again a major role in the Middle East. In fact, according to Carter administration officials (including Hermann Eilts, who was the United States Ambassador to Egypt at the time), Sadat welcomed and applauded the Soviet–American statement of October 1, 1977. Eilts recalled Sadat as having said on hearing of it, "Brilliant.

Brilliant."[31] It seems likely, however, that Sadat's enthusiasm diminished as it became evident that the joint statement did not represent a carefully planned strategy on the part of the United States and, in any event, owing to the domestic political uproar it provoked, was not going anywhere. These factors, rather than the policy represented by the joint statement itself, may have propelled Sadat toward his famous initiative.

Only a few dissenters from the prevailing consensus recalled the Soviet-American initiative of October 1977 as a lost opportunity. Nahum Goldmann, recently retired as president of the World Jewish Congress, wrote in 1978: "The Soviet Union is certainly not strong enough to impose a peace agreement in the Middle East, but it is well capable of sabotaging any settlement reached without it. For that reason the Vance-Gromyko agreement of October 1977 was a piece of real statesmanship, and it is regrettable that Israel's opposition and that of the pro-Israel lobby in America rendered the agreement ineffective."[32]

SCHOOLS OF THOUGHT

Fears of Soviet involvement in the Middle East derive only in part from the actual record of Soviet policy toward the Arab-Israeli conflict. They are also rooted in general perceptions of the nature of Soviet communism, and particularly in the conviction that the Soviet Union remains, as it proclaimed itself to be in Lenin's time, a world revolutionary power, committed to fomenting turmoil and revolution. There is much in the record of Soviet behavior—in abetting conflict between the two Yemens, in supporting coups and invading Afghanistan, in the meddlings of Cuban surrogates in Africa, in the imposition of Soviet domination over Eastern Europe in Stalin's time and the harsh suppression of freedom movements in Poland, Hungary and Czechoslovakia—to give solid basis for fears of Soviet power. Nevertheless, there is strong evidence to support the conclusion that, having been shocked and disappointed by Soviet expansionism after World War II, and by the refusal of the Soviets to cooperate in building a world security system based on the United Nations, American policy makers began to think *deductively* from general conclusions they drew at that time about Soviet motives and aims rather than pragmatically on the basis of discrete occurrences. In 1950 State and Defense Department officials prepared a document—known as "NSC–68"—that became highly influential on American policy making in that period and that remains, in attenuated form, a significant influence. NSC–68 said, "The Soviet Union, unlike previous aspirants to hegemony, is animated by a new fanatic faith, antithetical to our own, and seeks to impose its absolute authority over the rest of the world." The document went on to say that the Soviet Union was "inescapably militant," that its "fundamental design" was to subjugate the free world, and that the USSR, therefore, "mortally challenged" the United States.[33]

Gradually and intermittently, beginning with the second Eisenhower administration in the late fifties, a competing school of thought gained credibility and respectability although it has never attained dominance. The "détente" school holds that the Soviet Union since Stalin's time, although still committed to the ideology of revolution, has become cautious and even conservative in its foreign relations. The détente school proposes that Soviet leaders attach high value to the maintenance of a stable, businesslike relationship with the United States—partly because of the economic advantages of American trade and investment, partly because they are attracted to the idea of great power condominium in world affairs, but most of all because of a deep-seated fear of war born of the two German invasions of Russia in the twentieth century. In this perspective, as exposited by George F. Kennan, the Soviet leaders are not the "monsters" some Americans portray—who would run any risk or extract any sacrifice from their people to establish their domination over us or destroy us—but rather "quite ordinary men," victims to some extent of their own ideology but shaped primarily by their responsibilities as leaders of a great country. They are, Kennan suggests, "highly conservative men, perhaps the most conservative ruling group to be found anywhere in the world, markedly advanced in age, approaching the end of their tenure, and given to anything but rash adventure." In addition, Kennan suggests, they "share the horror of major war that dominates most of the Soviet people," and "have no desire to experience another military conflagration and no intention to launch one. . . ."[34]

In the United States, after more than thirty years of debate, no definitive consensus has formed as to which of the two schools of thought more accurately defines Soviet behavior. Accordingly, although the view of the Soviet Union as an agent of disruption and subversion commands wider support than the détente school, no final decision has been reached either as to whether it is wise or foolhardy, prudent or dangerous, necessary or avoidable, to invite the Soviet Union into a cooperative effort to bring peace to the Middle East. In making this decision, the United States must consider two closely related questions: Is the Soviet Union able and willing to enter such a partnership? And if so, is it to the interest of the United States to have the Russians as partners in Middle East peacemaking? These questions are related but not identical. Assuming Soviet willingness to cooperate, the desirability of cooperation increases accordingly, but the question would still remain whether there is more to be gained from collaboration than from a successful rivalry. Both questions turn on the larger, still unresolved question of superpower détente—whether it is feasible at all and, if so, how far it is desirable and advantageous to carry it.

Even the more anti-Soviet officials and scholars in the mainstream of American debate no longer contend that it is impossible to do business with the Russians; they readily acknowledge that the Soviet Union has evolved since Stalin's time and that it is not only possible but necessary to cooperate with the Soviets in strategic arms control, trade, and the containment of regional disputes. What remains at issue between the supporters of détente and its skeptics is not the fact of change in Soviet attitudes and policy but the nature of the changes that have taken place—whether they are tactical and opportunistic or fundamental and more or less permanent. Assuming, as it seems reasonable to do, that no responsible official or scholar or citizen would prefer unending cold war, an unrestrained arms race, and periodic confrontations of lesser or greater magnitude in place of a measure of cooperation with the other superpower, the question still comes down to: What are the post-Stalin Russians really like? Are they the same incorrigible reprobates they seemed to be in Stalin's time, more cautious, skilled, and flexible in their methods but still committed to their world revolutionary goal? Or has revolutionary zeal drained away, leaving a more or less traditional great power, ready and willing to expand its influence when the opportunity arises and the risk seems not too great, but also ready to retreat when prudence dictates, and with a growing, unacknowledged, but increasingly vested interest in major aspects of the global status quo?

Views on this question as it affects the Middle East vary not only with doctrinal orientation—for or against détente—but also with concerns such as human rights, past and present Russian anti-Semitism, and restrictions on Jewish emigration from the Soviet Union. Anti-Soviet feeling on the part of Israeli and American Jews derives not only from Soviet support of Israel's Arab enemies but also from deep-seated resentment of past and present anti-Semitism in Russia. From the fierce pogroms of the late nineteenth century under the tsars to the trials and imprisonment of Soviet Jewish dissenters in the 1970s, Jews have been subjected to officially sponsored discrimination and persecution in Russia. Indeed a large portion of the Jewish population of the United States are the children and grandchildren of Jews who fled from Russia and became Americans because of the poverty, discrimination, and recurrent violence that were visited on them by act or consent of the rulers of Russia. The oppressed Jews of Russia, Amos Elon wrote, found three avenues of escape: emigration (primarily to America), political radicalism within Russia, and Jewish nationalism. While a million and a half Jews left Russia for America between 1900 and 1914, a small fraction of that number went to Palestine as pioneers.[35] Russian anti-Semitism was thus a major factor in the rise of political Zionism in the early twentieth century; it is hardly surprising that the fear and mistrust of Russia survive as a major influence on Zionist thought, American Jewish attitudes, and Israeli life and culture.

To Israelis and to American Jews, restrictions on Jewish emigration from the Soviet Union are a modern manifestation of a baneful tradition of oppression. Although Soviet policies play on and thus encourage old-fashioned Russian anti-Semitism, the Soviet leaders themselves do not appear to be anti-Semitic in the traditional sense. Jews played a prominent role in the Bolshevik Revolution and the shaping of the Soviet state; official discrimination against Soviet Jews today—for what little solace it may be to its victims—appears to be directed not against Jews as a religious or ethnic group but against Jews as devotees of a foreign nationalism and therefore as a threat to the monolithic Soviet system as well as a complicating factor in Soviet dealings with the Arab world. It is worth noting in this respect that, unlike the tsars, who singled out the Jews for persecution ("But we must never forget that the Jews crucified our savior and shed his precious blood," the tsar scribbled on a late-nineteenth-century report on the condition of the Jews[36]), the Soviet leaders fear and restrict *all* national minorities within the Soviet Union, none of whom, *except the Jews*, are permitted to emigrate in significant numbers. To the extent that Soviet Jews are more conspicuously harassed and restricted than other dissidents and national minorities, the cause would appear to lie in their more active role as dissidents and in the greater force of their nationalism, with its strong support from the United States.

The level of Jewish emigration from the Soviet Union has risen, fallen, and then risen again—largely according to the state of Soviet-American relations. It rose from 15,000 in 1971, to 30,000 in 1972, and almost to 35,000 in 1973—the years of the Nixon-Kissinger détente policy—and then, following the adoption in 1974 of the Jackson-Vanik amendment making equal trade treatment contingent on dropping emigration controls, fell to about 15,000 in 1975 and remained the same in 1976. Emigration rose again significantly in 1978 and in the early months of 1979, with the SALT II treaty nearing completion and the prospect of a lifting of trade and credit controls for both the Soviet Union and China, rose to an all-time record level, indicating an annual rate of about 50,000.[37] Emigration dropped again with the deterioration in Soviet-American relations in 1980 and 1981, reaching a ten-year low in the summer of 1981. Emigration has been used by the Soviet Union not only as a signal to the United States but, in the view of Arie Lova Eliav, also as a signal to Israel, saying in effect, "We are not interested in your destruction, and under certain conditions dialogue with you would become possible."[38]

Despite such signals and despite the occasional release of leading Jewish dissidents, Russia has remained, in Israeli and Jewish eyes, the great "prison of nations" Lenin had spoken of early in the twentieth century. In an addition to the revised edition of his memoir written in 1972, Menachem Begin wrote: "Tens of thousands of Jews in the Soviet Union sing and call out: 'To return to the land of our fathers.'. . . Since I came, or returned, to Eretz Israel, I have not ceased to express hope, or faith, that there would be a return to Zion from Russia as well."[39] In April 1979 the Soviet and American governments carried out an agreement to exchange five prominent Soviet dissidents for two Soviet spies serving prison sentences in the United States. The exchange, which took place at Kennedy International Airport in New York, included two dissidents whose release had long been sought by American Jewish organizations, Eduard S. Kuznetsov and Mark Dymshits, both of whom had been convicted in 1970 as leaders of a failed attempt to hijack a Soviet plane to escape to Israel. "Could I have stayed on in the Soviet Union if I had a choice?" Dymshits said in New York. "Absolutely not! I couldn't bear it any longer—I couldn't bear the anti-Jewish policy and the Soviet approach to Middle East policy."[40] The released dissidents expressed hope for the release of other "prisoners of ideas" still held in the Soviet Union,[41] including Anatoly B. Shcharansky, a leader of the Jewish emigration movement, whom President Carter personally had declared innocent of the espionage charge on which he was convicted, and who, at the end of his trial in Moscow, had defiantly repeated the ancient vow of dispersed and persecuted Jews, "Next year in Jerusalem."[42] To the consternation of Israeli officials, an increasing proportion of Jewish emigrants from the Soviet Union—reaching 65 percent in 1980—chose to go to places other than Israel, with most going to the United States.[43]

For the Soviet Union as for the United States, albeit in quite different ways, the Middle East conflict thus has major domestic as well as international consequences. It has given rise to the most significant, effective and, from the Soviet standpoint, dangerous dissident movements in postwar

Soviet history. To allow it free play, in emigration and public expression, is to encourage other national minorities to assert themselves against the monolithic Soviet system, and to some degree also to antagonize the Soviet Union's Arab allies, who fear and resent the strengthening of Israel through immigration. On the other hand, suppressing the dissident movement, by provocative political trials such as those of Shcharansky and Alexander Ginzburg in July 1978, or by drastically cutting back emigration, has cost the Soviet Union heavily in desired trade and credits from the United States, played a part in the Senate's failure to ratify the second SALT treaty, and has generally jeopardized the détente with the United States. Typical U.S. Senate reactions to the July 1978 trials were those of the Minority Leader, Senator Baker, who called for the temporary suspension of SALT negotiations, and Senator Don Riegle, Democrat of Michigan and a past proponent of negotiations with the Soviet Union, who called the trials the work of "sick and twisted bureaucratic midgets" and said he could not imagine "a SALT treaty I could support with a nation that terrorizes its own people."[44] The Soviet leaders have dealt with this excruciating dilemma over the years by vacillating, according to their perceived needs of the moment, between suppression and conciliation. In something of an understatement Arie Lova Eliav observes: "It so happens that the two greatest Jewish Diasporas are to be found within the two superpowers. Each of these Diasporas vastly complicates the life of its superpower on account of the Arab-Israel problem."[45]

The overall effect of the Soviet Union's clumsy and often brutal attempt to deal with its "Jewish problem" has been to strengthen the school of thought that regards the Soviet Union as a dangerous and unworthy partner in the effort to bring peace to the Middle East. American supporters of détente, and a minority—probably no more than a small minority—in Israel, would share the view of Professor Marshall Shulman, adviser to Secretary of State Cyrus Vance on Soviet affairs during the Carter administration, that the easing of repression in the Soviet Union would be "more likely to result from evolutionary forces within the society under prolonged conditions of reduced international tension than from external demands for change and the siege mentality they would reinforce,"[46] or the more emphatic assertion of Nahum Goldmann that the failure of détente would mean "the end of hopes of peace in the Middle East, the immediate halting of emigration from the USSR, leaving more than three million Jews in Soviet Russia in a worse situation. . . ."[47] The majority view, however, in the United States as well as Israel, has been against the feasibility of détente as an inducement to Soviet good behavior. In this dominant view the suppression of human rights in the Soviet Union speaks for itself, indicating a predatory as well as oppressive regime that can, perhaps, be dealt with in specific ways for specific purposes, but only when agreements are backed by reliable sanctions. That conception underlies the Jackson amendment, which relies on economic sanctions to induce a liberal Soviet emigration policy; it also underlies the policy of diligent exclusion of the Soviet Union from the main arena of Middle East diplomacy.

Influenced by dislike of the Soviet system and suspicion of Soviet motives on the one hand, and by the periodic need for cooperation and appreciation of Soviet power on the other, American policy makers have tended more to fear than welcome Soviet offers of collaboration toward peace in the Middle East. It has been generally agreed that the Soviet Union could not be excluded entirely because of its influence on some of the parties, its superpower status, and its consequent ability to impair or prevent a settlement in which it had no part or of which it disapproved. Beyond that minimal consensus, American policymakers—prior to the Reagan administration—and scholars have remained divided and uncertain as to whether the Russians really wanted a settlement and as to the extent of Soviet involvement in Middle East peacemaking that was necessary and safe. Efforts to resolve these uncertainties have turned in large part on inferences concerning Soviet motives drawn from Marxist-Leninist ideology, from three decades of superpower rivalry, and from Soviet internal practices. Equally pertinent to a soundly based assessment of what can be expected of the Soviets in the future is a taking into account of what in fact they have done in the past with respect to the Arab-Israeli conflict.

THE SOVIETS AND THE ARAB-ISRAELI CONFLICT

On May 14, 1947 the Soviet representative to the United Nations Security Council and deputy foreign minister, Andrei Gromyko, told the General Assembly that, although the Soviet Union saw greater merit in a single binational Arab-Jewish state in Palestine, the partition of Palestine into separate Arab and Jewish states also warranted consideration if Arab-Jewish hostility made a unified state unfeasible. "We must bear in mind," Gromyko said, "the incontestable fact that the population of Palestine consists of two peoples, Arabs and Jews. Each of these has its historical roots in Palestine."[48] Soon thereafter the Soviet press stopped publishing anti-Zionist material. On October 13, 1947 the Soviet delegate, in a speech before the General Assembly, gave unequivocal endorsement to the concept of partition. The Soviet Union and the United States both actively supported the resolution to partition Palestine, which was adopted by the General Assembly on November 29, 1947. On May 17, 1948, three days after its proclamation by the Jewish Agency, the Soviet Union accorded full recognition to the new state of Israel. In the ensuing war of independence the Soviet Union, through Czechoslovakia, sold sizable quantities of arms to the hard-pressed Israelis.[49]

The highly probable reason for the sudden shift of Soviet policy in late 1947 and 1948, the crucial period in the making of the Israeli state, was that the Soviet Union perceived an opportunity, by supporting the expulsion of British imperial power from Palestine, to inject its own influence into the Middle East, possibly by means of Soviet participation in an international police force constituted to implement the partition. The Russians may have hoped that the new Jewish state would be highly nationalistic and anti-Western, and possibly even communist, or they may have calculated that Arab-Jewish hostility arising from the creation of the Jewish state would offer opportunities for communist penetration and the expansion of Soviet influence in the Arab world.[50] Whatever the motivation of the change of Soviet policy in 1947 and 1948, it gave crucial assistance to the Zionist cause at the climactic period of the struggle for a Jewish state. Menachem Begin believed that the change of Soviet policy was no sudden thing. "During the years of revolt," he wrote in his memoir, "we met and talked with official and unofficial representatives of the Soviet Union and her friends. We learnt that as a result of our struggle for liberation, the attitude of Russia to our striving for Jewish National independence was changing." Begin also wrote: "It is noteworthy that the American, Warren Austin,[51] in supporting the demand for the replacement of British rule in Eretz Israel by a new regime, used language almost identical with that of the Russian, Gromyko."[52]

Soviet enthusiasm for the new Jewish state was short-lived. With imperial Britain removed from Palestine—all too willingly, as it turned out—Stalinist Russia turned to the frustrated, embittered Arab states as fertile fields for cultivation. In addition, the new state of Israel exerted a powerful magnetism on the Jews of the Soviet Union, arousing Stalin's ire against both. Thus, having contributed substantially to the success of the Zionist cause, the Soviet Union quickly reverted to its traditional anti-Zionism and became the political and military patron of Israel's Arab enemies. At no time, however, did the Soviet Union withdraw its recognition from the Jewish state, call for its dissolution, or challenge its right to exist. The official Soviet position has been consistent since 1948 in support of Israel's right to exist and consistent since 1967 in support of Israel's right to a secure national existence, as called for in Security Council Resolution 242, within its 1967 borders. The basic Soviet position on a general Middle East settlement was spelled out by President Brezhnev in a speech to the sixteenth Congress of Trade Unions on March 21, 1977, in which he called for Israeli withdrawal to the borders of 1967; Palestinian self-determination; guarantees of the right of all states and peoples of the region, including Israel, to independence, peace and security; and, on the completion of Israeli withdrawal, termination of the state of war and the establishment of normal relations between Israel and its neighbors.[53] The Soviet Union has also offered to guarantee Israel. On April 23, 1975 Foreign Minister Gromyko, at a dinner in Moscow for Syrian foreign minister Abdel Halim Khaddam, said, "Israel may get, if it so wishes, the strictest guarantees with the participation—under an appropriate agree-ment—of the Soviet Union."[54] The offer to participate with the United States in a general guarantee of a Middle East settlement was reiterated in the joint statement of October 1, 1977.

In the absence of access to the internal discussions in the Kremlin, the reasons for the Soviet Union's consistent support—at least verbal, official support—of Israel's right to a secure national existence can only be specu-lated on. The most commonly heard explanation is that Israel is the essential avenue to Soviet influence in the Arab world—a thesis diametri-cally opposed to the contention that Israel serves as a barrier to Soviet influence in the Middle East. Nahum Goldmann wrote in 1974 that "the existence of Israel is vital to the USSR's position in the Arab world because, in view of the strong hostility to communism felt by most of the Arab people, had it not been for Russia's support for the Arabs in their conflict with Israel the Arabs would have become clients of the West."[55] A parallel view was expressed by a Saudi official who observed in October 1978 that a solution to the Palestinian problem would "close all the windows" to the Soviet Union and to communism in the Middle East, because the Arabs "could not be communist by nature."[56] The premise of this interpretation is that it is not the preservation of Israel that interests the Soviet Union but the perpetuation of conflict and turmoil to which Israel's presence in the Middle East gives rise. It is not entirely clear, however, how the conflict would be perpetuated were a settlement along the lines repeatedly urged by the Soviet Union accomplished—unless it is assumed that the Soviets make their proposals for settlement in full confidence that they will never be accepted or implemented. Further doubt is cast on the premise of Israel's essentiality to Soviet aims by the fact that the United States has largely displaced the Soviet Union in influence in the Arab world precisely because, by contrast with the Soviet Union, it can, if it chooses, bring leverage to bear on Israel. In this respect the perpetuation of conflict has worked to increase American and diminish Soviet influence. A further question with respect to the basic premise has been raised by historian Charles Issawi of Princeton University, who has suggested that Islam is not necessarily incompatible with communism, that indeed, with their common emphasis on the group as against the individual, they might even make a happy marriage under the rubric of "Islamic Communism."[57]

Soviet long-term aims in the Middle East—predatory, benign, or improvisatory—can only be guessed at. The Soviet record, however, which is available for examination, suggests certain generalizations: that the Soviets have played a crucial role on critical occasions in the past and almost certainly will continue to play a critical role; that their efforts to build influence in the Arab world, though untiring, have met with only limited success and a number of spectacular failures; that, like the United States, they have suffered repeated and severe frustration at the hands of their Middle Eastern clients; that they have been careful to avoid confrontation with the United States; that on a number of important occasions they have shown an interest in joint action with the United States; that, on the whole, however, they, like the United States, have treated the Middle East as an arena of great power rivalry rather than of cooperation. If any single theme can be identified as underlying Soviet policy in the Middle East since World War II, it has been the drive to secure recognition of the Soviet Union as a Middle Eastern power, entitled to be consulted on major issues—a power whose consent and participation is essential to the solution of the Arab-Israeli problem as well as other major regional issues.

Having given the Russians the opportunity to become involved in the Middle East, the Arab-Israeli conflict, from the outset, has rewarded them with little else. The Soviet Union began providing arms to Egypt and Syria in 1955. When Israel, in alliance with Britain and France, attacked Egypt in late October 1956, the Russians, who at the time were engaged in suppressing a popular uprising in Hungary, immediately withdrew their advisers from Egypt. On November 5, 1956, after British and French landings in the Suez canal area and Israeli occupation of most of Sinai, the Soviets threatened nuclear retaliation against Britain and France, but on the same day proposed joint Soviet-American intervention to end the aggression in the Middle East. When a United Nations cease-fire went into effect, the Soviet Union threatened to send "volunteers" to compel the withdrawal of British, French, and Israeli troops, but this threat too was unaccompanied by action. After the war the Soviets replaced Egypt's military losses and thereafter became Egypt's principal military supplier, providing, however, only limited quantities of distinctively offensive weapons.[58]

In the spring of 1967, following Syrian provocations of Israel and Israeli retaliatory attacks, the Soviet Union encouraged a more militant policy on the part of Egypt, possibly as a way of reducing the pressure on Syria without active Soviet involvement in its defense. Events quickly passed out of Soviet control as an overconfident President Nasser, going beyond Soviet expectations, demanded the withdrawal of the United Nations Emergency Force that had been placed in the Sinai after the 1956 war and also, on May 22, 1967, blockaded the Strait of Tiran at the mouth of the Gulf of Aqaba. The Soviets then tried to keep matters in hand by warning Israel they would come to the aid of the Arab states if Israel attacked them, while warning Egypt and Syria that they could not count on Soviet support except in the event of direct American intervention. Israel called the Soviet bluff, launched its lightning attack on June 5, ignored Soviet demands for a cease-fire, and went on to win its greatest military victory. The Soviet Union made no serious effort to resupply the Arab combatants during the brief conflict, although warnings conveyed through Washington may have restrained the Israelis from attacking Damascus.[59]

Having suffered a severe foreign policy defeat in the Six Day War, the Soviet Union thereupon undertook to replace the Arab military losses. This massive resupply operation, augmented by an influx of Soviet military advisers to retrain the Egyptian and Syrian armies, had profound political consequences. It enabled the Arab states to escape the necessity of making peace on the basis of the military situation produced by the war and, at their Khartoum summit meeting in September 1967, to adopt a rejectionist policy of no concessions or dealings with Israel. Israel, in turn, was robbed of the opportunity, had she wished to take it, of offering to return territory in exchange for a general settlement.[60] The Six Day War demonstrated the limits of Soviet power to control conflict in the Middle East; the aftermath demonstrated the extent of Soviet power to alter the consequences of conflict once it had occurred.

Bolstered by Soviet arms, military advisers, and technicians, President Nasser (who had barely survived in power after the 1967 debacle) in 1969 launched the "War of Attrition" along the Suez Canal. By early 1970 Egypt was being battered by Israeli "deep penetration" raids, and the Soviet Union, offering careful explanations to the United States, began to take over Egypt's air defense with Soviet missile crews and Soviet-piloted fighter planes. Israeli deep penetration raids thereupon ceased; SAM missile sites were reconstructed; Israeli planes were shot down; and Soviet aircraft began to operate over the Suez Canal zone. On July 30, 1970 the Israelis, abandoning caution, engaged the Soviet aircraft and shot down five MIG–21s. The Russians chose not to publicize the incident and made no threats of retaliation, concentrating thereafter on building up ground-to-air defense missiles along the canal while avoiding further encounters with Israeli pilots.[61] An American-mediated ceasefire went into effect along the canal on August 8, 1970, suspending the War of Attrition, but leaving the Soviets with almost full responsibility for Egypt's air defense.

For their considerable efforts the Russians were rewarded in 1971 and 1972 with mounting Egyptian ingratitude and complaints. Fearing another rash or disastrous military venture, the Russians kept their clients on short rations, withholding offensive weapons and even ammunition. On July 8, 1972 President Sadat ordered most of the Soviet personnel out of the country; the Russians complied quickly, quietly, and, by some accounts, gladly.

The Egyptians thereupon began planning for a new war and in early 1973 the Soviets, no longer heavily involved on the ground, began to supply Egypt, and also Syria, with large quantities of strategic and tactical offensive weapons. Whether or not the Soviet leaders gave their consent or expected war to ensue is unclear; there is no doubt, however, that Soviet weapons, especially for air defense, and years of Soviet training of Egyptian and Syrian forces made possible the war of October 1973. During the war the Soviets maintained a heavy flow of supplies to the combatants by air and sea.[62] During the weeks of fighting the Russians reinforced their Mediterranean fleet and, when the war began to go against the Arabs, sent military personnel to try to reconstruct Egypt's SAM missile sites and also placed Soviet airborne divisions on alert.

As the Egyptian and Syrian military positions worsened, the Soviets sought, with mounting urgency, American cooperation to bring about a cease-fire. The United States readily agreed, but both superpowers then faced the task of imposing the cease-fire. Under heavy Soviet pressure Syria agreed, and under American pressure Israel agreed, but the cease-fire in Egypt quickly broke down and the Israelis threatened to destroy the Egyptian Third Army trapped on the east bank of the Suez Canel. The ensuing crisis in Soviet-American relations (to be discussed in the following section), in which the Soviets came close to unilateral intervention, culminated in joint action by the superpowers to enforce the cease-fire, in consequence of which the Third Army was saved and the fighting brought to an end.[63] Having provided the essential military equipment to enable Egypt and Syria to go to war, having sustained the Arab armies with emergency supplies during the war, and finally having acted boldly to save them from defeat, the Soviet Union stood, at the end of the October War, at a high point of prestige and influence in the Middle East.

Soviet influence fell precipitously thereafter. Recognizing that the United States, as the only power with real influence on Israel, held "99 percent of the cards"—as he was to repeat many times—President Sadat had little further use for the Russians. Increasingly excluded from the diplomatic process as Secretary of State Henry Kissinger took center stage with his "step-by-step" policy of limited disengagement agreements, the Soviets cut back on arms deliveries and refused debt concessions to Egypt, while President Sadat, for his part, became ever less inhibited in making known his dislike of the Russians. In March 1976 Sadat denounced the Soviet-Egyptian Treaty of Friendship and Cooperation of 1971.[64] While Syria retained close—though by no means subservient—relations with the Soviet Union in the years following the October War of 1973, Egypt moved steadily into the American orbit, becoming, in the wake of Camp David and the peace treaty of March 1979, a near-equal to Israel in closeness to and reliance on the United States and something more than Israel's equal in the frequency and fervor of its imprecations against the Soviet Union.

After three decades of active involvement in the Arab-Israeli conflict, the Soviet Union had clearly established itself as a Middle East power. In a few peripheral areas, notably South Yemen and Libya, it had become the paramount, though by no means assuredly permanent, outside influence. In two major countries, Iraq and Syria, the Russians had established long-term significant influence, although neither of these countries became subservient to Soviet power or even receptive to communist ideology. A Soviet ambassador in Damascus, indeed, was credited with the observation that the Syrians took everything from the Russians except advice.[65] In the central arena of Soviet interest and effort, however—the Arab-Israeli conflict—the Soviets after thirty years retained a degree of influence which, though significant, fell far short of proportionality to the cost and effort incurred in its attainment. In this respect the Soviet experience has paralleled that of the United States: neither has been able to exercise influence commensurate with the costs, risks, and responsibilities incurred on behalf of its respective clients. Although both have exercised restraining influence at times, neither has been able to prevent recurrent military encounters—encounters that either could not have occurred or would have been much reduced in scale without their support, encounters that on several occasions, notably October 1973, set them against each other in circumstances neither had desired or foreseen, for causes outside of their own bilateral relations, and as the outgrowth of decisions neither had made and actions neither had initiated.

Meager though the rewards have been for Soviet policy in the Arab-Israeli conflict, that policy has been consistent over three decades in certain fundamentals: first, Soviet policy has been marked by caution at times of crisis—even crises the Soviet Union had helped precipitate such as the Six Day War of 1967—by carefully limiting its own support and involvement and otherwise trying to restrain its Arab allies from rash and dangerous action. Second, although sometimes heavy-handed as in the period of their large scale military presence in Egypt between 1967 and 1972, the Russians at no time tried to impose their own military or ideological domination over Egypt or Syria, as they had in eastern Europe, but rather contented themselves with political influence, a military presence, and great power prestige. Third, although they have been the principal arms supplier to the Arab confrontation states, the Soviets have consistently sought a political rather than purely military settlement of the Middle East conflict, as evidenced by the strict limits maintained on the quantity and kinds of arms supplied,[66] and by their involvement in the diplomacy of the Arab-Israeli conflict from the partition plan of 1947 to the drawing up of Security Council Resolution 242 in 1967 and the convening of the abortive Geneva Conference in 1973. Fourth—and closely related—the Soviet Union has, since the creation of the state of Israel in 1948, upheld the right of Israel to exist as a permanent, recognized state. Professor Hisham Sharabi observed in 1978, from a Palestinian perspective, that the Soviet Union had been "amazingly consistent" in this respect. "It has gone against the objectives of many Arab states, including the PLO in various phases, alienating many of its friends by consistently adopting the position that the Israelis are there to stay and that the idea of changing this fact by a war of liberation or by the replacement of Israel with a democratic secular state is politically impossible and practically not feasible."[67] Finally, as will be seen in the next section, Soviet policy has been characterized by the careful avoidance of confrontation with the United States, by periodic efforts to involve the United States in joint undertakings as with the joint statement of October 1, 1977, and by a demonstrated appreciation of the fact that the Middle East is an area of vital interest to the United States, with respect both to the survival and security of Israel and the oil resources of the Arabian peninsula.

A review of Soviet policies and actions in the Middle East since 1947 casts doubt on, although it does not disprove, prevailing views as to long term Soviet objectives in the Middle East. There is no question that, as a supporter of Palestinian nationalism and advocate of Israel's withdrawal to its borders of 1967, the Soviet Union is a "revisionist" rather than status quo power in the Middle East. The same, however, may be said of the United States, to the extent that it supports some degree of Israeli withdrawal and some degree of Palestinian self-rule. More open to question is whether Soviet "revisionism" is rooted in an active, operational commitment to Marxist-Leninist goals. John Campbell, former Director of Studies at the Council on Foreign Relations, wrote in 1978 that there is "a basic Soviet assumption of continuing conflict, in the Middle East as elsewhere, between the forces of imperialism and reaction led by the United States and the forces of socialism and progress led by the USSR; and although the course of events may be marked by tactical adjustments, compromises and temporary defeats, confidence in the ultimate victory of socialism informs middle range aims and policies." Campbell asserts too that, although the Soviet Union has become in many respects a conservative power, "its leadership does not seek in the Middle East stability, settlement of local conflict or political solutions for their own sake or as a contribution to world order."[68] In the absence of more than fragments of information as to the discussions that take place within the Kremlin, these propositions can be tested only as they manifest themselves in Soviet policies and actions, but even a close examination of the record of Soviet behavior provides only limited clues as to what is taking place within the *minds* of policy makers in the Kremlin. After how many years, for example, does a series of adjustments, each of which was *intended* to be tactical, form a pattern of settled behavior, in practice if not intent? When too does an "assumption of continuing conflict," intermittently acted upon, begin to pass from a principle of policy to liturgy? It may also be asked: Does it matter whether solutions are sought "for their own sake," or for purposes of contributing to world order, as long as they are sought? Campbell raises the "perennial question" whether the Soviets really want an Arab-Israeli settlement. His answer is, "They have committed themselves publicly, again and again, to the proposition that they do," and their proposed terms, "on the surface anyway, are not so different from those the United States Administration has in mind. . . ."[69]

In their hearts and minds the Kremlin policymakers may indeed still dream of world empire. Such restraint as they have shown, and the proposals they have made for cooperation with the United States, may reflect only the lack of power or opportunity to act otherwise. Alternately, the "quite ordinary men" of Kennan's description who inhabit the Kremlin, aged and conservative, tempered by the great and often intractable problems of running a great country, may have lost much or most of their zeal for adventure, beyond that minimum required for propitiating the gods of their ideological temple. Crane Brinton, an historian of revolution, wrote, "there is no eternal fanaticism or, at any rate, there has not yet been an eternal fanaticism."[70] On the basis of events and performance, a plausible case can be made that, until and unless the global power equation changes greatly, Soviet aims in the Middle East, at least in practice, do not exceed the attainment of equality of influence or perhaps a kind of condominium with the United States. Still another possibility, never to be underrated in evaluating the motives of politicians, is that the Kremlin policy makers are best understood as improvisors, who wish to make their presence felt but otherwise lack long-term goals, or at least goals of sufficient precision to serve as operative guides to policy. At the very least, it can be safely concluded that there is a discrepancy between theory and practice in Soviet policy in the Middle East and that in this discrepancy lie opportunities for American policy.

DÉTENTE AND CONFRONTATION

It was suggested in chapter 2 that the United States has a major national interest in the avoidance of confrontation and enlistment of Soviet collaboration wherever possible for the maintenance of world order. It would not seem essential to demonstrate a high probability of nuclear war arising from some future crisis in the Middle East to establish the value of a stable superpower relationship in that volatile region. The very possibility of so great a catastrophe would seem to justify major exertions to prevent it. Past events have shown that a global catastrophe could indeed arise out of a superpower confrontation over the Middle East, and that would seem reason enough to try to put superpower relations on some basis more solid than periodic resort to "crisis management." Even the most skillfully conducted crisis diplomacy carries the danger, greatly magnified in the nuclear age, that Kissinger recognized in Bismarck's agile improvisations: "In the hands of others lacking his subtle touch, his methods led to the collapse of the nineteenth century state system. The nemesis of power is that, except in the hands of a master, reliance on it is more likely to produce a contest of arms than of self-restraint."[71]

As Peter Mangold observed in his study published in 1978, *Superpower Intervention in the Middle East*, every major Middle East crisis has "raised the specter of superpower confrontation."[72] The fact that these confrontations, including the American nuclear alert of October 25, 1973, were probably less dangerous than the Berlin crises of earlier years and the Cuban missile crisis of 1962, does not alter the basic fact: they were dangerous enough. The initial American response to the air attack on the American intelligence-gathering ship *Liberty* in the Mediterranean during the 1967 war was to believe that the Soviet Union—and not, as it turned out, Israel—was responsible.[73] During the War of Attrition, in 1969 and 1970, the threat of a direct clash between Soviet and Israeli forces kept open the possibility of American involvement if the Israelis found themselves in real trouble. In fact, as noted in the previous section, Israeli and Soviet planes did clash on July 30, 1970, but the Israelis got much the better of that encounter—and the Russians, for reasons, one supposes, of sensitivity to the larger issue as well as of embarrassment, chose not to publicize the occurrence. In a television interview on July 1, 1970, President Nixon had spoken of the Middle East as being "terribly dangerous, like the Balkans before World War I, where the two superpowers, the United States and the Soviet Union, could be drawn into a confrontation that neither of them wants."[74] National Security Adviser Henry Kissinger had called up the same analogy five days earlier, noting that both regional belligerents were allied to superpowers, "each of them to some extent not fully under the control of the major country concerned."[75]

The superpowers came closer still to a direct confrontation in the 1973 war, although exactly how close remains in dispute. On October 19, with Israeli forces advancing on the west bank of the Suez Canal and threatening to envelop the Egyptian Third Army on the east bank, Soviet Ambassador Dobrynin presented to Secretary Kissinger an invitation from General Secretary Brezhnev to fly to Moscow for "urgent consultations on the Middle East." Fearing Soviet unilateral action and judging the situation therefore to be "murderously dangerous," Kissinger promptly accepted. On the same day, President Nixon sent a special message to Congress requesting an emergency grant of $2.2 billion in military supplies for Israel; the Middle East, Nixon said, had become "a flash point for potential world conflict." The next day, October 20, as Kissinger flew to Moscow, Saudi Arabia joined other Arab states in announcing an oil embargo against the United States. The following day agreement was reached between the United States and the Soviet Union calling for a cease-fire, and on October 22, on Soviet-American recommendation, the United Nations Security Council adopted Resolution 338 calling for an immediate cease-fire in place and reaffirming Security Council Resolution

242 of November 1967. Each superpower undertook to secure the compliance of its respective clients; Brezhnev won Sadat's agreement to the cease-fire and to direct talks with Israel, but only after promising that the Soviet Union would, if necessary, act alone to enforce the cease-fire.[76]

The cease-fire failed to take hold as each side blamed the other for violations. A second Soviet-American sponsored cease-fire went into effect early on October 24, but by that time, much to Kissinger's dismay, the Israelis had enveloped the Egyptian Third Army on the east bank of the Suez Canal. On that same day intelligence reports showed that seven Soviet airborne divisions had been placed on alert and that eighty-five Soviet ships were then in the Mediterranean. On the evening of the 24th President Nixon received a "very urgent" message from Brezhnev, a message that Nixon later wrote "represented perhaps the most serious threat to U.S.-Soviet relations since the Cuban missile crisis eleven years before."[77] Accusing Israel of "drastically" violating the cease-fire, Brezhnev urged that the two leaders "urgently dispatch Soviet and American contingents to Egypt," and he added: "If you find it impossible to act together with us in this matter, we should be faced with the necessity urgently to consider the question of taking appropriate steps unilaterally. Israel cannot be allowed to get away with the violations."[78]

A hastily convened meeting of the president's top national security advisers convened at 11:00 P.M. on the night of October 24 in the White House "Situation Room," where they considered the situation on the basis of advice received from three panels of experts that there was a "high probability" of some kind of "unilateral Soviet move." On the unanimous recommendation of the national security advisers, word went out in the course of the night to American conventional and nuclear forces around the world placing them on varying degrees, although not the most extreme degree, of military alert. Allowing the Russians time to detect the American alert by their own electronic devices, Nixon fired off a message to Brezhnev advising him that his proposal for joint Soviet-American military intervention was "not appropriate in the present circumstances," and that "in these circumstances, we must view your suggestion of unilateral action as a matter of the gravest concern involving incalculable consequences." Nixon said he would agree to Soviet and American non-combatant personnel being included in a United Nations truce observation force, but "You must know, however, that we would in no event accept unilateral action. . . ."[79] Kissinger held a news conference on October 25 in which he angrily rejected suggestions that the alert might have been called to divert attention from the burgeoning Watergate crisis—Nixon's infamous "Saturday Night Massacre" had occurred the previous weekend—and Kissinger also said, speaking of the Soviet Union and the United States: "We possess, each of us, nuclear arsenals capable of annihilating humanity. We, both of us, have a special duty to see to it that confrontations are kept within bounds that do not threaten civilized life. Both of us, sooner or later, will have to realize that the issues that divide the world today, and foreseeable issues, do not justify the unparalleled catastrophe that a nuclear war would represent."[80]

The Russians backed off. Abandoning the idea of either Soviet or American participation in a peacekeeping force, they acquiesced, on October 25, 1973, in Security Council Resolution 340, which mandated the establishment of a United Nations Emergency Force to be composed of personnel from countries other than the permanent members of the Security Council.[81] At a meeting with the bipartisan congressional leaders on October 25, President Nixon gave his evaluation of the interplay of détente and confrontation in the Middle East war: "I have never said that the Soviets are 'good guys.' What I have always said is that we should not enter into unnecessary confrontations with them."[82]

A considerable controversy arose as to how dangerous the superpower confrontation really had been on the night of October 24–25, 1973. Kissinger, who judged the situation "murderously dangerous" at the time, later referred to the alert as "our deliberate overreaction."[83] Secretary of Defense Schlesinger, in a news conference on October 26, 1973, strongly defended the alert but stated his opinion that "we were very far away from a confrontation," and also said that there had been "mixed reactions and different assessments" of the likelihood that Soviet forces were actually en route to Egypt on October 24. The whole episode, Schlesinger said, had underscored the strengths of détente as well as its limitations.[84] Whether or not accounts at the time exaggerated the gravity of the crisis of October 1973, and whether in fact the situation in the Middle East was as dangerous in the summer of 1970—as Nixon and Kissinger contended—as the situation in the Balkans had been in the summer of 1914, there can be no doubt that there was *some* risk in these and other crises, appreciable if not acute, and a trip to the very brink of nuclear war would not seem essential to instilling an appreciation of the desirability of efforts to avoid it.

Efforts to head off great power confrontation in past, successive Middle East crises have been in the nature of highly improvisational "crisis management" rather than manifestations of preplanned consultation under the aegis of détente. Neither the United States nor the Soviet Union actually *wanted* the wars of 1967 and 1973 to take place; neither indeed was consulted or specifically forewarned of the initiation of hostilities. Both, however, were drawn, with less than deliberate consent, into the role of noncombatant cobelligerents; both were drawn into deep, costly, and frustrating involvement in the consequences of these wars; and in 1973, and perhaps too in the War of Attrition in 1970, they were brought within range, lesser or greater, of unplanned, unwanted confrontation with each other. Through diplomatic improvisation, the careful reading of each other's urgent messages, and the urgent imposition of restraint on their respective clients at critical moments, the superpowers have managed to sustain peace with each other and stalemate between the regional combatants. Neither, however, has been able or willing to use the power that they undoubtedly possess, if not to prevent conflict in the Middle East entirely, then greatly to limit its scale and circumscribe its consequences. They have been unable to do this because, on one level, neither has been willing to leave a client to its fate, to suffer the full consequences of defeat or to reap the rewards of victory, and because, on the more basic level, the superpowers have been unable to identify a common interest of their own—or a "special duty," as Kissinger put it,[85] to protect the world from nuclear war—that would override the geopolitical advantages each might hope to derive from treating the Middle East as an arena of great power rivalry. Convinced as they apparently have been of the unretractable character of their own rivalry, the superpowers have, perforce, become in important respects, the creatures rather than the controllers of their respective clients, improvisers rather than arbiters, crisis managers rather than trustees of world order, in the search for a stable peace.[86]

We return inevitably to the question, still open after three decades of Soviet-American preponderance in world affairs, of what kind of people the Soviet leaders really are—the "quite ordinary men" of Kennan's perception, or "aspirants to hegemony" under the banner of a "fanatic faith."[87] In more concrete terms: how far are the Russians willing to go, how far would they dare to go, how greatly or little do they desire to destroy Western interests in the Middle East? In a farewell speech as secretary of energy on August 16, 1979, James Schlesinger said that the energy crisis provided "a new dimension to the political and ideological competition between the United States and the Soviet Union." Citing the steady growth of Soviet military power, Schlesinger called for a "new and effective response" to Soviet pressures in the Middle East, "a region to which Russia has aspired since the days of Peter the Great." He warned: "Soviet control of the oil tap in the Middle East would mean the end of the world as we have known it since 1945 and of the association of free nations."[88] Earlier in the summer of 1979 the director of the Soviet Institute for American and Canadian Studies, Georgy A. Arbatov, had spoken to the same subject: "The Soviet government would certainly not interfere with Western oil supplies from the Middle East, whether this were done by intimidating the oil producing countries not to export oil to the West or by strangling the sea routes. These would be very hostile acts, close to a declaration of hostilities." Arbatov added: "I could not conceive of a scheme the Soviet Union might apply to deprive the West of oil from the Middle East without realizing what this would mean to the whole world situation."[89] It would not seem essential—even if it were possible—to determine whether Arbatov or Schlesinger was more accurate in defining Soviet intentions to decide on whether or not the United States ought to maintain a rough balance of military power with the Soviet Union in the Indian Ocean and the Persian Gulf. That would seem the course of prudence in either case. An approximate evaluation of Soviet intentions would seem highly pertinent, however, to basic political decisions as between détente and confrontation, attempts to build partnership or relentless rivalry, the inclusion of the Soviet Union in the diplomacy of the Arab-Israeli conflict or its rigorous exclusion so far as that is possible.

With the collapse of the SALT II treaty, the invasion of Afghanistan, the inauguration of the Reagan administration, and the turning away from détente, American official opinion—and to a lesser degree, academic opinion—has become increasingly weighted against the feasibility of Soviet-American partnership in the affairs of the Middle East or other areas of world politics. This remains the case despite a longstanding Soviet interest in a kind of superpower condominium in the Middle East. The Soviet Union had proposed joint Soviet-American intervention to impose partition in 1948, again to end the fighting in the Suez war of 1956, to enforce the cease-fire in 1973, and to bring about a general settlement through the joint statement of October 1, 1977. When Brezhnev visited the United States in the summer of 1973, by his account, "I kept Nixon up almost all night on the Middle East, trying to convince him of the need to act together. Otherwise there would be an explosion."[90] Dismissing such proposals as self-serving devices for Soviet penetration of the Middle East, American officials have tended to assume that Soviet involvement would inevitably be followed by Soviet efforts at disruption and subversion, the operating premise being that, whatever the Russians might be up to, they were surely not up to any good.

Only infrequently have influential voices been raised to suggest that cooperation with the Soviets, whatever its risks, might also yield dividends for the broader purpose of maintaining world order. Secretary of State Kissinger suggested as much when he called attention, on October 25, 1973, to the superpowers' "special duty" to keep their confrontations "within bounds that do not threaten civilized life," although he himself proceeded to exclude the Russians as much as possible from the "step-by-step" diplomacy that followed the 1973 war. During that same period, in the aftermath of the 1973 war, Senator Fulbright, Chairman of the Senate Foreign Relations Committee, suggested that the crisis of the night of October 24–25 had pointed up the necessity rather than the futility of Soviet-American détente:

> The fact that détente is fragile does not mean that it is futile. Quite the contrary: every time the two great nuclear powers come to a point of confrontation, the necessity of détente is reinforced. What the detractors cannot seem to get through their heads is that there is no alternative except endless conflict. We and the Russians have to get along with each other, because, in matters of world peace, neither can get along without the other.[91]

PUBLIC ENEMY NUMBER TWO

Long-standing mistrust of Soviet motives has convinced American policy makers of the *necessity* of excluding the Russians from the Middle East so far as possible. A corollary belief that key Arab countries shared this mistrust to the extent of fearing Russia more even than Israel, despite lip service to the contrary, seems to have convinced some American policy makers that excluding the Soviets—and uniting the major nations of the Middle East against them—was *feasible* as well as desirable. This outlook is expressed in an amorphous but identifiable school of thought holding that there exists an implicit, unacknowledged alliance among Israel, Egypt, Saudi Arabia, and the Gulf emirates, and, before the fall of the shah, Iran, against Soviet-sponsored radicalism. It is further believed that this "alliance," to which Israel is said to contribute by fostering an environment in which moderate regimes can survive and radical ones are contained, can be strengthened by an American policy of unstinting support of Israel. Senator Henry Jackson of Washington, after a trip to the Middle East in 1972, reported that he found Israel, Iran, and Saudi Arabia united, paradoxically, by common interests. "While neither Israelis nor Saudis are in a position to acknowledge the degree to which they have interests in common," the senator said, "the many issues on which they have a shared perspective—despite those on which they differ—have about them a compelling logic that would lead an outside observer to that very conclusion."[92]

The Jackson premise in large part underlay the Camp David agreements. Israelis and their supporters in the United States, eager to find a way for Israel to break out of the ring of Arab-imposed isolation, had long been intrigued by the notion of a subterranean alliance of Israel and the moderate Arab states against the radical Arabs and their Soviet sponsors. Egypt in turn, having broken with the Soviet Union after the 1973 war and then, in 1977, embarking on the road to its separate peace with Israel, lent strong additional support and persuasiveness to the idea of the feasibility of a de facto alignment of Israel and the moderate Arabs against Soviet-sponsored radicalism. "In a metaphorical sense," reporter Jim Hoagland wrote at the time, "the Russian Menace occupied the fourth chair at Camp David."[93] The framers of the Camp David agreement proceeded, therefore, with considerable confidence, on two basic assumptions: that no one except the Palestine Liberation Organization—and perhaps Libya and Iraq and one or two other less influential Arab countries—really wanted a Palestinian state, and that, except for these, protestations to the contrary notwithstanding, the Arab states in general had far less real fear of Israel than of the Soviet Union and its radical clients. On the basis of these assumptions, the Camp David partners expected Saudi Arabia and Jordan, if not actively to join the painstakingly constructed peace process, then at least to take no stand against it and allow it to proceed with their tacit consent. It was a considerable shock and disappointment to all three of the Camp David partners, especially the United States, when Saudi Arabia and Jordan not only denounced the Camp David accords but actively associated themselves with the "rejectionist" alignment at the meetings in Baghdad in November 1978 and, after the signing of the Egyptian-Israeli treaty, in March 1979.

Even after the Egyptian-Israeli treaty, hope if not confidence survived that Jordan and Saudi Arabia might still lend their support to the Camp David autonomy plan for the West Bank and Gaza. Strains between Syria and Iraq, recently and temporarily reconciled, along with indications that the Baghdad-imposed sanctions against Egypt were having less damaging effect than had been anticipated, gave new life to hope within the Carter administration that the Arab world could be further fragmented and new support won for the Camp David autonomy plan. President Carter, in an interview in Tampa, Florida, on August 30, 1979, declared that he had "never met an Arab leader that in private professed the desire for an independent Palestinian state." As for the Saudis, the president said that they attached great importance to the United States as a "stabilizing factor." "They have an abhorrence of the Soviet Union," Carter said, "because it's atheistic and because it's communist and because they encourage sometimes radicalism and turmoil and violence, and they know that we are a religious nation and they know we are a democratic nation. . . ."[94] The Saudis responded to the president's statement with a strong reaffirmation of their support for a Palestinian state.[95]

Confronted with the difficult, unwelcome choice between Israel and the Soviet Union as their premier enemy, the Saudis, without too great hesitation, chose Israel. As against the perceived threat of encirclement by Soviet-supported radical regimes in South Yemen and Ethiopia on the one hand and the clear and present danger, as the Saudis perceived it, of alienating Iraq and Syria, incurring the wrath of the PLO, further fragmenting the Arab *umma*, and breaking Islamic legitimacy in the wake of the Iranian revolution, the Saudis reluctantly made the choice, against Camp David and the United States, that they had fervently hoped to avoid. The Soviets, recognizing opportunity, tentatively suggested in January 1979 that the time might be ripe for Soviet-Saudi rapprochement. An officially sanctioned article in the Soviet weekly, *Literary Gazette*, noted that the Soviet Union and Saudi Arabia had never come into conflict despite different social systems, and the author commented, "I think that the strongly exaggerated ideas of the anti-Sovietism of Saudi Arabia are deliberately created by Western European and American journalists." The article recalled that the late King Faisal, as Crown Prince, had visited the Soviet Union in 1932 and quoted him as having said at that time that the two nations were tied together "by the strongest links of friendship." The *Literary Gazette* article of January 1979 contrasted notably with an earlier reference to Saudi Arabia, in *Izvestia* in April 1978, as "Israel's fellow traveler . . . in carrying out U.S. aims."[96]

The Saudis responded, in their style, to the Soviet flirtation. In an interview published on March 3, 1979 in the Beirut magazine *Al Hawadess*, the Saudi foreign minister, Prince Saud al-Faisal, acknowledged the Soviet Union's "important role in world politics" and also said: "We wish to emphasize that the absence of diplomatic ties does not mean we don't recognize the Soviet Union. On the contrary we have often expressed our gratitude for the positive policy adopted by the Soviet Union toward Arab issues." Disavowing any Saudi interest in aligning itself with either of the superpowers to deal with the affairs of the Persian Gulf, Prince Saud said that the real threat to the region and its stability was not the upheaval in Iran but "the Zionist danger." "The way to reestablish calm and stability in the area," he added, "is by having Israel withdraw from the occupied Arab territories, return Jerusalem and recognize the Palestinian people's right to self-determination."[97]

There is some evidence that the senior princes and officials of Saudi

Arabia—at least since the death of King Faisal in 1975—have been more receptive than they have seen fit to indicate publicly to the possibility of some form of Soviet involvement in the peace process. An American who has spent many years in Saudi Arabia and has intimate ties with members of the royal family wrote in 1980:

> I can clearly recall in early 1976, many months before the Soviet-American joint statement of October 1st, 1977, discussing with Crown Prince Fahd the practical advantages that would derive both to the Arabs and to the U.S. if we were able to achieve some level of effective cooperation between the USSR and the U.S. in reassuring Israel of its security vis-à-vis a Palestinian state. Surprisingly, Fahd warmed to the subject and added some quite original and creative thoughts of his own, which he then asked me to forward to President Ford. I did, but was flatly rebuffed. . . . [The rebuff came from intermediaries] on the grounds that Kissinger would not appreciate any such suggestion. . . .[98]

The Saudi overture to the Russians in early 1979 was, most probably, in some degree disingenuous, more an expression of displeasure with the United States than a genuine bid for rapprochement with the Soviet Union. The amenities exchanged in early 1979 were not followed by further tangible steps toward the establishment of formal relations between the Soviet Union and Saudi Arabia. The Saudis, despite Prince Saud's bold disclaimer, remained anxious and alert to the possible fallout effects of the Iranian revolution; as noted in chapter 3, this concern was undoubtedly a factor in the Saudi decision, in the wake of Camp David and Egypt's separate peace with Israel, to align themselves solidly with the cause of Arab unity and Islamic legitimacy. Nor, despite suggestions to the contrary, is it plausible that the Saudis had suddenly thrown off their longstanding, deep-seated fear of Soviet Communism and atheism or of Soviet penetration of the Arab world. Their apparent, indeed obvious intent in raising the possibility of détente with the Soviet Union was to disabuse American policy makers of their solid conviction that the Saudis feared the Russians more than anyone and that this fear made them pliable for other purposes, notably for supporting or acquiescing in American policy with respect to the Arab-Israeli conflict. The Saudis, to be sure, had themselves instilled and encouraged this conviction on the part of American policy makers: an American embassy official in Jidda in November 1978 quoted Prince Fahd as having said, "If the Soviet Union goes to heaven, we don't want to go."[99] Having encouraged the Americans in this belief, the Saudi leaders—or at least some of the younger, American-educated ones—had come to find it inconvenient, robbing them of leverage and allowing the Americans to take them for granted. They thereupon undertook, to the well-founded astonishment of American officials, to downgrade the Soviet Union, at least slightly, in their gallery of demons while confirming Israel in its position of unchallenged primacy among the kingdom's enemies.

In the early months of 1979 the Carter administration undertook to assuage Saudi objections to Camp David by providing highly visible support against the perceived threat of Soviet encirclement through the penetration of South Yemen, Afghanistan and the horn of Africa. In January the Carter administration, having first dispatched, but then held back, a carrier task force from the Persian Gulf for fear of exacerbating the convulsion in Iran, sent a dozen unarmed F–15 fighter planes and three hundred Air Force personnel on a brief "show-the-flag" mission to Saudi Arabia. In March the United States provided $500 million in emergency supplies to Saudi-supported Yemen to bolster it against attack by Marxist South Yemen—an action with which the Saudis, according to a senior official, were only "mildly impressed." On February 10, 1979, according to press reports, Secretary of Defense Harold Brown, visiting Riyadh, offered extensive new Saudi-American security arrangements, including the establishment of American bases on Saudi territory. In return, it was reported, the United States hoped to elicit from the Saudis a commitment to increased oil production, increased Saudi investments to support the U.S. dollar, and a more favorable attitude toward the Camp David "peace process." Startled by the sweeping nature of the American proposal, unwilling to become involved as a client in an overt great power alliance, mindful of the failure of American-supplied weapons to save the Shah of Iran, and distinctly unattracted to an arrangement suggesting even indirect association with Israel, the Saudis, according to press accounts, politely but firmly turned aside Secretary Brown's proposal. "We want to cooperate in the economic field, but don't push us in the political field. We can't go down that road with you," a Saudi petroleum official told an American reporter.[100] President Carter denied that the United States had proposed to establish bases or assign American troops to Saudi Arabia.[101] Prince Saud, however, referred to Brown's reported proposals in his Beirut interview of March 3, 1979: "The Americans feel that the Soviet Union is trying to take advantage of the changing conditions in the region. They believe the Soviets are trying to enhance conflicts and encourage violence. They regard this as dangerous because it tends to disturb the international balance. We explained . . . that we have nothing to do with international strategies."[102]

Disdaining the crafted euphemisms favored by the Saudis, King Hussein of Jordan rejected with undisguised asperity American efforts to entice Jordan into an alignment of Israel and Arab moderates against Soviet-sponsored radicalism through support of the Camp David agreements. Following National Security Adviser Brzezinski's visit to Amman prior to the signing of the Egyptian-Israeli treaty in March 1979, the king pointedly told American reporters that Jordanian-American relations had deteriorated so far that "we will have to look around" for alternative sources of military supply. The dominant threat perceived by Arabs, the king said, was not communism but the Israeli occupation of Arab lands and, as he described it, Israel's militaristic mentality. There was a basic difference between Jordan and the United States in this respect, King Hussein said: Brzezinski had pressed on him the American contention that the real threat to Jordanian and American interests in the Middle East was "radicals and communists," and the king, reminding the reporters that on a clear day they could see Jerusalem from the terrace of his palace, recalled that he had replied to Brzezinski, "We asked which threats are we facing? Zionism or communism? Where does Israel fit into this threat?"[103]

Caught between conflicting interests in Israel and the Arab world, American political leaders have periodically sought to reconcile their dilemma by drawing Arabs and Israelis into common cause against Soviet-sponsored radicalism in the Middle East. Based more on hope than on factual evidence of its validity, the thesis of the "secret alliance" has always found greater receptiveness among elected officeholders in the United States, subject as they are to domestic political pressures, than among foreign policy professionals and Middle East specialists in and out of government. The latter have recognized the deepseated mistrust of most Arabs for the Soviet Union, its ideology and its aims, and they have also recognized—and on occasion made good use of—the strong Arab cultural attraction to America and Americans. The Russians, as American professionals have recognized, have to work harder and sometimes spend more to try to match American influence in the Middle East because, as a Jordanian official put it, "they're not as pretty as the Americans."[104] At the same time, the professionals—or "State Department Arabists" as they are known to their detractors—have remained unconvinced, the Egyptian-Israeli treaty notwithstanding, that the major remaining Arab parties to the conflict with Israel—Saudi Arabia, Jordan, Syria, and surely the Palestinians—could be dislodged from their position by promises of American support, still less by suggestions of de facto alliance with Israel, against the Soviet communist menace. This is not to say that the conservative Arab states have come either to like or trust the Russians, but rather, quite simply, that, however much they fear and mistrust the Soviet Union, they fear and mistrust Israel more. The thesis of the "secret alliance" would seem to be the product not of hard-headed geopolitical analysis as its proponents claim, but rather of wishful thinking, super-power rivalry and a natural tendency to project one's own predilections onto others, of sympathy for Israel and the strong desire to help Israel extricate itself further from isolation, and of the equally strong desire of American officeholders to extricate themselves from the conflicting pressures of national interest on the one hand and domestic political concerns on the other.

"STRATEGIC CONSENSUS"

Despite all lack of encouragement from the Arab parties, the idea of the "secret alliance" gained new life with the collapse of Soviet-American détente in the late seventies and even more with the accession in 1981 of the Reagan administration. The fall of the shah in January 1979, the ensuing revolutionary chaos in Iran, the seizure of American hostages by the Iranian revolutionaries in November 1979, and the Soviet invasion of Afghanistan in December 1979, taken together, significantly altered the American strategic position in the Persian Gulf. Whether and to what degree these events also posed a clear Soviet threat to the industrial world's access to Persian Gulf oil was and remains in doubt. The Carter administration, however, perceived the threat as great and perhaps imminent. In his State of the Union address on January 23, 1980, President Carter said that the Soviet invasion of Afghanistan "could pose the most serious threat to the peace since the Second World War," and that the Soviet Union was "now attempting to consolidate a strategic position . . . that poses a grave threat to the free movement of Middle East oil." He thereupon announced the policy that came to be known as the Carter Doctrine: "An attempt by any outside force to gain control of the Persian Gulf region will be regarded as an assault on the vital interests of the United States of America. And such an assault will be repelled by any means necessary, including military force."[105]

The Soviets, for their part, denied any ambition to threaten the non-communist world's oil "lifeline" to the Persian Gulf. President Brezhnev, in an address to the Indian parliament on December 10, 1980, stated that "the U.S.S.R. has no intention of encroaching upon either the Middle East oil or its transportation route," and he went on to propose some specifications of a multilateral agreement for the demilitarization and neutralization of the Persian Gulf region.[106] Brezhnev reiterated this proposal on February 23, 1981, offering to extend the agreement to apply to the international but not the internal status of Afghanistan; Brezhnev also called for negotiations to bring peace to the Middle East and for an "active dialogue" with the United States, including a summit meeting between himself and President Reagan.[107]

The newly installed Reagan administration showed little interest in Brezhnev's proposal. Instead, as Secretary of State Haig explained to the House Foreign Affairs Committee on March 18, the new administration undertook, while relegating the Palestinian question and other local issues to a lower order or priority "to begin to develop a consensus of strategic concerns throughout the region among Arab and Jew and to be sure that the overriding danger of Soviet inroads into this area are not overlooked." The "strategic consensus," as envisioned by Haig, would include Pakistan and Turkey as well as Egypt, Israel, and the Arab Gulf states.[108]

As enunciated and developed in its early months, the Reagan administration's policy represented an expansion of the Carter Doctrine based on a clear, strongly held conception of Soviet motives and aims—the conception spelled out in "NSC–68," referred to above.[109] President Reagan elaborated on it on January 29, 1981, in his first news conference after taking office. From the time of the Russian Revolution until the present, Reagan said, Soviet leaders had reiterated "their determination that their goal must be the promotion of world revolution and a one world Socialist or Communist state. . . ." They have "openly and publicly declared," Reagan continued, "that the only morality they recognize is what will further their cause: meaning they reserve unto themselves the right to commit any crime; to lie; to cheat, in order to obtain that. . . ." When you do business with them, the president added, "you keep that in mind."[110]

Reasoning deductively from this broad conception, the Reagan administration tended to dismiss Soviet disclaimers of aggressive intent and calls for an international conference on the Persian Gulf as dishonest and self-serving. Brezhnev reiterated in May 1981 his call for an international conference on the Middle East including the Persian Gulf and Afghanistan but the proposal elicited no response. Meanwhile the Reagan administration began to develop plans to enable the armed forces, in the event of a Soviet attack in the Persian Gulf, to strike back at Soviet forces not only in the Persian Gulf but in other areas as well, especially those, such as Cuba, in which their forces would be vulnerable. Secretary of Defense Caspar W. Weinberger advised the Senate Armed Services Committee that American deterrent capability in the Persian Gulf "is linked with our ability and willingness to shift or widen the war to other areas."[111] In September 1981 the United States and Israel, on the occasion of Prime Minister Begin's visit to the United States for his first meeting with President Reagan, announced plans for a new "strategic relationship" to encompass such collaborative measures as a joint air defense system, joint naval exercises in the Mediterranean, and the storage of medical supplies in Israel for possible use by American forces assigned to the Middle East in an emergency. Although American officials emphasized that the measures contemplated were directed not at Arab countries but at the Soviet Union, speculation was widespread that the primary target was Congress, which was about to consider the proposed sale to Saudi Arabia of four AWACS radar surveillance planes, and which, it was thought, would be less likely to disapprove the sale if it were assured that cooperation with Israel was proceeding in other areas.[112]

Whatever reassuring effect the new "strategic relationship" had on Israel and on Congress, it had an unsettling effect on the Arabs. Saudi Arabia quickly and indignantly contested a State Department announcement that Crown Prince Fahd, in a briefing in Madrid by Secretary Haig on the new arrangement with Israel, had offered "no expressions of disapproval." On the contrary, the official Saudi statement said, the new American arrangement with Israel would "impede peace" and plunge the region into a "terrible arms race." Syria announced that it would seek an enhanced strategic relationship with the Soviet Union.[113]

The Reagan administration, no less than its predecessor, encountered repeated rebuffs in its efforts to bring Arab countries to set aside or subordinate the Palestinian question and join in an American-sponsored "strategic consensus" against the Soviet Union. Inclined though they sometimes are to euphemism, evasion, and the polite if sometimes misleading response, Arab leaders were candid in their early response to the Reagan-Haig appeal. A delegation of senators led by Senator Howard Baker, the majority leader, visiting Saudi Arabia in April 1981, were forthrightly reminded that, although the Saudis recognized a Soviet threat to the security of the region, they regarded the Palestinian problem as primary, and further, regarded the lack of progress in resolving the Palestinian question as the primary reason the Soviet Union was able to gain influence in the region.[114] King Hussein of Jordan, once a staunch ally of the United States but increasingly alienated since Camp David, visited Moscow in May 1981 where he endorsed President Brezhnev's proposal for an international conference on the Middle East including the Palestine Liberation Organization.[115] "We are poles apart," King Hussein told an American interviewer in the summer of 1981.[116]

In the Middle East, no less than in other areas of superpower relations, the United States continues to deal with the Soviet Union largely on the basis of general conceptions of Soviet aims and motives drawn from the experience of the early years of the Cold War. A more pragmatic approach might allow of greater attention to the indigenous regional issue, including the strongly held concerns of the regional parties. It would also take dispassionate account of Soviet political and economic interests in the Middle East, at least testing the proposition that these are finite rather than apocalyptic. In the case of the Arab-Israeli conflict itself, conceding the Soviets a role of "equality" with the United States—if that were all they wanted—would seem an acceptable price to pay for progress toward a stable and equitable settlement.

In the case of the Persian Gulf, Soviet energy requirements would warrant consideration. Estimates drawn by the Central Intelligence Agency in the 1970s suggested that by the mid-eighties the Soviet Union would require sizable oil imports. It was in part on the basis of these estimates that the Carter Doctrine was framed and plans laid for a Rapid Deployment Force, to protect the oil producing region from Soviet incursions. In early 1981 Secretary of Defense Weinberger cited prospective Soviet oil needs as indicating an intention to deny access to oil by the West and therefore as a reason for increasing the American military presence in the Persian Gulf area.[117] More recent assessments, by the CIA and others, suggest that the Soviet Union will remain self-sufficient in oil at least through the decade of the eighties and probably for the remainder of the century. An Exxon Corporation report of late 1980 concluded that Soviet oil production "will be relatively stable, in the 11 to 12 million barrels per day range through 2000."[118]

These estimates suggest that, from the standpoint of economic self-interest, the Soviet Union has no pressing need to compete with the noncommunist industrial world for Persian Gulf oil. They also provide a basis—unless it is assumed that Marxist ideology alone guides Soviet policy—for allowing the possibility that the Soviet leaders, recognizing the extraordinary risk in threatening so vital a Western interest, are truthful in denying the intention of cutting off oil. From this perspective, a number of observers have suggested the usefulness of exploring President Brezhnev's proposal of an international agreement for the neutralization of the Persian Gulf region. Writing in *Foreign Affairs* in the summer of 1981, Christopher Van Hollen, a former deputy assistant secretary of state for Near Eastern and South Asian affairs, suggested the possibility of a combination of bilateral and multilateral agreements to include "guarantees of free passage, equal access to Persian Gulf oil for all nations, and possibly international endorsement of regional nonalignment."[119]

In similar vein, Senator George McGovern, writing in *The Atlantic* in June 1980, took note of the historically demonstrated usefulness of neutralization as a means of both protecting small countries and averting conflict between big countries. McGovern suggested the possibility of a general neutralization agreement to include the entire Persian Gulf region and also Afghanistan:

> Under such a general agreement the regional and nonregional powers, including the superpowers and the principal consumers of Persian Gulf oil, might pledge to respect the sovereignty and neutrality of the countries of the region and the inviolability of the sea-lanes through which the oil flows, with the single reservation, cautiously stated but clearly understood, that a clear and present danger to the oil supply would necessitate measures for its protection if requested by a producing country. Itself a prospective consumer of Persian Gulf oil, the Soviet Union could be expected to appreciate this necessity on the part of the United States and its allies.[120]

The potential usefulness of the approaches suggested by McGovern and Van Hollen would depend upon such factors as the amenability of the prospective parties, the specificity of the provisions and pledges to be drawn up, and the means and likelihood of their enforcement. How these in turn are assessed would depend in no small measure on the "school of thought" to which officials making the assessment subscribed—that represented by "NSC–68" and the Reagan news conference of January 29, 1981, or the "détente" school as defined by George Kennan.

A SOVIET-AMERICAN GUARANTEE

As noted earlier, American policy has been less than constant but also, over the years, less than adamant in its resolve to exclude the Soviet Union from the diplomacy of the Middle East. Just as the Russians, for whatever reasons of their own, have periodically shown an interest in some kind of superpower condominium in the affairs of the Middle East, the United States in turn has recognized that, however successful American diplomacy might be in excluding the Soviets from one arena or another of activity, there was an irreducible minimum beyond which Soviet influence could not be eliminated, and that even at its lowest ebb Soviet influence would remain sufficient to foment troubles if the Russians so chose and to obstruct the resolution of central problems, notably the Palestinian problem. There could, in short, be no general settlement without Soviet participation and consent. This proposition was recognized by Dr. Kissinger even in the halcyon days of his "step-by-step" diplomacy. Asked if a "real settlement" in the Middle East were possible without Soviet cooperation, Kissinger told the Senate Foreign Relations Committee on September 19, 1974: "It is correct that progress in the Middle East will be very difficult, if not impossible, except in the context of at least Soviet acquiescence." Further, Kissinger thought such acquiescence by no means beyond attainment. The Russians, he said, had given no active support to, but neither had they tried to block, his unilateral American efforts to achieve disengagement agreements between Israel on the one side and Syria and Egypt on the other in the months after the 1973 war: "Throughout these negotiations we kept in touch with them and we did not find it difficult to stay in touch."[121]

Beyond acquiescence, grudgingly and suspiciously sought as a matter of necessity, there remains the untested possibility of active Soviet-American collaboration for the achievement and enforcement of a general Middle East settlement. J. W. Fulbright, the former chairman of the Senate Foreign Relations Committee, has suggested the feasibility of a positive, self-reinforcing kind of "linkage" among the various issues, regional and global, in which the superpowers are mutually involved. He wrote in 1978:

> As currently practiced, linkage involves retaliation, or the threat of it, in one area for the failure of agreement in another. Its effect is to exacerbate disagreement—threatening SALT, for example, because we do not like what the Russians are doing in Africa. Were we instead to pursue a SALT agreement independently of other issues, and without excruciating bargaining over every last technical detail, we might then find ourselves in an improved position—on a new psychological plateau, so to speak—for enlisting Soviet cooperation for a settlement in the Middle East. And were we to do that, instead of trying to exclude the Russians from the Middle East, we might, conceivably, find them easier to deal with in regard to Ethiopia or Rhodesia.[122]

Secretary of State Kissinger put forth the same proposition in his testimony on détente in 1974: "Our approach proceeds from the conviction that in moving forward across a wide spectrum of negotiations, progress in one area adds momentum to progress in other areas."[123]

Linkage, so conceived, would take cognizance for constructive purposes of the common attribute of the United States and the Soviet Union that neither shares with any other country on earth: they alone are *global* powers, with power and interests extending to all regions of the world.

They alone, therefore—however qualified their leadership, however pertinent their national experiences—have the power and responsibility to maintain a measure of order in a turbulent world. They alone are in a position to deal with regional issues in a global context. "They alone," wrote Fulbright, "have the power, through collaboration, to put limits on the world's turbulence, to prevent great conflicts and contain small ones, to curb the excesses of nationalism and ambition, including their own, and by so doing to make the world as safe as it can be made in the thermonuclear age."[124]

Smaller countries tend to dislike and fear the idea of superpower condominium. With perceived interests confined to their own neighborhoods, and lacking the power in any event to influence events beyond their regions, they may regard the problems of other regions or the bilateral dealings of the superpowers as anything from an extraneous nuisance to a grave national danger. Israel, for example, accused the United States in the summer of 1979 of making a deal with the Soviet Union on supervising the implementation of the Egyptian-Israeli peace treaty in the Sinai for the unrelated purpose of avoiding a quarrel that might jeopardize the SALT treaty then being debated in the Senate. From the American standpoint the linkage of Sinai with SALT may be considered a rational and responsible course of action. From the Israeli standpoint SALT was extraneous and the United States was acting in bad faith by allowing it to intrude on the regional issue. Dislike of Soviet-American collaboration is by no means confined to Israel. Egypt under President Sadat has been hardly less outspoken than Israel in its fear and dislike of this collaboration. The attitude indeed is endemic to many less powerful nations, especially those engaged in local or regional quarrels. Having the superpowers set against each other not only allows the smaller countries greater freedom of action, it can afford them powerful leverage by allowing them to play the great powers against each other, to the extent, at times, of all but reversing the patron-client relationship. There can be no doubt that small states derive advantage from great power disunity. Whether it also serves their more basic long-term interests is very much to be doubted, to say nothing of the interests of the great powers themselves, or of the peace and stability of the world as a whole.[125]

Intermittently, through the years of Soviet-American rivalry, proposals have been advanced for active superpower collaboration, first to bring about a settlement in the Middle East and then to guarantee it. Without exception such proposals, including that contained in the joint statement of October 1, 1977, have been shot down by Israeli leaders and supporters of Israel in the United States, who have perceived in them the bugbear of an "imposed" settlement. The United States, in fact, has repeatedly disavowed the intention or desire to impose a settlement in the Middle East, confining occasional, cautious suggestions of a possible willingness to guarantee a general settlement with assurances that this would apply only to a settlement negotiated and agreed to by the Middle Eastern parties themselves. In suggesting the possibility of guarantees in which they might participate, the Soviet Union and the United States specified in the joint statement of October 1977 that such guarantees might be established only "should the contracting parties so desire."[126]

As the great power with paramount influence in the Middle East, the United States could, of course, offer itself as the sole guarantor of a general settlement, excluding the Soviet Union. To take this course would encourage the Soviet Union to play the spoiler, waiting in the wings for opportunities—which would not fail to arise in so volatile a region—to destabilize the settlement by encouraging social unrest, communal strife, and, occasionally, seizures of power. It seems unlikely, in any event, that the American people and Congress would support so far-reaching and unpredictable an undertaking, involving obligations that would be increased in scope and risk by the very fact of the exclusion of the Soviet Union. To include the Soviet Union, on the other hand, in guarantees of Israel and an independent or autonomous West Bank-Gaza unit, would represent an act of "positive linkage," giving the Soviets a political and psychological stake in the settlement, conceding their aspiration to a role of equality with the United States as the price of locking them into a responsible and constructive role. Indeed, given their three decades' record of caution in avoiding direct military encounters in the Middle East, the Soviet leaders, Israeli fears notwithstanding, could hardly be eager to acquire a unilateral military responsibility for so vulnerable a territory as the Palestinian West Bank, where the balance of military power would be overwhelmingly in favor of Israel.[127] But even if ill-advised adventurism were to tempt the Soviets otherwise, the *joint* involvement of the Soviet Union with the United States (and perhaps other major countries as well, such as Britain and France) would help keep both the Russians *and* the Palestinians out of trouble. "It would not be wise," John Campbell wrote in 1978, "to exaggerate Soviet ability to control or dictate to the PLO or to make a puppet out of a West Bank state in Palestine. Arafat's fate and that of his organization will be determined in the whirlpools of Palestinian and Arab politics rather than in Moscow."[128]

In geopolitical terms, accepting the Soviets as coguarantors would represent a kind of sacrifice for the United States—the waiving of its paramount great power role. Paramountcy, however, is not dominance, and the contention that the United States does not need Soviet cooperation to achieve peace and that it is therefore gratuitous to "invite" the Russians back into the Middle East, has been shown by events since Camp David and the Egyptian-Israeli peace treaty to be erroneous. Events seem clearly to have borne out the projection made in 1975 by the Brookings Middle East Study Group, composed of individuals of wide-ranging viewpoints and personal sympathies. "Since there is no question but that the USSR has a considerable capacity for obstructing a general settlement," the study group concluded, "and any settlement which it opposed would be likely to prove unstable, its involvement in the negotiating process and in the arrangements and guarantees following a successful negotiation would seem on balance to be an advantage rather than a disadvantage. . . ."[129] In the more pungent observation of Nahum Goldmann, "Every attempt to prevent the USSR from playing a role in the Middle East settlement— something that the United States has sometimes tried to do and sometimes still tries to do—is useless, and can only impede or prevent real solution."[130]

The logic of Soviet-American partnership for a general settlement in the Middle East and for the enforcement of that settlement is the logic of détente itself. As long as the Middle East conflict remains unresolved—or only partly resolved—there will remain the danger of superpower confrontation. That danger can be eliminated in only one of two ways. One would be the virtual abandonment by the great powers of their respective clients, who would then be left, without further support from outside, to work out or fight out their differences as they would. That course, however, for reasons of policy and principle, has been ruled out, because the United States under no conceivable circumstances would leave Israel to an uncertain fate. The alternative is collaboration by the great powers to make and enforce an equitable general settlement.

In an increasingly pluralistic world, the superpowers have a commensurately increased responsibility to maintain a measure of global order, to exert restraints on quarrelling clients even as they accept restraints on themselves. With the increase in the number of highly nationalistic independent states, and the proliferation among them of modern weapons, power has indeed become diffused in the world, and small states play an unprecedentedly large role in world affairs. The power they wield, however, being limited and local, is fundamentally disruptive from the standpoint of world order. They have neither the capacity, nor, it would seem in most cases, the will to fuse that power for collective action, through international institutions, to maintain and enforce peace and a measure of law in international affairs. That power, and the responsibility to exercise it, belongs, in the absence of effective international institutions, primarily to the superpowers. This fundamental fact, coupled with the essential similarity of official Soviet and American peace proposals for the Middle East, militates strongly in favor of Soviet-American partnership to resolve the world's most persistent and dangerous conflict.

CHAPTER SEVEN

Conclusion:
On Peace and How to Get It

In the history of the American republic it is unlikely that any issue of foreign relations has confounded and frustrated the nation's policy makers more completely, repeatedly, and over a longer period of time than the problems of the Middle East in the years since World War II. Since the United Nations resolved in 1947 to partition Palestine, the United States has tried and failed repeatedly to mediate lasting solutions, prevent the recurrence of crisis, stem the tide of chronic instability, and secure its own vital interests in the region that, from the standpoint of American national interest, has become the most important in the world. The United States has been unable to devise or arrange workable solutions in the Middle East not because the issues there have been complex beyond all others—those arising from each of the two world wars were at least as complex and far more comprehensive. Nor has the Middle East been the most internally disruptive foreign issue in recent American experience—Vietnam was more demanding morally and emotionally. These and other issues were nevertheless resolved or at least disposed of, whereas the Middle East, notwithstanding the enormous exertions and considerable achievements of the Carter administration, remains an arena of crisis and potential disaster—for the United States, for the peoples of the region, and for much of the rest of the world.

The root cause of the failure of American policy in the Middle East has been the inability of a succession of administrations, primarily because of domestic political factors, to reconcile and synthesize the nation's four fundamental interests in the Middle East—access to oil, the security of Israel, détente with the Soviet Union, and adherence to such principles as the peaceful settlement of disputes and the right of peoples to self-determination. Except for cooperation with the Soviets (which, as an aspect of the larger global question of détente, is genuinely controversial), none of these objectives is seriously contested as a soundly based American interest. What is contested—and that most vigorously—is the relative value of one interest as against another and the extent to which the less valued should be jeopardized for the sake of the more valued. The issue is essentially domestic—what it comes down to, in concrete terms, is that, owing to the unmatched influence of the Israel lobby in American politics, Israeli security (or, more exactly, the conceptions of Israeli security held by incumbent Israeli governments) has been permitted to *preempt* other vital interests in American policy. This, rather than the undoubted complexity of the issues, or the strategic, economic, or moral stakes of one case as opposed to another, has been the root cause of a chronically unbalanced policy that, despite certain tactical successes, remains a strategic failure.

WHAT NEEDS TO BE DONE

Obscured from view behind the charges and countercharges exchanged between Israel and its antagonists, between Israeli and American governments, and between supporters and critics of Israeli policy in the United States, has been the emergence of a *consensus* among moderates in the Arab world, the United States, and Europe—with some minority support in Israel as well—on the approximate terms of a viable and equitable comprehensive settlement in the Middle East. The essentials of the consensus of moderates are well known, approximating in most respects the *official* policy of the United States at least since the adoption of Security Council Resolution 242 in 1967 and the enunciation of the Rogers Plan in December 1969. The key elements are: Israeli withdrawal to the borders of 1967, with minor variations in Israel's favor; Palestinian self-determination within the West Bank and Gaza, conditional upon explicit, official Palestinian recognition of the permanence and legitimacy of Israel; some form of Arab sovereignty over the Muslim holy places in Jerusalem, with unimpeded access thereto; the establishment of demilitarized zones around all of Israel's borders, to be patrolled by United Nations forces that could not be removed except with the consent of both sides; an end to all hostile actions against Israel and the initiation by stages of normal political, economic, and cultural relations between Israel and the Arab states; and guarantees of the entire settlement by the United Nations, including the superpowers, supplemented, if desired, by an explicit American guarantee of Israel.

Outside of Israel, the United States, a few "rejectionist" Arab states, and certain groups within the PLO, support for a settlement along these lines approaches worldwide unanimity. Within Israel a small but articulate group of "doves" strongly supports a peace based on the terms described, and in the United States such a peace commands the open support of most Middle East specialists out of government and, by available indications, the discreet support of many within government. The consensus has been expressed in many forums, statements, and documents. The best known of these statements was the "Brookings Report" of 1975, drawn up and signed by a group representing a diversity of viewpoints and personal sympathies.[1] The basic terms of the consensus were spelled out and commended by Middle East specialists representing both academic and diplomatic experience of the region in extensive hearings before the Senate Foreign Relations Committee's Subcommittee on Near Eastern and South Asian Affairs in 1975 and 1976.[2] A settlement along the lines described has been endorsed by the American Friends Service Committee as long ago as 1970,[3] by major church groups in the United States,[4] and by leading participants in Middle East professional organizations.[5] It also represents, in key provisions, the official position of the nine members of the European Community, who, on the occasion of the signing of the Egyptian–Israeli peace treaty, issued a statement declaring that "the establishment of a just and lasting peace in the Middle East can only take place within the framework of a comprehensive settlement" and that such a settlement "must translate into fact the right of the Palestinian people to a homeland."[6]

Not to be overlooked either is the essential similarity of the moderate consensus to *official* American positions, except with respect to Palestinian self-determination. From the Rogers Plan of 1969 to the Soviet-American statement of October 1, 1977, successive American administrations have endorsed, in principle, a settlement based on Israeli withdrawal from much or most of the occupied territories, recompense in the form of a "*homeland*" of one shape or another to the Palestinians, mutual recognition by the parties, and international guarantees. President Carter, early in his term, endorsed in a qualified way the Rogers Plan formula; the president called for Israeli withdrawal to the 1967 borders with some "minor adjustments."[7]

On the matter of self-determination, the United States remains, as it has since President Wilson's time, ambivalent. The Aswan formula, which would permit the Palestinian people to "participate in the determination of their own future," is, in the present view, inadequate for purposes of both *equity* and *stability* in a general settlement. As an international norm the principle of self-determination means, simply, that a land belongs to the people who inhabit it and not to someone else, however ingenious the claimant's legal arguments, however great his real or perceived need of the land, however sincere his feeling of historical or religious attachment, and however greatly he has suffered and is therefore deserving of recompense. Applied to the West Bank and Gaza, self-determination implies the unencumbered right of the local population, who are mostly Arab, to decide the area's future. Attempting to split this unsplittable difference, the Aswan formula succeeds only in committing the United States to two irreconcilable positions and, in so doing, represents a damaging flaw in American policy. Because of the ambivalent, self-negating American position as embodied in the Aswan formula, it has proven impossible to draw the Palestinians into the Camp David peace process. When Secretary of State Vance, at the outset of the autonomy talks in Beersheba in May 1979, tried to entice Palestinians into the negotiations with the assurance that, "in the United States, we believe deeply in the proposition that governments derive their just powers from the consent of the governed,"[8] his statement was rendered less than convincing by President Carter's reaffirmation, four days later, that "we've never espoused an independent Palestinian state. I think that would be a destabilizing factor there."[9] The contradiction is the same one that Arthur Balfour perceived, in 1919, between President Wilson's advocacy of Zionism and his commitment to the principle of self-determination.[10]

Some considerable emphasis has been placed in these pages on Palestinian self-determination because, in the present view, it is one of the two rock-bottom requisites of a settlement both equitable and stable. Equity and force are the essential variables of stable peace settlements: neither may suffice in itself, but, in general, the more one is applied, the less is required of the other. Israel, backed to the hilt by the United States, could perhaps maintain its existence and hold its enemies at bay for an extended period by the rigorous, forcible suppression of Palestinian nationalism, but that seems unlikely. Forced solutions, to last, require the application of overwhelming force and the will and ability to apply it over long periods. They are the prerogative, by and large, of great and totalitarian powers, which have both the necessary force and the ability to suppress domestic opposition to its use. They tend not to work for small states, which lack overwhelming force, and for democracies, where internal dissent to undemocratic practices cannot be suppressed. Israel, by these standards, being both small and democratic, is a two-count loser. As the small, brave band of dissenters within Israel—heirs of the "Other Zionism"[11]—continue to warn, Israel has no choice: its future is in coming to terms with its rival claimant to the Holy Land, in accepting the legitimacy of Palestinian nationalism, in conceding the right of the Palestinian people to shape their own destiny in the 23 percent of the territory of old Palestine that remained outside of Israeli control prior to the 1967 war. Peace is Israel's "great necessity," David Ben-Gurion said in 1971 and, to get it, "we must return to the borders before 1967." Militarily defensible borders, although desirable, Ben-Gurion said, could not by themselves guarantee Israel's future. "Real peace with our Arab neighbors—mutual trust and friendship—that is the only true security."[12]

The other rock-botton requirement of a fair and durable settlement is a solid, explicit system of international guarantees of the entire settlement, including, if Israel so desires, a bilateral treaty between Israel and the United States guaranteeing Israel's independence and territory. Palestinian recognition of the permanence and legitimacy of Israel, in forms comparable to those spelled out in the Egyptian-Israeli treaty, would be an essential provision of a general settlement, but insufficient in itself. Too much bitterness, mistrust, and animosity have built up over the years for Israel to be expected to accept Palestinian promises at face value. A combination of multilateral and bilateral American guarantees was proposed by J.W. Fulbright, chairman of the Senate Foreign Relations Committee, in 1970. Suggesting that the United Nations Security Council be entrusted to enforce a general peace settlement "and all of its specifications," Fulbright suggested too that in practice primary responsibility for enforcing the peace would fall to the United States and the Soviet Union. In deference to Israel's long-standing lack of confidence in the United Nations, Fulbright also proposed a complementary, bilateral American-Israeli treaty that would "neither add to, nor detract from, nor in any way alter the multilateral guarantee of the United Nations," but "would obligate the United States to use force, if necessary, in accordance with its constitutional processes, to assist Israel against any violation of its 1967 borders which it could not repel itself. . . ." Israel in turn would be obligated, "firmly and unequivocally, never to violate those borders herself."[13] The Fulbright plan has been reiterated many times with variations in detail since 1970—in the Brookings Study Group plan of 1975, for example, and in the Soviet-American joint statement of October 1, 1977. The Brookings plan suggested that an American guarantee be restricted to "major violations of the agreements threatening world peace or the existence of states."[14]

Lesser threats to Israel, such as the mounting of terrorist raids from Palestinian territory, would be dealt with in part by the stationing of United Nations forces in a demilitarized zone straddling the Israeli-Palestinian border. Further restraints would be imposed by precisely defined restrictions on the armaments permitted the Palestinian state (or the Palestinian portion of a confederation with Jordan) and by placing on it, by international contract, the obligation to prevent and suppress terrorism. Beyond these arrangements the principal restraint on, and principal insurer of the good behavior of, a Palestinian government would be the overwhelming power, compared to its own, of Israel, with its demonstrated will and ability to use that power. The international guarantees provided as a part of a general settlement need not and should not be extended to protect the Palestinian state against clearly provoked Israeli punitive actions. Unlike the PLO in its Lebanese exile, an independent Palestine would have much to lose by irresponsible behavior. As Professor Walid Khalidi observed in his proposal for a sovereign Palestinian state, "any PLO leadership would take the helm in a Palestinian state with few illusions about the efficacy of revolutionary armed struggle in any direct confrontation with Israel. They would be acutely aware of its costs. They would have little incentive on national or corporate grounds to incur it."[15] Or, as Professor Hisham Sharabi observed, even if, after forming a West Bank-Gaza state, Palestinians were to continue dreaming their dream of a unified, democratic secular state of all Palestine, "What of it? What can they do about it?"[16]

In the long-term real peace—for Palestinians no less than Israelis, and also for Jordan and Syria, the remaining confrontation states—will come only with mutual acceptance, the development of normal relations, and the beginnings of trust and friendship as envisioned at various times by Ben-Gurion, by Nahum Goldmann, by Chaim Weizmann, and by President Sadat. The grudging, de facto acceptance of Israel offered by the PLO in the seventies was perhaps all that could have been expected at the time, but in the long term it will not suffice. Palestinians, who have pressed a well-founded case for redress of the wrongs that have been done them, must recognize that many things, including what is just and what is unjust, change over time, and that it would be no less an injustice now to dismantle the lovingly, painstakingly built Israeli state and nation than it was in 1948 to expel the Palestinian people from their country and their homes. There has to be a time limit on questions of justice and injustice; without it nothing would ever be solved. Israelis, for their part, may find their own attitudes altered, their fear of Palestinian nationalism diminished, and their confidence in their own survival enhanced by the experience of even partial peace. Many Israelis have predicted this, and Palestinians would have everything to gain by allowing the evolutionary process to advance.

The terms of a general settlement herein suggested represent something far short of the aspirations of both claimants to the land of old Palestine—they also represent something far short of an ideal settlement. The latter, if it has ever been approximated at all, is probably best represented by I.F. Stone's "Other Zionism" of the twenties and thirties with its aspiration to a unified, binational state in which Arabs and Jews would live together in freedom and equality. The development of Israel as a Jewish state and the palpable, passionate desire of the Israelis to keep it that, coupled with the rise of Palestinian nationalism, have rendered that conception obsolete and unfeasible. The alternative remains, as it has always been, partition—not, however, the partition of the territories occupied in 1967 as called for by the Allon Plan,[17] but the partition of old Palestine along the approximate lines of 1967. For Israelis this will mean the end of their dream for retrieval of the entirety of the "God-covenanted" land. For Palestinians it will mean the end of their dream for the "democratic, secular" state and settling instead for a truncated homeland in the West Bank and Gaza. Both will have to put their dreams away and, in a world in which the fulfillment of dreams is as elusive as the realization of justice, settle for more limited satisfactions.

HOW TO DO IT

From the standpoint of American interests, as well as equity to the parties, the problem is not what to do but how to do it. No issue in contemporary international affairs has been more thoroughly and more frequently scrutinized—by official task forces, congressional committees, and private study groups, in government, the universities, and research institutes—and the models of possible solutions have been all but exhausted. In brief there are three possibilities: a peace based on Israeli predominance, either in the form offered by Begin or in the form offered by the Labor opposition, which would necessitate the suppression of Palestinian nationalism; a peace of the kind envisioned by the PLO Charter and the "rejectionist" Arab states, which would necessitate the liquidation of Israel as a Jewish state; and a peace based on the consensus of moderates, which offers the only practical possibility of reconciling "the sons of Ishmael and the sons of Isaac,"[18] and therefore of durability.

If it is that obvious, that desirable, and also in keeping with the national interests of the United States, why has American policy so signally failed to achieve it? Why indeed have the superpowers, with all their power and with similar official aims in the Arab-Israeli conflict, found their own influence so limited? There would seem to be two reasons. One is the inability of the superpowers to cooperate, by reason of their chronic susceptibility to the temptation to carry their global rivalry into the Middle East arena—a susceptibility encouraged by both Israel and Egypt. The second and more fundamental reason for the failure of the United States to realize its interests in the Middle East has been the extreme reluctance of successive American administrations to use the multiform power of the United States to advance American interests. This reluctance has had nothing to do with the much-decried post-Vietnam reaction against military intervention or excessive commitment abroad. The refusal to apply pressure on Israel—which would surely mean economic not military pressure—long antedates Vietnam: no American president has applied or even seriously tried to apply such pressure on Israel since President Eisenhower compelled the Ben-Gurion government in 1957 to withdraw Israeli forces from Sinai after the Suez War. The reluctance to use American power in the Middle East has to do, instead, with the fear of domestic opposition and political reprisal. The statement attributed to Senator John Culver in explanation of his signature on the famous "letter of seventy-six," which effectively negated the Ford-Kissinger "reassessment" of Middle East policy in 1975, may stand as definitive: "The pressure was just too great. I caved."[19]

There are three rationales for the refusal to apply serious pressure on Israel: that it cannot be done; that it would not bring the desired result; and that it is illegitimate.

The first is based on the premise that the United States simply does not possess the necessary power to compel Israel's acquiescence in a peace of the kind endorsed in these pages. "What will you do if we maintain settlements?" Dayan asked Joseph Kraft. "Squawk? What will you do if we keep the army there? Send troops?"[20] The Israeli premise is not, in fact, that the United States could not apply the necessary pressure by withholding some of the military and economic assistance on which Israel so heavily depends but that no American president, for fear of Congress and the Israeli lobby, would *dare* to withhold aid. The Carter administration, like its predecessors, was at considerable pains to encourage Israel in that confidence at the same time that it suffered agonies of frustration over Israeli intransigence at various stages of the "peace process." In June 1977, to cite one of many examples, when the Carter administration still had hopes of a general settlement through a Geneva conference, Vice President Mondale said in a speech in San Francisco, "We do not intend to use our military aid as pressure on Israel."[21] In March 1978, when President Sadat's peace initiative seemed to be coming unglued, President Carter, in advance of a visit by Begin, said, "I don't have any intention to pressure Prime Minister Begin. I don't have any desire to do it and couldn't if I wanted to."[22] The Reagan administration, in its first months, evinced not the slightest intention of altering this approach. By constantly assuring Israel that the United States would never use its aid to pressure Israel to act against its own preferences, even when those preferences went against American interests, every American president since Eisenhower has reinforced, and apparently solidified, the conviction of Israeli leaders that it is both feasible and safe to defy the United States. And so indeed it has been—not, however, because the United States could not apply pressure but because American office-holders, fearing political reprisal, have acquiesced in the prohibition.

The second rationale for eschewing pressure is that it would not work anyway and could provoke even greater defiance. The premise underlying many elaborate assurances of the unconditionality of American support has been (aside from domestic political necessity) that military security would induce flexibility and more accomodating attitudes on Israel's part, whereas pressure and threats would provoke defiance by activating the Israeli penchant for "tenacious solitude." The validity of this thesis is, at best, arguable. Confidence in American support and its own military superiority may have been a factor in the concessions made by Israel to secure the Camp David agreements and peace treaty with Egypt. More probably, the Begin government made the concessions it had to make to secure the strategic prize aspired to by every Israeli government since the founding of the state: a separate peace with Israel's strongest enemy. Whatever its effects elsewhere, military strength and American support have produced no important concessions regarding the West Bank and Gaza and the Golan Heights. Henry Kissinger, who made frequent use of the argument that American military aid would encourage Israeli flexibility, complained in early 1975, a time when his peace efforts were faring badly, "I ask Rabin to make concessions, and he says he can't because

Israel is weak. So I give him more arms, and he says he doesn't need to make concessions because Israel is strong."[23] As for provoking defiance, there is no doubt that expressions of American displeasure confined to verbal reproach, as in the case of the West Bank settlements, have been defied and ignored frequently; it is by no means obvious that the credible threat of an aid cutoff would have the same result.

The third argument against pressure is that it is illegitimate, connoting the bugbear of an "imposed settlement." This objection is spurious on two counts, the first of which is that almost any conceivable settlement will be, in one way or another, and to one degree or another, imposed. A settlement reached between an Israel heavily armed by the United States and an Arab coalition of much inferior military capacity would no more represent a freely negotiated agreement among equals than would a peace made between the PLO, backed by its Arab supporters, and an Israel abandoned by the United States. As long as Israel denies Palestinian self-determination, it purports to impose a settlement based on Israeli military preponderance. Nor can the Camp David framework for the West Bank and Gaza, even if liberally implemented, be regarded as an arrangement freely contracted between Israelis and Palestinians. The Aswan formula of January 4, 1978 (of which the Camp David framework was an elaboration) by specifying that the Palestinians might "participate in the determination of their own future," also specified, in effect, that others would participate in making that determination, which means that, to one degree or another, the future of the Palestinians would be something that was *imposed* on them. The real issue is not whether the settlement will be imposed or not, but in what degree it will be imposed and by whom.

The second specious notion is that imposed settlements are by definition unjust and by nature unworkable. History provides numerous examples of imposed peace settlements that proved durable, some of which were reasonably equitable as well. Force and equity, as noted earlier, are the operating variables: although neither may be sufficient in itself, the more there is of one, the less, generally speaking, is required of the other. The peace imposed on France by the Congress of Vienna in 1815, for example, held up in its essential parts for a hundred years, during which there was no general European war; it held up because it was diligently enforced by the victorious alliance of European powers, and also because it left intact the national territory of the defeated state, restored France to equal membership in the Concert of Europe, and so gradually dissipated the lingering French appetite for revision and revenge. In the 1830s, to take another example, the European powers forcibly divested the Netherlands of its Belgian province, since which time the two separate states, Belgium and Holland, have lived together in uninterrupted peace if not flawless harmony. By contrast, the Treaty of Versailles collapsed within a few years and was followed by an even more destructive Second World War even though it had implemented the principle of self-determination by giving Europe the best ethnographic map it has ever had, before or since, deprived Germany of little if any territory to which it had just claim, imposed on Germany a reparations obligation well warranted by the aggression and destruction inflicted by Germany on Europe (and that Germany, in the event, did not pay), and, bequeathed to a war-ravaged world a League of Nations to prevent future wars. Denounced at the time as a diktat, the peace of Versailles failed not because it was imposed in the first instance but because it was not subsequently enforced. Had the victors of World War I remained united and had they enforced the peace, as they had the legal right and, until the late thirties, the power to do as well, there would have been no Second World War; there would have been no holocaust.

There is neither merit nor special morality in a national policy of abstention from the use of power to realize the national interest. This is especially true if the concept of national interest employed is of sufficient breadth to encompass principled behavior, compliance with law, loyalty to friends and commitments, and adherence to established international norms as codified in the United Nations Charter. So embedded in official liturgy, however, is the notion that imposed solutions are bad, and so great is the confusion about what this means, that President Carter, in April 1979, excused himself from more vigorous efforts to restrain Israel from its illegal settlements policy in the West Bank on the ground that "there's a limit to what we can do to impose our will on a sovereign nation,"[24] thus, in effect, extending the scope of Israel's sovereign immunity to include acts of coercion beyond its recognized frontier. The moral consideration expressed in the president's statement was misconceived, not only because a nation's sovereignty is not properly regarded as extending to the exercise of force against others, but because, too, the unlimited sovereignty of nations has become a dangerously obsolete concept. Limitations on the sovereignty of nations have become, in the twentieth century, a requisite for the protection of all nations.

The preferability of voluntary agreements to imposed solutions is beyond question. That, however, is not the real issue for the United States in Middle East peacemaking. Over six decades following the Balfour

Declaration—which would seem a fair trial period—Arabs and Israelis demonstrated conclusively that they were unable to reach agreements without heavy pressure from outside. The real choice is between the coercion of one local party by the other using military power provided by the United States, and the bringing to bear of American power more directly, to secure a settlement both equitable to the parties and compatible with American interests. The power required for this purpose, it should be emphasized again, is not physical coercion: it is not a question of training the guns of the American Sixth Fleet on Israel's coastal cities to compel Israeli acquiescence in Palestinian self-determination; still less is the pressure required comparable, as has been suggested, with the Vietnam War policy of bombing the North Vietnamese to the bargaining table. What is required, quite obviously, is the attachment of conditions to future American military and economic assistance, which, if not accepted, would result in the United States government telling Israel: "You are on your own."

The necessity of a forceful new American approach has been demonstrated by events and is testified to by experts. The Carter administration's diligence, good will, and extraordinary patience in mediating the Camp David accords and the Egyptian-Israeli peace treaty demonstrated both the rewards and limitations of the mediating role. "The easy part is over," a senior American diplomat in Israel said after the Camp David accords.[25] The far more difficult issues that remain seem unlikely to yield to American influence in the absence of a basic change in the American role, from mediator to arbiter of peace. Israeli governments have repeatedly asserted their defiance of American pressure; from this it has been inferred, wrongly, that no form of pressure will work. The pressure to which they have demonstrated their imperviousness has been verbal pressure, which is to say, persuasion; it has not been demonstrated that Israeli leaders would be impervious to a credible American threat to withhold aid. Wolf Blitzer, Washington correspondent of the *Jerusalem Post*, observed in a presentation at the annual conference of the Middle East Institute in October 1979 that Israelis did not greatly mind American criticism of their policies, such as placing new settlements in the West Bank; the real test of relations was the reliability of American aid, and in that respect, said Blitzer, they were well satisfied.[26]

Judging by the experience of preceding years, the cautiously phrased Brookings Study Group report of 1975 concluded that "the governments directly concerned must bear the responsibility for negotiation and agreement, but initiative, impetus and inducement may well have to come from outside."[27] Less cautiously, Nahum Goldmann, the former president of the World Jewish Congress and former president of the World Zionist Organization, writing in 1978, characterized the demand that the United States not "impose" a peace as "absurd" and as "a clever and demagogic formula." Goldmann wrote:

> International politics are based on permanent interference and pressures, and even Israel very often demands that the United States should influence its allies in NATO or pressure its adversaries like the Soviet Union. . . . America, by its reluctance to influence Israel and through having given in to too many Israeli demands . . . not only failed to help Israel but harmed it in the long run. With greater American interference, peace could have been brought about long ago. . . . Experience has shown that the Arabs and Israelis, left alone, will not achieve an agreement. The conflict is, in a certain way, a family affair between two Semitic peoples, who are characterized by stubbornness and lack of flexibility. The United States, which has intervened in many other conflicts and helped to bring about settlements, should not only have the right but the obligation to use all its influence in the Arab-Israeli issue, which has occupied the headlines of the world for thirty years.[28]

There was one occasion, as noted in chapter 2,[29] on which the United States did act effectively as "arbiter" in the Middle East. Following the Suez War in 1956, Great Britain and France complied with United Nations resolutions calling for withdrawal from Egyptian territory, but their collaborator, Israel, insisted on certain guarantees as conditions for its withdrawal. President Eisenhower made it clear that, if necessary, the United States would support UN sanctions against Israel to enforce the withdrawal resolution; he also raised the possibility of removing the tax deductibility of private gifts to Israel by United States citizens. Israeli forces were finally withdrawn from Sinai and the Gaza Strip in March 1957. Eisenhower later told an interviewer, "Finally, we had to be very tough with them, really, but finally they agreed."[30]

Eisenhower based his firm stand on the importance of upholding the integrity of the United Nations as a peace enforcement organization and as "our best hope of establishing a world order." Since that time confidence in the United Nations has fallen precipitously with the decline in the world organization's effectiveness and objectivity. The conception on which the UN is based, and which Eisenhower tried to uphold in 1957, however, remains valid and—more than valid—highly pertinent to the world's current needs. That conception is the necessity, in the wake of two world wars and in the nuclear age, of at least a minimal world security community, in the words of the preamble to the United Nations Charter, "to save succeeding generations from the scourge of war. . . ." No community can function without some capacity for coercion. The United Nations Charter spells out procedures and sanctions, graduated from political and economic to military, for the enforcement of peace, and every member of the organization, by its own consent as a signatory to the charter, is bound "to accept and carry out the decisions of the Security Council."[31] "The crucial distinction," Senator J. W. Fulbright wrote, "is not between coercion and voluntarism, but between duly constituted force, applied through law and as a last resort, and the arbitrary coercion of the weak by the strong."[32]

The rewards of American mediation may well have been exhausted with the Camp David accords and the Egyptian-Israeli peace treaty. Should that prove to be the case, and with interests of great magnitude still unsecured, an American president, sooner or later, will face the long-postponed and exceedingly difficult choice between continued futile pleadings with the intransigent parties and accepting once again, as Eisenhower did in 1956–57, the role of arbiter for peace in the Middle East. It could be done, as has been suggested in these pages, and probably must be done in collaboration with the Soviet Union and other nations, but the initiative necessarily lies with the United States, because the United States, as President Sadat so often reminded Americans, still holds "ninety-nine percent of the cards." Egypt did about as much as it could toward securing a peace based on the consensus of moderates; it settled for less because it had to, providing an example for all concerned of courage and moderation. The other Arab states, and the PLO, can create crises and disruptions, but they otherwise lack the power to alter the post–Camp David status quo. Israel possesses the power to change the status quo but, in its deep-seated fear of Palestinian nationalism, refuses to do so. With peace and normal relations with Egypt, that situation could change, as the Israeli "doves" have ardently hoped but not quite dared to predict. The United States alone, in the period following the Egyptian-Israeli peace treaty, possessed the untapped reservoir of power and influence to guide the negotiations on Palestinian self-rule toward self-determination and a general settlement.

To exercise that power an American president would have to resolve, or overcome, powerful domestic obstacles. Since the creation of Israel, and increasingly with the development of the powerful Israeli lobby in the United States in the sixties and seventies, virtually every American effort to defend and advance American interests in the Middle East—interests ranging from peace to détente to energy—has been immediately converted from a foreign to a domestic problem. That fact has been the principal obstacle to the formulation of an American policy based on the totality of American interests in a vital and dangerous region. To over-come it will require a sustained, purposeful campaign by the president and any other elected leaders who might care to step forward to educate the American people in the realities of the Middle East, the nature of American interests in the region, the relationship of these interests to each other, and the necessity of a policy that harmonizes these so far as possible. Even more important than apprising the American people of their interests in the Middle East would be a new effort, by private citizens no less than by public officials, to curb the excesses of the politics of faction, to retrieve the Congress from its recent role as a brokerage of interests to its proper role as a deliberative body committed to the general good, and most important of all, to place in positions of public trust those individuals, in Madison's definition, "whose enlightened views and virtuous sentiments render them superior to local prejudices, and to schemes of injustice."[33]

NOTES

1. THE LONG ROAD TO CAMP DAVID

1. Press conference in Jerusalem, November 21, 1977 (*New York Times*, November 22, 1977, p. 16).

2. Quoted by William E. Farrell in "An Ex-Legislator Roams the Halls of the Knesset to Lobby for Peace," *New York Times*, November 22, 1977, p. 17.

3. Address to the Knesset, November 20, 1977 (*New York Times*, November 21, 1977, p. 14).

4. News conference of President Sadat and Prime Minister Begin, Jerusalem, November 21, 1977 (*New York Times*, November 22, 1977, p. 16).

5. Address to the Knesset, November 20, 1977 (*New York Times*, November 21, 1977, pp. 13–14).

6. "Comment on Palestinians," *New York Times*, November 22, 1977, p. 16.

7. Interview with *October Magazine*, January 14, 1978, English translation in Foreign Broadcast Information Service (FBIS), Daily Report, *Middle East and North Africa*, January 16, 1978, p. D4.

8. "Excerpts from Sadat's Speech to Egyptian Parliament," November 26, 1977 (*New York Times*, November 27, 1977, p. 16).

9. "No Turning Back," *Washington Post*, December 23, 1977, p. A14.

10. "The Talk of the Town," *The New Yorker*, January 9, 1978, p. 19.

11. "Texts of Statements by Sadat and Begin and Their News Conference in Ismailia," *New York Times*, December 27, 1977, p. 16.

12. Ezer Weizman, *The Battle for Peace* (New York: Bantam Books, 1981), pp. 124, 129.

13. "Statement by Begin about the Ismailia Talks on His Return to Israel," *New York Times*, December 27, 1977, p. 16.

14. "Text of Begin's Plan for West Bank and Gaza Strip," *New York Times*, December 29, 1977, p. 8.

15. William E. Farrell, "Begin Insists Israel Must Keep Troops in West Bank Area," *New York Times*, December 29, 1977, pp. 1, 8.

16. "Text of Statements by Sadat and Carter Following Meeting in Aswan," *New York Times*, January 5, 1978, p. A4.

17. Henry Tanner, "Leaders Consult Briefly at Aswan and Agree on 'Most Issues'," *New York Times*, January 5, 1978, p. A1.

18. Interview with *October Magazine*, FBIS, Daily Report, *Middle East and North Africa*, January 16, 1978, pp. D1–8.

19. "Remarks by Begin at the Dinner for Participants in Jerusalem Talks," *New York Times*, January 19, 1978, p. A12.

20. "Transcription of Egyptian Statement on Halt in Talks," *New York Times*, January 19, 1978, p. A11.

21. Quoted by William E. Farrell in "Cabinet Acts Quickly," *New York Times*, January 19, 1977.

22. Interview with *October Magazine*, FBIS, Daily Report, *Middle East and North Africa*, January 16, 1978, p. D6.

23. Interview in New York, February 9, 1978, quoted by Henry Scott-Stokes, "Dayan Is Briefed by U.S. Official about Sadat Visit," *New York Times*, February 10, 1978, p. A3.

24. For a concise historical summary of the background of the Arab-Israeli conflict, see Fred J. Khoury, *The Arab-Israeli Dilemma* (Syracuse: Syracuse University Press, 1968), pp. 1–67.

25. Menachem Begin, *The Revolt* (London: W. H. Allen, 1951), p. 3.

26. Arie Lova Eliav, *Land of the Hart* (Philadelphia: Jewish Publication Society of America, 1974), pp. 9–12.

27. A maxim current in Zionist circles in the late 19th and early 20th centuries.

28. David Lloyd George, *The Truth About the Peace Treaties*, 2 vols. (London: Victor Gollancz, Ltd., 1938), vol. 2, pp. 1116–1122.

29. Ibid., pp. 1119–1120, 1137–1139.

30. George Antonius, *The Arab Awakening* (New York: G. P. Putnam & Son, 1946) pp. 261–264. Antonius believes the imperial motive for the Balfour Declaration was the dominant one.

31. Quoted by Seth P. Tillman in *Anglo-American Relations at the Paris Peace Conference of 1919* (Princeton: Princeton University Press, 1961), p. 225.

32. Address to a joint meeting of Congress, February 11, 1918, quoted ibid., pp. 32–33.

33. Ibid., p. 29.

34. Antonius, *The Arab Awakening*, pp. 286–287.

35. Memorandum by Frankfurter of a meeting in Paris, June 24, 1919, quoted in Tillman, *Anglo-American Relations* p. 226.

36. Ibid., p. 226; Harry N. Howard, *The King-Crane Commission* (Beirut Khayats, 1963), pp. 92, 224–225.

37. Begin, *The Revolt*, p. 26.

38. Antonius, *The Arab Awakening*, pp. 411–12.

39. John Snetsinger, *Truman, the Jewish Vote, and the Creation of Israel* (Stanford University: Hoover Institution Press, 1974), pp. 19–21.

40. Ibid., pp. 23–24; Khoury, *The Arab-Israeli Dilemma*, p. 34.

41. Snetsinger, *Truman, the Jewish Vote, and Israel*, p. 28.

42. Ibid., p. 42.

43. Ibid., pp. 84–85.

44. Ibid., pp. 85–94.

45. Khoury, *The Arab-Israeli Dilemma*, pp. 58–60, 63.

46. Snetsinger, *Truman, the Jewish Vote, and Israel*, pp. 104–111.

47. Dean Acheson, *Present at the Creation* (New York: W. W. Norton & Co., Inc., 1969), p. 169.

48. Harry S. Truman, *Years of Trial and Hope* (Garden City, N.Y.: Doubleday & Co., Inc., 1956), p. 133.

49. Quoted by Snetsinger in *Truman, the Jewish Vote, and Israel*, p. 135.

50. Begin, *The Revolt*, pp. 373–377.

51. Eliav, *Land of the Hart*, pp. 54–55.

52. Begin, *The Revolt*, pp. xi–xii.

53. Ibid., pp. 36, 46.

54. Eliav, *Land of the Hart*, p. 55.

55. Quoted by Thomas W. Lippman & Jonathan C. Randal in "Hard Issues May Be Put Off," *Washington Post*, January 8, 1978, pp. A1, A14.

56. I. F. Stone, "Holy War," in *The Arab-Israel Reader* (Walter Laqueur, ed., New York: Bantam Books, 1969), p. 324.

57. Quoted by Khoury in *The Arab-Israeli Dilemma*, p. 41.

58. Address to the United Nations General Assembly, November 13, 1974.

59. Wilfred Cantwell Smith, *Islam in Modern History* (New York: New American Library, 1957), pp. 103–104.

60. Quoted in Raphael Patai, *The Arab Mind* (New York: Charles Scribner's Sons, 1973), pp. 262–264.

61. Ibid., p. 265.

62. Seth Tillman, *The Middle East Between War and Peace, November-December 1973*, a Staff Report Prepared for the Use of the Subcommittee on Near Eastern Affairs of the Committee on Foreign Relations, United States Senate, March 5, 1974 (Washington, D.C.: U.S. Government Printing Office, 1974), p. 3.

63. Ibid., pp. 8–9.

64. Ibid., p. 39.

65. Interview with *October Magazine*, FBIS, Daily Report, *Middle East and North Africa*, January 16, 1978, pp. D3, D6.

66. Edward W. Said, *The Question of Palestine* (New York: Vintage Books, 1980), p. 69.

67. "President Carter's News Conference of January 30, 1978," *New York Times*, January 31, 1978, p. A10.

68. Office of the White House Press Secretary, "Transcript of an Interview with the President by Barbara Walters, Robert McNeil, Tom Brokaw and Bob Schieffer," December 28, 1977, pp. 5–6.

69. Marvine Howe, "Sadat Calls Begin 'the Only Obstacle' to Mideast Accord," *New York Times*, July 23, 1978, pp. A1, A4.

70. William E. Farrell, "Israel Turns Down Appeal from Egypt for Friendly Move," *New York Times*, July 24, 1978, pp. A1, A3.

71. Terence Smith, "Mondale Says Begin Agrees to a Parley with Egypt and U.S.," *New York Times*, July 3, 1978, pp. A1, A3.

72. Jim Hoagland, "Vance: U.S. Help Not Linked to Summit Results," *Washington Post*, August 15, 1978, p. A1.

73. Sidney Zion and Uri Dan, "Untold Story of the Mideast Talks," *New York Times Magazine*, January 28, 1979, p. 38.

74. Weizman, *The Battle for Peace*, pp. 367, 372.

75. Bernard Gwertzman, "Saudis Call Sadat's Effort for Mideast Peace a Failure," *New York Times*, August 3, 1978, p. A6.

76. "Framework for the Conclusion of a Peace Treaty Between Egypt and Israel," September 17, 1978.

77. "A Framework for Peace in the Middle East Agreed at Camp David," September 17, 1978.

78. Conversation with Tahseen Basheer, Egyptian representative to the Arab League, Cairo, October 14, 1978.

79. An Egyptian Foreign Ministry official, in a conversation in Cairo, October 15, 1978.

80. Interview with Ambassador Herman Eilts, Cairo, October 16, 1978.

81. Weizman, *The Battle for Peace*, pp. 190–191.

82. "Egypt Insists That Pact Is Linked to West Bank," *Washington Post*, October 21, 1978, p. A12.

83. Bernard Gwertzman, "Israel and Egypt Study U.S. Plan; Carter Terms Both Sides Stubborn," *New York Times*, November 14, 1978, pp A1, A6.

84. "Begin Rejects Plan for Link in Treaty to the Palestinians," *New York Times*, November 27, 1978, pp. A1, A3.

85. "Text of Sadat Talk at Nobel Ceremony," *New York Times*, December 11, 1978, p. 12.

86. "Text of Begin Speech Accepting Prize," *New York Times*, December 11, 1978, p. 12.

87. John M. Goshko, "Vance Imposes Cutoff on Middle East Shuttle," *Washington Post*, December 14, 1978, pp. A1, A19.

88. Terence Smith, "Carter Says Treaty Is up to Israel Now; U.S. May Curb Role," *New York Times*, December 15, 1978, pp. 1, 13.

89. Pranay Gupte, "U.S. Jews Charge Carter Abandons Mediator Role," *New York Times*, December 17, 1978, p. 3.

90. "Carter Blames the Jews," *New York Times*, December 18, 1978, p. 19.

91. Lee Lescaze, "Kissinger Raps White House for Blaming Israel on Impasse," *Washington Post*, December 19, 1978, p. A18.

92. "Egyptian-Israeli Treaty 'So Close,' Carter Says," *Washington Post*, February 27, 1979, p. A6.

93. John M. Goshko and Edward Walsh, "Begin Declares Peace Talks Are in 'Deep Crisis'," *Washington Post*, March 2, 1979, pp. A1, A7.

94. Bernard Gwertzman, "Carter Gives Begin Treaty Suggestions to Buoy the Talks," *New York Times*, March 5, 1979, pp. A1, A8.

95. Terence Smith, "President Sets Off on Mission of Peace to the Middle East," *New York Times*, March 8, 1979, pp. A1, A14.

96. Hedrick Smith, "Begin, With a Dinner Comment, Turns a Smiling Carter Ashen," *New York Times*, March 12, 1979, pp. A1, A8.

97. Jonathan Kandell, "Israelis Listen Silently to Carter; Heckle and Cry Angrily at Begin," *New York Times*, March 13, 1979, pp. A1, A11.

98. "Text of the President's Address and Excerpts from the Prime Minister's Reply," *New York Times*, March 13, 1979, p. A10.

99. "Statements by Carter and Begin on Mideast Talks," *New York Times*, March 14, 1979, p. A12.

100. Jonathan Kandell, "Begin Says Israel Will Never Allow Palestinian State in Occupied Area," *New York Times*, March 21, 1979, pp. A1, A9.

101. Jonathan Kandell, "Dayan Seeks U.S. Security Assurance," *New York Times*, March 23, 1979, p. A12.

102. Earleen Tatro, "Sadat Says He Wants Just One Pact Ceremony, Not 3," *New York Times*, March 17, 1979, p. A4.

103. *The Egyptian-Israeli Peace Treaty*, March 26, 1979 (United States Department of State Publication 8973, Near Eastern and South Asian Series 90, Bureau of Public Affairs, March 1979).

104. *Documents Pertaining to the Conclusion of Peace* (Embassy of Israel, Washington, D.C., April 1979).

105. Bernard Gwertzman, "Carter Gives Begin Treaty Suggestions to Buoy the Talks," *New York Times*, March 5, 1979, pp. A1, A8.

106. William Claiborne, "Israel Holds Firm," *Washington Post*, May 25, 1979, p. A29.

107. Thomas W. Lippmann, "Egypt Urges Accord," *Washington Post*, May 25, 1979, pp. A29, A30.

108. John M. Goshko, "Carter, Sadat Part After Talks on Resolving Palestinian Impasse," *Washington Post*, April 10, 1980, pp. A1, A25.

109. Terence Smith, "Two Mideast Leaders Agree on a Device for Autonomy Pact," *New York Times*, April 17, 1980, pp. A1, A5.

110. Henry Tanner, "Jordan Acts to Aid Iraq With Supplies for War With Iran," *New York Times*, October 7, 1980, pp. A1, A14.

111. Bradley Graham, "European Summit Urges PLO Role in Mideast Talks," *Washington Post*, June 14, 1981, pp. A1, A10.

112. "Israel Rejects PLO Role in Mideast Negotiations," *Washington Post*, June 14, 1981, p. A18.

113. John Kifner, "PLO Asserts Stand of the Europeans Misses Basic Points," *New York Times*, June 15, 1980, pp. A1, A5.

114. Questions submitted to the candidates by the Jewish Telegraphic Agency, *JTA Daily News Bulletin*, Vol. LVIII, No. 206, October 28, 1980.

115. Bernard Gwertzman, "Haig Says U.S. Seeks Consensus Strategy in Mideast Region," *New York Times*, March 20, 1981, pp. A1, A4.

116. Bernard Gwertzman, "Attempting to Recoup, Haig Works Hard to Score Points Abroad," *New York Times*, April 12, 1981, p. E2.

117. William Claiborne, "War or Compromise: Israelis Debate Syria's Missiles," *Washington Post*, May 14, 1981, p. A31.

118. David K. Shipler, "Begin Defends Raid, Vows 'Never Again' a New 'Holocaust'," *New York Times*, June 10, 1981, pp. A1, A12.

119. "Dayan Says Israel Has the Capacity to Produce A-Bombs," *New York Times*, June 25, 1981, pp. A1, A7.

120. David K. Shipler, "Israelis Insist Air Raid on Iraqis Was Justified," *New York Times*, June 11, 1981, pp. A1, A10.

121. David K. Shipler, "Begin Says Attack on Iraqis Made Him 'Feel a Free Man'," *New York Times*, June 15, 1981, p. A10.

122. Letter from Secretary of State Alexander M. Haig, Jr. to Speaker of the House Thomas P. O'Neill, *New York Times*, June 11, 1981, p. A14.

123. Bernard Gwertzman, "U.S., Citing Possible Violation of Arms Agreement, Suspends Shipment of 4 F–16's to Israel," *New York Times*, June 11, 1981, pp. A1, A14.

124. Michael J. Berlin, "U.N. Council Condemns Israeli Raid," *Washington Post*, June 20, 1981, pp. A1, A17.

125. David K. Shipler, "Begin and U.S. Aide 'Clarify' Positions on Reactor Raid," *New York Times*, July 14, 1981, pp. A1, A7.

126. "Middle East Absurdities," *Washington Post*, July 14, 1981, p. A12.

127. William Claiborne, "Israeli Election Results Signal Harder Line on Occupied Territories," *Washington Post*, July 9, 1981, p. A18.

128. William Claiborne, "Begin Widens Targeting to PLO Sites in Cities," *Washington Post*, July 18, 1981, pp. A1, A14.

129. "Reagan Reports 'No Decision' on Planes for Israel," *New York Times*, July 19, 1981, p. 13.

130. William Claiborne, "Israeli Fears of Guerrilla Buildup Triggered Beirut Strike," *Washington Post*, July 25, 1981, p. A18.

131. David K. Shipler, "For Israelis, a Toting Up," *New York Times*, July 27, 1981, pp. A1, A6.

2. AMERICAN INTERESTS AND THE AMERICAN POLITICAL SYSTEM

1. Lord Palmerston's speech before the House of Commons in defense of his foreign policy, March, 1848.

2. "National Commitments," *Report of the Senate Foreign Relations Committee on Senate Resolution 85,* 91st Congress, 1st Session (Calendar No. 118, Report No. 91–129, April 16, 1969), p. 9.

3. *Nomination of Henry A. Kissinger,* Hearings before the Committee on Foreign Relations, United States Senate, 93rd Congress, First Session, (Washington, D.C.: U.S. Government Printing Office, 1973), p. 7.

4. Quoted by Samuel Flagg Bemis in *A Diplomatic History of the United States,* 4th ed. (New York: Henry Holt and Co., 1955), p. 472.

5. Arthur H. Vandenberg, Jr., ed., *The Private Papers of Senator Vandenberg* (Boston: Houghton Mifflin Co., 1952), p. 340.

6. "Transcript of President's First News Conference on Foreign and Domestic Topics," *New York Times,* January 30, 1981, p. A10.

7. Excerpts from Text of an Interview with Carter on Foreign and Domestic Affairs," *New York Times,* December 5, 1977, p. C41.

8. Quoted by David A. Andelman in "Document That Omits Rights Is Adopted at Belgrade," *New York Times,* March 9, 1978, p. A7.

9. Quoted by Seth P. Tillman in *Anglo-American Relations at the Paris Peace Conference of 1919* (Princeton: Princeton University Press, 1961), p. 132.

10. Article 2, paragraph 3.

11. Article 2, paragraph 4.

12. Articles 39–42.

13. Article 25.

14. Article 1, paragraph 2.

15. Article 1, paragraph 3.

16. Article 2, paragraph 7.

17. Address to Congress, March 12, 1947. Quoted in Ruhl J. Bartlett, *The Record of American Diplomacy,* 3rd. ed. (New York: Alfred A. Knopf, 1954), p. 725.

18. Henry Kissinger, "Bismarck: The White Revolutionary," *Daedalus,* Summer 1968, p. 922.

19. Exxon Corporation, Exxon Background Series, *Middle East Oil,* 2nd. ed., September 1980, pp. 5–6.

20. Walter J. Levy, "Oil: An Agenda for the 1980's," *Foreign Affairs,* vol. 59, no. 5, Summer 1981, pp. 1082–3, 1100.

21. Joseph S. Nye, "Energy and Security," in *Energy and Security* (David A. Deese and Joseph S. Nye, eds., Cambridge, Mass.: Ballinger Publishing Co., 1981), p. 3.

22. "Excerpts from Begin's News Conference at National Press Club in Washington," *New York Times,* March 24, 1978, p. A10.

23. Quoted by Bernard Gwertzman in "Carter Rejects Plea to Delay Proposal on Jets for Arabs," *New York Times,* April 25, 1978, p. A9.

24. Department of State, Memorandum of Conversation, Meeting with Jewish Leaders, Hotel Pierre, New York, June 15, 1975, pp. 3, 10.

25. Figures provided by the Agency for International Development in July 1981 showed military assistance to Israel of $12,904,200,000 and economic assistance of $5,585,800,000 for the period from 1948 to the end of fiscal year 1980.

26. Quoted in *The Middle East,* 3rd ed. (Washington, D.C.: Congressional Quarterly, September 1977), p. 85.

27. Henry Fairlie in an article in *The New Republic,* February 5, 1977, quoted ibid. p. 9.

28. Nahum Goldmann, "The Psychology of Middle East Peace," *Foreign Affairs,* October 1975, pp. 113–114.

29. See chapter 1, p. 4.

30. In an interview with John Chancellor on CBS News, April 26, 1978.

31. A formal agreement between the United States and Soviet Union on the prevention of nuclear war, issued June 22, 1973 on the occasion of Brezhnev's visit to the United States of June 18–25, 1973.

32. Quoted in *A Select Chronology and Background Documents Relating to the Middle East*, 2nd revised ed., Committee on Foreign Relations, United States Senate, February 1975 (Washington, D.C.: U.S. Government Printing Office, 1975) pp. 249–250.

33. Quoted ibid., p. 266.

34. See chapter 6, p. 232.

35. Public Papers of the Presidents of the United States, *Dwight D. Eisenhower*, 1957 (Washington, D.C.: U.S. Government Printing Office, 1958), pp. 151–152.

36. Address to a joint meeting of Congress, February 11, 1918. Quoted in Ray Stannard Baker and William E. Dodd, eds., *The Public Papers of Woodrow Wilson, War & Peace*, 2 vols. (New York & London: Harper & Brothers, 1927), vol. 1, p. 180.

37. Speech of December 9, 1969, in *Background Documents Relating to the Middle East*, p. 266.

38. Statement at Clinton, Mass., March 16, 1977, in *Weekly Compilation of Presidential Documents, Jimmy Carter, 1977*, vol. 13, no. 12, March 21, 1977, p. 361.

39. "Text of Statements by Sadat and Carter Following Meeting at Aswan," *New York Times*, January 5, 1978, p. A4.

40. Seth P. Tillman, *Anglo-American Relations at the Paris Peace Conference of 1919* (Princeton: Princeton University Press, 1961), p. 226.

41. Interview with Anthony Lewis, reported in "Arafat Hints Easing of PLO's Attitude," *New York Times*, May 2, 1978, pp. A1, A8.

42. "Text of Carter-Desai Declaration," *New York Times*, January 4, 1978, p. A2.

43. *Middle East Peace Prospects*, Hearings before the Subcommittee on Near Eastern and South Asian Affairs of the Committee on Foreign Relations, U.S. Senate, 94th Congress, 2nd Session (Washington, D.C.: U.S. Government Printing Office, 1976), p. 106.

44. Remarks at an American Jewish Congress dinner honoring former Israeli Prime Minister Golda Meir, quoted in "End to US-Israel Uncertainties Urged," *Washington Post*, November 14, 1977, p. A12.

45. Senator Humphrey to Prime Minister Begin, January 11, 1978, *Washington Post*, March 27, 1978, p. A25.

46. *Toward Peace in the Middle East*, Report of a Study Group (Washington, D.C.: The Brookings Institution, 1975), p. 10.

47. Hope Eastman, *Lobbying: A Constitutionally Protected Right* (Washington, D.C.: American Enterprise Institute for Public Policy Research, 1977), p. 35.

48. Jacob E. Cooke, ed., *The Federalist* (Middletown, Conn.: Wesleyan University Press, 1961), no. 10, p. 57.

49. Ibid., p. 60.

50. Ibid., pp. 63–64.

51. Ibid., p. 62.

52. Ibid., p. 64.

53. William J. Lanouette, "The Many Faces of the Jewish Lobby in America," *National Journal*, vol. 10, no. 19, May 13, 1978, pp. 748–756. The words quoted appear ibid., p. 755. See also *The Middle East*, 3rd ed. (Washington, D.C.: Congressional Quarterly, 1977), pp. 96–101; Russell Warren Howe and Sarah Hays Trott, *The Power Peddlers*, (Garden City, N.Y.: Doubleday & Co., Inc., 1977), pp. 271–327.

54. Stephen D. Isaacs, *Jews and American Politics* (Garden City, N.Y.: Doubleday & Co., Inc., 1974), pp. 255–6.

55. Ibid., p. 256.

56. Edward R. F. Sheehan, *The Arabs, Israelis, and Kissinger* (New York: Reader's Digest Press, 1976), pp. 164–174.

57. Press release, with the text of the letter appended, issued by the offices of Senators Javits and Bayh, May 22, 1975. The text of the letter also appears in Sheehan, *The Arabs, Israelis, and Kissinger*, p. 175.

58. Quoted ibid., pp. 175–6.

59. Howe and Trott, *The Power Peddlers*, pp. 272–3.

60. Sheehan, *The Arabs, Israelis, and Kissinger*, p. 176.

61. Ibid., p. 202.

62. The term is used by Stephen D. Isaacs in *Jews and American Politics*, p. 263.

63. Concise summations of the origins and historical development of Jewish American and Arab American interest in Middle East politics are contained in essays in the *Middle East Journal*, vol. 30, no. 3, Summer 1976, entitled "The Holy Land: The American Experience." Helen Anne B. Rivlin writes on "American Jews and the State of Israel: A Bicentennial Perspective," pp. 369–389; Jacqueline S. and Tareq Y. Ismael write on "The Arab Americans and the Middle East," pp. 390–405.

64. William E. Leuchtenburg, "The American Perception of the Arab World," in *Arab and American Cultures* (George N Atiyeh, ed., Washington, D.C.: American Enterprise Institute, 1977), pp. 15–25.

65. Ismael and Ismael, "The Arab Americans and the Middle East," *Middle East Journal*, Summer 1976, p. 398.

66. Ibid., pp. 403–5.

67. *Middle East Arms Sales Proposals*, Hearings before the Committee on Foreign Relations, U.S. Senate (Washington, D.C.: U.S. Government Printing Office, 1978), pp. 162–190. See chapter 3 ("Special Relationships").

68. Lanouette, "The Many Faces of the Jewish Lobby in America," *National Journal*, May 13, 1978, p. 753.

69. Robert G. Kaiser, "Saudis Retain U.S. Firm to Lobby for Warplanes," *Washington Post*, March 29, 1978, p. A2.

70. I base this conclusion on my own experience as a professional staff member of the Senate Foreign Relations Committee from 1961 to 1977.

71. James Reston, "The New Diplomacy," *New York Times*, April 28, 1978.

72. Bernard Gwertzman, "Dayan and Vance Exchange Ideas on Ways to Revive Mideast Talks," *New York Times*, April 28, 1978, pp. A1, A7.

73. "PLO's Terzi Welcomes Whirl of Publicity in Young Affair," *Washington Post*, August 22, 1979, p. A4.

74. Meg Greenfield, "Pluralism Gone Mad," *Washington Post*, August 22, 1979, p. A25.

75. Robert J. Pranger, "The Decline of the American National Government," *Publicus*, vol. 3, no. 2, (Fall 1973), pp. 97–127.

76. Quoted ibid., p. 103.

77. "The Federalist No. 10" in *The Federalist*, p. 58.

3. SAUDI ARABIA: THE POLITICS OF OIL

1. Quoted in David H. Finnie, *Pioneers East* (Cambridge, Mass.: Harvard University Press, 1967), p. 2.

2. Quoted by Joseph J. Malone in "America and the Arabian Peninsula: the First Two Hundred Years," *Middle East Journal*, Summer 1976, p. 419.

3. Figures used by Emile A. Nakhleh in *The United States and Saudi Arabia* (Washington, D.C.: American Enterprise Institute, 1975), pp. 11–12.

4. *BP Statistical Review of the World Oil Industry 1979* (London, 1980). 1980 figures are based on preliminary estimates in *Oil and Gas Journal*, December 29, 1980.

5. *Ibid.*; Roger Stobaugh and Daniel Yergin, "Energy: An Emergency Telescoped," *Foreign Affairs: America and the World 1979*, vol. 58, no. 3, Council on Foreign Relations, 1980, pp. 578–9; Exxon Background Series, *World Energy Outlook*, December 1980, p. 22.

6. Energy Information Administration, United States Department of Energy, *Monthly Energy Review*, April 1981.

7. Walter J. Levy, "Oil: An Agenda for the 1980's," *Foreign Affairs*, vol. 59, no. 5, Summer 1981, p. 1084.

8. *The Middle East*, 3rd ed. (Washington, D.C.: Congressional Quarterly, 1977), p. 142.

9. *Ibid.*, p. 123.

10. Adeed I. Dawisha, "Saudi Arabia in the Eighties: The Mecca Siege and After," a paper presented at the Wilson Center, Smithsonian Institution, Washington, D.C., November 6, 1980, p. 16.

11. *The Middle East*, 3rd ed., p. 141.

12. Exxon Background Series, *World Energy Outlook*, December 1980, p. 20.

13. Source: United States Bureau of Mines, "Supply, Demand and Stocks by P.A.D. District, Annual," July 1977.

14. *Project Interdependence: United States and World Energy Outlook Through 1990*, A Summary Report by the Congressional Research Service, Library of Congress, June 1977 (Washington, D.C.: U.S. Government Printing Office, 1977), pp. 50–51.

15. Seth Tillman, *The Middle East Between War and Peace, November–December 1973*, a Staff Report to the Subcommittee on Near Eastern Affairs, Committee on Foreign Relations, U.S. Senate March 5, 1974 (Washington, D.C.: U.S. Government Printing Office, 1974), p. 17.

16. Malone, "America and the Arabian Peninsula," *Middle East Journal*, Summer 1976, pp. 418–19.

17. Data provided by ARAMCO, Washington, D.C. See also *The Middle East*, pp. 52–53.

18. See Dankwart A. Rustow, "United States-Saudi Relations and the Oil Crises of the 1980's," *Foreign Affairs*, April 1977, pp. 503–506.

19. Steven Rattner, "OPEC Freezes Price of Oil, Establishes Cuts in Production," *New York Times*, May 27, 1981, pp. A1, D13.

20. Walter J. Levy, "The Years That the Locust Hath Eaten: Oil Policy and OPEC Development Prospects," *Foreign Affairs*, vol. 57, no. 2, Winter 1978–79, pp. 291, 303.

21. "The Stand-Off in OPEC," *Washington Post*, May 27, 1981, p. A18.

22. Levy, "Oil: An Agenda for the 1980's," *Foreign Affairs*, Summer 1981, p. 1099.

23. Quoted in *The Middle East*, p. 51.

24. See Levy, "The Year That the Locust Hath Eaten," *Foreign Affairs*, Winter 1978-9, pp. 298–9, 304–5.

25. Abdul Kasim Mansur, "The American Threat to Saudi Arabia," *Armed Forces Journal International*, September 1980, p. 58.

26. *Middle East Arms Sales Proposals*, Hearings before the Committee on Foreign Relations, U.S. Senate (Washington, D.C.: U.S. Government Printing Office, 1978), p. 164.

27. Ibid., pp. 144–146.

28. Daniel Yergin, "The Real Meaning of the Energy Crunch," *New York Times Magazine*, June 4, 1978, pp. 98–99.

29. Dawisha, "Saudi Arabia in the Eighties: The Mecca Siege and After," pp. 1–5.

30. "The Sale of F–15's to Saudi Arabia," a trip report for the Senate Foreign Relations Committee by Hans Binnendijk and Bill Richardson, February 16, 1978, *Middle East Arms Sales Proposals*, pp. 249–250.

31. John Duke Anthony, "Westernization, Nationalism, Ideology," a lecture delivered at the Aspen Institute Mideast Project Seminar, "The Shaping of the Arab World," Punalu'u, Hawaii, January 19, 1979.

32. Nakhleh, *The United States and Saudi Arabia*, pp. 30–32, 46–47.

33. Figures quoted in *Open Doors*, edited by Alfred C. Julian and Robert F. Slattery (New York: Institute of International Education, 1978).

34. John M. Goshko, "Connally Outlines Proposal for Overall Mideast Peace," *Washington Post*, October 12, 1979, pp. A1, A4.

35. *Near East Report*, vol. 23, no. 41, October 17, 1979, p. 183.

36. "Merchants of Myth," *New York Times*, October 21, 1979, p. 20E.

37. Hearings before the Subcommittee on Near Eastern and South Asian Affairs of the Committee on Foreign Relations, U.S. Senate, *Middle East Peace Prospects* (Washington, D.C.: U.S. Government Printing Office, 1976), pp. 220–221.

38. Ibid., p. 216.

39. Quoted in *The Middle East*, p. 55.

40. Ibid., p. 71.

41. Senator Howard H. Baker, Jr., *Peace and Stability in the Middle East*, A Report to the Committee on Foreign Relations, U.S. Senate (Washington, D.C.: U.S. Government Printing Office, 1975), p. 17.

42. "Crown Prince Fahd," *Washington Post*, May 25, 1980, p. A22.

43. Hearings before Committee on Foreign Relations Subcommittee on Near Eastern and South Asian Affairs, *Middle East Peace Prospects*, pp. 222, 207.

44. Ibid., p. 219.

45. Ibid., p. 224.

46. He so informed the writer, then a member of the staff of the Senate Foreign Relations Committee.

47. *Congressional Record*, Senate, 93rd Congress, First Session, May 21, 1973, p. S 9445.

48. Ibid., p. S 9447.

49. Tillman, *The Middle East Between War and Peace*, p. 14.

50. Ibid., p. 22.

51. *The Middle East*, p. 123

52. Quoted in "Ship Rescue Toll 5 Killed, 16 Missing, 70–80 Hurt," *New York Times*, May 19, 1975, p. 4.

53. George C. Wilson, "New United States Military Plan: European, Persian Focus," *Washington Post*, January 27, 1978, pp. A1, A17.

54. Fern Racine Gold and Melvin A. Conant, *Access to Oil—The United States Relationship with Saudi Arabia and Iran*, printed for the use of the Committee on Energy and Natural Resources (Washington, D.C.: U.S. Government Printing Office, 1977), pp. 60, 63.

55. "Brown: U.S. Would Defend Oil Interests," *Washington Post*, February 26, 1979, p. A14.

56. Press Conference of April 26, 1978, *New York Times*, April 27, 1978, p. A20.

57. The letter was signed by Senators Frank Church (D-Idaho), Joseph R. Biden (D-Delaware), Paul S. Sarbanes (D-Maryland), Dick Clark (D-Iowa), Richard Stone (D-Florida), Claiborne Pell (D-Rhode Island) and Clifford P. Case (R-New Jersey).

58. Senators Howard Baker (R-Tennessee), James B. Pearson (R-Kansas) and Jacob Javits (R-New York).

59. James Reston, "How to Double Trouble," *New York Times*, January 27, 1978, p. A25.

60. Rowland Evans and Robert Novak, "Carter's Dilemma on Saudi Arms Sale," *Washington Post*, February 2, 1978, p. A19.

61. See chapter 2, p. 53.

62. Quoted by Bernard Weintraub in "Israel Says Sending United States Jet to Arabs Would Endanger Its Security," *New York Times*, May 15, 1978, p. A3.

63. "Beyond the Interim Agreement," Address to the Annual Conference of the Middle East Institute, Washington, D.C., October 3, 1975.

64. "Assurances from 15 Governments to Israel," in *Early Warning System in Sinai*, Hearings before the Committee on Foreign Relations, U.S. Senate, 94th Congress, October 6 and 7, 1975 (Washington, D.C.: U.S. Government Printing Office, 1975), p. 252.

65. See chapter 2, p. 52.

66. Quoted by William E. Farrell in "Begin and Other Israelis Deplore Senate Vote on Jets," *New York Times*, May 17, 1978, p. A3.

67. Peter Osnos and David B. Ottaway, "Yamani Links F–15's to Oil, Dollar Help," *Washington Post*, May 2, 1978, pp. A1, A10.

68. Foreign Broadcast Information Service, Arabian Peninsula, May 4, 1978, p. C2.

69. Don Oberdorfer and Bill Peterson, "Saudi Leader Appeals for F–15's for Defense," *Washington Post*, May 14, 1978, p. A1.

70. See, for example, the statement of Morris J. Amitay, Executive Director, American-Israel Public Affairs Committee, in *Middle East Arms Sales Proposals*, pp. 164, 168.

71. For a concise analysis of Saudi security interests see Dale R. Tahtinen, *National Security Challenges to Saudi Arabia*, (Washington, D.C.: American Enterprise Institute, 1978).

72. *Middle East Arms Sales Proposals*, pp. 163, 184.

73. Ibid., p. 166.

74. Ibid., p. 171.

75. Ibid., pp. 178–180. The word "commodity" in the last sentence quoted appears as "community" in the published hearings. Richardson advises that this was an error.

76. *Congressional Record*, 95th Congress, Second Session, May 15, 1978, pp. S7377–8.

77. Ibid., pp. S7382, S7384.

78. Ibid., pp. S7407–9.

79. Ibid., pp. S7409.

80. Ibid., p. S7417–8.

81. Ibid., p. S7426.

82. Ibid., p. S7428.

83. Ibid., p. S7429.

84. Ibid., pp. S7390–1.

85. Ibid., pp. S7395–6.

86. Ibid., pp. S7396–7.

87. Ibid., pp. S7398–9.

88. Ibid., pp. S7392–3.

89. Ibid., pp. S7393–5.

90. Ibid., pp. S7421–2.

91. This theme was exposited in a speech by the chairman of the Senate Foreign Relations Committee, Senator Frank Church of Idaho, who himself, however, had voted against the F–15 sale. "Return to the Path of Camp David," an address by Senator Frank Church before the Anti-Defamation League of B'nai B'rith, Palm Beach, Florida, February 1, 1979.

92. See chapter 5, pp. 201–210.

93. Bayly Winder in a panel of the 33rd Annual Conference of the Middle East Institute, of which the theme was, "The Middle East after Partial Peace: What Lies Ahead?" October 5, 1979.

94. See chapter 6, p. 263.

95. See chapter 1, pp. 36–37.

96. Jonathan C. Randal, "Arabs Approve Multi-Billion War Chest, Anti-Sadat Steps," *Washington Post*, November 6, 1978, p. A21.

97. Christopher S. Wren, "Sadat Seems Bitter at Arab Moderates," *New York Times*, November 21, 1978, p. A11.

98. Thomas W. Lippmann, "Economic Boycott of Egypt Imposed by Arab Countries," *Washington Post*, April 1, 1979, pp. A1, A26; Marvine Howe, "Arabs Agree to Cut All Cairo Ties in Retaliation for Pact with Israel," *New York Times*, April 1, 1979, pp. A1, A4; "Saudi Arabia-United States: That Special Relationship," in *Foreign Reports* (a newsletter on Saudi Arabia) April 25, 1979, p. 2.

99. Anthony Lewis, "Saudi Crown Prince Urges U.S. to Start Talks with PLO," *New York Times*, June 22, 1979, p. A2.

100. Thomas W. Lippmann, "Saudis to Close Arab Arms Firm to Punish Egypt," *Washington Post*, May 15, 1979, pp. A1, A14; Christopher S. Wren, "Saudis Scuttle a Billion-Dollar Arms Consortium with Factories in Egypt," *New York Times*, May 15, 1979, p. A3.

101. In testimony before the House Foreign Affairs Committee, May 8, 1979. "Vance Sees Decline in U.S.-Saudi Links," *New York Times*, May 9, 1979, pp. A1, A11.

102. James Reston, "A Spasm of Pessimism," *New York Times*, May 16, 1979, p. A27.

103. "The Saudis and the Camp David Three," *Washington Post*, May 16, 1979, p. A26.

104. Bernard Gwertzman, "Saudis and U.S. Act to Keep Close Ties," *New York Times*, May 16, 1979, p. A7.

105. "Vance Sees Decline in U.S.- Saudi Links," *New York Times*, May 9, 1979, pp. A1, A11.

106. Chapter 5, "Camp David, The Arabs and The Palestinians."

107. Christopher S. Wren, "Sadat Seems Bitter at Arab Moderates," *New York Times*, November 21, 1978, p. A11.

108. Interview with Fawzi Shubokshi, Director of Western Hemisphere Affairs, Foreign Ministry, Jidda, October 25, 1978.

109. Interview with Prince Turki al-Faisal, Director General of Intelligence, Jidda, October 25, 1978.

110. Martin Tolchin, "Carter Says No Top Arab He's Met Privately Backs a Palestinian State," *New York Times*, September 1, 1979, pp. 1, 5.

111. Jim Hoagland, "Saud Politely Disagrees on Palestinians," *Washington Post*, October 5, 1979, p. A5.

112. See chapter 6, pp. 266–267.

113. On the effects of the Iranian revolution on Saudi attitudes toward the Palestinians and Camp David peace process, see John K. Cooley, "Iran, the Palestinians, and the Gulf," *Foreign Affairs*, vol. 57, no. 5, Summer 1979, pp. 1026–31.

114. Paul Lewis, "OPEC Reaffirms Its Economic Power," *New York Times*, March 28, 1979, p. D11.

115. Anthony J. Parisi, "Oil Shortages: Then and Now," *New York Times*, May 16, 1979, pp. A1, A19.

116. Anthony Lewis, "The Riddle of the Saudis," *New York Times*, June 25, 1979, p. A17.

117. "Text of OPEC's Communiqué on Oil at End of Ministerial Meeting in Geneva," *New York Times*, June 29, 1979, p. D4; Youssef M. Ibrahim, "OPEC Increasing Oil Price 16%, Making Total for Year 50%; Carter Offers Import Limits," *New York Times*, June 29, 1979, pp. A1, D4.

118. Memorandum for the President from Stuart Eizenstat, June 28, 1979, "'Nothing Else Has So Frustrated the American People,'" *Washington Post*, July 7, 1979, p. A10.

119. Bernard Gwertzman, "Saudi Oil: Secret Deal or Shortage of Cash," *New York Times*, July 12, 1979, p. A3.

120. "Transcript of the President's Address to Association of Counties in Kansas City," *New York Times*, July 17, 1979, p. A14.

121. Bernard Gwertzman, "U.S. to Sell Saudis $1.2 Billion in Arms," *New York Times*, July 14, 1979, pp. 1, 3.

122. Hobart Rowen, "'A Hollow Ring,'" *Washington Post*, July 19, 1979, p. A19.

123. "The Issue Is Blackmail," *New York Times*, August 5, 1979.

124. Jack Anderson, "Desert Sheiks Use Oil to Punish U.S.," *Washington Post*, July 11, 1979, p. C23.

125. Herblock, "After All What Are Friends For?" *Washington Post*, July 12, 1979, p. A16.

126. Martin Tolchin, "Carter Says No Top Arab He's Met Privately Backs a Palestinian State," *New York Times*, September 1, 1979, pp. 1, 5.

127. Hedrick Smith, "U.S. Urging Speed in West Bank Talks," *New York Times*, August 2, 1979, pp. A1, A7.

128. Edward Cody, "Dayan Charges U.S. Shifts Policy to Ensure Oil," *Washington Post*, August 8, 1979, pp. A1, A12.

129. Maurice Carroll, "Moynihan Bars 'Sacrifice' of Israel," *New York Times*, August 9, 1979, p. A10.

130. "Transcript of President's State of the Union Address to Joint Session of Congress," *New York Times*, January 24, 1980, p. A12.

131. Nigel Harvey, "Saudis Tacitly Approve Rapid Deployment Force but Oppose Gulf Bases," *Washington Post*, March 25, 1981, p. A16.

132. Bernard Gwertzman, "Haig Ends Mideast Tour Saying Results Please Him," *New York Times*, April 9, 1981, p. A12.

133. Philip Geyelin, "A Saudi Quid for the F–15 Quo?", *Washington Post*, March 27, 1981, p. A17.

134. Bernard Gwertzman, "U.S. Decides to Sell Equipment to Saudis to Bolster F–15 Jets," *New York Times*, March 7, 1981, pp. 1, 7.

135. Bernard Gwertzman, "Saudis' AWACS: Afterthoughts," *New York Times*, April 16, 1981, p. A1.

136. A Report to the United States Senate by Senator Howard H. Baker, Jr., *A Senate Perspective on Spain and the Middle East*, June 1981 (Washington, D.C.: U.S. Government Printing Office, 1981), p. 9.

137. Rowland Evans and Robert Novak, "Reagan, Israel and the F–15s," *Washington Post*, February 13, 1981, p. A19.

138. William Claiborne, "Begin Assails AWACS Sale to Saudis," *Washington Post*, April 23, 1981, pp. A1, A30.

139. "It's Time to Get Off Our Knees America," *New York Times*, May 29, 1981, p. A11.

140. Richard Halloran, "Majority in Congress Urge Reagan Not to Sell AWACS to Saudi Arabia," *New York Times*, June 25, 1981, pp. A1, A4.

141. "Resolution on AWACS and Remarks at Capitol," *New York Times*, September 18, 1981, p. A10.

142. "Transcript of President's News Conference on Foreign and Domestic Matters," *New York Times*, October 2, 1981, p. A26.

143. Soliman A. Solaim, "A Saudi Viewpoint on AWACS," *Washington Post*, September 21, 1981, p. A13.

144. "Excerpts from Israeli Foreign Minister's Speech," *New York Times*, October 6, 1981, p. A10.

145. "Excerpts from Reagan Letter to Baker on AWACS," *New York Times*, October 29, 1981, p. B10.

146. *Congressional Record*, 97th Congress, First Session, October 28, 1981, p. S12401.

147. Howell Raines, "President Praises Senate's Action as Statesmanlike and Courageous," *New York Times*, October 29, 1981, p. B11.

148. David K. Shipler, "Begin Ridicules Idea of Saudi Help in Crisis," *New York Times*, May 19, 1981, p. A3.

4. ISRAEL: THE POLITICS OF FEAR

1. Quoted by Thomas W. Lippmann in "Sinai Gap 'Is Bridgeable,' " *Washington Post*, January 13, 1978, p. A20.

2. Amos Elon, *The Israelis* (New York: Holt, Rinehart and Winston, 1971), p. 213.

3. Yigal Allon, "Israel: the Case for Defensible Borders," *Foreign Affairs*, vol. 55, no. 1, October 1976, p. 39.

4. Arie Lova Eliav, *Land of the Hart* (Philadelphia: The Jewish Publication Society of America, 1974), p. 20.

5. Nahum Goldmann, "The Psychology of Middle East Peace," *Foreign Affairs*, vol. 54, no. 1, October 1975, p. 117.

6. Quoted by Jonathan Kandell in "Merchants of Jerusalem Live in Fear of Bombing," *New York Times*, January 24, 1979, p. A3.

7. Senator George S. McGovern, *Realities of the Middle East*, A Report to the Senate Foreign Relations Committee, United States Congress (Washington, D.C.: U.S. Government Printing Office, 1975), p. 28.

8. Edward R. F. Sheehan, *The Arabs, Israelis and Kissinger* (New York: Reader's Digest Press, 1976), p. 162. The account of this exchange was drawn from

briefings given Sheehan by State Department officials based on the secret, official record of the secretary's conversations with Israeli officials.

9. Ibid., p. 163.

10. Notes kept by the writer, who accompanied Senator McGovern on a tour of the Middle East. See McGovern, *Realities of the Middle East*, pp. 26–27.

11. Poll taken by Louis Guttman, director of the Israeli Institute of Applied Social Research, reported in "Polls Show Impact of Sadat Visit," *Washington Post*, December 9, 1977, p. A30.

12. Poll taken by the Israeli Institute of Applied Social Research and the Communications Institute of Hebrew University, reported in "72 Per Cent in Israel Back Settlements in Sinai," *New York Times*, January 23, 1978, p. A3.

13. Reported by H.D.S. Greenway in "Begin Defends Israel's Stand in Middle East Talks," *Washington Post*, January 20, 1978, p. A29.

14. Ezer Weizman, *The Battle for Peace* (New York: Bantam Books, 1981), pp. 386–387.

15. Chapter 1, p. 20.

16. Quoted by Peter Grose in "Israel and United States in a Game of 'Diplomatic Chicken,'" *New York Times*, March 21, 1971, p. 4E.

17. Goldmann, "The Psychology of Middle East Peace," *Foreign Affairs*, October 1975, p. 117.

18. See chapter 1, p. 19.

19. Elon, *The Israelis*, pp. 225–226.

20. Edward W. Said, *The Question of Palestine* (New York: Vintage Books, 1980), p. 231.

21. Menachem Begin, *The Revolt* (London: W. H. Allen, 1951), p. 3.

22. Ibid.

23. Ibid.

24. Ibid.; Uri Avnery, "Menachem Begin: The Reality," *Worldview*, vol. 21, no. 6, June 1978, p. 5.

25. Begin, *The Revolt*, pp. 4, 373.

26. Ibid., p. 335.

27. Ibid., p. 335.

28. See chapter 1, pp. 18–19.

29. Quoted by William E. Farrell in "Israel Turns Down Appeal from Egypt for Friendly Move," *New York Times*, July 24, 1978, p. A3.

30. Amos Perlmutter, "Israel's de Gaulle," *Newsweek*, August 15, 1977, p. 29.

31. Genesis, xii, 1–3.

32. Begin, *The Revolt*, p. 372.

33. Ibid., p. 374.

34. Ibid., p. 376.

35. Ibid., p. 311.

36. Prime Minister Begin's Address to the Knesset, November 20, 1977 (*New York Times*, November 21, 1977, p. 14).

37. Begin, *The Revolt*, chapter 4.

38. Begin's Address to the Knesset, November 20, 1977 (*New York Times*, November 21, 1977, p. 14).

39. Interview with Israeli television, September 18, 1978. Reported by Jim Hoagland in "Dispute on Israeli Settlements Snags Accord," *Washington Post*, September 20, 1978, p. A1.

40. "Excerpts from Begin's News Conference at National Press Club in Washington, March 23, 1978," *New York Times*, March 24, 1978, p. A10.

41. Section A, paragraph 2.

42. Quoted by Jim Hoagland in "Dispute on Israeli Settlements Snags Accord," *Washington Post*, September 20, 1978, pp. A1, A11.

43. Quoted in "Sadat, Begin Tout Accords before Friendly Audiences," *Washington Star*, September 21, 1978.

44. Statement issued by the Israeli Ministry of Foreign Affairs, Jerusalem, June 22, 1977.

45. Statement issued by Embassy of Israel, Washington, D.C., August 10, 1977.

46. Transcript of interview with Moshe Dayan on "Face the Nation," September 25, 1977, CBS News, Washington, D.C.; Foreign Broadcast Information Service, Daily Report, *Middle East and North Africa*, October 4, 1977, p. N4.

47. Foreign Broadcast Information Service, Daily Report, *Middle East and North Africa*, August 10, 1977, p. N2.

48. William E. Farrell, "Israel Schedules Policy Statement and Debate on Middle East Today," *New York Times*, November 28, 1977, pp. 1, 12.

49. Interview with the *Sunday Times* (London), June 15, 1969. Quoted in *Israelis Speak* (Larry L. Fabian and Ze'ev Schiff, eds., New York and Washington, D.C.: Carnegie Endowment for International Peace, 1977), p. 15.

50. Joseph Kraft, "A Fear of Peace," *Washington Post*, December 1, 1977, p. A17.

51. Chapter 1, p. 5.

52. "Principles of Negotiation," Embassy of Israel, Washington, D.C., April 6, 1968, p. 3.

53. Abba Eban, "Camp David—The Unfinished Business," *Foreign Affairs*, vol. 57, no. 2, Winter 1978/79, pp. 344, 351.

54. Interview at Hebrew University, Jerusalem, November 6, 1978.

55. Eban, "Camp David—The Unfinished Business," *Foreign Affairs*, Winter 1978/79, p. 352.

56. Interview of November 6, 1978.

57. Quoted by William Claiborne in "Begin Urges Acceptance of Accords," *Washington Post*, September 26, 1978, pp. A1, A12.

58. William Claiborne, "West Bank, Golan Settlements to Be Enlarged, Begin Says," *Washington Post*, October 26, 1978, p. A27.

59. William Claiborne, "Israel Stresses Claims to Occupied Territories," *Washington Post*, October 27, 1978, p. A1.

60. John M. Goshko, "U.S., Israel at Odds on West Bank Settlements," *Washington Post*, October 27, 1978, pp. A1, A14.

61. William Claiborne, "Begin Reaffirms Settlement Policy in Reply to U.S.," *Washington Post*, October 30, 1978, p. A1.

62. William Claiborne, "Israel Stresses Claims to Occupied Territories," *Washington Post*, October 27, 1978, pp. A1, A14.

63. Interview in Jerusalem, November 6, 1978.

64. Interview at Bir Zeit University, West Bank, November 4, 1978.

65. Interview in Damascus, October 28, 1978.

66. "NAAA Trip Report and Recommendations," December 28, 1978.

67. Quoted by David Landau in "Will Israel Accept a Palestinian State?" *Washington Post*, October 20, 1978, p. A17.

68. Elon, *The Israelis*, p. 324.

69. Marvine Howe, "Sadat Calls Begin 'The Only Obstacle' to Mideast Accord," *New York Times*, July 23, 1978, pp. A1, A4.

70. The "Rogers Plan" of December 9, 1969, set forth this criterion. See chapter 2, pp. 56–57.

71. This summary of the "Allon Plan" is based on an address by Yigal Allon at the Hebrew University, June 3, 1973 and on a description contained in *The Allon Plan* by Yoram Cohen (1972), translated from the Hebrew. Both quoted in *Israelis Speak*, pp. 207–212.

72. Ibid., p. 211.

73. Ibid., p. 208.

74. Allon, "Israel: The Case for Defensible Borders," *Foreign Affairs*, October 1976, p. 48.

75. Ibid., p. 38.

76. McGovern, *Realities of the Middle East*, p. 22.

77. Ibid.

78. Allon, "Israel: The Case for Defensible Borders," *Foreign Affairs*, October 1976, pp. 44–48.

79. Ibid., p. 50.

80. "Prospects for Peace," *Newsweek*, September 11, 1978, p. 42.

81. Shimon Peres, "Herut and Labor," *New York Times*, August 6, 1978, p. E17.

82. Abba Eban, "Begin's Choice: Peace—or Party Platform," *Washington Post*, March 24, 1978, p. A12. For a fuller exposition of the "partition logic," see Eban, "Camp David—The Unfinished Business," *Foreign Affairs*, Winter 1978/79, pp. 343–354.

83. "It's just not true" that Egypt's policy would be governed by Israel's settlements policy and other matters affecting the West Bank, a foreign ministry official stated in an interview. Egypt's stake in peace, he said, would be determined by its "domestic agenda." Interview with Gad Ranon, Director, North American Division, Ministry of Foreign Affairs, November 6, 1978.

84. William Claiborne, "Israel to Repeat Earlier Proposal at Camp David," *Washington Post*, August 28, 1978, pp. A1, A18.

85. Quoted in "For the Record," *Washington Post*, September 3, 1978, p. C7.

86. McGovern, *Realities of the Middle East*, p. 24.

87. Interview with Mark Bruzonsky in *Worldview*, vol. 21, nos. 1–2, January-February 1978, p. 8.

88. Interview of Professor Hisham Sharabi with Mark Bruzonsky, "Forum," *The Middle East*, August 1978, p. 41.

89. Elon, *The Israelis* p. 156.

90. Ibid., p. 159.

91. Quoted by Said in *The Question of Palestine*, p. 13.

92. Quoted in *Israelis Speak*, p. 15.

93. Said, *The Question of Palestine*, p. 19.

94. Elon, *The Israelis*, pp. 156–157.

95. Quoted in "President and Golda Meir Disagree," *New York Times*, November 9, 1977, p. A8.

96. "Remarks by Begin at the Dinner for Participants in Jerusalem Talks," *New York Times*, January 19, 1978, p. A12.

97. "Excerps from Interview with Begin on the Prospects of the Cairo Conference," *New York Times*, December 14, 1977, p. A20.

98. One notable example is former Foreign Minister Abba Eban, who concedes the validity of Palestinian nationalism but stops well short of advocating Palestinian self-determination for the West Bank and Gaza, arguing instead for partition of the occupied territories and some ultimate undefined form of Arab sovereignty in "large areas west of the River." See, for example, Eban's article, "Camp David—The Unfinished Business," cited previously in *Foreign Affairs*, Winter 1978/79, pp. 343–354.

99. Eliav, *Land of the Hart*, p. 120.

100. Ibid.

101. Goldmann, "The Psychology of Middle East Peace," *Foreign Affairs*, October 1975, p. 121.

102. From a series of articles by Nahum Goldmann in the Israeli newspaper *Ha'aretz*, November 8–13, 1974, entitled "Israeli Policy: Proposals for Action." Reprinted in *Journal of Palestine Studies*, vol. IV, no. 2, Winter 1975, p. 129.

103. Meir Merhav, "The Palestinian Reality," *New York Times*, November 7, 1977, p. 37.

104. Joint interview with Flapan and Avnery in Tel Aviv, November 3, 1978.

105. Interview with Eliav in Tel Aviv, November 3, 1978.

106. Ibid.

107. Ibid.

108. Ibid.

109. For a full exposition of Peres's position, see Shimon Peres, "A Strategy for Peace in the Middle East," *Foreign Affairs*, vol. 58, no. 4, Spring 1980, pp. 887–901. The words quoted are on p. 893.

110. David K. Shipler, "On Israel's Ultimate Issue, Peres Is No Radical," *New York Times*, December 21, 1980, p. E5.

111. William Claiborne, "Begin Discloses Dayan Met with King Hussein," *Washington Post*, June 6, 1980, pp. A1, A20.

112. "Israelis Preparing Political Campaign," *New York Times*, August 7, 1980, p. A11.

113. Henry Tanner, "Jordan Acts to Aid Iraq With Supplies For War With Iran," *New York Times*, October 7, 1980, pp. A1, A14.

114. Jordan-Georgetown Seminar, Amman, Jordan, January 7, 1981.

115. David B. Ottaway, "Hussein Disavows 'Jordanian Option', Criticizes Tour by Kissinger," *Washington Post*, January 30, 1981, p. A17.

116. William Claiborne, "Election Rival Says Begin Timed Raid to Win Votes," *Washington Post*, June 11, 1981, pp. A1, A28.

117. Anthony Lewis, "Once and Future King?" *New York Times*, June 25, 1981, p. A19.

118. Terence Smith, "Administration's Discovery: Israelis Put Security First," *New York Times*, July 26, 1981, p. E1.

119. U.S. assistance to Israel represented 49 percent of total U.S. world assistance for the fiscal years 1973–1978. Outright grants to Israel represented 60 percent of total world grants in fiscal 1977 and 63 percent in fiscal 1978. Source: "U.S. Assistance to Israel," U.S. Department of State, updated June 23, 1978. Between 1948 and the end of fiscal 1980, Israel received $12,904,200,000 in U.S. military assistance and $5,585,800,000 in economic assistance. Source: Agency for International Development, July 1981.

120. Source: "Foreign Economic Trends and Their Implications for the U.S.: Israel," prepared by U.S. Department of State and released by U.S. Department of Commerce, July 1978, p. 8.

121. Quoted in the first section of this chapter.

122. I. L. Kenen, "A Forum: Voices Before the Summit," *Washington Star*, September 3, 1978, pp. D1, D4.

123. "Excerpts from Interview with Begin on the Prospects of the Cairo Conference," *New York Times*, December 14, 1977, p. A20.

124. "Excerpts from Begin's News Conference at National Press Club in Washington," *New York Times*, March 24, 1978, p. A10.

125. Interviews with Senator George McGovern, accompanied by the writer, April 1975.

126. Eliav, *Land of the Hart*, p. 237.

127. Kennett Love, *Suez* (New York: McGraw-Hill, 1969), p. 664.

128. Anthony H. Cordesman, "How Much is Too Much?" *Armed Forces Journal International*, October 1977, pp. 32–39.

129. Jim Hoagland, "Israeli Contingency Plan Readied," *Washington Post*, October 26, 1977, pp. A1, A9.

130. Deborah Shapley, "CIA Report Says Israel Secretly Obtained A-Matter," *Washington Post*, January 28, 1978, p. A2.

131. William Claiborne, "Israel, Early to Recognize Peking, Quiet on U.S. Move," *Washington Post*, December 27, 1978, p. A8.

132. William Claiborne, "Oil Affects Israeli Stance," *Washington Post*, February 23, 1979, pp. A1, A26.

133. Jonathan Kandell, "Iran's Exile Leader Warns West on Oil," *New York Times*, December 14, 1978, p. A8.

134. Wolfgang Saxon, "Arab Leaders Call Iran Shift Historic," *New York Times*, February 14, 1979, p. A9.

135. "Khomeini Assails Iranian Marxists for 'Evil' Aim in Continuing Fight," *New York Times*, February 20, 1979, pp. A1, A4.

136. Paul Hoffman, "Israeli Says Iranian Crisis Means Sinai Pact Must Include Oil Deal," *New York Times*, February 4, 1979, p. A16.

137. "Text of the President's Address and Excerpts from the Prime Minister's Reply," *New York Times*, March 13, 1979, p. A10.

138. Ibid.

139. "State Department Explains U.S.-Israeli Memo," *Washington Post*, March 30, 1979, p. A18.

140. Quoted by Stephen S. Rosenfeld in "The Language and the Chemistry," *Washington Post*, March 30, 1979, p. A23.

141. Goldmann, "The Psychology of Middle East Peace," *Foreign Affairs*, October 1975, p. 118.

142. Quoted by Elon in *The Israelis*, p. 214.

143. Eliav, *Land of the Hart*, p. 218.

144. Quoted in *The Middle East*, 3rd. ed. (Washington, D.C.: Congressional Quarterly, September 1977), p. 94.

145. Foreign Broadcast Information Service, *Middle East and North Africa*, Daily Report, vol. V, no. 192, October 4, 1977, p. N6.

146. "Begin Tells U.S. Jews His Visit was Success," *New York Times*, March 8, 1979, p. A14.

147. Eliav, *Land of the Hart*, p. 236.

148. Hedrick Smith, "Begin, with a Dinner Comment, Turns a Smiling Carter Ashen," *New York Times*, March 12, 1979, pp. A1, A8.

149. The Civilians Convention of August 12, 1949, Relating to Protection of Civilian Persons in Time of War (1955), 6 UST 3516—TIAS 3365 75 UNTS 287.

150. "Jewish Settlements in the Areas Administered by Israel," distributed by the Information Department of the Embassy of Israel, Washington, D.C., under cover of a letter dated October 25, 1977.

151. Seth Tillman, "The West Bank Hearings," *Journal of Palestine Studies*, vol. VII, no 2, Winter 1978, pp. 75–77.

152. United Nations General Assembly, October 28, 1977, General Assembly Document 32/5.

153. Kathleen Teltsch, "Egypt Denounces Israel at UN for Settlements in Arab Lands," *New York Times*, October 27, 1977, p. A3.

154. Tillman, "The West Bank Hearings," *Journal of Palestine Studies*, Winter 1978, pp. 77–78.

155. President Carter's News Conference of July 28, 1977, *Weekly Compilation of Presidential Documents*, vol. 13, no. 31, August 1, 1977, p. 1121.

156. President Carter's News Conference of August 23, 1977, *Weekly Compilation of Presidential Documents*, vol. 13, no. 35, August 29, 1977, p. 1243.

157. President Carter's News Conference of January 30, 1978, *New York Times*, January 31, 1978, p. A10.

158. Bernard Gwertzman, "Carter Voices Worry to Israel on Settlement," *New York Times*, January 30, 1978, pp. A1, A4.

159. William E. Farrell, "Three Israeli Outposts Built on West Bank Will Go to Settlers," *New York Times*, February 1, 1978, pp. A1, A7.

160. Terence Smith, "Israel Is Said to Have Altered Dayan Pledge to Carter on Settlements," *New York Times*, January 31, 1978, p. A3.

161. Moshe Brilliant, "Dayan Denies Pledge," *New York Times*, February 2, 1978, pp. A1, A4.

162. "Those Creeping Israeli Settlements," *New York Times*, February 2, 1978, p. A28.

163. "Settlements or Settlement?" *Washington Post*, February 2, 1978, p. A18.

164. See, for example, Anthony Lewis, "In Occupied Territory," *New York Times*, May 25, 1978, p. A23; William E. Farrell, "Israeli Court Halts a Settlement on Arab Land Pending an Appeal," *New York Times*, May 26, 1978, pp. A1, A4; H. D. S. Greenway, "Struggle for a 'Twice-Promised Land'," *Washington Post*, May 31, 1978, p. A22; "Two Standards of Justice," *Time*, vol. 112, no. 8, August 21, 1978, p. 25; William Claiborne, "Israeli Court Blocks Work on a West Bank Settlement," *Washington Post*, September 18, 1978, p. A14; William Claiborne, "Arabs Charge Israelis Defy Court on West Bank Project," *Washington Post*, October 19, 1978, p. A30.

165. "Israeli Site Set for Dig is Actually for Homes," *New York Times*, May 31, 1978, p. A14.

166. Douglas Watson, "Israel Approves Settlements," *Baltimore Sun*, August 14, 1978, pp. A1, A2.

167. Yuval Elizur, "Settlements Held Up," *Washington Post*, August 15, 1978, pp. A1, A8.

168. John Vinocur, "Begin, in Geneva, Says New U.S. Arms to Egypt Would Raise War Peril," *New York Times*, February 10, 1978, p. A3.

169. "Israel Group Demands Seizure of Arab Lands," *New York Times*, June 8, 1978, p. A9.

170. Text of President Carter's Address to Congress, " 'Impossible Dream Now Becomes a Real Possibility'," *Washington Post*, September 19, 1978, p. A14.

171. See p. 134.

172. Jim Hoagland, "Dispute on Israeli Settlements Snags Accord," *Washington Post*, September 20, 1978, pp. A1, A11; Jim Hoagland, "Dispute over Settlements Puts Pact in Limbo," *Washington Post*, September 21, 1978, pp. A1, A14.

173. See p. 136.

174. Edward Walsh, "Carter Disputes Begin on West Bank Settlements," *Washington Post*, September 28, 1978, p. A25.

175. Jim Hoagland, "Conference Sought on Lebanon War," *Washington Post*, September 29, 1978, p. A10.

176. "Excerpts from President's Comments at News Conference," *Washington Post*, September 29, 1978, p. A11.

177. William Claiborne, "Begin Rules Out Palestinian State on West Bank," *Washington Post*, March 21, 1979, p. A1.

178. Kathleen Teltsch, "U.N. Group to Study Israeli Settlements," *New York Times*, March 23, 1979, p. A12.

179. Bernard Gwertzman, "Two New Settlements Approved by Israel," *New York Times,* April 24, 1979, pp. A1. A4.

180. "Vance Opposes Immediate Lift of Rhodesia Sanctions," *Washington Post,* April 27, 1979, p. A36.

181. Joseph Kraft, "Building the Temple," *Washington Post,* March 27, 1979, p. A19.

182. "Transcript of the President's News Conference on Foreign and Domestic Matters," April 30, 1979, *New York Times,* May 1, 1979, p. A18.

183. Bernard D. Nossiter, "U.S. Votes at U.N. to Rebuke Israelis over Settlements," *New York Times,* March 2, 1980, pp. A1, A8.

184. Edward Walsh and John M. Goshko, "Carter Says Error Lead to U.S. Vote Against Israelis," *Washington Post,* March 4, 1980, pp. A1, A12; David K. Shipler, "Israelis Criticize U.S. for U.N. Vote and Say Resolution is 'Repugnant'," *New York Times,* March 5, 1980, p. A12; Bernard Gwertzman, "An Issue of U.S. Credibility," *New York Times,* March 5, 1980, pp. A1, A12.

185. Bernard Gwertzman, "U.S. Assails Israelis for Seizure of Land Outside Jerusalem," *New York Times,* March 13, 1980, pp. A1, A10.

186. *Congressional Record-Senate,* June 17, 1980, pp. S7161–4.

187. Ibid., p. S7170.

188. Ibid.

189. Ibid.

190. Ibid., p. S7172.

191. Ibid., p. S7173.

192. Ibid., p. S7175.

193. Ibid., p. S7173.

194. Ibid., pp. S7175–6.

195. William Claiborne, "Israel Rules Out Change on Jerusalem," *Washington Post,* August 12, 1980, pp. A1, A7.

196. United Nations Security Council Official Records, 1483rd meeting, July 1, 1969, p. 11.

197. Bernard D. Nossiter, "Muskie Rebukes Security Council As It Votes 14–0 to Censure Israel," *New York Times,* August 21, 1980, p. A1; "Excerpts from Muskie's Speech to Security Council," *New York Times,* August 21, 1980, p. A5.

198. Quoted by William Claiborne and Edward Cody in "Israel Shapes Immutable Future for West Bank," *Washington Post,* September 7, 1980, pp. A1, A14.

199. "Excerpts from President Reagan's Answers in Interview with Five Reporters," *New York Times,* February 3, 1981, p. A14.

200. See Shai Feldman, "Peacemaking in the Middle East: The Next Step," *Foreign Affairs,* vol. 59. no. 4, Spring 1981, pp. 756–780.

201. Elon, *The Israelis,* pp. 239, 263–264.

202. Gad Ranon, Director, North American Division, Ministry of Foreign Affairs, Interview in Jerusalem, November 6, 1978.

203. Interview in Jerusalem, November 6, 1978, with Shlomo Avineri, Professor of Political Science, Hebrew University, and former director general of the Ministry of Foreign Affairs.

5. THE PALESTINIANS: NATION IN DIASPORA

1. See chapter 4, p. 146.

2. For an analysis of the nature of nationalism, see Hans Kohn, *Nationalism: Its Meaning and History* (Princeton: N.J.: D. Van Nostrand Co., Inc., 1955). The words quoted appear on p. 2.

3. From "The Plight of the People of Palestine," a leaflet issued by American Near East Refugee Aid, Inc., Washington, D.C.

4. Quoted in *A Select Chronology of Background Documents Relating to the Middle East*, Committee on Foreign Relations, United States Senate (Washington D.C.: U.S. Government Printing Office, 1975), p. 199.

5. Source: American Near East Refugee Aid.

6. *The Middle East*, 3rd. ed. (Washington, D.C.: Congressional Quarterly, 1977), pp. 5, 112.

7. See, for example, "The Case for Palestinian Rights," a paid advertisement of the Arab Information Center of the League of Arab States, *Washington Post*, October 26, 1977, p. F12.

8. *Congressional Record*, 93rd Congress, First Session, July 18, 1973, pp. 24465–68.

9. Amos Elon, *The Israelis* (New York: Holt, Rinehart and Winston, 1971), p. 264.

10. Interview with Eric Rouleau in *Le Monde*, January 7, 1975, quoted in *The Middle East*, p. 113.

11. See Rosemary Sayigh, "Sources of Palestinian Nationalism," *Journal of Palestine Studies*, vol. VI, no. 4, Summer 1977, esp. pp. 21–23.

12. Interview in Damascus, October 28, 1978.

13. Ibid.

14. Hisham Sharabi, "Liberation or Settlement: the Dialectics of Palestinian Struggle," *Journal of Palestine Studies*, vol. II, no. 2, Winter 1973, p. 44.

15. Chapter 1, p. 20.

16. John K. Cooley, *Green March, Black September* (London: Frank Cass, 1973), pp. 89–92.

17. Quoted ibid., p. 99.

18. Sharabi, "Liberation or Settlement," *Journal of Palestine Studies*, Winter 1973, p. 35.

19. Cooley, *Green March, Black September*, pp. 100–101.

20. See chapter 4, p. 146.

21. Senator George S. McGovern, *Realities of the Middle East*, a Report to the Senate Foreign Relations Committee, United States Congress (Washington, D.C.: U.S. Government Printing Office, 1975), p. 11.

22. *The Middle East*, p. 113.

23. Interview with Eric Rouleau in *Le Monde*, January 7, 1975, quoted ibid.

24. McGovern, *Realities of the Middle East*, p. 11.

25. See chapter 1, p. 21.

26. Quoted by I. F. Stone in his essay "The Other Zionism," in *Underground to Palestine: And Reflections Thirty Years Later* (New York: Pantheon Books, 1978), pp. 242, 246–247. *Underground to Palestine*, an account of Stone's journey to Palestine with Jewish refugees aboard an illegal ship after World War II, was first published in 1946.

27. *The Middle East*, pp. 109–110.

28. Moshe Brilliant, "Fatah Admits Raid," *New York Times*, March 12, 1978, pp. A1, A12.

29. Marian Howe, "Raid Jeopardizes Sadat Peace Initiatives; Palestinians Expect Reprisal," *New York Times*, March 12, 1978, pp. A10.

30. Henry Kamm, "Begin Hints Strongly at Reprisal as Death Toll in Raid Reaches 37," *New York Times*, March 13, 1978, p A10.

31. William E. Farrell, "Major Fighting Ends," *New York Times*, March 16, 1978, pp. A1, A16.

32. "Begin Vows Israeli Units Will Remain Until Peace," *New York Times*, March 16, 1978, p. A16.

33. William Claiborne, "Aftermath of Invasion," *Washington Post*, June 15, 1978, pp. A25, A26.

34. James M. Markham, "PLO Said to Reap Gains from Israeli Push into Lebanon," *New York Times*, June 25, 1978, p. A10.

35. "A Lebanon Balance Sheet," *New York Times*, April 17, 1978, pp. A22.

36. Quoted by H. D. S. Greenway in "Doubts in Israel on Lebanon Campaign," *Washington Post*, April 30, 1978, p. B3.

37. "Vance's Letter to Congress on Israeli Use of U.S. Arms," *New York Times*, April 6, 1978, pp. A14.

38. Bernard Gwertzman, "U.S. Says Israelis in Lebanon Used Cluster Bombs, Breaking Pledge," *New York Times*, April 8, 1978, pp. A1, A4.

39. "Arafat Charges Carter Ignores Mideast Civilian Toll," *Washington Post*, July 31, 1978, pp. A13.

40. "Israeli Attacks upon Lebanon," statement by Senator J. W. Fulbright, *Congressional Record—Senate*, August 22, 1974, pp. S15628.

41. Ibid.; Jim Hoagland, "Israel Widens Scale of Raids in Lebanon," *Washington Post*, June 21, 1974, pp. A1, A36.

42. "Yesterday's Raid Biggest but Not First by Israelis," *Washington Post*, March 16, 1978, pp. A16.

43. Moshe Brilliant, "Israeli Jets Strike Lebanon to Avenge Bombing in Tel Aviv," *New York Times*, August 4, 1978, pp. A1, A3.

44. "Arab Gunmen in London Hit Israeli Crew," *Washington Post*, August 20, 1978, pp. A1, A20.

45. Edward Cody, "Israeli Navy Hits Syrian Positions in West Beirut," *Washington Post*, October 6, 1978, pp. A1, A20.

46. Warren Brown, "Dayan: No Troops to Southern Lebanon," *Washington Post*, October 9, 1978, p. A18.

47. William Claiborne, "Dayan Intensifies Israeli Warnings over Lebanon," *Washington Post*, September 1, 1978, pp. A1, A13.

48. United Nations Security Council, Resolution 425 (1978), adopted by the Security Council at its 2074th meeting, March 19, 1978.

49. Ihsan A. Hijazi, "Forty Reported Killed in Attack by Israel," *New York Times*, January 20, 1979, pp. A1, A3; "Israeli Forces Attack Villages in Lebanon," *Washington Post*, January 19, 1979, p. A17.

50. "Alert Declared in Northern Israel," *New York Times*, January 20, 1979, p. A3.

51. Jonathan Kandell, "Warning to Israeli Arabs," *New York Times*, January 24, 1979, p. A4.

52. "Begin, Thousands Mourn Raid Victims," *Washington Post*, April 24, 1979, p. A16.

53. Marvine Howe, "Lebanese Continue Fleeing North in Spite of Truce," *New York Times*, April 28, 1979, p. 3.

54. Kathleen Teltsch, "U.S., at U.N., Calls Upon Israelis and PLO to End Lebanon War," *New York Times*, August 30, 1979, pp. A1, A7; "Begin Decries U.S. Criticism of Israeli Raids on Lebanon," *Washington Post*, August 31, 1979, p. A22.

55. David K. Shipler, "5 Are Killed in Palestinian Attack on Jewish Settlers in West Bank," *New York Times*, May 3, 1980, pp. A1, A5; David K. Shipler, "A Palestinian Guerrilla Describes Taking Combat Training in Soviet," *New York Times*, October 31, 1980, pp. A1, A4.

56. David K. Shipler, "3 West Bank Arabs Deported by Israel in Slaying of Jews," *New York Times*, May 4, 1980, p. A1.

57. David K. Shipler, "3 West Bank Bombs Maim Two Mayors; Jews Are Suspected," *New York Times*, June 3, 1980, pp. A1, A8.

58. Edward Cody, "West Bank Welcome," *Washington Post*, July 10, 1980, pp. A1, A23.

59. John Kifner, "Israeli Jets Leave 50 Dead on the Roads of Lebanon," *New York Times*, July 23, 1981, p. A12.

60. An account of the Munich episode is contained in Cooley, *Green March, Black September*, pp. 125–128.

61. Professor George Giacaman, quoted by Nicholas Gage in "Israel's Invasion of Lebanon Dims Hope on West Bank for End of Occupation," *New York Times*, March 30, 1978, p. A12.

62. Arafat's address to the United Nations General Assembly, November 13, 1974, quoted in *The Middle East*, p. 113.

63. Menachem Begin, *The Revolt* (London: W.H. Allen, 1951), pp. 59–60.

64. Quoted by Sally Quinn in "The Dove: 'A Voice in the Wilderness,' " *Washington Post*, October 12, 1978, pp. D1, D6.

65. Senator Howard H. Baker, Jr., *Peace and Stability in the Middle East*, A Report to the Committee on Foreign Relations, U.S. Senate (Washington, D.C.: U.S. Government Printing Office, 1975), p. 11.

66. Seth Tillman, *The Middle East Between War and Peace, November-December, 1973*, Staff Report, Subcommittee on Near Eastern Affairs, Committee on Foreign Relations, U.S. Senate (Washington, D.C.: U.S. Government Printing Office, 1974), pp. 26–27.

67. Baker, *Peace and Stability in the Middle East*, p. 10.

68. Ibid. p. 11.

69. Ibid. p. 10.

70. Menachem Begin, *The Revolt*, revised ed. (New York: Nash Publishing, 1977), pp. 216–22.

71. Ibid., p. 290.

72. See, for example, Fred J. Khouri, *The Arab-Israeli Dilemma* (Syracuse: Syracuse University Press, 1968), pp. 123–24.

73. Begin, *The Revolt*, revised ed., p. 164.

74. Stone, "The Other Zionism," in *Underground to Palestine: and Reflections Thirty Years Later*, pp. 258–59.

75. Quoted ibid., p. 258.

76. Mohammed Hallaj, Dean of Arts, Bir Zeit University, interview of November 4, 1978.

77. Sharabi, "Liberation or Settlement," *Journal of Palestine Studies*, Winter 1973, p. 34.

78. Edward Said, *The Question of Palestine* (New York: Vintage Books, 1980), pp. xiv, 26, 37-38, 194.

79. Quoted in *The Middle East*, p. 112.

80. "Excerpts from State Department Reports on the Status of Human Rights Abroad," *New York Times*, February 10, 1978, p. A14.

81. "Excerpts from U.S. Report on Human Rights in Israel and the Occupied Lands," *New York Times*, February 8, 1979, p. A8.

82. T. R. Reid and Edward Cody, "U.S. Reports Indicate Israeli Abuse of Palestinians," *Washington Post*, February 7, 1979, pp. A1, A18.

83. Ibid. Instances of the abuses reported in Johnson's reports are cited in Edward Cody, "Palestinians Allege Torture by Israelis," *Washington Post*, February 7, 1979, p. 19.

84. "Israeli Statement on U.S. Reports," *Washington Post*, February 7, 1979, p. A18.

85. Paul Hoffman, "Israel Sees 'Smear' in Charge of Abuse," *New York Times*, February 9, 1979, p. A5.

86. "Begin Assails Post Report Citing Torture in Israel," *Washington Post*, February 12, 1979, p. A12.

87. Edward Cody, "Israel and U.S. Jewish Groups Criticize Printing of Arab Torture Allegations," *Washington Post*, February 8, 1979, p. A23.

88. "A Tortured View of Israel's Conduct," *New York Times*, February 9, 1979, p. A30.

89. William Claiborne, "Red Cross Role Seen Limited in Israeli-Occupied Areas," *Washington Post*, March 4, 1979, p. A11.

90. "Allegations of Torture," *Washington Post*, February 8, 1979, p. A24.

91. "Israeli Jobs Failing To Win Arabs," *New York Times*, November 1, 1977, p. C20.

92. Tillman, "The West Bank Hearings," *Journal of Palestine Studies*, Winter 1978, p. 79.

93. Conversations in the home of a Palestinian family, West Bank, November 2, 1978.

94. Summary impressions based on conversations with West Bank Palestinians in November 1978 and January 1981. There are many American newspaper accounts of daily life, protest, repression, and arbitrary arrest under the occupation, including, for example, a series by Sally Quinn in the *Washington Post*, Sept. 29–Oct. 15, 1978.

95. Tillman, "The West Bank Hearings," *Journal of Palestine Studies*, Winter 1978, p. 79.

96. Interview with Hanna Nasir in Amman, October 31, 1978.

97. Excerpts from U.S. Report on Human Rights in Israel and the Occupied Lands," *New York Times*, February 8, 1979, p. A8.

98. Interview with Mayor Mohammed Milhem in Halhoul, November 2, 1978.

99. William Claiborne, "Israeli Curfew Closes Town in West Bank," *Washington Post*, March 26, 1979, pp. A1, A12; "Israel Ends Curfew in West Bank City," *Washington Post*, March 31, 1979, p. A11.

100. William Claiborne, "West Bank's Water Is Autonomy Issue," *Washington Post*, May 2, 1979, p. A24.

101. Interview with Hikmat al-Masri in Nablus, November 4, 1978.

102. Interview with Mayor Karim Khalaf in Ramallah, November 4, 1978.

103. See chapter 1, p. 19.

104. Sally Quinn, "West Bank Imbroglio," *Washington Post*, October 9, 1978, pp. B1, B3.

105. Christopher S. Wren, "West Bank Calm Hides Simmering Resentment of Israel," *New York Times*, July 25, 1978, p. A2.

106. "Open West Bank Colleges," a statement issued by Palestine Human Rights Campaign, Washington, D.C.

107. Interview with Mohammed Hallaj, Dean of Arts, and four professors of Bir Zeit University at Bir Zeit, November 4, 1978.

108. Ibid.

109. Fahd Qawasmeh and Mohammed Milhem, "Equity for Palestinians," *New York Times*, May 31, 1981, p. E 19.

110. Sharabi, "Liberation or Settlement," *Journal of Palestine Studies*, Winter 1973, p. 43.

111. "'Impossible Dream Now Becomes a Real Possibility,'" text of President

Carter's address to Congress, September 18, 1978, *Washington Post*, Sept. 19, 1978, p. A14.

112. "Arafat Denounces Agreement as 'Dirty Deal' at Summit," *Washington Post*, September 20, 1978, p. A10.

113. "Statement by the Saudi Council of Ministers on the Camp David Agreements, Issued in Riyadh, September 19, 1978," *Journal of Palestine Studies*, vol. VIII, no. 2, Winter 1979, p. 179.

114. Ibid., p. 180; Milton R. Benjamin, "Saudis, Jordan Assail Parts of Accords," *Washington Post*, September 20, 1978, pp. A1, A10.

115. Statement of Karim Khalaf, Mayor of Ramallah, September 20, 1978, Press Release by Palestine Human Rights Campaign, Washington, D.C.

116. Jonathan C. Randal, "King Is 'Shattered' by Egypt's Action," *Washington Post*, September 24, 1978, pp. A1, A24.

117. Thomas W. Lippmann, "Israelis Jubilant but Arabs Are Critical, Cautious," *Washington Post*, September 19, 1978, pp. A1, A12.

118. See chapter 4, p. 138.

119. Interview with Hanna Nasir in Amman, October 31, 1978.

120. Interview with Mayor Fahd Qawasmeh in Hebron, November, 2, 1978.

121. Interview with Mayor Mohammed Milhem in Halhoul, November 2, 1978.

122. Interview with Mayor Karim Khalaf in Ramallah, November 4, 1978.

123. Interview with Mayor Bassam Shaka' in Nablus, November 4, 1978.

124. Interview with Mayor Elias Freij in Bethlehem, November 4, 1978.

125. See chapter 4, p. 148.

126. Interview at Bir Zeit University, November 4, 1978.

127. See chapter 4, pp. 137–139.

128. Interview with Mayor Milhem in Halhoul, November 2, 1978.

129. President Carter so indicated in a news conference on December 15, 1977. "Transcript of the President's News Conference on Foreign and Domestic Matters," *New York Times*, December 16, 1977, p. A28.

130. Interviews with United States Embassy officials, Jidda, October 24, 1978.

131. Interview with Prince Turki al-Faisal, Director General of Intelligence, Jidda, October 25, 1978.

132. This view was expressed by Prince Turki, and also by Fawzi Shubokshi, Director of Western Hemisphere Affairs in the Saudi Foreign Ministry, in Jidda, October 25, 1978.

133. Interview with Raymond H. Close in Jidda, October 25, 1978.

134. Christopher Wren, "Man on the Spot," *New York Times Magazine*, April 8, 1979, pp. 17–19, 64.

135. "Hussein Seeks U.S. Response on Many Issues," *Washington Post*, October 2, 1978, p. A16.

136. Rowland Evans and Robert Novak, "The Answers to Hussein's Questions," *Washington Post*, October 30, 1978, p. A23. The State Department confirmed the accuracy of Evans' and Novak's information.

137. See chapter 4, p. 138.

138. Marvine Howe, "Hussein Criticizes the U.S.," *New York Times*, March 21, 1979, pp. A1, A7.

139. Interview with U.S. Ambassador Talcott Seelye in Damascus, October 26, 1978.

140. Interview with Riad Siage, Head of the Department of American Affairs, Ministry of Foreign Affairs, Damascus, October 29, 1978.

141. David B. Ottaway, "Hussein Disavows 'Jordanian Option,' Criticizes Tour by Kissinger," *Washington Post*, January 30, 1981, p. A17.

142. William Claiborne, "Disillusionment on the West Bank," *Washington Post*, September 27, 1978, pp. A1, A16.

143. Interview with Hanna Nasir in Amman, October 31, 1978.

144. See p. 201.

145. This view was expressed, for example, by Prince Turki al-Faisal, Saudi Director General of Intelligence. Interview in Jidda, October 25, 1978.

146. Interview with Mayor Milhem in Halhoul, November 2, 1978.

147. Senator Howard H. Baker, Jr., *Peace and Stability in the Middle East*, A Report to the Committee on Foreign Relations, U.S. Senate, August 1975, (Washington, D.C.: U.S. Government Printing Office, 1975), p. 18.

148. Anthony Lewis, "Saudi Crown Prince Urges U.S. to Start Talks with PLO," *New York Times*, June 22, 1979, p. A2.

149. See Said, *The Question of Palestine*, pp. 220–221.

150. *The Middle East*, 3rd ed., p. 113.

151. McGovern, *Realities of the Middle East*, p. 11.

152. Baker, *Peace and Stability in the Middle East*, pp. 10–11.

153. McGovern, *Realities of the Middle East*, pp. 10, 12.

154. Baker, *Peace and Stability in the Middle East*, pp. 11, 14.

155. Statement at Clinton, Mass., March 16, 1977. *Weekly Compilation of Presidential Documents: Jimmy Carter, 1977*, Vol. 13, No. 12, March 21, 1977, p. 361.

156. Sabri Jiryis, "On Political Settlement in the Middle East: The Palestinian Dimension," *Journal of Palestine Studies*, vol. VII, no. 1, Autumn 1977, pp. 4–7.

157. Ibid., p. 7; "Secretary of State William P. Rogers, Statement before the Galaxy Conference on Adult Education, Washington, December 9, 1969 (Excerpts on Middle East Peace)," in *A Select Chronology and Background Documents Relating to the Middle East*, Committee on Foreign Relations, U.S. Senate, February 1975 (Washington, D.C.: U.S. Government Printing Office, 1975), p. 266.

158. See chapter 1, p. 22.

159. Jiryis, "On Political Settlement in the Middle East," *Journal of Palestine Studies*, Autumn 1977, pp. 7–10, 24.

160. Walid Khalidi, "Thinking the Unthinkable: A Sovereign Palestinian State," *Foreign Affairs*, Vol. 56, No. 4, July 1978, pp. 697–99.

161. Ibid., pp. 699–705.

162. Ibid., p. 707.

163. Ibid., pp. 711–13.

164. Jiryis, "On Political Settlement in the Middle East," *Journal of Palestine Studies*, Autumn 1977, p. 13.

165. Address to the United Nations General Assembly, November 13, 1974, quoted in *The Middle East*, p. 113.

166. Interview with PLO Chairman Yasser Arafat, his deputy "Abu Iyad," and Khalid Fahoum, Chairman of the Palestine National Council, in Damascus, October 28, 1978.

167. Ibid.

168. Interview with Prince Turki al-Faisal in Jidda, October 25, 1978.

169. Interview in Damascus, October 28, 1978.

170. Press Release issued by Congressman Paul Findley, "Arafat Pledge Opens Door for U.S. Talks with PLO," December 1, 1978.

171. Statement of Representative Paul Findley before the Seventh Annual Convention of the National Association of Arab Americans, Mayflower Hotel, Washington, D.C., May 5, 1979.

172. "Palestinians, Reacting to the Pact, Go on Strike and Denounce Egypt," *New York Times*, March 27, 1979, pp. A1, A10.

173. Private meeting with Shafik al-Hout at the Middle East Institute, Washington, D.C., April 12, 1979.

174. Sally Quinn, "The Dove: 'A Voice in the Wilderness,'" *Washington Post*, October 12, 1978, pp. D1, D6.

175. Letter from John P. Richardson to Shafik al-Hout, April 12, 1979.

176. Stephen S. Rosenfeld, "Can the PLO Risk a Cease-Fire?" *Washington Post*, April 13, 1979, p. A13.

177. *Weekly Compilation of Presidential Documents: Jimmy Carter, 1977*, vol. 13, no. 12, March 21, 1977, p. 361.

178. So said Mayor Milhem of Halhoul. Interview in Halhoul, November 2, 1978.

179. *Weekly Compilation of Presidential Documents: Jimmy Carter, 1977*, vol. 13, no. 20, May 16, 1977, p. 706.

180. See page 191.

181. *Weekly Compilation of Presidential Documents: Jimmy Carter, 1977*, vol. 13, no. 20, May 16, 1977, p. 706.

182. See chapter 2, pp. 58–61.

183. For example, in a press conference on July 12, 1977. *Weekly Compilation of Presidential Documents: Jimmy Carter, 1977*, vol. 13, no. 29, July 18, 1977, p. 990.

184. Office of the White House Press Secretary, Transcript of an Interview with Barbara Walters, Robert McNeil, Tom Brokaw and Bob Schieffer, December 28, 1977, p. 5.

185. Ibid.; *Weekly Compilation of Presidential Documents: Jimmy Carter, 1977*, vol. 13, no. 29, July 18, 1977, Press Conference of July 12, 1977.

186. See chapter 4, pp. 135–136.

187. "Text of Statements by Sadat and Carter Following Meeting at Aswan," *New York Times*, January 5, 1978, p. A4.

188. See chapter 2, pp. 58–61.

189. "Text of Statements by Sadat and Carter Following Meeting at Aswan," *New York Times*, January 5, 1978, p. A4.

190. Henry Tanner, "Leaders Consult Briefly at Aswan and Agree on 'Most Issues,'" *New York Times*, January 5, 1978, pp. 1, 5.

191. "Begin Sees Benefit in Aswan Remarks," *New York Times*, January 5, 1978, p. A3.

192. "PLO Ridicules Carter Remark," *New York Times*, January 5, 1978, p. A3.

193. "President Carter's News Conference of March 9, 1978," *New York Times*, March 10, 1978, p. D12.

194. Interview with Trude B. Feldman, a writer for Jewish publications. Quoted by Bernard Gwertzman in "Begin Arrives in U.S. and Will See Carter about Mideast Issues," *New York Times*, May 1, 1978, pp. A1, A4.

195. "A Framework for Peace in the Middle East Agreed at Camp David," September 17, 1978.

196. William J. Lanouette, "The Many Faces of the Jewish Lobby in America," *National Journal*, vol. 10, no. 19, May 13, 1978, pp. 754–755.

197. "Memorandum of Agreement Between the Governments of Israel and the United States: the Geneva Peace Conference," September 1, 1975, in *Early Warning System in Sinai*, Hearings before the Committee on Foreign Relations, U.S. Senate, 94th Congress, First Session, October 6–7, 1975 (Washington, D.C.: U.S. Government Printing Office, 1975), p. 252.

198. Ibid., pp. 210–211.

199. *Panama Canal Treaties*, Report of the Committee on Foreign Relations, U.S. Senate, 95th Congress, First Session (Washington, D.C.: U.S. Government Printing Office, 1978), pp. 9–10.

200. *Weekly Compilation of Presidential Documents: Administration of Jimmy Carter, 1977*, vol. 18, no. 31, August 1, 1977, p. 1123.

201. Office of the White House Press Secretary (Plains, Georgia), "Information Question and Answer with the President," August 8, 1977, p. 2.

202. "Transcript of the President's News Conference on Foreign and Domestic Matters," *New York Times*, September 30, 1977, p. A18.

203. Conversation with former Ambassador to Egypt Hermann Eilts, May 8, 1981; Said, *The Question of Palestine*, pp. 226–227.

204. "Excerpts from Sadat's Speech to Egyptian Parliament," November 26, 1977 (*New York Times*, November 27, 1977, p. 16).

205. "Transcript of the President's News Conference on Foreign and Domestic Matters," *New York Times*, December 16, 1977, p. A28.

206. Marvine Howe, "Behind Its Slogans, PLO Is Worried about Losing Peace Role," *New York Times*, January 6, 1978, p. A3.

207. Interview with David Hirst of the Manchester Guardian on January 2, 1978, "Arafat Assails U.S. 'Flagrant Bias' Toward Israel," *Washington Post*, January 3, 1978, p. A13.

208. "Transcript of the President's News Conference on Foreign and Domestic Matters," *New York Times*, December 16, 1977, p. A28.

209. Interview in Damascus, October 28, 1978.

210. Ibid.; Jim Hoagland, "Now Comes the Selling of the Camp David Pact," *Washington Post*, September 27, 1978, p. A20.

211. Excerpts from Interview with Ambassador Andrew Young, by the staff of *The Inter Dependent*, a publication of the United Nations Association, January 9, 1979.

212. Bernard Gwertzman, "Carter Wants Palestinian Tie, Calls PLO a 'Problem,' " *New York Times*, March 24, 1979, pp. A1, A3.

213. Ibid.

214. *Early Warning System in Sinai*, p. 252.

215. "Begin Says Israelis Will Stay in Golan," *New York Times*, May 3, 1979, p. A5.

216. "Excerpts from President Reagan's Answers in Interview with Five Reporters," *New York Times*, February 3, 1981, p. A14.

217. Bernard Gwertzman, "Sadat Bid Reagan Drop U.S. Refusal to Talk to P.L.O.," *New York Times*, August 6, 1981, pp. A1, A5; Don Oberdorfer, "Reagan Rejects Sadat Plan on Contacts with P.L.O.," *Washington Post*, August 7, 1981, pp. A1, A20.

218. "Text of President's Statement on Trade Sanctions against Rhodesia," *New York Times*, June 9, 1979, p. A4.

219. Fawaz Turki in "A Forum: Voices Before the Summit," *Washington Star*, September 3, 1978, p. D1.

220. Elihu Root, "A Requisite for the Success of Popular Diplomacy," in *Fifty Years of Foreign Affairs* (Hamilton Fish Armstrong, ed., New York: Praeger Publishers, 1972), p. 6.

221. Stone, "Confessions of a Jewish Dissident," in *Underground to Palestine: And Reflections Thirty Years Later*, p. 238.

6. THE SOVIET UNION: PREDATOR OR PARTNER?

1. Dean Acheson, *Present at the Creation* (New York: W.W. Norton & Co., 1969), p. 219.

2. Quoted by Daniel Yergin in *Shattered Peace* (Boston: Houghton Mifflin Co., 1977), p. 296.

3. See chapter 2, p. 55.

4. "Text of Soviet-American Statement on the Mideast," *New York Times*, October 2, 1977, p. 16.

5. See chapter 2, pp. 56–57.

6. Secretary of State Rogers's speech of December 9, 1969, in *A Select Chronology and Background Documents Relating to the Middle East*, 2nd revised ed., Committee on Foreign Relations, United States Senate, February 1975 (Washington, D.C.: U.S. Government Printing Office, 1975), p. 266.

7. *RN: The Memoirs of Richard Nixon* (New York: Gosset & Dunlap, 1978), p. 479.

8. Ibid.

9. William E. Farrell, "U.S. Move on Mideast Rejected by Israel, Welcomed by Arabs," *New York Times*, October 3, 1977, pp. A1, A7.

10. Bernard Gwertzman, "Carter, Dayan Reach Agreement on Procedures for Geneva Talks," *New York Times*, October 5, 1977, pp. A1, A12.

11. William E. Farrell, "Fear They May Be a Pawn in Carter's Global Game," *New York Times*, October 4, 1977, p. A3.

12. Shlomo Avineri, "Peacemaking: The Arab-Israeli Conflict," *Foreign Affairs*, vol. 57, no. 1, Fall 1978, p. 60.

13. "Mideast Peace Initiative Provokes Criticism in U.S.," *New York Times*, October 3, 1977, p. 6.

14. "Carter's Stance on Palestinians Turns Off Jewish Contributors," *Washington Post*, October 6, 1977, p. A16.

15. "The Geneva Express (Via Moscow)," *New York Times*, October 4, 1977, p. 37.

16. William Safire, "Selling Out Israel," *New York Times*, October 6, 1977, p. 41.

17. "PLO Welcomes Declaration," *New York Times*, October 2, 1977, p. A16.

18. See chapter 5, pp. 216–217.

19. Anthony Lewis, "Arafat Hints Easing of PLO's Attitude," *New York Times*, May 2, 1978, pp. 1, 8.

20. S. M. Rogov, "The American Jewish Community and Israel," 1978, typescript English translation provided by the author.

21. "Transcript of President Carter's Address to United Nations General Assembly," *New York Times*, October 5, 1977, p. 20.

22. Bernard Gwertzman, "Carter, Dayan Reach Agreement on Procedures for Geneva Talks," *New York Times*, October 5, 1977, pp. A1, A12.

23. "Joint U.S.-Israel Statement of October 1, 1977," Public Information Series, Bureau of Public Affairs, Department of State, October 7, 1977.

24. Sidney Zion and Uri Dan, "Untold Story of the Mideast Talks," *New York Times Magazine*, January 21, 1979, pp. 46–47. See also Bernard Gwertzman, "U.S. Reports Accord with Israel Raises Hope of Peace Talks," *New York Times*, October 6, 1977, pp. A1, A12.

25. Ibid.

26. Conversation with State Department officials, May 8, 1981.

27. "Transcript of the President's News Conference on Foreign and Domestic Matters," *New York Times*, December 16, 1977, p. A28.

28. Remarks of Senator Howard H. Baker, Jr. before the World Jewish Congress, November 1, 1977, Washington, D.C., "The United States, the Middle East and the World."

29. *Congressional Record*, 95th Congress, Second Session, May 15, 1978, p. S7381.

30. Ibid., pp. S7382–3.

31. Conversation with Ambassador Hermann Eilts, May 8, 1981.

32. Nahum Goldmann, "Zionist Ideology and the Reality of Israel," *Foreign Affairs*, vol. 57, no. 1, Fall 1978, p. 80.

33. "NSC–68," A Report to the National Security Council (Washington, D.C.: National Security Council, 1950), p. 4.

34. George F. Kennan, "A Current Assessment of Soviet-American Relations," remarks at a meeting of the Council on Foreign Relations, Washington, D.C., November 22, 1977.

35. For an account of Jewish life in Tsarist Russia and its political consequences see Amos Elon, *The Israelis* (New York: Holt, Rinehart and Winston, 1971), pp. 33–81.

36. Ibid., p. 52.

37. Figures are approximate and vary somewhat according to sources. See J. William Fulbright, "The Significance of SALT," *AEI Defense Review*, Vol. 2, No. 4, 1978, p. 10; Bernard Gwertzman, "Jewish Emigration Sets Soviet Record," *New York Times*, April 4, 1979, pp. A1, A3.

38. Arie Lova Eliav, *Land of the Hart* (Philadelphia: The Jewish Publication Society of America, 1974), p. 273.

39. Menachem Begin, *The Revolt*, revised edition (New York: Nash Publishing, 1977), p. xvi.

40. Pranay B. Gupte, "Five Released Dissidents Express Joy, Hope That Soviet Will Free Others," *New York Times*, April 29, 1979, pp. 1, 30.

41. Ibid.

42. " 'Next Year in Jerusalem'," from notes taken at Shcharansky's trial by his brother, Leonid, *New York Times*, July 15, 1978, p. A1.

43. David K. Shipler, "Soviet Jews Choosing U.S. Put Israelis in a Quandary," *New York Times*, September 13, 1981, p. E5.

44. Robert G. Kaiser and Walter Pincus, "Trials Provoke Anger on Hill," *Washington Post*, July 12, 1978, pp. A1, A13.

45. Eliav, *Land of the Hart*, p. 243. For a brief account of Soviet attitudes toward Zionism and Soviet Jews since the Russian Revolution, see ibid., pp. 259–270.

46. Marshall Shulman, "On Learning to Live with Authoritarian Regimes," *Foreign Affairs*, vol. 55, no. 2 (January 1977), p. 334.

47. Nahum Goldmann, "Israeli Policy: Proposals for Action," a series of articles published in the Israeli newspaper *Ha'aretz*, November 8–13, 1974. Translated and published in the *Journal of Palestine Studies*, vol. IV, no. 2, Winter 1975, p. 124.

48. "Excerpts from Speeches of Gromyko, el-Khouri," *New York Times*, May 15, 1947, p. A8.

49. Eliav, *Land of the Hart*, p. 248.

50. Fred J. Khouri, The *Arab-Israeli Dilemma* (Syracuse: Syracuse University Press, 1968), pp. 43, 50–51.

51. U.S. ambassador to the United Nations.

52. Begin, *The Revolt*, revised ed., pp. 56–58.

53. O. Alov, "For a Settlement in the Middle East," *International Affairs*, September 1977, pp. 61–70.

54. Christopher S. Wren, "Gromyko Offers Israel Guarantee," *New York Times*, April 24, 1975, p. A5; David Astor and Valerie Yorke, *Peace in the Middle East* (London: Corgi Books, 1978), p. 75, 81 (fn. 38).

55. Goldmann, articles in *Ha'aretz*, November 8–13, 1974, in *Journal of Palestine Studies*, Winter 1975, pp. 128–9.

56. Interview with Fawzi Shubokshi, Director of Western Hemisphere Affairs of the Saudi Foreign Ministry, Jidda, October 25, 1978.

57. Comment by Prof. Charles Issawi at an Aspen Institute Mideast Project Seminar, "The Shaping of the Arab World," Punalu'u, Hawaii, January 12, 1979.

58. Peter Mangold, *Superpower Intervention in the Middle East* (New York: St. Martin's Press, 1978), pp. 116–17.

59. Ibid., pp. 117–119.

60. Ibid., pp. 119–20, 146.

61. Ibid., pp. 121–124.

62. Ibid., pp. 124–8.

63. Ibid., pp. 128–130.

64. Ibid., pp. 130–131.

65. Ibid., p. 115.

66. Ibid., p. 169 and, generally, chapter 7, pp. 115–141.

67. Micheline Hazou, "Road to Nowhere," an interview with Professor Hisham Sharabi, *Monday Morning*, Beirut, July 10–16, 1978, pp. 28–29.

68. John C. Campbell, "The Soviet Union in the Middle East," *Middle East Journal,* vol. 32, no. 1, Winter 1978, pp. 3–4.

69. Ibid., pp. 7–8.

70. Crane Brinton, *The Anatomy of Revolution* (New York: Vintage Books, 1965), p. 234.

71. Henry Kissinger, "Bismarck: The White Revolutionary," *Daedalus*, Summer 1968. Quoted by James Chace in *A World Elsewhere* (New York: Charles Scribner's Sons, 1973), pp. 33–34.

72. Mangold, *Superpower Intervention in the Middle East,* p. 164.

73. Ibid., p. 167. A detailed account of the attack on the *Liberty*, by one of the ship's officers, is contained in James M. Ennes, Jr., *Assault on the Liberty* (New York: Random House, 1979).

74. Murrey Marder, "U.S. Seeking to Oust Soviet Units in Egypt," *Washington Post*, July 3, 1970, pp. A1, A23.

75. Background Briefing, San Clemente, California, June 26, 1970, p. 20.

76. Marvin Kalb and Bernard Kalb, *Kissinger* (Boston: Little, Brown & Co., 1974), pp. 481–6; Nixon, *RN*, pp. 931–3, 936.

77. Nixon, *RN*, p. 938.

78. Kalb and Kalb, *Kissinger*, pp. 486–90; Nixon, *RN*, pp. 936–8.

79. Nixon, *RN*, pp. 939–40; Kalb and Kalb, *Kissinger*, pp. 490–92.

80. Kalb and Kalb, *Kissinger*, pp. 495–6.

81. Committee on Foreign Relations, United States Senate, *A Select Chronology and Background Documents Relating to the Middle East*, 2nd. revised ed., February 1975 (Washington, D.C.: U.S. Government Printing Office, 1975), p. 286.

82. Nixon, *RN*, p. 941.

83. Edward R. F. Sheehan, *The Arabs, Israelis, and Kissinger* (New York: Reader's Digest Press, 1976), p. 38.

84. "Secretary of Defense Schlesinger's News Conference, October 26, 1973 (Excerpts Regarding U.S. Military Alert)", in *Background Documents Relating to the Middle East,* pp. 292–3, 296.

85. Press Conference of October 25, 1973, in Kalb and Kalb, *Kissinger*, pp. 495–6.

86. See Mangold, *Superpower Intervention in the Middle East*, pp. 168–72.

87. See chapter 6, p. 239.

88. James R. Schlesinger, "America's Energy Destiny," *Washington Post,* August 23, 1979, p. A21; Steven Rattner, "Schlesinger, in Farewell, Demands Balance with Russians in Mideast," *New York Times*, August 17, 1979, p. A8.

89. Henry Brandon, "Soviets Won't Provoke Oil Clash, Official Says," *Washington Star*, July 25, 1979, p. A1.

90. Mangold, *Superpower Intervention in the Middle East*, pp. 38, 41 (fn. 41), 116.

91. Senator J. W. Fulbright, "Détente and the Middle East," *Congressional Record, Senate*, 93rd Congress, First Session, vol. 119, November 9, 1973, pp. 36478–36480.

92. Senator Henry Jackson, "The Middle East and the Energy Crisis," *Congressional Record, Senate*, 93rd Congress, First Session, vol. 119, May 21, 1973, pp. S9446–7.

93. Jim Hoagland, "Carter Has Moved into Center of Arab-Israeli Chessboard," *Washington Post*, September 24, 1978, p. A19.

94. Martin Tolchin, "Carter Says No Top Arab He's Met Privately Backs a Palestinian State," *New York Times*, September 1, 1979, pp. 1, 5.

95. Jim Hoagland, "Saud Politely Disagrees on Palestinians," *Washington Post*, October 5, 1979, p. A5.

96. Kevin Klose, "Soviet Union Suggests Ties with Saudis," *Washington Post*, March 4, 1979, pp. A1, A15.

97. Thomas W. Lippman, "Saudis Signal Wish for Link with Soviets," *Washington Post*, March 4, 1979, pp. A1, A20.

98. Letter to the author dated October 19, 1980.

99. Interview with American Embassy officials in Jidda, October 24, 1978.

100. Don Oberdorfer, "Frustration Marks Saudi Ties to US," *Washington Post*, May 6, 1979, pp. A1, A18.

101. "Transcript of the President's News Conference on Foreign and Domestic Matters," *New York Times*, February 28, 1979, p. A16.

102. Lippman, "Saudis Signal Wish for Link with Soviets," *Washington Post*, March 4, 1979, pp. A1, A20.

103. Jonathan C. Randal, "Jordan's Hussein Criticizes US on Peace Treaty," *Washington Post*, March 21, 1979, pp. A1, A20; Marvine Howe, "Hussein Criticizes the US," *New York Times*, March 21, 1979, pp. A1, A7. See also chapter 5, p. 208.

104. Interview with an adviser to the Jordanian royal family, Amman, October 31, 1978.

105. "Transcript of President's State of the Union Address to Joint Session of Congress," *New York Times*, January 24, 1980, p. A12.

106. "Excerpts from Soviet Leader's Speech to Parliament in New Delhi," *New York Times*, December 11, 1980, p. A12.

107. "Excerpts from Address by Brezhnev to the Soviet Communist Party Congress," *New York Times*, February 24, 1981, p. A6.

108. Bernard Gwertzman, "Haig Says U.S. Seeks Consensus Strategy in Mideast Region," *New York Times*, March 20, 1981, pp. A1, A4.

109. See chapter 6, pp. 238–239.

110. "Transcript of President's First News Conference on Foreign and Domestic Topics," *New York Times*, January 30, 1981, p. A10.

111. George C. Wilson, "U.S. May Hit Soviet Outposts in Event of Oil Cutoff," *Washington Post*, July 17, 1981, pp. A1, A11.

112. Bernard Gwertzman, "New Gamble in Mideast," *New York Times*, September 12, 1981, pp. A1, A3; George C. Wilson and John M. Goshko, "Begin Sketches New Relationship in Strategic Plans," *Washington Post*, September 12, 1981, pp. A1, A15.

113. John Kifner, "New U.S.-Israeli Step May Isolate Arab Allies," *New York Times*, September 16, 1981, p. A3.

114. *A Senate Perspective on Spain and the Middle East*, A Report to the U.S.

Senate by Senator Howard H. Baker, Jr. (Washington, D.C.: U.S. Government Printing Office, 1981), pp. 10–12.

115. Serge Schmemann, "King Hussein, in Moscow, Endorses Brezhnev's Call for Mideast Parley," *New York Times*, May 27, 1981, p. A10.

116. Anthony Lewis, "'We Are Poles Apart'," *New York Times*, July 9, 1981, p. A23.

117. "Excerpts from Weinberger Statement on Military Budget Outlay," *New York Times*, March 5, 1981, p. B11.

118. Exxon Background Series, *World Energy Outlook*, December 1980, p. 36.

119. Christopher Van Hollen, "Don't Engulf the Gulf," *Foreign Affairs*, vol. 59, no. 5, Summer 1981, p. 1075.

120. George McGovern, "How to Avert a New 'Cold War'," *The Atlantic*, vol. 245, no. 6, June 1980, p. 57.

121. *Détente*, Hearings before the Committee on Foreign Relations, United States Senate, 93rd Congress, Second Session (Washington, D.C.: U.S. Government Printing Office, 1975), pp. 263, 265.

122. J. William Fulbright, "The Significance of SALT," *AEI Defense Review*, vol. 2, no. 4, August 1978, p. 8.

123. *Détente*, p. 240.

124. Fulbright, "The Significance of SALT," *AEI Defense Review*, August 1978, p. 13.

125. On this aspect of the Israeli-American relationship see George Ball, "How to Save Israel in Spite of Herself," *Foreign Affairs*, vol. 55, no. 3, April 1977, pp. 467–8.

126. "Text of Soviet-American Statement on the Mideast," *New York Times*, October 2, 1977, p. 16.

127. So argues Walid Khalidi, a Palestinian intellectual with ties to the PLO, in "Thinking the Unthinkable: A Sovereign Palestinian State," *Foreign Affairs*, vol. 56, no. 4, July 1978, p. 711.

128. Campbell, "The Soviet Union in the Middle East," *Middle East Journal*, Winter 1978, p. 9.

129. *Toward Peace in the Middle East*, Report of a Study Group (Washington, D.C.: The Brookings Institution, 1975), p. 18. See also David Astor and Valerie Yorke, *Peace in the Middle East*, (London: Corgi Books, 1978), pp. 51–53, 62–64. A valuable discussion of the possible forms of superpower collaboration in enforcement of a Middle East peace settlement is contained in this study.

130. Goldmann, "Israel Policy: Proposals for Action," a series of articles published in the Israeli newspaper *Ha'aretz*, November 8–13, 1974, in *Journal of Palestine Studies*, Winter 1975, p. 124.

7. CONCLUSION: ON PEACE AND HOW TO GET IT

1. *Toward Peace in the Middle East*, Report of a Study Group (Washington, D.C.: The Brookings Institution, 1975).

2. *Priorities for Peace in the Middle East*, Hearings before the Subcommittee on Near Eastern and South Asian Affairs of the Committee on Foreign Relations, United States Senate (Washington, D.C.: U.S. Government Printing Office, 1975); *Middle East Peace Prospects*, Hearings before the Subcommittee on Near Eastern and South Asian Affairs of the Committee on Foreign Relations, United States Senate (Washington, D.C.: U. S. Government Printing Office, 1976).

3. *Search for Peace in the Middle East*, a study prepared by an interfaith working party (Philadelphia: American Friends Service Committee, 1970).

4. See *Where We Stand*, Statements of American Churches on the Middle East Conflict (Allan Solomonow, ed., New York: The Middle East Consultation Group, 1977).

5. See, for example, *The Middle East After Partial Peace: What Lies Ahead?* A Summary Record of the 33rd Annual Conference of the Middle East Institute (Washington, D.C., October 5–6, 1979).

6. Statement by the European Nine, March 26, 1979.

7. President Carter's News Conference of March 9, 1977. *Weekly Compilation of Presidential Documents: Jimmy Carter, 1977*, vol. 13, no. 11, March 14, 1977, p. 330.

8. Bernard Gwertzman, "Vance Reports U.S. Will Make Overture to the Palestinians," *New York Times*, May 27, 1979, pp. 1, 11.

9. "Transcript of the President's News Conference on Foreign and Domestic Matters," *New York Times*, May 30, 1979, p. A12.

10. See chapter 1, p. 11.

11. See chapter 5, p. 178.

12. Quoted by Senator J. W. Fulbright in "The Clear and Present Danger," an address delivered at Westminster College, Fulton, Missouri, November 2, 1974.

13. J. W. Fulbright, "Old Myths and New Realities—II: The Middle East," *Congressional Record*, August 24, 1970, p. 29809.

14. *Toward Peace in the Middle East*, p. 23.

15. Walid Khalidi, "Thinking the Unthinkable: A Sovereign Palestinian State," *Foreign Affairs*, vol. 56, no. 4, July 1978, p. 713.

16. Hisham Sharabi, at a "Face-to-Face" dinner, sponsored by the Carnegie Endowment for International Peace, June 13, 1979.

17. See chapter 4, pp. 140–141.

18. See chapter 1, p. 28.

19. See chapter 2, pp. 66–67.

20. See chapter 4, p. 166.

21. Address by Vice President Walter Mondale before the World Affairs Council of Northern California, "A Framework for a Middle East Peace," *Department of State News Release*, June 17, 1977.

22. "President Carter's News Conference of March 9, 1978," *New York Times*, March 10, 1978, p. D12.

23. Edward R. F. Sheehan, *The Arabs, Israelis, and Kissinger* (New York: Reader's Digest Press, 1976), p. 199.

24. See chapter 4, p. 166.

25. Interview with United States Embassy Officials, Tel Aviv, November 3, 1978.

26. *The Middle East After Partial Peace: What Lies Ahead?* A Summary Record of the 33rd Annual Conference of the Middle East Institute, Washington, D. C., October 5–6, 1979, p. 53.

27. *Toward Peace in the Middle East*, p. 21.

28. Nahum Goldmann, "Zionist Ideology and the Reality of Israel," *Foreign Affairs*, vol. 57, no. 1, Fall 1978, pp. 80–81.

29. See chapter 2, p. 57.

30. Kennett Love, *Suez: The Twice-Fought War* (New York: McGraw-Hill Book Co., 1969), p. 633.

31. United Nations Charter, Articles 25, 39–42.

32. J. William Fulbright, *The Crippled Giant* (New York: Vintage Books, 1972), p. 108.

33. See chapter 2, p. 64.

INDEX

Abd al-Aziz, King, 15, 73, 79
Abdullah, King, 23
Abourezk, Senator James, 68, 161, 162, 195, 196
Abu Iyad. *See* Khalaf, Salah
Acheson, Dean, 17–18, 230–31
Afghanistan, 265–66
Akins, James E., 95
Alaskan North Slope, 74
Allon, Yigal, 124, 140, 154, 233
Allon Plan, 140–44, 151, 281
Altermann, Nathan, 123
American Friends Service Committee, 277
American-Israel Public Affairs Committee, 65, 84, 102
American Jewish Committee, 65, 99
Amitay, Morris J., 66, 68, 84, 102
Anderson, Jack, 115
Anglo-American Committee of Inquiry, 15–16
Anthony, John Duke, 91, 94
Anti-Defamation League of B'nai B'rith, 65, 120, 155
Antonius, George, 14
Arab Americans: and lobbying, 67–69
Arab Information Centers, 69
Arab-Israeli conflict: and Soviet Union, 244–53
Arab-Israeli War, 1948, 17
Arab League, 108, 109, 176
Arab Organization for Industrialization, 109
Arabs: and Palestine history, 8–9; and Jews, 20–23; and Camp David accords, 201–10; and Soviet Union, 264–65; and strategic relationship, 267
Arafat, Yasser, 70, 121, 139, 156; and unified Palestine, 21; and independent Palestinian state, 59; on his home, 174; and state of Palestine, 177; and General Assembly, 179; on Palestinian terrorist attack, 179; on terrorists, 187, 189; and Camp David accords, 201; and PLO, 210–19; and Soviet-American statement, 1977, 234

ARAMCO, 73–74, 79, 88
Arbatov, Georgy A., 258
Armed conflict: and Palestinians, 173–79
Armed Forces Journal International, 154
Arim, Professor Yehuda, 195
Association of Arab American University Graduates, 67
Aswan formula, 221, 227, 228, 278
Attlee, Clement, 15
Austin, Warren, 16, 245
Avineri, Shlomo, 137, 233
Avnery, Uri, 148
AWAC, 52, 118–21

Baghdad meetings, 1978–79, 108–109, 111
Baker, Senator Howard, 92, 188, 211, 212, 237, 243, 267
Balfour, Arthur, 10, 11, 53, 59, 278
Balfour Declaration, 10, 12, 285–86
Baroody, Joseph, 69
Begin, Menachem, 127, 283; and Sadat's visit, 2, 126; and Ismailia meeting, 3; 1977 plan of, 3–4, 24, 25, 133, 142; and idea of Israel, 8; in World War II, 13; and founding of Israel, 18–19, 130; on the "fighting Jew," 19–20; on Arabs in Israel, 20; and Camp David summit, 26; on Israeli attack on Iraq, 38–39; and F-15 sale, 100; policies of and Congress, 106; life of, 128–32; and independent Palestinian state, 136, 139; on Palestinians, 147; on guarantees, 153–54; on American Jews, 158; and Palestinian terrorist attack, 179–80; and terrorism, 189; and Aswan formula, 221; and PLO, 226–27; on Jews in Russia, 242; on Soviet policy, 245
Bellmon, Senator, 106
Ben-Gurion, David, 13, 146, 149, 280; and Arabs, 21; on U.S. guarantees, 158; on peace, 279
Bentsen, Senator, 106
Betar, 128
Bevin, Foreign Secretary, 16
Bir Zet University, 199–200, 210; and Camp David accords, 202, 204

DATE DUE

MAR 3 '86			